The Yorùbá God of Drumming

The Yorùbá God of Drumming

TRANSATLANTIC PERSPECTIVES ON THE WOOD THAT TALKS

. . . .

Edited by Amanda Villepastour

Preface by J. D. Y. Peel

UNIVERSITY PRESS OF MISSISSIPPI • JACKSON

www.upress.state.ms.us

The University Press of Mississippi is a member of the Association of American
University Presses.

Copyright © 2015 by University Press of Mississippi
All rights reserved
Manufactured in the United States of America

First printing 2015

∞

Library of Congress Cataloging-in-Publication Data

The Yorùbá god of drumming : transatlantic perspectives on the wood that talks / edited
by Amanda Villepastour.
pages cm
Includes bibliographical references and index.
ISBN 978-1-4968-0293-4 (cloth : alk. paper) — ISBN 978-1-4968-0350-4 (ebook)
1. Yoruba (African people)—Music—History and criticism. 2. Drum language—
Religious aspects. 3. Orishas—Songs and music. I. Villepastour, Amanda, 1958– editor.
ML3760.Y67 2015
786.9089'96333—dc23
2015015799

British Library Cataloging-in-Publication Data available

I dedicate this book to my friend and mentor,
Michael Marcuzzi

Contents

III. GENDERS

IV. IDENTITIES

V. SECONDARY DIASPORAS

Acknowledgments

· ·

In the mid-2000s, Michael Marcuzzi and I hatched a plan to co-edit a volume about the Yorùbá god of drumming. This collection is the product of a transatlantic community of academics, musicians, and priests who have forged intellectual alliances and deep friendships around our shared passion for Yorùbá music in Nigeria and Cuba and its enduring drumming ancestor. After several years of sporadic work, Michael handed the project over to me due to ill health, which tragically took him away from us aged only forty-seven in September 2012. My dedication of this book to Michael Marcuzzi not only acknowledges his brilliant scholarship and the many hours of labor he gave to this volume in its early stages of development, but it preserves the memory of the kind and compassionate friendship he shared with most of our contributors. Little over a year later in 2013, our dear friend Katherine Hagedorn died after only a short illness, also in her prime at fifty-two. This edited collection is a testament to the encouragement and support I received from these two wonderful friends and colleagues. I am further privileged to have the sagacious ear and critical voice of J. D. Y. Peel throughout my research, the preparation of this book, and up to the present. The contributors also feel honored to "share the stage" with such a prestigious scholar of Yorùbá studies.

My love of the Yorùbá language compels me to present it with optimum linguistic precision, an ambitious aspiration often avoided by Yorùbá scholars themselves and publishers wishing to avoid the quagmire of fonts and fickle diacritics. Beyond the technical typesetting challenges, the language is like a beautifully cut diamond; meanings transform depending on where the light hits constellations of Yorùbá words. The archaic "deep" (ìjìnlẹ̀) Yorùbá of drummers cannot be easily translated, and many a week has been spent on a single line of poetry within these chapters. The Yorùbá-English translations in several of the essays emerged only after layered engagement with the many Àyàn drummers who sounded the messages, consultation with priests versed in religious language (Táíwò Abímbọ́lá, Kẹ́hìndé Abímbọ́lá, Ifáfẹ́mi Awóníran, Ògúnlékè Abímbọ́lá of Ọ̀yọ́, and Adédoyin 'Fáníyì of Òṣogbo) and Yorùbá linguists (Akin Oyètádé and Túndé Adégbọlá). These cultural insiders have then had to tolerate the musings and debates of foreign scholars such as myself, armed with our collection of dictionaries and an enduring curiosity and passion for their mother tongue. Special mention must go to Clement Odòjé, who agreed to the labor-intensive task of copy-editing the Yorùbá and overseeing the translations across the entire book in the final stages of its preparation.

Several key musicians and caretakers of Àyàn (Añá) have been situated on the crossroads of our transatlantic drumming network, and indeed their names pop up across chapters of this book and the wider Nigerian and Cuban musical literature. Ẹ ṣé and *gracias* to the Àyàn and Añá drummers who continue to educate me: Chief Rábíù Àyándòkun of Èrìn-Òṣun and Ángel Bolaños from Havana. A *dúpẹ́* to all of those who have passed to the ancestors since this book was conceived, and who were wise enough not to take all of their esoteric knowledge (*awo*) with them. Some were contributors whose last writings appear posthumously here: Kawolèyin Àyángbẹ́kún (d. 2007, Ògbómọ̀ṣọ́), Akínṣọlá Akìwọwọ (1922–2014), Michael Marcuzzi (1966–2012), and Katherine Hagedorn (1961–2013). Other departed people who enlightened and enriched most of us herein include my first bàtá teacher Àyánwálé Àyángbémigá (dates unknown) from Ọ̀yọ́, and from Cuba, Regino Jiménez Saez (1948–2005), Fermín Nani Socarrás (d. 2007), Estéban Vega "Cha Chá" (1925–2007), Armando Pedroso "El Surdo" (1945–2013), and the lone female voice of Amelia Pedroso (1946–2000). One can only imagine the music resounding in their heavenly sphere, no doubt led with military precision by the junior one who knew them all during his short time with us, percussionist, trumpeter, composer, arranger, and priest, Michael Marcuzzi 'Fágbénró.

Preface

A Drummer's Tale: Àjàká of Òtà

J. D. Y. Peel

• •

During my first period of research in Yorùbáland in the mid-1960s, which was on Aládúrà churches such as the Cherubim and Seraphim, I was struck that while they took great pride and joy in the African idioms of their worship—which included dancing and the use of drums to accompany many of their hymns and choruses—the form of drum mainly used was a simple rectangular frame with the membrane stretched across one side.[1] I also saw in use, for some outdoor parades, the use of a side drum beaten with two sticks, of the kind played in military bands, which must have been introduced by the Salvation Army or the Boys Brigade, a church youth organization. These both became popular in the 1920s. Musical indigenization did not then extend to using the kinds of drums played by professional Yorùbá drummers in religious and ceremonial contexts, such as the conical drums used in the three-drum *bàtá* ensemble, or the hourglass *dùndún* "talking drum" with a variable pitch, beaten with a single curved stick. The reason was that indigenous drums were still felt to be too associated or tainted with the *òrìṣà* worship that was their main occasion of public use, and themselves (as objects) too bound in with sacrifices and "*jùjú*" (medicine).[2] In the 1960s, the bulk of Christians were still of the first- or second-generation, and needed to put space between themselves and the "idolatry" they had left behind but whose potency many of them still felt.[3] Who can know what troubling emotions were stirred in the souls of these Christians striving to be true to their new faith, when they heard the complex rhythms of the bàtá ensemble or the evocative rise and fall of the dùndún's voice?

The relationship between Christianity and Yorùbá musical culture was first sharply raised by some of the "native agents" of the missionary societies in the last three decades of the nineteenth century, a period which saw the first emergence of an indigenous hymnody.[4] Outstanding among these men was the Revd. James White of the Church Missionary Society (Anglican) (CMS), from whose letters and journals virtually all the material in this preface is drawn. It says something that when I started my complete reading of the CMS archive, I was quite unaware of White's name, and he is virtually absent from the two classic studies of the missions' impact on the Yorùbá, by Àjàyí (1965) and Àyándélé (1966).[5] Yet when I came to compile the index of my *Religious Encounter and the Making of the Yoruba*, I found I had made more references to White than to any other missionary agent. This was because of the sheer quality of his reportage—its detail, range, and insight—of the mundane activities of the people among whom he worked, of the indigenous religion that he strenuously opposed, of his own evangelistic encounters, and above all (for our present purposes) of the aesthetic and artistic dimensions of Yorùbá life. Under the last heading comes an account of his conversion of a drummer, Àjàká, which shows a remarkable insight into the nature of Yorùbá drumming itself. It is also the earliest contemporary account of drumming in relation to a named individual that we have.

· · ·

It is important to say something about this relatively unknown pastor, since everything we know about Àjàká is strongly framed though his writing. James White was born in Sierra Leone in the early 1820s, the child of Yorùbá parents—his mother was an Owù and he had uncles in the Owù section of Abéòkúta—and was educated there: three years at the CMS Grammar School, where he was selected for further training as a teacher.[6] In 1850 he was posted as a teacher to Badagry, but was soon transferred to Lagos. Though his hopes to be allowed to take his education further in England went unfulfilled, he learned enough Greek to be able to read the New Testament and used his visit to Sierra Leone in 1864 for his ordination to immerse himself in theological reading.[7] White's command of English is evident in the vigorous and assured prose of his journals, but his language skills went further, for Bishop Crowther invited him to serve as one of his assistants in the great project of translating of the Bible into Yorùbá. White was responsible for the first versions of several books of the Old Testament.[8] From 1854 to 1880 he served as pastor of the Àwòrí town of Òtà, thirty miles northwest of Lagos on the road to Abéòkúta.

It was not an easy posting. Òtà was prone to acute factional politics which sometimes came close to civil war, with one party linked to the interest of ex-king Kòsọ́kọ́ of Lagos, the other pro-Ègbá and generally more sympathetic to the mission. Converts came very slowly and (as in other Yorùbá towns) were much more drawn from slaves, strangers, and migrants than from Ọ̀tà indigenes. Year after year White recorded in his "Annual Letters" his feelings of discouragement at the lack of progress.[9] It must have been very frustrating—for a man who was not only a vehement evangelical Christian, convinced of the folly of "heathenism" and zealous to see its extirpation, but an African anxious for the moral uplift, cultural advance, and material advancement of his race—that his lot was to labor among a people whom he described in a letter to the CMS Secretary Henry Venn as "after the Popoes [the Ègùn of Badagry] [. . .] the most given to pleasure, the most superstitious and idolatrous, and the bitterest enemy of true religion."[10] Even in Freetown, he noted, the Ọ̀tàs "retire from the respectable part of the town to the grassfields that they may better carry on their country fashions [traditional religious practices]. . ." Of forty returnees from Sierra Leone to Ọ̀tà, only four joined his congregation. It was one of these who persuaded the chiefs to ask for a mission to be established in their town, but their motive was purely pragmatic. In Ọ̀tà's precarious situation, suspended between Abẹ́òkúta and Lagos, it was good political insurance to have an *òyìnbó* (white person) resident in the town, but it did nothing to make its people want to become Christians themselves.[11]

Granted the respective religious outlooks of the two sides—White so damning of the Ọ̀tàs' idolatry and they so dismissive of his Christianity—it is impressive that he was moved to write in such detail about the life around him, and so often with such an objective tone about cultural practices he disapproved of. From his perspective there was a lot to condemn, but where he could, he praised, for he was also looking for points on which a Christian culture that was both modern and indigenous could be grown. There must also be a purely personal element, a wonder and curiosity peculiar to him as an individual, that shows itself in quite small observations. He liked to name names and put down the very words that people used. Thus it is White who records the earliest Yorùbá carver we know by name, Kúdóró, a master of Gẹ̀lẹ̀dẹ́ masks; and in contrast to the dozens of *babaláwo* (Ifá divining priests) who pass through the pages of the CMS journals unnamed, he mentions one whose predictions were so accurate that he was called Adọbakúnlẹ̀ ("He whom the king kneels to"), being much consulted by Kòsọ́kọ́ of Lagos. If the words of a song appeal to him, he will quote it, even if they criticize the mission, as with the women who prepared the mud for the walls of the mission-house under his predecessor:

Daddy o! O le pania, awa teyepe, k'a fe di ara orun pupo
Mammy o! Aya re, wá ban'te ille yi o
(Oh Daddy, he could kill a man, we compress mud, till we only want to
be dead.
Oh Mammy, his wife, come and help me compress this earth)[12]

In his very first quarterly journal from Ọ̀tà,[13] White notes the particular
devotion of its people to the òrìṣà Èṣù or Ẹlégbára—"(the Devil)," he
casually adds in parenthesis—and goes on to describe in detail the performances given in Èṣù's honor:

> Sculptors and painters use all their skill "to present to the public [. . .]
> elaborate masterpieces of masks intended to delineate as nearly as possi-
> ble the human features." These were of stock types, such as "the woman
> with plaited hair," "the man with shorn head," "the old man with white
> hair," "the Mohammedan with big beard and head-dress." The actors
> wore silk and velvet costumes, some of which were borrowed for the oc-
> casion from other towns, and wore iron or brass rings on their ankles. If
> an actor fell during the performance he was severely punished. [Though
> White speaks of "actors," they were clearly dancers, and as such must
> have been accompanied by drummers, though he does not mention this].
> Unlike Eẹ́gún ancestral masquerades, these ones are not identified with
> the deceased, but are subject to critical evaluation by the spectators of
> the "game"—"this stick is handsomely dressed," "this stick knows how
> to dance well"—and are rated against one another.[14] The performances
> are funded by public subscription, and anyone who does not contrib-
> ute is disgraced and "even excluded from the society of his respect-
> able companions." The Chiefs play a major role and "not even are they
> ashamed to appear in public as actors." In sum, the Ọ̀tàs' "industry at
> trade and agriculture is not prompted so much for the sake of satisfying
> their wants as to be enabled to join in these games."

White does not expressly identify this as a performance of Gẹ̀lẹ̀dẹ́,
though this can be inferred from a second description he gave fifteen
years later:[15]

> "Today there was a grand play in this town which may be called the
> Gẹ̀lẹ̀dẹ́ exhibition, the principal amusement of the nation . . . [Its aim
> is] to display the skill of the artists in producing the best workmanship
> in carving and painting, and the wealth of that particular section of the
> town." People flock from all the neighbouring towns to see the show,
> which White thinks this year is the "grandest I have witnessed since my

residence in this town." The best mask he saw was one carved with a ba-
nana tree bearing fruit, some painted red to show their ripeness and finished off with parrots perched on their ends. He missed seeing another
even more spectacular mask "with the figures of two children attached
to their sides, all showing motion, as if they were living creatures."

After White's evident appreciation of the artistic skill that went into
Gèlèdé performance and his recognition of its importance in the life of
the community, the harshness of his critique comes as a shock:

> It is a great pity to see the interest and zeal manifested by each individu-
> al and the considerable amount of money lavished on mere fleeting, mo-
> mentary and unprofitable pursuits and gratifications, whereas the great
> and important truth of their being great sinners in the sight of God [. . .]
> is treated with as much indifference as a child's plaything. How forcible
> are the words of Scripture "They spend their money for that which is not
> bread and their labour for that which satisfieth not."

What is notable here is that the main thrust of his objection is not their
idolatrous character as such—his only reference to religion is that the
"games" or "play" were in honor of Èṣù.[16] It is rather grounded in two
attitudes deep-set in the moral culture of bourgeois Evangelicalism: utilitarianism (or more prosaically, a horror of waste) and a distrust of show,
display, or mere appearance.

It is worth elaborating a little on how these attitudes were rooted in
the Evangelical tradition, which so profoundly shaped White. At first
glance he puts us rather in mind of Mr. Gradgrind in Charles Dickens's
Hard Times (1854), who represents the fusion of utilitarianism and phi-
listinism in Victorian England.[17] But White was no philistine in the sense
of being indifferent to the arts or hostile to them as such—as he showed
not only in his appreciative descriptions of Gèlèdé, but in his aspiration
to develop a Christian musical tradition from the culture of the Àwórì.
We might even see in him something akin to the musical trajectory of
Handel in eighteenth-century London, when he moved from writing op-
eras in the Italian style, showy performances redolent of Catholicism and
the loose morals of the aristocracy, to oratorios, Bible-based choral music like *Messiah* or *Jephtha*, that appealed to the sober Evangelical piety
of a Protestant middle class. That was very much in line with White's
taste.

White's mixed attitudes are to be seen in two other fascinating passages of cultural description in his journals. The first concerns what he
calls the "theatres" in Igbèsà, another Àwórì town, where he had gone

to support Williams, the scripture reader, who was having a hard time in the town.[18] These were two-storey oblong buildings made of mud-brick and thatch in the usual way, walled at the back and sides but open to the front. The upper story was supported on pillars and had a wooden floor, made of boards held in place by a low brick wall or parapet above the pillars; between the pillars were carved images. The "theatres" were of various sizes, but one was forty feet long, sixteen feet high, and fourteen feet deep. For decoration, European plates and mirrors were set in their walls, which gave them their Yorùbá name: *ilé àwo* ("plate house"). People gathered in them "when their public plays or amusements" were exhibited; and they were also used by those who came to the service White conducted. As far as I am aware, nothing like these buildings is described for any other Yorùbá town, and assuredly none has survived. The other is a description of a mechanical device deployed by a priest of the òrìṣà Ọsanyìn, an image attached to a rope suspended about six feet above ground, which could be manipulated to move along the rope and produce a nasal sound at intervals that the priest interpreted.[19] White could not resist rising to the challenge of this marvel, which he did by attaching a toy duck to some bellows and, hiding it under a cloth, got it to produce a whispering sound; and then revealed the trick. The onlookers, who had initially been amazed at both performances, fell about with laughter and the priest was shamed for his deception.

All these descriptions focus in one way or another on performance, and White surely got the ethos of his own Yorùbá culture dead right in giving it such prominence in his account, to a greater extent than any other CMS journal-writer. Yet as an Evangelical Christian, he also had deeply ambivalent feelings about it, not only extrinsically, as regards the ends to which it was directed, but also intrinsically, as implying insincerity and deception. And if he nevertheless takes pain to show the skill, artistry, ingenuity, and intelligence of which Ọ̀tà people were capable in their performances, it was in large part to argue that these abilities were misdirected. One aim of his mission was to get them directed aright. His conversion of a drummer called Àjàká seemed a golden opportunity.

• • •

White records their first meeting on February 24, 1855, when Àjàká called to visit him. Àjàká was a man of some standing in the town, for he was a grandson of a former king of Ọ̀tà (the Ọlọ́tà), and his name indicates that he belonged to the royal lineage of Ọ̀yọ́, some of whose members had long been settled in this southwestern corner of Yorùbáland.[20] They had a long talk in which Àjàká told him how God had given him many blessings—wealth, wives, and slaves—but not any children. He had applied to òrìṣà priests for help in getting them, and also to the Muslims. They had taken his money, but no children had come. White spoke of "the Author and Giver of every good and perfect gift, who if he sees fit will satisfy his desires"; but he did not promise him a child or take any money. Àjàká was "delighted" to hear White's citation of the Biblical precedents of Abraham, Hannah, and Zachariah. Three days later White paid a return visit to Àjàká. Over the next few months, there were more mutual visits between them, and Àjàká started attending church regularly.[21] By July his resolve to abandon his òrìṣà was growing and White speaks of him as "Àjàká, my convinced friend."[22] Finally, he smashed the image of his Ẹlẹ́gbára (Èṣù) with a cutlass—apparently in White's presence—and showed him his Ifá wrapped up in a corner, asking White to note that it had not had a sacrifice recently. He said he would keep it as "food for some day to come to chew with my corn."[23]

Àjàká's new Christian identity took some time to become consolidated. In September he told White he was now at peace, whereas before he was always "disquieted in quest of a child."[24] For the rest of the year and well into 1856 there is a lull in references to Àjàká in White's journals. Perhaps it is because White had other things to write about: a visit to Lagos and then an outbreak of civil conflict in Ọ̀tà (though he notes a conversation in which Àjàká explained to him about the disputes in the town). It was not till May that Àjàká's religious quest resumed, with the report that one Sunday after the service his wife had handed over her òrìṣà: Ẹlẹ́gbára, Ifá, and Elere.[25] At some point in the year he generously gave thatch for the church, for which White thanked him in his Annual Letter.[26] In July there occurred what may have been a key turning point. White paid a visit to Àjàká, showed him a Bible, and tried to convince him it was God's book.[27] This in itself was strange: had not this been central to White's message all along, and could Àjàká have got this far without accepting it? That White felt he had, as it were, to go back to basics in this way implies they had reached some critical sticking point. (What this almost certainly was will shortly become clear.) Àjàká then "told me that two nights before, he saw in a dream a person resembling myself, telling him these same things and that there is nothing untrue in all I told him—that he was very uneasy all the while till he consulted his Ifá which told him it was all for good." So it was that the Ifá, which he had set aside, finally sanctioned Àjàká's conversion. It is rather curious that White does not expressly tell us in his journal when Àjàká was baptized. But we can infer that he was among the six adults and four children whom Bishop Crowther baptized on December 7, before a congregation of three hundred, since in the journal entry that next mentions him, January 10, 1857, he is called for the first time by his Christian name, as "Abraham Àjàká, one of our converts." Soon he was accompanying White on his rounds about Ọ̀tà.[28] But one decisive act of his conversion yet remained.

In all the journal entries from which I have reconstructed Àjàká's story so far, his occupation as a drummer is mentioned only once, in passing, as if it were of minimal significance. But in September 1857, White wrote a long letter to Venn, the CMS Secretary, giving an account of Àjàká's conversion in which his role as a drummer is pivotal.[29] Àjàká did not come from the Àyàn drumming lineage.[30] Indeed, his expressed wish to become a drummer was first met with the objection that it was a lowly occupation "as all drummers are beggars"; and, perhaps for that reason, he went to train as a drummer with a man called Aṣàdé at Adó Odò, another Àwòrí town. He duly became known as the finest drummer in Ọ̀tà. He drummed in time of war "to rouse the drooping spirits of the soldiers," and without his presence "the idolatrous [. . .] devotion of the pagans would be cold and devoid of life, for them it was necessary to drum the attributes of the various deities and to awaken them to be propitious to them." His third main public function was to play at funerals. He would also go to the houses of chiefs and big men, to play their praises, and from this he would get cowries for his maintenance.

Unsurprisingly, Àjàká's initial reaction to the Gospel had been one of open hostility, and he once punished a nephew for listening to White's preaching in the street. After he had turned toward Christianity and renounced his òrìṣà, "one of his inquiries always was whether our religion forbade drumming." White's response had to be carefully considered. "Finding that a direct answer would be repulsive to his feelings and occasion a relapse *(for he loves it as his god and actually sacrifices to it)*,[31] I told him not to be in a hurry about that, but that he should not beat it on the Lord's day." Àjàká still sometimes did so by stealth, but he found that if he did so, the skin of his drum would break, as if "God saw him and his hand was against him." So he strictly stopped drumming on Sundays. Later—in November 1856, sometime after his dream—he raised the issue with White again: did Christianity disallow drumming? White now felt that Àjàká's faith was strong enough for him to be told it straight. He reconstructed the exchange thus:

> "Whose praise do you celebrate with those sounds you make with your drum?"
> "The gods."
> "How would you like to have a child who sides with your enemies and uses all [his] efforts to extol and magnify them?"
> "I would be very indignant."

"Can you be a true child of God when you espouse the cause of his greatest enemy the Devil, and do you not in effect recognize idols to be something?"

White told Àjàká that he could not compel him to give up drumming, but asked him to ponder as to whether it really now became him. Àjàká soon left off drumming altogether, though many friends and companions begged him with presents and entreaties to continue. In May or June 1857 he brought his drum—it seems the big ìyá ìlù of a bàtá ensemble—and handed it over to White, saying: "'God is great. I never thought anyone could take my affections from this my favourite pursuit, but God has done so. Take it and do what you want with it. I paid 15 heads of cowries for it. I have been offered much more for it but I refused.'"

White took the drums—two smaller ones went with the ìyá ìlù—but wondered what to do with them. A few months later the veteran English missionary from Abẹ́òkúta, Henry Townsend, was passing through, and offered to buy them. Àjàká refused to sell them, saying "Abraham of old sacrificed his only son to God. I have no child but I give this." So Townsend just took the drums to send to Venn in London. Later a messenger came from Àjàká's old teacher Aṣàdé, now a chief at Adó, with a bottle of rum, to ask if he would sell the drums to him.

After this extraordinary sacrifice, Abraham Àjàká settled into the life of Òtà's small Christian community, and for several years all but disappears from White's journal. Four years later White mentions meeting him discussing the Word of God with some others.[32] Then, in 1870, Àjàká makes a dramatic re-entry in the context of a furious dispute with White, who now described him as "a man of a very vain, boisterous, contentious and covetous disposition."[33] He had gone around town, alleges White, bad-mouthing him—and anyway, he was always quarrelling with someone or other. The dispute arose from a perennially sensitive issue in the Yorùbá Mission, namely the holding of domestic slaves by church members. Àjàká and his wife jointly owned a slave-girl: she had cost a hundred and thirty-four heads of cowries, his wife having provided a hundred and twenty while Àjàká lent her the remaining fourteen. Àjàká liked the girl and wanted to buy out his wife's share, but she declined, offering to pay back the fourteen instead.[34] White was away at the time, so the church members tried to mediate. But they took the wife's side, and White, on his return, agreed with them. The Ọló̩tà (who was Àjàká's uncle) offered to settle the matter privately, but Àjàká refused. He told his wife to go away to Igbèsà, which she did, taking the slave-girl with her and refusing White's pleas to return. Àjàká's anger now turned on White, whom he charged with driving his wife away and taking two of his slaves. All this came to the ears of the Ọlọtà, who again offered to settle things privately; but Àjàká insisted on a public hearing. This would be expensive, but White knew he had to "go public," since he needed to clear his name. Àjàká went around the chiefs to give them money to declare in his favor, which some accepted and some declined. Both parties had to produce a session fee of twenty-two heads and a hearing fee of thirty-three heads of cowries. The hearing lasted from 9:00 a.m. to 4:00 p.m., and finally the verdict was delivered: first by the elders, then by the chiefs, and finally by the Ọlọtà, before a large concourse of people. White was absolved, and the money he had paid was returned to him, but he divided it with the Ọlọtà and chiefs, with his thanks.

For Àjàká, worse was to come. Two days later, Olóru, the greatly feared executive arm of the chiefs, came out at night and announced that he was to leave town for contempt of the Ọlọtà in refusing to have the matter settled privately, but instead forcing everyone to spend a whole day in the burning sun listening to the dispute.[35] He would have been punished by death, as had happened on two previous occasions, but for White's sake the sentence was commuted. His exile was not permanent: he paid an indemnity and was back within the year. Àjàká now spoke against the Christians, trying to dissuade a man from following the prompting of a dream that drew him toward White, and accusing him and the Christians of helping his slaves abscond to Lagos.[36] That is the last we hear of Àjàká. We have no idea whether he gave up Christianity completely or ever took up drumming again.

• • •

A conversion story is a very individual thing, even if its basic components recur in many stories: the personality of the individual, the social and ideological context, the triggers of change, the build-up to a crisis, the establishment of a new identity. The only such story in the CMS archive that bears comparison with the story of Àjàká for its length and detail is that of the babaláwo Akíbọdé, converted by White's friend Samuel Pearse at Badagry in 1863.[37] In both cases the subject was a man who combined an exceptional personality with the command of an important area of cultural knowledge—which meant, in the Yorùbá context, some connection with the òrìṣà. To convert a babaláwo or a drummer was something special! It is widely considered that in Yorùbá culture there are systematic correspondences between personality type, occupation, and òrìṣà-affiliation.[38] The self-mastery and learned authority of a babaláwo were very different from the exuberance and self-projection of a drummer.

Now it so happens that White converted another drummer, Tifá by name. (He gives no indication that the two men were connected with one another or entered one another's stories, though surely they must have known one another.) So how much did Tifá, and his story, resemble Àjàká and his? White first mentions his name in 1857—about the time that Àjàká was having his struggle to give up drumming—while Tifá was encountering family opposition to his interest in Christianity.[39] He had attended the class for baptismal candidates for nine years, when a change of heart suddenly started to show itself.[40] White thought him a clever man, who had learned to read but was prone to levity, vainglory, and sensuality, which one might suppose to be rather drummerly qualities. He once rushed out of church when his friends called him to join them drumming by playing his name on the dùndún. Tifá had two wives and children. Early in 1865 he fell sick, but recovered after his family bought medicine and made sacrifice; but he became uneasy and started "uttering things which appeared strange to his relatives, so much so that he became unmanageable by them." They consulted oracles, who said that his behavior was due to a madness sent by Ifá and Ọwọ̀.[41] When White and a senior church member went to see him, Tifá told them: "'I want no medicine but I have no rest within me. I am seeing strange things. It is no dream. I see them as clearly as can be, though no one else sees them. My heavenly father has given orders to some celestial being to fetch me. He has bound me with fetters and is ready to take me away.'"

Tifá was brought to lodge at the teacher's house, where they thought him deranged. He talked constantly of his sin and said he had no pleasure anymore in his wives. He kept pressing for baptism and said that God had already baptized him as Michael. "He gave a description of what he saw of God, of angels, of heaven, of devils and of wicked men and of hell, all of which accord with the description given in Holy Writ." He was taken home by his relatives, whom White admonished not to give him poison and then say he had been killed by the gods. For a while he was restrained and gagged, but they freed him when at last he started talking sense again. For some time he would not eat. But members of the congregation kept visiting him, and he delighted in their prayers and praises. Gradually Tifá recovered and became quite a different person: "zealous, humble, sober, teachable and affectionate"—a positive catalogue of Evangelical virtues. He released both his wives to choose other husbands, and became active in preaching about the town. Soon after his recovery he handed over to White his Ifá, and also his father's Òsù, "the household god."[42] A couple of later entries suggest his zeal as a Christian was maintained.

Though the personal qualities of Àjàká and Tifá overlap considerably, both being extroverts and egotists given to self-gratification, their
conversion narratives are utterly different. Whereas Àjàká's starts from
a strong and culturally intelligible motive—his childlessness—that led
him to Christian conversion within a couple of years, we have no idea
what may have set Tifá on his spiritual quest, though it took nine years
for him to reach the crisis episode. The psychotic breakdown that over-
took him apparently wrought a radical and permanent change in his personality. White appears to have been a virtual bystander to it, though
his preaching over several years must have laid the foundation for the
eschatological angst that seems to have been at its core. Yet what Tifá
renounced, in the process of making himself a new man, he did entirely
on his own initiative. Àjàká underwent nothing so personally dramatic
or far-reaching in its psychological consequences, and his great act of
renunciation was something artfully pressed on him by White. Perhaps
part of the reason for his eventual relapse was that he remained more
completely his old self in his passage through Christianity and never, at
the deepest level, was reconciled to the loss of his drum.

Notes

1. Editor's note: This was likely the *aṣíkò* or *sámbà* drum (interchangeable terms), developed
from *gumbe* frame drums brought by maroons exiled from Jamaica to Sierra Leone in the late
eighteenth century. This family of drums is of unique construction and was diffused through
West and Central Africa by Kru sailors and, in the current context, Yorùbá-speaking Saros from
Freetown. The gumbe and its associated local forms constitutes one of the earliest musical examples of "diaspora in reverse" (see Waterman 1990, 39–41; Bilby 2011).

2. Editor's note: Drums consecrated with Àyàn must be two-headed like the bàtá and dùndún,
or single-headed without an aperture such as the bowl-drum *gúdúgúdú* so the drumming spirit can
be hermetically sealed inside. Single-skin frame drums such as the aṣíkò or sámbà, or European-
derived drums such as the military snare, were likely favored in the church for this reason.

3. For the record, mainline churches nowadays generally allow dùndún (but less so bàtá)
drums to be used, especially to accompany Yorùbá-style choruses in the less formal parts of their
services, though neo-Pentecostal churches like Deeper Life still do not allow them.

4. On how this later fed into Nigerian popular music, see Waterman (1990).

5. White appears in one footnote in Àjàyí and is absent from Àyándélé.

6. White to Venn, November 25, 1850. This and all other documents prior to 1880 are to be
found in the CMS (Yorùbá Mission) Archives, Birmingham University Library, ref. CA2/O 87.
Documents from 1880 onward have the reference G3/A2. For fuller details, see Peel (2000).

7. White to Venn, June 10, 1864.

8. Between 1864 and 1867 White translated Joshua, I Kings, II Kings, and II Chronicles. The
way they worked was that White would write his translation "in the contracted form the language

is spoken," and Crowther would correct as he "prefers the words written out" (Journal, December 14, 1864).

9. For example, in 1870, he writes of "nothing but discouragement," in 1874 of his dejection at what he's achieved in twenty years, in 1875 he reports the people as "hardened as ever," in 1878 he says the Àwórì are the most "stubborn" of all tribes. After twenty-six years of service, he says, he had conducted 110 baptisms, of which two thirds were of non-natives of Ọ̀tà.

10. White to Venn, February 3, 1864.

11. Òyìnbó means "white person" but often in a cultural rather than a racial sense. In the nineteenth century the native agents of the CMS were regarded as "white men," particularly on account of wearing European dress, as White himself noted on a visit to Ìjẹ̀bú Òde (Journal, October 28, 1852). Even today African Americans typically count as òyìnbó.

12. The Yorùbá text is as White wrote it and the translation is mine (White, Journal, May 3, 1855).

13. White, Journal, December 31, 1855. At that point he had been in Ọ̀tà less than three weeks.

14. "Stick" is White's rendering of igi (tree, wood, wooden carving), which is what Gẹ̀lẹ̀dẹ́ masks were called (see Lawal 1996, 193).

15. White, Journal, January 13, 1871.

16. Perhaps, because he had just arrived in Ọ̀tà, White was not yet aware of the main objective of Gẹ̀lẹ̀dẹ́, to assuage the malign potential of women as witches—though Èṣù certainly has a role, initially as a potential "spoiler" of the ritual, but also as an òrìṣà connected with markets and witches (see Lawal 1996; Drewal and Drewal 1983).

17. It is noteworthy that Dickens (who loved amateur theatricals himself) counterposes to Mr. Gradgrind a group of circus people, "players" like the Gẹ̀lẹ̀dẹ́ dancers and drummers, who stand for spontaneity and feeling against the calculating rationality of utilitarianism. It is surely not accidental, either, that he intensely disliked Evangelical do-goodery, and satirized it in the person of the sanctimonious Mrs. Jellyby in *Bleak House* (1853), who is full of schemes for the improvement of the natives of West Africa. He parodied the freed-slave and trading settlement of Lọ̀kọ́ja as "Borrioboola-Gha."

18. White, Journal, February 16, 1862.

19. White, Journal, January 18, 1855, at Òkè Ọdàn.

20. Àjàká was the mythological brother of Ṣàngó, as well as both his predecessor and successor as Aláàfin (king) of Ọ̀yọ́ (Johnson 1921, 148–54). The names Àjùwọ̀n and Àjàká were "given to males of the Ọ̀yọ́ Royal Family" (Abraham 1958, 40). Ọ̀yọ́ had extended its imperial control in a southwesterly direction as far as the coast in connection with its involvement in the transatlantic slave trade. Several Ẹ̀gbádò towns were directly founded and ruled by Ọ̀yọ́ princes, while other formerly independent towns (like Ọ̀tà) became tributary to Ọ̀yọ́ (see Morton-Williams 1964; Law 1977, 90–96).

21. White, Journal, May 29, July 5, July 10, 1855.

22. White, Journal, July 17, 1855.

23. White, Journal, August 2, 1855. The point of Àjàká's jocular remark about "chewing" his Ifá, is that it took the form of a set of sixteen or more consecrated palm-nuts (ikin).

24. White, Journal, September 18, 1855.

25. White, Journal, May 25, 1856.

26. White to Straith, Annual Letter, January 1, 1857.

27. White, Journal, July 12, 1856.

28. White, Journal, April 8, 1857.

29. White to Venn, September 1, 1857.

30. However, there does seems to have been an Àyàn drumming lineage at Ọ̀tà, if we can make that inference from the name of a man called Àyánbíyì—who, however, is not identified as a drummer (White, Journal, August 7, 1856).

31. My italics. It is strange that these crucial words were struck out in pencil on White's manuscript by the CMS editor who prepared it for publication.

32. White, Journal, October 22, 1861.

33. White, Journal, May 23, 1870.

34. A quarrel over a slave-girl need not be inconsequential—after all, European literature begins with one, the quarrel between Achilles and Agamemnon which drives the plot of Homer's *Iliad*. This led on to the famous characterization of Achilles in Horace's *Ars Poetica*, as "impiger, iracundus, inexorabilis, acer" (energetic, quick to anger, inexorable, keen)—not so different from Àjàká's character.

35. White, Journal, May 25, 1870. Olóru means "the Owner of the Night," and was personified as a fearsome spirit.

36. White, Journal, September 29, 1870 and January 9, 19 1871.

37. See Peel (1990, 338–69).

38. See Barber (1981, 724–45) and Horton (1983).

39. White, Journal, 18, May 20, 1857.

40. White, Journal, May 14, 1865.

41. Ọwọ̀ was a local òrìṣà that discerned and killed witches. For detailed descriptions of its operation, see White, Journal, March 5, 1865 and Annual Letter for 1878.

42. Òsù or Òsùn is a sacred staff possessed by Ifá priests that embodies the òrìṣà Òsùn and is closely tied in with traditional medicine in the Ifá, Ọ̀sanyìn, and Erinlẹ̀ cults. White described it as "a long piece of iron, branched at the end like a candlestick." It also occurs among the idols given up on his conversion by the babaláwo Philip Jose Meffre: Samuel Pearse, Journal, November 7, 1868 (CA2/ O 76). Tifá's name indicates that he too was a babaláwo wielding the Òsùn staff.

References Cited

Abraham, R. C. 1958. *Dictionary of Modern Yoruba*. London: University of London Press.

Àjàyí, J. F. Adé. 1965. *Christian Missions in Nigeria 1841–1891*. London: Longman.

Àyándélé, E. A. 1966. *The Missionary Impact on Modern Nigeria 1842–1914*. London: Longman.

Barber, Karin. 1981. "How Man Makes God in West Africa: Yoruba Attitudes Toward the 'Orisa.'" In *Africa* 513: 724–45.

Bascom, William Russell. 1972. *Shango in the New World*. Austin: African and Afro-American Research Institute, University of Texas at Austin.

Bilby, Kenneth. 2011. "Africa's Creole Drum: The Gumbe as Vector and Signifier of Trans-African Creolization." In *Creolization as Cultural Creativity*, eds. Robert A. Baron and Ana C. Cara. Jackson: University Press of Mississippi. 137–77.

Drewal, H. J., and M. T. Drewal. 1983. *Gẹ̀lẹ̀dẹ́: Art and Female Power among the Yorùbá*. Bloomington: Indiana University Press.

Johnson, Samuel. 1921. *The History of the Yorùbás: From the Earliest Times to the Beginning of the British Protectorate*. Lagos: CMS Bookshop.

Horton, Robin. 1983 [1959]. "Social Psychologies: African and Western." In *Oedipus and Job in West African Religion with an Essay* by Meyer Fortes and Robin Horton. Cambridge: Cambridge University Press. 41–82.

Law, Robin. 1977. *The Ọ̀yọ́ Empire c. 1600–c. 1836: A West African Imperialism in the Era of the Atlantic Slave Trade*. Oxford: Clarendon Press.

Lawal, Babátúndé. 1996. *The Gẹ̀lẹ̀dẹ́ Spectacle: Art, Gender, and Harmony in an African Culture*. Seattle: University of Washington Press.

Morton-Williams, Peter. 1964. "The Ọ̀yọ́ Yoruba and the Atlantic Trade, 1670–1830." In *Journal of the Historical Society of Nigeria* 3: 25–45.

Peel, J. D. Y. 1990. "The Pastor and the Babalawo." In *Africa* 60 (3): 338–69.

———. 2000. *Religious Encounter and the Making of the Yorùbá*. Bloomington: Indiana University Press.

Waterman, Christopher. 1990. *Jùjú: A Social History and Ethnography of an African Popular Music*. Chicago: University of Chicago Press.

The Yorùbá God of Drumming

Introduction

Asọ̀rọ̀ Igi (Wood That Talks)

Amanda Villepastour

● ●

> *Ìwọ Àyàn Àgalú*
> *Asọ̀rọ̀ 'gi*
> *Àwọn ọmọ ẹ tí wọ́n ńgbé ọ kọ́rùn yí o.*
>
> (You, Àyàn Àgalú
> The wood that talks
> Your children carry you around their necks.)[1]

Àyàn is most commonly described as the god of drumming, the spirit of the wood or the first Yorùbá drum maker and drummer. Àyàn's "children" referred to in this opening *oríkì* (praise poem) are drummers, those devotees who sling his sacred wooden vessel over their neck, and through whom the god of drumming talks. The first time in a day that Àyàn drummers pick up their instrument, they praise their god with oríkì such as this one. The Yorùbá words *asọ̀rọ̀ igi*, which frequently resonate in the drummed vocabulary of Àyàn musicians, may even stand in for a drummer's usual name. Asọ̀rọ̀ igi can be translated as "wood that talks," "the speaking tree" (*igi* means both "wood" and "tree"), "[one] who speaks through the medium of wood" (Ọlọrúnyọmi 2003, 5), or "speaker through wood" (Euba 1990, 90). Àyàn is believed to reside in wood and to carve words from it, for Yorùbá drums are usually instruments of speech surrogacy, mimicking and coding natural language into musical talking (Villepastour 2010). Láoyè (1966, 36) attributed human-like powers to the drum wood: "[. . .] if a piece of timber from a tree nearest a roadside is used in carving out a drum, the drum will be able to imitate human tones better, as it is believed that trees like human

3

beings have ears and can hear people talk as they go along the road." For Yorùbá traditionalists, Àyàn, like their other deities, is omnipresent and omniscient.[2]

Àyàn is an òrìṣà, one of the Yorùbá spiritual beings straddling the esoteric and phenomenal worlds.[3] The òrìṣà may be deified human ancestors and historical personalities, as is the original drummer Àyàn, or they may be forces of nature or esoteric energies that were never earthbound, such as the Ẹgbẹ́, a cluster of spirits believed to be one's heavenly accomplices that can protect or cause havoc for the living. To encapsulate the òrìṣà of drumming, the late Susanne Wenger[4] employed the phrase "the linguist and vocal emissary of heaven" (Wenger and Chesi 1983, 203), for Àyàn is believed to speak for all òrìṣà by transforming their esoteric energy into a musical language that rouses congregants to partake in their most powerful acts of communal worship: singing and dancing. Wenger's portrait of Àyàn slips between describing on one hand an invisible spiritual force, and on the other the contemporary Yorùbá drummer, who both represents and enacts the god of drumming. As function links to identity, the drummer in action *becomes* Àyàn. However understood and defined, Àyàn is one of the most salient forces in the ritual life of transnational Orisha Devotion, though enigmatic in comparison with other "major" orishas.[5] With the growing global pervasiveness of Orisha Devotion and music, Àyàn's importance for transnational devotees is continually revealed in new constellations of meaning.

Àyàn is one of many orishas (symbolically said to number four hundred and one) remembered or imagined as having once been human. From their esoteric world, the orishas communicate with humans through divination, possessed human bodies, dreams, and musical performance. Àyàn's primary human agents are drummers who themselves may be referred to by name as "Àyàn" or by kind, as "the Àyàn." The orisha of drumming that lives in and talks with wooden apparatus—the drum—is routinely humanized but is deemed supernatural; Àyàn may be both male and female but has no human body of his/her own and occupies humans through spirit possession from time to time. Asòrò Igi (one of Àyàn's nicknames) is both known and mysterious, tangible and unquantifiable, for wood is solid and sound is ephemeral.

Àyàn, the wood that talks, is known as Añá in Cuba, where descendants of West African slaves (re)produced their spiritual universe.[6] Such is this oricha's centrality in Afro-Cuban (Lucumí) worship (known as Santería, Regla de Ocha, Ocha, or simply *el religión*) that no initiation into the oricha priesthood is complete without a special ceremony called "the presentation to Añá."[7] Equally remarkable is that Àyàn did not manifest in other Yorùbá diasporas, along with the multitude of orishas which were reborn and renamed across Latin America and the Caribbean. Notwithstanding, in the late twentieth century Añá emigrated out of Cuba in the hands of drummers into religious and musical spheres of influence across the Caribbean and Latin and North America into secondary diasporas, for drumming is one of the most powerful, unifying elements in diverse forms of global Orisha Devotion.

Àyàn, Añá and the Orishas

Orisha Devotion has taken diverse yet related forms throughout the Americas, the most populous traditions being Candomblé in Brazil, Santería in Cuba, Shango in Trinidad, Vodou in Haiti,[8] and their diasporic and fused practices in North America and increasingly Europe. More marginal and less-documented diasporic forms that evolved during slavery and have seen recent cultural reclamations (such as Kele in Saint Lucia) are scattered across the Caribbean. Indeed, the export of the òrìṣà out of West Africa into sites of mass slavery in the Americas has resulted in a twenty-first-century orisha diaspora that far exceeds the homeland in terms of sheer numbers of devotees (though not orishas, which tend to have contracted in number). Diverse systems of Orisha Devotion across transatlantic sites have much in common with one another in terms of beliefs, practices, and the centrality of ceremonial drumming. Devotees believe that the orishas have the power to intercept the phenomenal world in order to facilitate healing, aid conception and childbirth, and solve worldly troubles such as problems with relationships and money. Accordingly, the orishas can be petitioned for wealth, children, and other blessings. Morally neutral, they are also believed to have potentially destructive power should the spirits feel offended or neglected; devotees routinely appease the orishas through prayer, praise, music, and sacrificial offerings (ẹbọ) to bring forth their benevolent side. As divination is a central practice wherever orishas are found, devotees consult with expert diviners regularly or learn to divine for themselves. Diligent devotees spend time and energy learning the divination literature, invocatory repertoire, songs, and ritual gestures and dances in order to be socially and spiritually effective.

Given that the various diasporic forms of Orisha Devotion overlap in terms of values, practices, spiritual symbols, material culture, and music, one can only speculate as to why the sacred Yorùbá bàtá drums and their guardian òrìṣà, Àyàn—both so central to African devotion—only developed into a drum-god tradition in Cuba, where Añá resides in their own, creolized batá drums. Other diasporas, where there were also large populations of peoples who fervently worshipped the orishas, do not nurture a Yorùbá drumming god. Àyàn's absence in Trinidad and Brazil in particular is curious and worthy of further research, given the strength and obvious Yorùbá influence in their African-derived religious traditions.[9] Leobons (this volume)—a Brazilian born into the local *orixá* practice, Candomblé, and who is also a priest and drummer initiated into the Cuban oricha tradition—speculates about the absence of a drumming orixá in the numerically second-largest "black country" in the world after Nigeria, while describing his role in bringing Añá from Cuba into Rio de Janeiro. Yet Leobons's insider view cannot explain everything.

Considering the question of Àyàn's absence in most Yorùbá diasporas leads one to formulate a hypothesis. In searching for explanations about cultural transfer or indeed the absence of it, one should be cautious of approaches that attempt to measure ethnic impact based purely on population numbers, an approach still prevalent in both general orisha studies and musical research. Using Shango orisha worship in Trinidad as a case study, Trotman (1976) argues against conflating population numbers with ethnic influence while referring to homeland–diaspora musical transfers, while Kubik (1999, 13) reminds us: "*One* charismatic personality will suffice to release a chain reaction. *One* virtuoso musician can end up being imitated by hundreds. This fact has often been neglected by researchers proceeding from a collectivistic perception of culture." The musician (though not explicitly named) informants of the Cuban ethnographer Fernando Ortíz appeared to understand Kubik's assertion that launching tradition in a new place requires only a small group of knowledgeable, creative, and charismatic (if not forceful) brokers surrounded by a group of compliant participants. Ortíz's resulting inscription of Añá's Cuban beginnings at the hands of just three men, Añabí (an Àyàn drum lineage member), Atandá (a wood carver), and the later involvement of Adechina (a *babalao* divining priest), remains the dominant testimony (1954, 315–16).[10] With no supporting evidence, Ortíz faithfully reported his informants' claim that Añabí and Atandá consecrated the very first Añá batá drums in 1830. Recent struggles for reterritorialization of Añá in new sites of Orisha Devotion such as New York, Venezuela, and Brazil described by Amira, Quintero, and Leobons (respectively) in this volume have obviously been faced with different challenges from those encountered by distant nineteenth-century priests in Cuba. On one hand, the contemporary accounts in the current volume offer insight into how past histories may have been successfully constructed; on the other, they are a testament to the porous interface between oral history and historiography.

Binary models of "transmission through lineage [in Africa] and dissemination through proximity [in the diaspora]" (Dianteill 2002, 122) abound in diasporic orisha studies, often assuming that African priests and musicians are invariably born into traditions while blood lineages in Cuba have been entirely replaced by ritual ones. Yet Barber (1981) and Peel (2000, and this volume) illustrate that free will and proximity were always important determinates in individuals' entry into and exit from òrìṣà cults in Africa. Àyàn lineage members in Nigeria today do have endogamous tendencies, preferring to marry their own kind and to intermarry with members of the Òjẹ̀ lineage of masqueraders (see Klein, this volume). As Peel's preface illustrates and my own fieldwork confirms, non-lineage members do become drummers and initiates of Àyàn for a range of reasons. The loss of Àyàn's consanguineous connection in Cuba may indicate that few agnate members of Àyàn families arrived there during the slave trade. One can only speculate, but the diasporic fracturing of lineage may also be due to the fact that those who did arrive in Cuba were not sufficiently clustered in order to merge the collective knowledge required for the continuation of Yorùbá lineage practice. Marcuzzi (2005, 203) suggests, "criteria such as performance acumen and expertise in drum construction and consecration—areas open to drumming experts from other lineages, artisans (e.g., carvers), and the axiomatic expertise of the Ifá divination cult—dominated the burgeoning cult at the expense of the lineage bearers." Yet in contemporary Cuba, lineage also plays an important role in the transmission of Añá. Though initiation into Cuban oricha and Ifá cults are primarily ascribed by divination, entry into the Añá brotherhood is frequently determined by proximity to family traditions; many a master drummer has trained and initiated his own sons. Initiation into the brotherhood also frequently involves divination, in which devotees with no hands-on experience of drumming can be "marked" for initiation with a recommendation of a musical life.

Beyond methods of transmission, there is no doubt that profoundly divergent practices have developed around the god of drumming in Nigeria and Cuba over two centuries. Drummers on both sides of the Atlantic have been only vaguely aware of each other's practices and beliefs; indeed, significantly less exchange has taken place between drummers in Nigeria and Cuba than between priests of other orisha cults. The escalation of cooperative exchange, competition, and ideological conflict between Nigerian- and Lucumí-initiated orisha priests detailed by Palmié (2013) has had a negligible impact on the distinct musical traditions of devotional drumming, perhaps primarily because most Nigerian Àyàn drummers are Muslims (Villepastour 2009). Transatlantic orisha collaborations have been overwhelmingly dominated by the powerful priests called *babaláwo* (Yorùbá) or *babalaos* (Lucumí) in the Ifá divining cult. In comparison with the diversity of other orisha cults, both domestically and in transatlantic perspective, Ifá tends to have considerably more global coherence in terms of form and content. Reflecting this diversity of orisha cults, the Àyàn lineage and Añá brotherhood also have very different drumming and ritual practices. Notwithstanding, for sacred drummers on both sides of the Atlantic, whether they be nominal or even devoted Yorùbá Muslims who uphold Àyàn rites in private or devout oricha priests who attend Catholic mass on occasion, there cannot be two Àyàns any more than there can be two Muhammads, Jesuses, or Ifás. In line with this emic view, the alternate use of the names Àyàn and Añá or the conjoined Àyàn/Añá throughout this volume distinguishes only ritual practices, sites of worship, and historical contexts but does not designate distinct mythohistorical characters or spiritual beings. By presenting multi-vocal narratives, this volume chips away at rigid, hegemonic understandings of a trans-ethnic, transnational, ambiguously gendered deity. The drumming god's oríkì and rhythms are infinitely creative and fluid; so too are the histories, stories, and characterizations of the Yorùbá drumming god. Just as the drummer's technology of speaking with wood is not simple, endeavors to describe and inscribe the entity resonating within the drums are complicated.

Inscribing the Orishas

The earliest written accounts about the area now called Yorùbáland straddling Nigeria and Benin were those of early European explorers, the Scot Hugh Clapperton and Englishman Richard Lander (1966 [1829]) and later Lander and his brother John (1965 [1832]). Alongside European travelers and scholars across disciplines, the proto-Yorùbá[11] have been self-documenting for over one hundred and fifty years, starting with indigenous missionaries, many of whom were Western-educated Yorùbá-speaking returnees from Sierra Leone who came to be known as Saros.[12] The Church Mission Society (CMS) archives have proved to be a veritable goldmine of documentation about nineteenth-century Òrìṣà Tradition (see McKenzie 1997 and Peel 2000, for example), but curiously seem to be widely overlooked by many contemporary scholars of the Yorùbá diaspora. It is also interesting that Àyàn is not explicitly described by the missionaries. Although passing mentions of drumming do appear, James White's detailed entries about the drummer Àjàká stand out. Peel (1990,

345–46, 359) reports that the missionaries had a bias for babaláwo, the divining priests they considered to be intellectually more "sophisticated" than other òrìṣà priests (*àwòrò*), often deemed "fetish priests" and "corrupt and ignorant deceivers." An entry in Samuel Crowther's *Vocabulary of the Yoruba Language* (1843, 61) reveals a similar contempt for drummers: "A great many batá drummers are beggars." The particularly low social status of drummers may largely explain their absence from the religious and scholarly literature. Notwithstanding, it is in the journals of the Yorùbá-speaking Saro missionary James White that the first known ethnography of a Yorùbá professional drummer emerges (as detailed by Peel, this volume). Although Àyàn is not explicitly named, we are told that Àjàká loved his drum "as his god and actually sacrifices to it." Biographical details indicate that he was from an Ọ̀yọ́ royal line rather than the Àyàn drumming craft lineage, and despite objections to his choice of what was considered "a lowly occupation"—especially, one imagines, for a prince from whom musicians would normally seek patronage—Àjàká was in fact driven toward Àyàn by the desire for a child. In various phases he sought help from Muslim imams, òrìṣà priests, and finally Christian missionaries, but since no path delivered a child, we have no Àjàká descendants to call upon. Hence White's handwritten pages become even more valuable.

The beginning of Yorùbá scholarship (and collective Yorùbá identity itself) was perhaps marked in earnest by Rev. Samuel Johnson's tome, *The History of the Yorubas*, written in the late nineteenth century and published in 1921. Expansive in its description of the òrìṣà and their historical interface with kingship, Johnson dedicates only a page to music with no mention of Àyàn (120–21). The late-nineteenth to mid-twentieth century saw a surge of indigenous religious scholarship about "traditional" pre-Christian and -Islamic Yorùbá practices, which served to shape contemporary understandings of "Yorùbá religion" among a population already predominantly Christian and Muslim. In North America in particular, where various forms of Orisha Devotion burgeoned during the 1960s civil rights movement and later increased following a large influx of Cubans over the following two decades, contemporary religious scholars and devotees alike appropriated early English-language texts about the Yorùbá. Ironically, most texts were compiled by religious outsiders (often Christian clergy) but were regarded as authoritative sources from which to discover and reconstitute "the root" in the orisha diaspora (Clarke 2004; Palmié 2013).

Àyàn was notably minimized or entirely sidelined in these early texts. For example, in a book about the òrìṣà by Lucas (1996 [1948], 162), Àyàn makes a rare appearance under "The Minor Òrìṣàs" in a section called "Igi (Trees)." The author states: "The tree is sacred to Ṣàngó, the god of lightning. It is from its hard timber that the club or axe of Ṣàngó is made."[13] Lucas, however, fails to mention drums or a drumming god. Another Yorùbá religious "classic" is Ìdòwú's *Olódùmarè* (1962), which became something of a handbook in African American reconstructions of Orisha Devotion (Clarke 2004). Ìdòwú's lesser-known contemporary, E. A. Adé Adégbọlá, made perhaps the more significant scholarly contribution in an unpublished thesis (1976), which also does not mention Àyàn. Yet another notable monograph of the same period, which helped define Yorùbá òrìṣà religion as it is now widely understood, was Awólàlú's *Yorùbá Beliefs and Sacrificial Rites* (1979), again bypassing Àyàn. Produced by an elite group of Christian Yorùbá scholars, these books self-consciously generated a systematized "pantheon" of òrìṣà by presenting an archaic "religion" in monotheistic terms with Olódùmarè (god almighty) at the helm. The underpinning aspiration of such scholars in the newly independent nation of Nigeria was to assert Òrìṣà Tradition in favorable terms alongside the world religions, while forging a retrospectively constructed religious identity that was, in reality, at odds with the notion of Yorùbá as a new identity solidified in the 1890s (Horton 1979; Waterman 1990; Palmié 2013). With every new publication and cross-referenced list, the "Yorùbá pantheon" recycled itself into an almost biblical inventory that did not include Àyàn.

The Yorùbá òrìṣà are possibly now the best-known African deities outside of their homeland, for they have been globalizing for at least two hundred years. Not only did devotees, who were violently torn from their homelands in the course of the transatlantic slave trade, take the knowledge and technology of òrìṣà into the diaspora, but the mainland Yorùbá have been one of the most studied and documented peoples in Africa since the mid-nineteenth century, boasting copious literature about their art, spirituality, philosophy, language, social and political life, history, and to a lesser extent, music. The prestige generated by this scholarly attention has led diasporic traditions, such as Regla de Ocha and Candomblé, to "(re)Yorùbárize" their practices and ritual vocabularies.[14] Over time this has resulted in competing African "nations" in diaspora being supplanted by Yorùbá-derived spiritual systems (Parés 2004; Matory 2005). In the extreme, so-called Yorùbá traditions have been strategically and even fraudulently fabricated.[15]

Employing this road-tested sacro-entrepreneurial style, a self-proclaimed *maestre* and personal guardian of Ayom (apparently a lusophone transliteration of Àyàn) attempted to launch this "lost" orixá in Brazil in the first decade of the 2000s. The said individual approached me several years ago in pursuit of my Nigerian fieldwork materials, and had also approached Fernando Leobons around the same time (see his description of the encounter in the final chapter of this volume). Several years on, an online survey suggests that Ayom is still a one-man tradition for which its founder (now also presenting himself as an ethnomusicologist) has apparently devised a drummed repertoire for his excavated god. Perhaps the "ethnographic interface" cooked up by scholarly priests and priestly scholars, forensically critiqued by Palmié (2013, 7–11), is beginning to loop back into academic and ritual communities in new ways. Just as upwardly mobile, imaginative spiritual entrepreneurs seek the unpublished research resources, institutional authority, and means of dissemination of the academy, scholars are becoming more vigilant about the inventive processes and ambitious social aspirations of their research collaborators.

The circular processes of enquiry and documentation swirling between researchers and religious communities described by such authors as Clark (2004), Parés (2004), Matory (2005), and Palmié (2013) have given rise to a sequence of edited collections that focus on a single orisha. The first such scholarly collection was Sandra Barnes's landmark *Ogun: An Old God for a New Age* (1980)[16]—apparently creating a model, as orisha collections have proliferated, including volumes focused on Ọ̀ṣun (Murphy and Sanford 2001), Ṣàngó (Tishken, Fálọlá, and Akínyẹmí 2009), Èṣù (Fálọlá 2013), and Yemọja (Otero and Fálọlá 2013). This present collection about a relatively obscure orisha in transatlantic perspective not only makes the most audible of Yorùbá gods more visible, but it enters into the scholar-devotee loop where "a future pregnant with new pasts" (Palmié 2013, 219) may stimulate a Yorùbárized Añá, engender increased female involvement, empower marginal practices (such as Iyesá in Matanzas, Cuba), and even attract charges against the editor of inappropriate involvement in an all-male tradition and covert political agendas. Indeed, one of the contributors in this volume, the late Katherine Hagedorn, shared with me that she received a death threat via email soon after the publication of her monograph, *Divine Utterances* (2001). The god of drumming is known for heightening emotions and raising temperatures.

The African-Cuban link between Àyàn and Añá has not had an accurate or comprehensive treatment that other transatlantic orishas have enjoyed. Perhaps the resemblance of Yorùbá and Cuban pronunciations and transliterations of "the major" orishas such as Ògún/Ogún, Ọ̀ṣun/Ochún, Ṣàngó/Changó, Èṣù/Echú, Yemọja/Yemayá, and Ọbàtálá/Obatalá render them easier to correlate than Àyàn and Añá. Ortíz (1954, 208) not only revealed the unfamiliarity of his informants with Añá's mainland African precedent and parallel but demonstrated a false confidence in his dictionary excavation methods. Ortíz deemed "*áña* or *añá*" to be a Creole corruption of *dza* or *adza* (words he said are from a Yorùbá dialect), offering the glosses "to wage war," "warrior," "fighter," "dog," or amusingly, "a goblin or spirit that fights with witchcraft." Ortíz errantly collected this material from Bowen's *Grammar and Dictionary of the Yoruba Language* (1858):[17] "adźa, *a dog*, lit. *a fighter*, from dźà, *to fight*" (page 5); "a-dźa, *n. a dog; a fairy skilled in medicine*" [italics Bowden's] (8), glossed in Spanish by Ortíz as "un duende o espíritu que pelea con brujería"; and "dźà, *v. to fight, quarrel, strive; to rage, as a storm*" (28). Bowen used an unenduring orthography where *ź*a represented /j/; the Yorùbá words Bowen refers to are written in contemporary orthography as *jà* (a verb meaning "fight"), *ìjà* (a noun for "fight," "quarrel," or "war"), and *ajá* ("dog"), none of which are remotely related to Àyàn. Ortíz's etymological dog-fight exemplifies his "philological overkill [. . .] from someone who had no firsthand knowledge of the African languages he so insistently exploited" (Pérez Firmat 1985, 198).[18] Kubik (1993, 432) more generally cautions, "If a researcher's method is to compare lexemes that sound 'African' with their apparent counterparts by consulting dictionaries of African languages that happen to stand on his shelves, then he has entered a twilight zone." Considering the authority Ortíz had attained by the time he published his 1954 treatise on the batá and its rituals, as well as the enduring confidence in his written output, this particular red herring—Añá as dog-goblin—may have in fact provided a substantial setback to the pursuit of this diasporic god's ritual lineage and linguistic and spiritual meaning.

Where less could go philologically wrong with two very similar words, Ortíz and other scholars were more successful in cross-referencing the Yorùbá bàtá and the Cuban batá (Bascom 1951; Ortíz 1954; Rouget 1965). Only since the 1990s have researchers begun to acknowledge the link between Àyàn and Añá (e.g., Mason 1992, 6–7; Ramos 2000, 131–34; Hagedorn 2001, 91, 96) and make more comprehensive comparisons (Marcuzzi 2005; Vincent 2006). Perhaps it is this very dearth of literary attention within the spiraling scholar-devotee ethnographic interface of orisha studies that has allowed Àyàn and Àñá drummers to quietly coexist outside of the occasional transatlantic skirmishes between the Big Men of Orisha Devotion (Villepastour 2009). The assembly of liminal scholar-priests (academics who have undergone initiations in the course of their research) and priest-scholars (devotees who have sought academic training) in this volume threatens to stir the pot "in which heterogeneous ingredients—people, practices, modes of thought—are being stewed into each other on the hearth of history" (Palmié 2013, 29).

Stepping back from yet another speculative (or even divined) future, let us rewind to the existing literature about the Yorùbá god of drumming.

More recent literature includes only small sections within articles, theses, and books that focus specifically on Àyàn and Añá.[19] Unlike the vast literature about other orishas, the number of pages dedicated to the orisha of drumming is easily quantifiable; the attention given to this omnipresent orisha is generally fleeting and limited to passages within larger, other-focused texts. Ultimately, it is noteworthy that writings relevant to Àyàn and Añá are scant in relationship to a significant body of scholarship about Orisha Devotion while the sound of drumming and its cultural significance cannot be ignored. Further to the reasoning outlined above, I propose several explanations for Àyàn's conspicuous absence from the transatlantic orisha literature.

An Obscure Orisha

It can easily be argued that Àyàn is as commonplace and omnipresent as those often deemed "the major orishas" in the pantheon such as Ògún, Yemoja, Òṣun, Ṣàngó, Èṣù, Obàtálá, and Ifá. Although the Àyàn drummer exists in the public sphere, his orisha is not visible in the same manner as the rest of the pantheon. There are no obvious Àyàn symbolic accoutrements brandished by devotees, such as the iron cutlass of Ògún, the brass fan of Òṣun, or wooden double-axe of Ṣàngó. Àyàn has no identifying color-coded clothing, bracelets, or ritual crowns associated with most orishas. The identifying artefact for the god of drumming is the drum itself; Àyàn worship is aural and performative. Musical knowledge and know-how equals ritual expertise, and drumming is both a form of worship and a medium to facilitate the worshipping gestures of others. Yet Àyàn's own rhythms and songs—the musical liturgy Àyàn priests perform for their god—are not heard in the main orisha rites, which sequentially "salute" each orisha with musical signifiers.[20] Àyàn's own repertoire on both sides of the Atlantic is private and guarded.

In both Nigeria and Cuba, the orisha of drumming can be distinguished from other major orishas in several respects. The fact that almost all Nigerian drummers self-identify as Muslim is a primary difference. This is not to say that the plural and layered religious practices of Islam, Christianity, and Òrìṣà Tradition do not exist in other òrìṣà cults, for intermarriage and religious tolerance has been a remarkable feature of Yorùbá culture.[21] Beyond this religious plurality among Àyàn drummers (as Àjàká's biography attests), and unlike other òrìṣà cults, Islam is now the core religious and cultural orientation of drummers over which other traditions may be layered (see Klein, this volume). As my primary teacher, Chief Alhaji Rábíù Àyándòkun, once put it, "Islam is my religion and òrìsà is my culture," as marked by the naming sequence of his chieftaincy title "Agbásà Èrìn-Òṣun" (the ambassador of culture in Èrìn-Òṣun), his Mecca pilgrimage title (Alhaji), his Muslim name (Rábíù), and finally his drum lineage appellation Àyándòkun.[22] Contemporary Àyàn drummers provide their services year-round for private events in small communities of òrìsà worshippers as well as for larger, public annual religious and folkloric festivals and events connected to traditional kingship. As Òrìsà Tradition in Nigeria continues to lose ground in the face of religious conversion to the world religions and modernization, most of the work of a contemporary Àyàn drummer in Nigeria now takes place at the secular events of Muslims and Christians such as naming ceremonies, weddings, and funeral celebrations. In urban centers, Àyàn drummers survive primarily by playing popular music in *jùjú, fùjì*, highlife, afrobeat, and Westernized pop outfits. Sacred repertoires are increasingly peripheral to contemporary Àyàn drummers' performances, though those who are internationally active tend to be more focused on òrìsà rhythms, perhaps even learning sacred drumming for the first time to satisfy a very different musical market in Europe and the United States (Klein, this volume).

Behind the scenes, Muslim Àyàn drummers may attend to their òrìsà and ancestor Àyàn, paying homage through drummed or spoken oríkì,[23] consecrating drums by sealing a "secret" inside the shell, or by making sacrificial offerings to the drum of food, herbs, or animal blood. Many Àyàn drummers participate only sparingly in such rites but return to the traditional ways during troubled times. Muslim Àyàn drummers can be tight-lipped about such affairs, as they exist in a liminal space between two distinct religious worlds. While they must be discreet about traditional practices among their "modern" Muslim and Christian peers, the relative rarity of ẹbọ (sacrifice) and other ritual practices in their lives may either be underplayed or overtly performed when among interested foreigners, many of whom are themselves orisha devotees. Hence, Àyàn's absence from the scholarly òrìsà literature may reflect on one hand the obscuring of the drumming god by the overlay of Islam, and on the other the general decline of Àyàn as a "living" òrìsà who is regularly and publicly celebrated in the manner of the more prevalent (and increasingly commoditized) deities in Nigeria and Cuba.

A more rudimentary difference between Àyàn worship and that of other òrìsà cults is the mode, or even absence of initiation in Àyàn compounds. Most orishas in Cuba and Brazil, as in Nigeria, are symbolically placed within the head of devotees in a seven-day ceremony called the *ìdóṣù* in Nigeria, *kariocha* or *asiento* in Cuba, and *adoxu* in Brazil. While variation exists between orisha cults and local practices in these three transatlantic sites, the first day of an initiation to orishas such as Oshun, Ogun, or Shango is marked by a ceremony in which the initiate's head is shaved, painted, and "seated" with their tutelary orisha by placing the orisha vessel (that is, the pot or calabash containing stones and other consecrated accoutrements containing the energy of the orisha) on the crown of the head of the initiate. Hence, initiated devotees are often deemed "crowned" in orisha vernacular in the Americas. By this ritual action, the connection between the orisha's *ashe* (life force)[24] and the neophyte's head and inner being (*orí inú*) is activated with sacrifice (ẹbọ), medicinal substances (*oògùn*), and powerful incantations (*ọfọ̀*), forging an irreversible link between the person and their orisha. The initiate and the orisha enter into a lifelong mutual commitment.

The ìdóṣù ceremony is now rare (although not unheard of) within Muslim Àyàn compounds. Àyàn lineages that never converted to Islam or Christianity are most likely to uphold the ìdóṣù ceremony for Àyàn, yet drummers whose primary allegiance is to the òrìṣà are now rare within Muslim Àyàn families in Nigeria. The Àyàn "òrìṣà men" such as Àyánṣọọlá and Àyángbékún (this volume) hold a tenuous legacy. In Cuba, no one has ever been "crowned" with Añá, not even in distant memory. Añá initiations are more systemized and uniform in comparison with the variegated landscape in Nigeria, yet Añá initiations are distinct from other oricha initiations in Cuba, which for some calls into question the very taxonomy of Añá as oricha (see Vélez 2000, 48; Hagedorn, this volume).

Spirit possession is connected with the practice of placing the orisha "in the head." Hence, in Nigeria Àyàn can possess the bodies of humans, though this is now a rare and marginal practice generally restricted to the funerals of Àyàn drummers (see Villepastour, this volume). In Cuba, where Añá is never crowned, possession by the oricha of drumming is not regarded as a possibility, perhaps again threatening Añá's status as oricha. Due to their initiation practices, Àyàn and Añá do not "live" in vessels that are easily recognizable in relation to more common orisha practices. When a devotee of pantheon orishas such as Ọ̀ṣun/Ochún, Ṣàngó/Changó, and Ògún/Ogún is "seated" with their orisha, they will then be known as an *iyàwó/iyawó* (a "bride" of the orisha) for a period following the ceremony. The iyàwó receives and takes home a sacred vessel, usually of clay, wood, glass, or gourd, containing the consecrated stones and accoutrements of their òrìṣà to which they are expected to prostrate, make offerings, and pray. In the vast majority of

Àyàn compounds in Nigeria, no such vessel exists. Rather, the god of
drumming is ritually placed inside sealed drums in a closed ceremony, as
with Añá in Cuba.[25]

Another difference between Àyàn and other orishas is that Àyàn has
no color-coded, blood- and herb-consecrated beads, which customarily
mark other orisha initiations. As well as providing spiritual protection
and keeping the energy of the orisha close to the initiates, coded beads
act as an identity marker. This is not so with the orisha of drumming;
Àyàn is not identified visually, but projects aurally from a dark, resonating wooden vessel.

The Sacred Drummer

Like the many òrìṣà that derive from mythological personalities, the
Yorùbá god of drumming straddles categories. Àyàn is remembered as
an historical personality, deemed to be the first Yorùbá drummer and
drum maker in service to Ṣàngó when he was king of Ọ̀yọ́ in the fifteenth
century. Multifarious appellations and descriptions of Àyàn are simultaneously applied to encompass the òrìṣà, the ancestor (eégún), and the
spirit of the àyàn wood. Àyàn can designate a male and female figure
of either Yorùbá or foreign (non-Yorùbá) extraction. In reference to the
drumming ancestor and first drum maker, Àyàn is always designated as
male. The cultural logic is that because all Yorùbá drummers are male,
Àyàn must obviously be male. But when imagined as an esoteric entity,
Àyàn and Añá are frequently cast as female (Hagedorn, Villepastour, this
volume). Àyàn is at once a deified human and a humanized deity, his/her
mythological identity intertwining with the contemporary lives of Àyàn
drummers. Beyond the variegated narratives of who the òrìṣà of drumming is or was, perhaps the common thread throughout Yorùbáland and
the òrìṣà diaspora is that Àyàn was the first drummer and/or drum maker.
Láoyè (1959, 10) reports that Àyàn "taught some Yorùbá families the
art of drumming and he was so loved by them that they deified him after
his death." Similarly, some Cuban Ifá texts depict the drumming oricha as an ancestral carpenter who made the first consecrated bátá drum
(Vincent 2006, 153).

Deriving from this oral history, Àyàn is at the center of a contemporary craft lineage: the drumming trade. Just as a pan-African "sacred iron complex" probably emerged out of iron-making technology
(Barnes 1997; Herbert 1993), so too one often finds drum deities and
spirits where drum-carving technologies are culturally important. Other

òrìṣà-led trade lineages among the Yorùbá include Ògún (hunting and smithing), Ìyámòpó (pottery), Ọbàlùfòn (weaving), and Òrìṣà Oko (farming). But Àyàn is now the only musical lineage among the Yorùbá where others have faded, such as that of the òrìṣà of wealth, Ajé, represented by West Africa's former currency, cowrie shells. Ajé's devotees traditionally specialized in the production and performance of the ṣèkèrè (the shell-clad gourd idiophone). Ògún's blacksmiths were once musicians, making hocketed music with their iron forges, yet only vestiges of this rich musical tradition remain. It is not unique that the Yorùbá have an ancestral god of drumming. Many West and Central African peoples have their own drum spirits, such as the ancestral spirits Shija, Gwakume, and Gbatumen who taught the Tiv (in eastern Nigeria) the mysteries of drumming. In many West African cultures, the tree and the spirit of the drum are one and the same. To the Akan in Ghana, Odùm is both a tree and a deity, and for the Ewe, the same tree and spirit is named Logo. In Christianized areas of Ghana, these trees are intentionally chopped down as "witch trees" (pers. comm., James Burns, December 20, 2007) as are Yorùbá ìrókò (African teake) trees, an object of traditionalist worship. Drum spirits are also not exclusive to the Lucumí in Cuba; Haitians, for example, consecrate drummers with Adya Hounto (see Amira, this volume). However, it is Àyàn's contemporary success and dominance in contemporary life that is remarkable. The ancestral Àyàn presides over the craft lineage associated with making and playing drums. He is simultaneously imagined as a force of nature that resides in living trees and the sonorous wood of drums. Within these intersecting imaginaries, Àyàn does not exist outside of the drumming trade. Àyàn and Añá devotees, initiates, descendants, and aficionados almost always drum, whereas Ògún devotees, for example, are no longer obliged to smith in order to be considered fully fledged Ògún priests.

Like all òrìṣà, Àyàn is known by many names. Among the most common is Àyàn Àgalú, which is frequently elided to Àyàngalú or abbreviated to Àgalú. These names are often used interchangeably, but I have also collected conflicting explanations from Yorùbá drummers. I have heard that Àgalú can denote Àyàn's father, Àyàn's mother, Àyàn's wife, or Àyàn's oríkì (praise name) depending on the storyteller and the context of the narrative. Àgalú may even be used as a nickname for a humanized Bàtá (see Àyángbékún with Villepastour, this volume). Contemporary Ọ̀yọ́ drummer Jàre Àyánkọ́sọ̀ọ́ uniquely claims that Àyàn was originally called Sàátẹ́ and was the attendant for the Aláàfin (king) of Ọ̀yọ́. It was Sàátẹ́'s role (as it is for contemporary Àyàn drummers) to let the king know about the arrival of visitors. Àyánkọ́sọ̀ọ́ argues that the name Àyàn derives from *yàn* (to choose) and that the etymology of Àyàn means "the one who chooses."[26] It is this intersection of function and identity that marks Àyàn as the progenitor and ancestor of the Àyàn craft lineage.

While there is a general consensus that Àyàn was an ancestral drummer and/or drum maker, his place of origin has less cohesion. Oral narratives about Àyàn most commonly locate him in Ọ̀yọ́, the kingdom of his mythological friend and royal benefactor, Ṣàngó. Láoyè (1959, 10) nudges the narrative further north, designating Àyàn a native of Saworo (a town that now exists only in oral literature) in Ìbàrìbá in northwest Yorùbáland. Other oral recitations place Àyàn's origin and life north of the Niger River among the Nupe people (Wenger 1983, 203; Thieme 1969, 183) or even Hausaland (Marcuzzi 2005, 165; 2011). Less commonly, Àyàn's life is situated in Ilé-Ifẹ̀, the purported cradle of civilization of the Yorùbá, while Àyánṣoolá (this volume) provides an idiosyncratic narrative that closely positions the historical figure Àyàn with the details of his own family history in Ìjẹ̀bu, a southernmost region of Yorùbáland.

The òrìṣà wield significant moral power among believers, where *ìwà pẹ̀lẹ́* (good character) is said to richly reward devotees with wealth, health and longevity. When one has transgressed, however, the god of drumming is no less swift and brutal in retributions than any other deity. Although Àyàn has many facets, two aspects of this òrìṣà are recurring: Àyàn is a "hot" òrìṣà, and he is insistent upon honesty and justice. Devotees categorize the òrìṣà on a continuum of the hottest spirits, such as Ògún the blacksmith who works with fire, Ṣàngó who manipulates lightning, and Ṣọ̀pọ̀nnọ́, the òrìṣà of smallpox who first manifests with a fever; at the other end of the spectrum, the coolest òrìṣà include the agriculturalist Òrìṣà Oko, whose livelihood depends on rain, and Ọ̀ṣun, Yemọja, and Ọ̀tìn, who reside in the cool water of the river and are all female. "Hot" often evokes male-ascribed occupations, such as blacksmithing and war (Ògún) and hunting (Ọ̀ṣọ́ọ̀sì), while "cool" is associated with the *òrìṣà funfun* (white òrìṣà) whose occupations are more benign, such as Ọbàtálá (the etymology of which is "king of the white cloth," the òrìṣà of creativity) and Ọbàlùfọ̀n (the òrìṣà of weaving) who were turned to for protection against fire, both literally and metaphorically (Peel 2002, 98). Yet the òrìṣà eternally resist neat binaries such as hot/cold, black/white, and male/female. Attesting to the complex ambiguities of òrìṣà and the tendency to counter every formula with an opposite, the female river òrìṣà Ọya is considered to be hot. Indeed, she is said to have taught Ṣàngó the secrets of fire. "Cool-headedness" is a revered feminine attribute among the Yorùbá, while "hot-headedness" is regarded as a male inclination and a feared and negative female tendency, as expressed by the witches (àjẹ́). As a hot òrìṣà, Àyàn's devotees (drummers) are advised to resist the temptation to be hot headed, causing them to argue and fight. As devotees are believed to both naturally encapsulate and develop the traits of their tutelary òrìṣà, perhaps it is Àyàn's heat that gives many drummers the reputation of being volatile. Àyángbẹ́kún cautioned, "The moment you get angry, Àyàn will escalate the situation and there may be a problem because when Àyàn is angry, all other òrìṣà will join in the fight" (pers., comm., August 2003). Echoing such terrifying portraits of Àyàn, Cuban Carlos Aldama declares, "When Añá takes to the streets it is *para contraversiar* (to find conflict, raise hell) with the dancers, the singers, and to attract the spirits with this commotion [. . .] Añá is a devil (*un diablo*)" (Vaughan and Aldama 2012, 28). Such outbursts of the god of drumming are frequently framed as a response to unfairness. Like Ògún, Àyàn is universally regarded as being an òrìṣà associated with justice and may be called upon to mediate and curb dishonesty, for devotees believe that Àyàn punishes deceit and can even kill in the name of justice. In disputes, adversaries may be asked to put their head to an Àyàn drum and proclaim the truth. Lying in the presence of Àyàn, I have been told on numerous occasions by a range of drummers, may result in a bad headache at best and death at worst.

Making Sense of Àyàn Utterances

As Àyàn is continually reconstructed through human and drummed utterances, we inevitably encounter disparate, contradictory yet intersecting images and narratives of this òrìṣà. In surveying the array of Yorùbá oral genres and secondary sources that speak of Àyàn, one might ask for example, how can Àyàn simultaneously originate in the towns of Ọ̀yọ́, Nupe, Ilé-Ifẹ̀, or even the Nigeria's northern region of Hausaland? How do we make sense of Àyàn's intermittent appearances as a husband, father, wife, and concubine? Which accounts are authentic, and how does a student or devotee of Àyàn process this outpouring of conflicting information? Who or what should one believe?

To survey the performed and written texts about Àyàn (or any other òrìṣà) and attempt to smooth over the dissonance of incompatible identities and histories in order to generate a consonant and authoritative "life of Àyàn" would be misguided, if not misleading. As Barber (1990, 317) masterfully demonstrates, "Inconsistency, fragmentation and merging of òrìṣà need to be treated not as accidental and regrettable untidiness, but as central features of Yorùbá religious thought and practice." Yet as the dynamism of Yorùbá spiritual beings is not unique, it is helpful to survey the relationship between the performance of text as a medium and source of history, and an utterance's relationship to the larger context of tradition.

Vansina (1985, 12–14) suggested that oral history is a recitation of sequenced past or present events, whereas oral tradition comprises intergenerational messages, which may or may not be chronologically organized. He theorized that personal anecdotes both become and derive from family traditions, while multifarious accounts over more than one generation may become fused into more stable narratives of events and people. As an example of Vansina's category of oral history, Àyánṣoolá (this volume) recites the names of his Àyàn ancestors back to the eighteenth century, while simultaneously placing himself into a lineage deriving from the first Àyàn, the Àyàn. Àyánṣoolá locates Àyàn's descent from heaven into the Nigerian town of Ilé-Ifè, from where he says the drumming progenitor traveled to the towns of Ọ̀yọ́, Ìbàdàn, and finally to Ògúnmógbó near the birthplace of his (Àyánṣoolá's) father, simultaneously inserting his family into Àyàn's myth and incorporating Àyàn into his own lineage history. From his final stop in Ògúnmógbó during his time on earth, Àyánṣoolá tells us that Àyàn ascended back to heaven. When lining up Àyánṣoolá's account with some established historical facts, Àyàn's decent into Ilé-Ifè could feasibly have been earlier than 1000 CE, as the town was likely founded prior to this time (Horton 1979, 97). If Àyánṣoolá's story coheres with the most popular accounts of Àyàn, the original drummer was a contemporary of the fourth Ọ̀yọ́ king, Ṣàngó, whose time of reign remains vague, sometime in the fourteenth or fifteenth century (Thieme 1969, 14–19, 183–86). Àyánṣoolá tells us that Àyàn's next move was to Ìbàdàn, which could not have been earlier than the 1820s, when the first military settlements began to coalesce there after the demise of old Ọ̀yọ́ (Watson 2003, 16). Àyàn's earthly pursuits, according to Àyánṣoolá, terminated in his own hometown, Ògúnmógbó, which may project an unlikely antiquity onto this contemporary Ìjèbu town. Àyàn's history is both temporally compressed and geographically diverted in order to raise the significance of the narrator's town, thus centralizing his own family's historical proximity to Àyàn. As anything beyond the remembered past is cast into time immemorial (látijọ́) in Yorùbá narratives, lineage status trumps historical accuracy, or as Peel (1968, 139) puts it, "the past is perceived as entirely the servant of the needs of the present." There is also the added layer of performing for foreign ethnographers. Of Àyàn's history in relation to the dùndún, Thieme (1969, 19) notes:

In evaluating the legends and statements taken from oral tradition quoted above, it may be stated that only one of them is widely reported: the one connecting the history of the <u>dundun</u> drums to the Yoruba creation myth. This belief may be said to have somewhat of the character of a "revised standard version." That is, it is the one generally accepted "for outside consumption" (i.e., by visitors, or "outsiders"). The other versions may be said to have primarily local currency, among the drummers (or "insiders") [. . .] This, of course, does not bring one any closer to the ultimate truth of the matter.

Ìtàn (stories, narratives, histories) are fluid by nature, and one can likely find hundreds of variants of the "life of Àyàn" throughout Nigeria as narrators centralize their own family lineage and town in uttered performances. Although each narrator may insist on the authenticity and historical accuracy of his own account, variation nevertheless abounds. Yet beyond inconsistency, it is the intersection points of diverse narratives and the emergence of recurring themes that begin to define Àyàn and standardize this òrìṣà's history. Indeed, lineage status is one of the most prevalent themes. For Añá cult members in Cuba, where agnate lineage was severed through slavery, it is initiation lineages and one's allegiance to eminent sets of drums which largely shape contemporary narratives (see, in particular, Quintero, this volume). The most prestigious Añá lineage in Cuba leads back to three African-born slaves, Añabí, Atandá, and Adechina. It is this narrative—committed to print by an authoritative ethnographer, Fernando Ortíz—that has virtually usurped the possibility of alternative Añá histories, at least up until now.

The fluid and ephemeral nature of orality becomes fixed when documented via recordings and/or print. A case in point, Ortíz's unnamed informants were likely those centralized in the text.[27] As the first written account of an oral history said to have been 120 years old at the time of publication (1954, 315–21), Ortíz's document has become *the* (virtually uncontested) historical account of Añá's beginnings in Cuba. Yet when the time frame is smaller and the gap between observation and authorship is closed, as in the contemporary histories of Añá in Venezuela, Brazil, and New York reported by the authors at the nucleus of these narratives (Quintero, Leobons, and Amira, respectively), the accounts may become less problematic, at least in terms of alternative local histories. Whether contemporary or past, the narrator has the power to assemble events and aspirations into a "schema of long-term actions" (Peel 1995, 587). Just as Ortíz's informants steered Añá's Cuban history in a direction that immortalized their own agency, Quintero, Leobons, and Amira (and Nigerians Àyánṣoolá and Àyángbékún) both determine and become part of the history they write. The main differences, however, between these contemporary contributors and Roche, Torregrosa, Díaz, Pérez, Hinojosa, Ramírez, and Piña is that the contributors to this volume are credited and significantly less mediated, rendering the ethnographic interface more porous than cyclic.

Beyond written sources, the Yorùbá and their descendants in Cuba have a range of oral performance genres within which Àyàn and other òrìsà are continuously realized. Perhaps the best-known genre is the Ifá divination corpus comprising 256 subsets of memorized and recited "chapters" called *odù*. Verses (*ẹsẹ*) of Ifá are harnessed by contributors across this volume to describe the drumming orisha. The corpus of cowrie shell diviners, the less-documented but highly significant *dínlógún*, also has much to say about the òrìsà of drumming, as Àyángbékún (this volume) virtuosically demonstrates. Both Ifá and the dínlógún comprise memorized texts in the form of chanted divination verses (ẹsẹ), praise poetry (oríkì),[28] songs (*orin*), and oral stories or histories (referred to as *ìtàn* in Nigeria and *pataki* in Cuba). Despite these typologies, the broad genres named above frequently borrow from one another and overlap (Amherd 2010). Barber (1990) argues that ìtàn are adjuncts to oríkì, in that one is embedded in the other. The words of memorized chanted or sung texts such as ẹsẹ, oríkì, and orin reside within poetic or musical arrangements, which limit variation of the text. By contrast, ìtàn are spoken stories that are by nature more open to reinterpretation and improvisation, and although internally consistent, can vary greatly between different narrators or even the repeated performances of a single storyteller. So while, for example, Àyánsọolá's family version of Àyàn's life in the form of ìtàn may be regarded as oral history, it is not oral literature, nor are his propositions supported by oral literature. By contrast, Àyángbékún interpolates stylized oral literature in the form of chanted oríkì and dínlógún verses between freer, spoken ìtàn. While oral literature can be oral history (as in the case of Àyángbékún) oral history is not necessarily oral literature, nor is it necessarily supported by oral literature.

In viewing the array of source materials and methodologies employed in this volume resulting in multifarious accounts of Àyàn and Añá, how can the reader begin the task of tying the variegated oral sources together in order to form a holistic image of Àyàn? How can one understand Àyàn's ever-shifting identity, which may effortlessly oscillate between the historical first Yorùbá drummer and the esoteric wife of Èsù, who is the òrìsà between heaven and earth? How are we to process Àyàn's promiscuous conjugal relationships (Àyángbékún with Villepastour), moral constitution and family identity (Klein), ambiguous or switching gender (Hagedorn, Villepastour), and varying and contested functions (Delgado)?

Barber (1990, 331) rationalizes the conflicting strands by pointing out, "As long as the proposed relationships put the òrìṣà in a favorable position, the details seem not to matter very much." That is, the narrative's primary function is to elevate both Àyàn and the narrator himself or herself, rather than to utter irrevocable fact or truth. While narratives can represent a real or presumed past, they may be "sketches of possibilities, prophecies, or scenarios for things that might be" (Peel 1995, 584). Firstly, Àyàn is placed in favorable proximity to historical characters (for example, as the male close friend of or wife of Ṣàngó, the king of Ọ̀yọ́). Àyàn may also be represented as being more powerful than or morally superior to other òrìṣà (Àyángbékún). Secondly, the narrator places himself through his family lineage and often his town in proximity to a once-living Àyàn. Contemporary Nigerian Àyàn drummers recite their lineage credentials and geographical proximity to Àyàn in order to promote their authority, orthodoxy, and employability (Àyánṣoolá): "Just as narrative is an expression of power, it also works to empower those who can achieve it" (Peel 1995, 593).

In order to make sense of the multifarious descriptions of Àyàn in this volume, one might distinguish on the one hand, contradictory material that functions to elevate the òrìṣà and the narrator, and on the other, intersecting, repeated themes that describe Àyàn. Whether male or female (Villepastour, Hagedorn), a native of Ọ̀yọ́ or Nupe, on the warfront, crossing the Niger on a divining tray or waiting naked between heaven and earth (Àyángbékún), residing inside a batá or iyesá vessel (Delgado) or a human cranium, Àyàn is never far from a drum. The resonating membranophone is the communication instrument mediated by Àyàn and mastered by his devotees, transmitting messages between people, òrìṣà and this world and the other.

Histories Herein

In the absence of copious references, such as those at the fingertips of contributors in other orisha collections, many authors in this volume have negotiated the onerous task of reconstructing Àyàn and Añá with few secondary sources. It is this pioneering volume that compiles histories and descriptions of the orisha of drumming for the first time. With the inclusion of cross-references in the main text and endnotes, the chapters intertwine with one another in interesting ways. The inter-relatedness of the texts and some of their authors offers a multidimensional view of Àyàn/Añá, helping the reader grasp the essence of an orisha who continues to adapt to new environments and situations.

This collection is multidisciplinary in nature, encompassing religious studies, ethnomusicology, anthropology, history, linguistics, and gender studies. The contributing authors come from a wide and overlapping range of backgrounds (initiates, scholars, and drummers), nationalities (Nigerian, Cuban, Venezuelan, Brazilian, U.S. American, Canadian, British, and Australian) and call on a diverse range of methods and approaches. Some authors are scholars and cultural outsiders (Amherd, Delgado, Hagedorn, Schweitzer, Klein, Marcuzzi, and Villepastour), though all have been musically immersed and some religiously involved and have collated and analyzed oral sources collected through fieldwork against the limited existing literature. Other writers in this volume are non-academic spiritual and musical insiders (Amira, Leobons, Quintero) who organized and sequenced their own memories and experiences into an authored form. Yet other cultural insiders (Àyángbẹ́kún, Àyánṣoolá, Akìwọwọ and Font-Navarrete) constructed more reflective accounts through internalized observations and musings. Despite their diversity, all of the above authors have been active in transatlantic conversations and/or travels.

Peel's preface is unique to the collection as it is based entirely on the personal journals of missionaries excavated from the Church Missionary Society (CMS) archive held in Birmingham, though his interpretation is seen through a lens conditioned by decades of ethnographic research among the Yorùbá. Echoing his landmark essay *The Pastor and the Babalawo* (1990), Peel portrays the first Yorùbá drummer, Àjàká, to be named and fully characterized in European writing. Through close study of the journals of the African man who converted him to Christianity, Reverend James White, Peel concludes that Àjàká was never "reconciled to the loss of his drum." Perhaps he never recovered from the surrender of the entity he "*loves* [. . .] *as his god.*"[29] If White was as successful in extracting Àjàká from the drumming profession as he was in removing the drums, he neither eradicated the lineage nor its god. As Klein argues, "being Àyàn" can be distinct from Àyàn worship, just as contemporary "Àyàn-identified" Muslim converts negotiate the changing social and religious terrain through performance craft. Klein developed a detailed ethnography by living with the families of her Nigerian research collaborators for an extended period, while other contributors apprenticed themselves to the practical drill of drumming (Villepastour, Font-Navarrete, Delgado, Hagedorn, Schweitzer, Amira, Leobons). While scholars routinely claim the power of constructing the narrative form, Peel (1995, 583) reminds us, "Whether it is the outsider-analyst or the insider-subject's narrative that predominates in an account, neither kind of narrative can stand without quite a deal of the other." The asymmetrical duality of "scholar" and "informant" is collapsed into shared authorship in three chapters of this volume, in which several interviews with Àyángbékún were edited and illuminated by Villepastour (ch. 2), Amherd organized and refined Àyánsoolá's autobiographical written essay (3), and Quintero's conversations and emails were assembled by Marcuzzi into a compelling narrative form (10).

The chapters are organized into five broad themes. The opening section titled "Cosmologies" uncovers some of Àyàn's esoteric world. Akìwowo and Font-Navarrete partnered to describe the òrìsà of drumming as spiritual insiders, one an elderly Nigerian babaláwo and prestigious sociologist, the other a musician and ethnomusicologist of Cuban and Puerto Rican descent who is an initiated drummer and caretaker of Añá's sacred vessels. Àyángbékún knew Àyàn intimately as a bàtá drummer, Sàngó and Àyàn priest, Egúngún masquerader, and master dínlógún (shell) diviner. With the blessing of his family, I have organized his virtuosic divination recitations into cohesive strands intertwined with explanatory prose, giving the reader access to a performance mode and oral literature corpus that is increasingly rare, as are Àyàn priests such as Àyángbékún who have no allegiance to Islam or Christianity.

Although all of the chapters refer to Àyàn's past, the thematic section "Histories" presents two very different angles. The first, from Àyánsoolá with Amherd, describes an Àyàn lineage history outside of the Òyó bàtá/Àyàn hegemony. While Àyánsoolá's narrative appears to dispute Àyàn's mainstream identity as a native of Òyó, we are presented with a typically malleable account that places the narrator, his kin, and his hometown in the center of Àyàn's human-life history. On the other side of the Atlantic, Delgado contests the received history authorized in print by Fernando Ortíz (1954) that Añá exists exclusively within bátá drums. Presenting evidence to the contrary, Delgado challenges this oricha's historiography.

"Genders" presents essays from Villepastour and Hagedorn about Àyàn and Añá, respectively. Villepastour's essay presents the contrasts between transatlantic Àyàn-Añá traditions in terms of their gender framing. Drawing on Nigerian fieldwork and critiquing the transatlantic commentary about the orisha of drumming, she describes a more relaxed and inclusive attitude in Africa in comparison with the Cuban diaspora. Focusing on Cuba, Hagedorn employs Añá's gender representation in secondary and oral sources to critique the discourse gleaned from her own fieldwork. Countering hooks' complaint that "ethnocentric white values have led feminist theorists to argue the priority of sexism over racism" (1986, 131), Hagedorn examines the gender hierarchy in Añá musical and ritual performance in relation to race and nationality. Villepastour and Hagedorn illustrate that the gender discourse in Nigeria and Cuba has been generated by cultural and religious insiders, despite contemporary assumptions that resistance to female and homosexual exclusion originates with the feminist interventions of foreigners (Villepastour 2013).

Schweitzer's contribution to "Identities" both dovetails and contrasts with the former section as he reflects on being a initiated member of an all-male brotherhood, whose prohibitions are "largely unaffected by modern feminist influences." Like Hagedorn, Schweitzer broadens the discussion to the issue of race, though not in relation to gender. He correctly asserts that "discourse regarding the lack of access permitted to women has been largely propagated by fraternity outsiders" and as a (foreign) cult insider, describes bonding strategies, community formation, and space maintenance in the Añá fraternity. In an essay drawing on over twenty years' careful ethnography, Klein provides a transatlantic counterpart to Schweitzer, reporting and analyzing what it means to be a Yorùbá master drummer in terms of ethnic and religious identity in contemporary Nigeria. Her intergenerational research findings are in some respects at odds with the more idealized presentation of the Àyàn drummer presented by Akìwowo and Font-Navarrete. Klein contests the North American "naturalized" notion of the Yorùbá Àyàn drummer as òrìsà worshipper, largely gleaned from contemporary Cuban practices (as described, for example, by Schweitzer) and superseded Yorùbá scholarship. Rather, Klein offers insight into the socially complex world of Muslim Àyàn drummers, laying bare their plural religious experience and survival strategies within an endangered musical and cultural tradition.

The final section, "Secondary Diasporas," collates accounts of Añá's instigation in new territories. Amira's chapter about Añá's beginnings in New York offers an insider's story that exudes musical drive and desire. In explaining events as he remembers them, Amira's account both expands and challenges the existing historiography of early batá drumming in New York. That Amira—a white New Yorker whose agency helped establish the tradition in his own city—is missing from written sources penned by African Americans and Latinos considered to be authoritative (e.g., Mason 1992; Vega 1995) perhaps speaks of the essentialist environment into which Añá was "born"—Civil Rights–period New York. Chapters 10 (Quintero, with Marcuzzi) and 11 (Leobons) lay out the contemporary histories of Añá's entry into Venezuela and Brazil respectively. Quintero and Leobons are Cuban-trained and initiated Añá drummers offering very personal narratives of Añá's beginnings in their home countries. The three final chapters, set in New York, Venezuela, and Brazil, reflect an overarching chronology of Añá's fragile reterritorialization processes. From the firmly established locations of the USA and Venezuela, where consecrated batá drums are now too numerous to tally, Leobons details his personal agency and creativity, as well as vicissitudes as owner of the only working batá drums in his huge nation of Brazil, ending the book with an uncertain history-in-the-making.

Although ambitious in its scope, this volume is far from comprehensive and acts more as a subject primer than an all-inclusive compilation of Àyàn and Añá identities and histories. Readers will need to reach for the more generalized texts cited by contributors (many in their own name) to form a holistic picture of the orisha of drumming. There are, of course, many important stories missing, such as Añá's instigation in other nations throughout the Caribbean, Latin America, Europe, and now in my home nation, Australia (Windress 2011). These new diasporic stories resemble those documented in New York, Venezuela, and Brazil. Each site has their Big Men (Barber 1981) and contested oral histories. Indeed the stories in "Secondary Diasporas" may act as models for documenting novel developments in existing and new Àyàn and Añá diasporas.

As the following chapters commit many oral narratives to print for the first time, Àyàn's utterances may be momentarily transformed from sacred stories into authoritative histories. Yet all of the following interpretations will doubtlessly be contested; there is always another story (or Big Man) lurking in the wings. Like Àyàn's rhythms, his utterances are regional, hocketed, improvised, changing, dynamic, and ultimately ephemeral. The following pages say much about the god of drumming but cannot possibly resolve the mystery of asọ̀rọ̀ igi.

Notes

1. Drummer Àyánkúnlé, as quoted by (Euba 1990, 90) and Akìwọwọ and Font-Navarrete (this volume), translation mine.

2. Yorùbá people devoted to the òrìṣà generally self-identify in English as "traditionalists."

3. The Yorùbá word òrìṣà (singular and plural) is spelled *oricha(s)* in Cuba, *orixá(s)* in Brazil, and orisha(s) in English. Throughout the volume, local transliterations will be used where appropriate, while English spellings will be employed when referring to global contexts. (See the glossary for parallel terms and explanations.)

4. Austrian artist Susanne Wenger (1915–2009) was initiated in the 1950s and spent the rest of her life in and around Òṣogbo in southwest Nigeria, where she was a highly revered priestess until her death January 12, 2009.

5. When referring collectively to diverse global practices, I use the capitalized, English spelling "Orisha Devotion" as a generic term to include all forms of orisha worship in any time and place. I use "Òrìṣà Tradition" as a collective designation for mainland African òrìṣà practices and "òrìṣà cult(s)" for discrete sects of Òrìṣà Tradition, though without the pejorative connotations of "cult."

6. I suggest "(re)produce" to complicate popular and scholarly narratives of a neat, unilateral forced migration of Yorùbá slaves into a diaspora faithful to homeland understandings and practices. See for example Matory (2005), Capone (2010), and Palmić (2013) for extensive texts that problematize the very notion of "the Yorùbá diaspora" and the formation of "Yorùbá religion" in Brazil and Cuba.

7. This is a short but crucial ceremony that requires new initiates to dance before consecrated Cuban *batá* drums. With no evidence of a past or present cognate ceremony in Nigeria, this is likely a twentieth-century Cuban development. See Cornelius (1995) for a detailed description of the ceremony and Marcuzzi (2005, 414–15) for a convincing argument against its antiquity claimed by devotees.

8. Unlike Candomblé and Shango, in which Yorùbá deities and practices dominate, Yorùbá influence is significant but shared with Fon (Benin), Igbo (Eastern Nigeria), and Congolese (Central Africa) elements in Vodou.

9. Ryan Bazinet (2013) offers significant research about orisha music in Trinidad. In my estimation, Shango drums (referred to as orisha drums by Trinidadian musicians) are remarkably close in construction and ensemble configuration to *bèmbé* drums in Òṣogbo, which are not consecrated with Àyàn.

10. See Marcuzzi (2005, 372–422) and Vincent (2006, 126–33) for a critique of Ortíz's historiography.

11. By proto-Yorùbá, I refer to those people speaking mutually intelligible regional dialects who have been grouped under the collective term Yorùbá since the 1890s. Prior to this time, Yorùbá referred to the language and people of Òyó, deemed "Yorùbá proper" since the 1890s. See Law 1977, Horton 1979, Peel 2000, and Palmić 2013 for comprehensive expositions on the formation of Yorùbá identity.

12. After abolition in 1807, slaves (many of whom were Yorùbá speakers) were returned from the Americas or were rescued from interrupted slave ships in British Atlantic coastal patrols and repatriated to Freetown, Sierra Leone. The Saros were among the first European-educated Africans.

13. Due to regional availability and deforestation, various species of wood are deemed to be *àyàn* wood in different places and times. "Àyàn wood" is also used to make *bàtá* drums. See Vincent (2006, 169–72, 367–70) for more detail on woods.

14. See Palmić (2013, 49–57) for a summary of how notions of Yorùbá superiority originated in Brazil and were appropriated by Ortíz in "the making of a Cuban Yoruba tradition."

15. See, for example, the well-documented case of the Twelve Obas of Xangô, a 1930s invention of tradition said, at the time, to be revived from an ancient Òyó practice by the resourceful priest Martiniano Eliseu do Bomfim (1859–1943). Though never substantiated with African historical material, several Brazilian scholars sanctioned Martiniano's invented tradition, which succeeded in "Yorùbárizing" and therefore authorizing the Opô Afonjá *terreiro* (ritual house) over the following decades. This particular example of past diasporic invention has been given substantial scholarly attention (e.g., Lima 1966; Butler 2001; Parés 2004; Matory 2005; Palmić 2013), while contemporary change and proliferating inventions that deserve the same scrutiny seem to be circumvented by culturally and politically sensitive scholar-priests.

16. A revised collection, *Africa's Ogun: Old World and New* was published in 1989, followed by a second, expanded edition in 1997.

17. Ortíz had access to a range of African glossaries and dictionaries (Pérez Firmat 1985, 198) and is known to have used Crowther's *Vocabulary of the Yoruba Language* (1843), Bowen's *Grammar and Dictionary of the Yoruba Language* (1858), and Ellis's *The Yoruba-Speaking Peoples of the Slave Coast of West Africa* (1894) (Palmić 2013, 49, 291).

18. On the methodology of the amateur linguist (partly quoted by Palmié 2013, 90), Pérez Firmat continues:

Ortiz's procedure was to ransack dictionaries and grammars of African tongues (most of these works written in English or French; hence the peculiar-looking—to Spanish eyes—transcriptions of the African roots) in search of homonyms or paronyms of words used in Cuba. Having found them, he then tried to confect a semantic link between the African word and the Spanish one. Once this connection was established, the rerooting (and re-routing) was complete. Needless to say, etymologies thus elaborated are far from reliable, especially in view of Ortiz's fanciful interpretive leaps [. . .] the excesses of his method are apparent even to the nonspecialist. (1985, 198–99)

19. Sources that discuss Àyàn include Láoyè 1959, 10; Thieme 1969, 15, 17–19; Bánkọ́lé et al. 1975, 49–50, 53–54, 56; Wenger and Chesi 1983, 203; Euba 1990, 90–93, 97, 103; Thompson 1993, 169–70; Abímbọ́lá 1997, 139–40; Marcuzzi 2005, 142–220; and Vincent 2006, 83–87, 147–49. Discussions of Añá can be found in Ortíz 1954, 284, 288–91; Friedman 1982, 104; Mason 1992, 6–7; Vélez 2000, 48–49, 117–18, 123–25; Ramos 2000, 131–38; Hagedorn 2001, 91, 96; Schweitzer 2003, 125; Marcuzzi 2005, 142–220; Vincent 2006, 116–19, 150–57; and Vaughan and Aldama 2012, xi, 28–30.

20. On both sides of the Atlantic, ceremonies may begin with a corpus of rhythms that invoke the orishas. This repertoire is known as the ilù ṣíṣẹ̀ in Nigeria and the oro seco in Cuba.

21. I write "has been" as, over the last decade, more stringent forms of Islam and Evangelistic Christianity have become increasingly aggressive, competitive, and repressive of Òrìṣà Tradition.

22. The low tone of the second syllable shifts to a high tone when preceding a verb, as in Àyándòkun.

23. See Ògúndùgbà with Amherd, Akìwọwọ and Font-Navarrete, and Àyángbẹ́kún with Villepastour, this volume, for examples of oríkì Àyàn.

24. Àṣẹ/aché/axé may be more expansively translated as vital power, sacred potential, power, authority, vital force, or the power of transformation.

25. There are lineages in Nigeria that place Àyàn's medicines in a clay pot, but to my knowledge, this is a marginal practice.

26. In his foreword in Vaughan and Aldama (2012, xi), John Mason authoritatively glosses Àyàn as "The Chosen," though apparently without any emic input or etymological logic.

27. Pablo Roche, Trinidad Torregrosa, Raúl Díaz, Jesús Pérez, Aguedo Hinojosa, Santos Ramírez, and Agustin Piña.

28. Barber (1990, 315) describes oríkì as "attributions or appellations: epithets, elaborated or concise, which are addressed to a subject and which are equivalent to, or alternatives to, names."

29. White to Venn, September 1, 1857. CMS (Yorùbá Mission) Archives, Birmingham University Library, ref. CA2/O 87.

References Cited

Abímbọ́lá, 'Wándé. 1997. Ifá Will Mend Our Broken World: Thoughts on Yorùbá Religion and Culture in Africa and the Diaspora. Massachusetts: Aim Books.

Adégbọlá, E. A. Adé. 1976. Ifá and Christianity among the Yorùbá: A Study in Symbiosis and in the Development of Yorùbá Christiology, 1890–1940. PhD thesis, University of Bristol.

Amherd, K. Noel. 2010. *Reciting Ifá: Difference, Heterogeneity, and Identity.* Trenton and Asmara: Africa World Press.

Awólàlú, J. Ọmọ́ṣadé. 1979. *Yorùbá Beliefs and Sacrificial Rites.* Essex, UK: Longman.

Bánkọ́lé, Ayọ̀, Judith Bush, and Sadek H. Samaan. 1975. "The Yorùbá Master Drummer." In *African Arts* 8 (2): 48–56, 77–78.

Barber, Karin. 1981. "How Man Makes God in West Africa: Yoruba Attitudes Toward the 'Orisa.'" In *Africa* 513: 724–45.

———. 1990. "Oríkì, Women and the Proliferation and Merging of Òrìṣà." In *Africa* 60: 313–37.

Barnes, Sandra T., ed. 1980. *Ogun: An Old God for a New Age.* Philadelphia: Institute for the Study of Human Issues.

———. 1997. *Africa's Ogun: Old World and New* [2nd Expanded Edition]. Bloomington: Indiana University Press.

Bascom, William. 1951. "The Yoruba in Cuba." In *Nigeria* 37: 14–20.

Bazinet, Ryan. 2013. *Two Sides to a Drum: Duality in Trinidad Orisha Music and Culture.* PhD diss., City University of New York.

Bowen, Thomas J. 1858. *Grammar and Dictionary of the Yoruba Language: With an Introductory Description of the Country and People of Yoruba.* Washington: Smithsonian Institution.

Butler, Kim. 2001. "Africa in the Reinvention of Nineteenth Century Afro-Bahian Identity." In *Rethinking the African Diaspora*, eds. Kristin Mann and Edna Bay. London: Frank Cass. 135–54.

Capone, Stefania. 2010. *Searching for Africa in Brazil: Power and Tradition in Candomblé.* Durham, NC: Duke University Press.

Clapperton, Hugh, with Richard Lander. 1966 [1829]. *Journal of a second expedition into the interior of Africa from the Bight of Benin to Soccatoo to which is added the journal of Richard Lander from Kano to the sea-coast partly by a more easterly route.* London: Frank Cass.

Clarke, Maxine Kamari. 2004. *Mapping Yorùbá Networks: Power and Agency in the Making of Transnational Communities.* Durham & London: Duke University Press.

Cornelius, Steven Harry. 1995. "Personalizing Public Symbols Through Music Ritual: Santería's Presentation to Añá." In *Latin American Music Review* 16 (1): 42–57.

Crowther, Samuel. 1843. *Vocabulary of the Yoruba Language: Part I. English and Yoruba. Part II. Yoruba and English. To which are prefixed, the grammatical elements of the Yoruba language.* London: Printed for the Church Missionary Society.

Dianteill, Erwan. 2002. "Deterritorialization and Reterritorialization of the Orisha Religion in Africa and the New World (Nigeria, Cuba and the United States)." In *International Journal of Urban and Regional Research* 26 (1): 121–37.

Ellis, A. B. 1966 [1894, 1964]. *The Yoruba-Speaking Peoples of the Slave Coast of West Africa: Their Religion, Manners, Customs, Laws, Languages, etc.* Oosterhout, Netherlands: Anthropological Publications.

Euba, Akin. 1990. *Yorùbá Drumming: The Dùndún Tradition.* Bayreuth: Bayreuth African Studies.

Fálọlá, Tóyìn, ed. 2013. *Èṣù: Yoruba God, Power, and the Imaginative Frontiers.* Durham, NC: Carolina Academic Press.

Friedman, Robert. 1982. *Making an Abstract World Concrete: Knowledge, Competence and Structural Dimensions of Performance among Batá Drummers in Santería.* PhD diss., Indiana University.

Hagedorn, Katherine. 2001. *Divine Utterances: The Performance of Afro-Cuban Santería.* Washington, DC: Smithsonian Institution Press.

Herbert, Eugenia W. 1993. *Iron, Gender, and Power: Rituals of Transformation in African Societies.* Bloomington: Indiana University Press.

hooks, bell. 1986. "Sisterhood: Political Solidarity between Women." In *Feminist Review* 23: 125–38.

Horton, Robin. 1979. "Ancient Ife: A Reassessment." In *Journal of the Historical Society of Nigeria* 9 (4): 69–149.

Ìdòwú, E. Bọ́lájí. 1994 [1962]. *Olódùmarè: God in Yorùbá Belief.* Brooklyn: A & B Books.

Johnson, Rev. Samuel. 1921. *History of the Yorùbás.* Lagos: Church Missionary Society.

Kubik, Gerhard. 1993. "Transplantation of African Musical Cultures into the New World— Research Topics and Objectives in the Study of African-American Music." In *Slavery in the Americas*, ed. Wolfgang Binder. Würzburg: Verlag Königshausen und Neumann. 421–52.

———. 1999. *Africa and the Blues.* Jackson: University of Mississippi Press.

Lander, John, and Richard Lander. 1965 [1832]. "1832 *The Niger Journal of Richard and John Lander.*" Edited and abridged with an introduction by Robin Hallet. New York: Frederick A. Praeger.

Láoyè I, Tìmì of Èdè. 1959. "Yorùbá Drums." In *Odù* 7: 5–14.

———. 1966. "Music of Western Nigeria: Origin and Use." In *Composer* 19: 34–41.

Law, Robin. 1977. *The Oyo Empire, c. 1600–1836.* Oxford: Clarendon Press.

Lima, Vivaldo da Costa. 1966. "Os Obás de Xangô." In *Afro-Ásia* 2 (3): 5–36.

Lucas, J. 1996 [1948]. *The Religion of the Yorùbás: Being an Account of the Religious Beliefs and Practices of the Yorùbá Peoples of Southern Nigeria, Especially in Relation to the Religion of Ancient Egypt.* Brooklyn: Athelia Henrietta Press.

McKenzie, Peter. 1997. *Hail Orisha! A Phenomenology of a West African Religion in the Mid-nineteenth Century.* Leiden, New York, and Köln: Brill.

Marcuzzi, Michael David. 2005. *A Historical Study of the Ascendant Role of Bàtá Drumming in Cuban Òrìṣà Worship.* PhD diss., York University, Toronto.

———. 2011. "Writing on the Wall: Some Speculations on Islamic Talismans, Catholic Prayers, and the Preparation of Cuban Bata Drums for Orisha Worship." In *Black Music Research Journal* 31 (2): 209–27.

Mason, John. 1992. *Orin Òrìṣà: Songs for Selected Heads.* New York: Yorùbá Theological Archministry.

Matory, J. Lorand. 2005. *Black Atlantic Religion: Tradition, Transnationalism, and Matriarchy in the Afro-Brazilian Candomblé.* Princeton, NJ: Princeton University Press.

Murphy, Joseph, and Mei-Mei Sanford, eds. 2001. *Òṣun Across the Waters: A Yorùbá Goddess in Africa and the Americas.* Bloomington: Indiana University Press.

Olórúnyọmi, Ṣọlá. 2003. *Afrobeat!: Fela and the Imagined Continent.* Trenton, NJ: Africa World Press.

Ortíz, Fernando. 1954. *Los Instrumentos de la Música Afrocubana, vol. IV.* Havana: Editoriales Cárdenas y Cía.

Otero, Solimar, and Tóyìn Fálọlá, eds. 2013. *Yemoja: Gender, Sexuality, and Creativity in the Latina/o and Afro-Atlantic Diasporas.* Albany: SUNY Press.

Palmié, Stephan. 2013. *The Cooking of History: How Not to Study Afro-Cuban Religion* Chicago: University of Chicago Press.

Parés, Luis Nicolau. 2004. "The 'Nagôization' Process in Bahian Candomblé." In *Yorùbá Diaspora in the Atlantic World*, ed. Tóyìn Fálọlá. Bloomington: Indiana University Press. 185–208.

Peel, J. D. Y. 1968. "Syncretism and Religious Change." In *Comparative Studies in Society and History* 10 (2): 121–41.

———. 1990. "The Pastor and the Babalawo: The Interaction of Religions in Nineteenth-Century Yorùbáland." In *Africa: Journal of the International African Institute* 60 (3): 338–69.

———. 1995. "For Who Hath Despised the Day of Small Things? Missionary Narratives and Historical Anthropology." In *Comparative Studies in Society and History* 37 (3): 581–85.

———. 2000. *Religious Encounter and the Making of the Yoruba*. Bloomington and Indianapolis: Indiana University Press.

———. 2002. "Yorùbá Religion and Gender." In *Journal of Religion in Africa* 32, Fasc. 2: 136–66.

Pérez Firmat, Gustavo. 1985. "The Philological Fictions of Fernando Ortíz." In *Notebooks in Cultural Analysis* 2: 190–207.

Ramos, Miguel. 2000. *The Empire Beats On: Oyo, Batá Drums and Hegemony in Nineteenth-Century Cuba*. MA thesis, Florida International University.

Rouget, Gilbert. 1965. "Notes et Documents pour Servir à L'étude de la Musique Yoruba." In *Journal de la Société des Africansistes* 35 (1): 67–107.

Schweitzer, Kenneth. 2003. *Afro-Cuban Batá Drum Aesthetics: Developing Individual and Group Technique, Sound and Identity*. DMA diss., University of Maryland, College Park.

Thieme, Darius L. 1969. *A Descriptive Catalogue of Yorùbá Musical Instruments*. PhD diss., Catholic University of America, Washington, DC.

Thompson, Robert Farris. 1993. *Face of the Gods: Art and Altars of Africa and the African Americas*. Munich: Prestel.

Tishken, Joel E., Tóyìn Fálọlá, and Akíntúndé Akínyẹmí, eds. 2009. *Ṣàngó in Africa and the African Diaspora*. Bloomington: Indiana University Press.

Trotman, David. 1976. "The Yorùbá and Orisha Worship in Trinidad and British Guinea: 1830–1870." In *African Studies Review* 27: 55–67.

Vansina, Jan. 1985. *Oral Tradition as History*. Madison: University of Wisconsin Press.

Vaughan, Umi, and Carlos Aldama. 2012. *Carlos Aldama's Life in Batá: Cuba, Diaspora, and the Drum*. Bloomington: Indiana University Press.

Vega, Marta Moreno. 1995. "The Yoruba Orisha Tradition Comes to New York City." In *African American Review* 29 (2): 201–6.

Vélez, María Teresa. 2000. *Drumming for the Gods: The Life and Times of Felipe García Villamil, Santero, Palero, and Abakuá*. Philadelphia: Temple University Press.

Villepastour, Amanda. 2009. "Two Heads of the Same Drum? Musical Narratives within a Transatlantic Religion." In *Journal of Transatlantic Studies* 7: 343–62.

———. 2010. *Ancient Text Messages of the Yorùbá Bàtá Drum: Cracking the Code*. Farnham: Ashgate.

———. 2013. "Amelia Pedroso: A Cuban Priestess Leads from the Inside." In *Women Singers in Global Contexts: Music, Biography, Identity*, ed. Ruth Hellier. Urbana: University of Illinois Press. 54–72.

Vincent [Villepastour], Amanda. 2006. *Bata Conversations: Guardianship and Entitlement Narratives about the Bata in Nigeria and Cuba*. PhD thesis, School of Oriental and African Studies, University of London.

Waterman, Christopher. 1990. "'Our Tradition Is a Very Modern Tradition': Popular Music and the Construction of Pan-Yoruba Identity." In *Ethnomusicology* 34 (3): 367–79.

Watson, Ruth. 2003. *"Civil Disorder Is the Disease of Ibadan": Chieftaincy & Civic Culture in a Yoruba City*. Athens: Ohio University Press.

Wenger, Susan, and Gert Chesi. 1983. *A Life with the Gods in Their Yorùbá Homeland*. Wörgl, Austria: Perlinger Verlag.

Windress, Kent. 2011. "The Outsider Going In: Research and Participation in Batá Drumming and Santería Ritual." In *Context* 35 (36): 153–65.

I
COSMOLOGIES

1

Awo Àyàn: Metaphysical Dimensions of the Òrìṣà of Drumming

Akínṣọlá A. Akìwọwọ and David Font-Navarrete

• •

While increased scholarly attention has recently been focused on some musical dimensions of Àyàn drumming in West Africa and the Caribbean (where the same deity is known as Añá), this article explores and focuses on some metaphysical aspects of Àyàn.[1] We use the term metaphysics to mean the theoretical or first principles of things, including various abstract concepts such as being, knowing, and identity. Metaphysics are central to even the most basic understanding of Àyàn in social, musical, and spiritual terms. Specifically, we discuss: 1) Àyàn as an *òrìṣà* (deity), a deified ancestor, and a progenitor of an extended family; 2) some of the orature regarding the apotheosis of Àyàn and the process by which human beings become òrìṣà; 3) the family model in Àyàn devotion; and 4) some ways in which Àyàn interacts with drummers and listeners.[2]

We approach this article from a cooperative perspective, which is both Yorùbá and Lucumí, both "Old" World and "New," and we assert a fundamental analogy between the Yorùbá Àyàn and the Lucumí Añá. Although this article focuses primarily on West African tradition, we use the designations "Àyàn" and "Añá" merely for the sake of clarity, maintaining that various forms of Àyàn and Añá worship across locales are part of a continuum of devotional strategies and modes. The strands of tradition woven together in this article are drawn from mythical, legendary, historical, and biographical sources, including our personal experiences.

This article is the product of intensive conversations between the authors—an elder grounded primarily in Yorùbá tradition and a junior grounded primarily in Lucumí tradition—over the course of several years. An *ẹsẹ odù* Ifá (sacred divination verse) from the divination sign Ọ̀sá Ìrẹtẹ̀ characterizes our collaborative approach to this article:[3]

Ọmọ dé gbọ́n	Children possess wisdom
Àgbà gbọ́n	Elders possess wisdom
Ni a fí dá Òtu Ifẹ̀.	This principle was used to establish the city of Ifẹ̀.[4]

In this sense, our collaboration, which was based on cooperation and dialogue, is an attempt both to write about Àyàn and to embody the spirit of Àyàn. Our mutual intention is to offer our thoughts on some aspects of the *awo* (mystery) of Àyàn. Although awo can also be understood as "esoteric knowledge" or "initiate" (one who possesses esoteric knowledge), our focus on nuanced, metaphysical matters does not presume to make our subject less mysterious, much less offer the reader esoteric knowledge. Rather, our intention is to explore and share some essential, abstract concepts regarding Àyàn. Our individual contributions as authors reflect the respective stages in our lives (elder and youth), and the form and content of the article embodies a dynamic dialogue between us and our experiences.

It is also worth mentioning that the vast majority of Àyàn drummers in present-day West Africa are Muslims; consequently, many of them regard some spiritual aspects of their pre-Islamic tradition (and traditionalist òrìṣà worship as a whole) with varying degrees of uneasiness or skepticism. In a contemporary African context, the metaphysical dimensions of Àyàn described in this article can therefore be regarded as somewhat idealized. Nonetheless, the principles and dynamics described in this article are easily and widely recognized by Àyàn and Aña devotees in Africa and the Americas, regardless of their formal religious affiliations.

Àyàn as Òrìṣà, Deified Ancestor, and Ẹbí (Extended Family)

Àyàn is approached by devotees as 1) an òrìṣà, 2) a deified ancestor, and 3) a collective of ancestral and living drummers and their families. As we begin our discussion of Àyàn, we are obligated to assert that the òrìṣà Àyàn—like other òrìṣà such as Ọbàtálá, Ọrúnmìlà, Ṣàngó, Ọ̀sun, Ògún, et al.—is a mysterious, divine force. However, given the abstract nature of sound—Àyàn's primary medium—it is important to keep in mind that a definitive answer to the question of Àyàn's essence is impossible.

Like many other òrìṣà, Àyàn is conceived as both human and divine, or ancestral and primordial. Examining mythical accounts of Odùduwà (the progenitor of the Yorùbá people), Awólàlú (1979, 27) observes that

Yorùbá followers or devotees of an outstanding leader may deify him upon his death, as well as name him "after a primordial divinity whose worship he had encouraged. [. . .] Odùduwà is portrayed as a primordial divinity and as a deified ancestor." The deification of Àyàn can be conceived in analogous fashion to the òrìṣà Odùduwà, Ọrúnmìlà (the seminal diviner in the Ifá tradition), and Ṣàngó (the deified king of Ọ̀yọ́), all of whom are continually immortalized and revered for the divine *and* human qualities that they embodied in the course of transforming the devotional traditions of their times.

Àyàn devotion, like devotion to other òrìṣà, synthesizes primordial forces, deified ancestors, and living devotees into a unified whole. The mention of Àyàn involves an immediate connection to sacred drumming (and, more generally, music), the *aláròfọ̀* Àyàn and his descendants, and the contemporary community of Àyàn drummers and devotees.[5] This integration is central to traditional Yorùbá philosophy and exemplified by Àyàn worship. In a discussion of Yorùbá rituals and their connection to primordial forces, Adégbìtẹ́ (1988, 18–19) writes:

> [Devotees] believe that nature is alive and that there are certain forces or powers superior to man which direct and control the course of nature and of human life in it. In many cases these powers that are superior to man inhabit prominent natural objects such as mountains, rivers and trees. These are generally regarded as the temples or abodes of gods and spirits. But the world of nature is not seen as a separate entity. The world of gods and goddesses, the world of ancestors and heroes, the world of human beings and the world of nature form a unity. Each world is alive, inter-related, and dependent upon each other in one vast circling stream of power in which visible and invisible forces interact.

The role of Àyàn is to connect these forces through drum music. Through sound and the human endeavors to organize it—music, dance, and language—Àyàn drumming adds to the media through which *ara ayé* (earth dwellers) and *ara òrun* (dwellers of heaven) may communicate and commune. Àyàn is an òrìṣà who brings vitality to the transitional spaces of human experience, where these two worlds come together. The unique voice of Àyàn connects what lies on either side of these transitional spaces, and Àyàn drums and drummers are media and agents for this voice. In both a musical and metaphysical sense, Àyàn drummers are instruments of the òrìṣà Àyàn. Drummers on both sides of the Atlantic assert that the link between the òrìṣà Àyàn and Àyàn drummers is as real as the wood used to carve drums. Without the òrìṣà of their devotion, Àyàn drummers would lack divine support, authority, and inspiration; without drummers and devotees, the energy and voice of òrìṣà Àyàn would lack an earthly manifestation.

An essential mystery of Àyàn lies at the intersection of speech, drumming, and the notion of "talking drums"—musical instruments that convey spoken language through surrogate speech. A particularly important intersection of speech and drumming is found in chanted and drummed *oríkì*.[6] The word oríkì can be translated into English in various ways such as praise poems, praise names, poetic naming, citation poems, citatory songs, or epitaphs, but can also be thought of as a recitation of essence, or a metaphysical expression of identity through sound. An oríkì Àyàn tells us that Àyàn is *asọ̀rọ̀ igi*, "the wood that speaks." The description of Àyàn as asọ̀rọ̀ igi can be understood as an integrated spiritual and sonic collective, which includes its disembodied voice and spiritual energy, its tangible musical and ritual vessels, and its drummers and devotees.

Àyàn Orature and Ancestorization

In order to cultivate a clearer understanding of the role of Àyàn as a spiritual and musical whole, it is useful to begin with Àyàn drummers' understanding of their òrìṣà. A Yorùbá *òwe* (proverb) states,

Kò sení	There is no one
mọ èdè Àyàn	who understands the language of Àyàn
bí ẹni tí ó mu pòpá lọ́wọ́.	like the one who holds the drum stick.

To varying degrees, all Àyàn families and initiates may trace their genealogy to a common eponymous ancestor whose detailed history is lost to antiquity. However, an important function of oríkì is often the tracing of one's ancestry, thereby establishing connections to the moral and ethical qualities of progenitors. According to Adégbìtẹ́ (1991, 45–50):

Sound [. . .] may be described as the vehicle for articulating an abstract idea in concrete form (i.e., for communicating "thought" as matter). [. . .] sound is evocative; that is, it has mystical powers which can be used to evoke psychic forces of tremendous potency [and form] a bridge between ideas and phenomena. It is also believed that there is a correspondence between musical sound and cosmic phenomena. [. . .] the textual contents of music are not just mere words but have mystical potency and can be used in many practical ways to produce concrete observable results. [. . .] there is a belief among the Yorùbá that sound is evocative and that the Orisa are lovers of music. Therefore, they communicate with their Orisa through music.

Chanted, sung, or drummed, the texts of oríkì Àyàn performed by drummers provide poetic, philosophical, historical, and metaphysical insights into Yorùbá worldviews. The invocation through homage (ìjúbà) of divine energies—including Olódùmarè (the creator god), òrìṣà, and ancestors—is an essential means of connecting the past and the future. These invocations are intended to secure necessary spiritual support in the face of the challenges we face in our phenomenal world. Àyàn drummers articulate this principle in their own orature. For example, the musicologist Euba (1990, 92) quotes an ìjúbà by a drummer named Àyánkúnlé that is dedicated to Adélabú, an ancestral drummer:

Adélabú, òrẹ́ Lásùnlé	Adélabú, Lásùnlé's friend
Ibà rẹ	I acknowledge you
n tó o gbé lémi lọ́wọ́	for this gift that you placed in my hands
Adáṣe ní hun mọ	A child fails when s/he tries to do something by him/herself
Ibà ò gbọ́dọ̀ hun mọ o	A child cannot fail when s/he acknowledges [the support of one's fathers]
Ibà pẹ́tẹ́ ẹsẹ̀ o	I acknowledge the sole of the foot
Ibà àtẹ́lẹsẹ̀	I acknowledge the sole of the foot
tí ò hun run tí ó e dé pọnpọn tan o	that does not deprive hair growth all the way up to the thigh
Má jẹ bà ó hun mí o.	Let this acknowledgment lead to my success.

It would be difficult to overstate the importance of ancestral drummers in the worship of Àyàn. In the Lucumí tradition, remembrances of deceased initiates (particularly those in one's ritual lineage) play an essential part in all rituals performed by òrìṣà devotees, including those of Añá drummers. Likewise, the following recitation is part of an oríkì of the ancestors of the late Chief Àyánlékè Adépòjù of Èruwà, Ọ̀yọ́ State, Nigeria.[7]

Mo ríbà bàbá mi	I pay homage to my father
Afọlábí, Sekoni	Afọlábí, Sekoni
Àbá ò di tẹni	Another person's wish can never be our own

Ènìyàn ò	No one has found
lóògùn ọrọ̀	the medicine for wealth
Boolórọ̀ tóò lówó lọ́wọ́	When a man is filthy rich
Bàbá táni ń yá ni lówó?	Does he go about lending money?
À ń jọrìn	We all walk the path of life together
A à meri	We do not know
olówó	the one destined to be rich
Afọlábí, bàbá Adédigbà	Afọlábí, father of Adédigbà
Eégún tó be gbeni	It is the ancestor who supports one
Láà fún lọ́tí	That one offers strong liquor
Òrìṣà tó bá gbeni	It is the òrìṣà that supports one
Láà sìn	To whom one is devoted
Afọlábí, Àyìndé	Afọlábí, Àyìndé
O ní òun o gbè mí	You declared you would support me
Tòun ò ni padà lẹ́ẹ̀hìn mi	You said you won't turn away from me
Didibíowú	Didibíowú
Agbọ́mábínnú	Agbọ́mábínnú
	(He-who-bears-offenses-in-silence)
Kọ̀lọ̀-kọ̀lọ̀ iba kú	Let the fox die
adìẹ ò sọkún	and the fowls will not cry
Ikúrúnilójú Àkànbí	Ikúrúnilójú Àkànbí
Oníwòo agbejo a fi ìdodo wu	Whose attractive navel
ni bí i tọmọ titun	is tender like that of a newborn
Kèlèbè	You are the mucus
balẹ̀ dira mú	that grips when it touches the ground
Adékàńbí Àkànbí	Adékàńbí Àkànbí
Alára	It is the being inhabiting a body
ló mọ̀ pé kò le	that knows where it aches
Ikúrúnilójú, ọmọ Agbọ́mábínnú	Ikúrúnilójú, offspring of Agbọ́mábínnú
múra ìjà	who responds to a fight
Bí amọ̀télẹ̀	Like one who had advance warning
Gúdúgúdú	[You are like] Gúdúgúdú
kìi turaálẹ̀ lẹ́ẹ̀kan	who never reveals himself all at once
Adégbìtẹ́ o!	Adégbìtẹ́!
Erígitọ́lá	Erígitọ́lá
Ọmọ Agbómábini, ibà	Offspring of Agbómábini, I pay homage
Àkekèé Iberekodo	Scorpion of Iberekodo
Adégbìtẹ́, máà ta mi	Adégbìtẹ́, please do not sting me
Ọmọ ẹlòmí i ni o ta	You may sting someone else
Àtàndá onílù	Àtàndá, the master drummer
Ọkọ Ògúnfúńkẹ́	Husband of Ògúnfúńkẹ́
Erigitọ́lá	Erigitọ́lá

Ọmọ oni ṣẹ́ṣẹ́ ẹfun	Offspring of the owner of white shells [sea goddess]
Àgbàlá Adégbìtẹ́	The courtyard of Adégbìtẹ́
ó ju oko bàbá tẹlòmíì lọ	is larger than some peoples' farmland
Ojówonibíkaakú, ìbà	Ojówonibíkaakú, I pay homage
Ọmọ Jọláadé	Child of Jọláadé
Ọ̀rọ̀ àgbò tí ń bí ìkokò nínú	The wolf is always agitated by the sheep's presence
Àlàbí,	Àlàbí,
onílù reki ẹlẹ́ẹ́bẹ̀	owner of the symmetrical ẹlẹ́ẹ́bẹ̀ drum
Ẹyẹ Òrìṣàńlá	[You are like] the bird of Òrìṣàńlá [Ọbàtálá]
Abàṣẹ lẹ́nu	who has àṣẹ (divine force) in his mouth
Ọmọ Agbọ́mábini	Offspring of Agbọ́mábini
Adérigbe	Adérigbe
Ọmọ Agbọ́mábini	Offspring of Agbọ́mábini
Akíntáyọ̀ o! Ibà	Akíntáyọ̀! I pay homage
Ẹlẹ́ẹ́bẹ̀ òpá	Stick of the ẹlẹ́ẹ́bẹ̀ drum
A bara yọ igi lẹ́nu	Your arm protrudes like the mouth of the stick whose body disturbs the tree
Ìṣòlá tẹ́mi í lẹ̀	Ìṣòlá, spread me on the floor
bó ò rẹ́ní	if you cannot find a mat
Ohun tí mo bá wá jorí ẹní lọ.	What I come for is more than a mat.

This recitation to Chief Àyánlékè's lineage includes poetic images, metaphors, symbolism, and glorification of his ancestors. The recitation itself is a means of remembering and honoring those who came before him, though some specific passages and ideas are worth particular mention here. The salutation of Afọlábí—"It is the ancestor who supports one / That one offers strong liquor / It is the òrìṣà that supports one / To whom one is devoted"—clearly illustrates the reciprocal relationship between his ancestors, the òrìṣà, and drummers. And Chief Àyánlékè closes this section by reminding his ancestors of their responsibility: "I pay homage / You declared you would support me."

Ikúrúnilójú is compared to the gúdúgúdú drum whose mysteries are never revealed "all at once." Àlàbí is addressed as the "owner of the symmetrical drum, ẹlẹ́ẹ́bẹ̀." The word ẹlẹ́ẹ́bẹ̀, also used to describe the chief of messengers or town criers, is most likely a reference to the dùndún drum's role in conveying important messages through its fluid melodic rendering of the Yorùbá language. In a more mystical vein, Chief Àyánlékè mentions Ikúrúnilójú's ability to transmit spiritual energy (àṣẹ) through sound, "like the bird of Òrìṣàńlá [Ọbàtálá] / who speaks with àṣẹ in its mouth." The power of sound in speech and music can move energy in both spiritual and concrete ways. Through his recitation, Chief Àyánlékè is thereby invoking his own inheritance: the ability to empower his own words—drummed, sung, or spoken—with the metaphysical energy of òrìṣà and his ancestors. It is noteworthy that Chief Àyánlékè closes his recitation with a bawdy exhortation to his wife Ìṣọlá; while this is a relatively lighthearted conclusion, it also speaks directly to the continuation of his lineage.

Another recitation of oríkì Àyàn by Ganiyu Senusi Àyánwálé Àyánléyẹ includes the following mention of specific qualities of gúdúgúdú and all *ìyáàlù* drums:

Gúdúgúdú kan	One gúdúgúdú
Ìyáàlù kan	One ìyáàlù
Ìwọ ni odídẹrẹ́	You are the African grey parrot
Párá niyi àwòdì	Speed is the prestige of the African black kite
Ká rí ogun	Never retreating from a fight
Mọ́sàá niyì ọkùnrin.	Is the honor of a man.[8]

Note how the drums are addressed directly, metaphorically equated with *odídẹrẹ́*, the African grey parrot endowed with a unique, primordial power of speech. Also, the drums are equated with *àwòdì*, the fierce hawk who never retreats from a fight (*káríógun mọ́sàá*). Despite the feminine quality clearly implied in the name of the ìyáàlù (literally, "mother drum"), it is invoked as male (*ọkùnrin*)—a seemingly paradoxical integration of male and female energies embodied in the drums, though one indicative of the pervasive mutability of Àyàn's gendered constructions.

Àyánwálé commented on this oríkì by saying, "This recalls a host of other oríkì in the memory. If we keep on reciting the oríkì of Àyàn, it will be nightfall before we finish."[9] Therefore, the recitations of oríkì Àyàn are many and extensive, implying that each recitation contributes to an ongoing, evolving chain of exultation, ancestral support, and the repertoires of orature that have effected its realization.

The Family Model in Àyàn Worship

Ọmọ Àyàn (children of Àyàn) use the family as a model of social organization, balancing independence and family, or more broadly, community. As we will see below, oríkì Àyàn extol the tremendous independence and privileged access that drummers enjoy. However, this independence is not absolute. A Yorùbá proverb states, "Always keep in mind whose offspring you are."[10] For members of an Àyàn family, this proverb implies that they should remember that they are the offspring of Àyàn and that their conduct should reflect their distinction; in this sense, privilege and independence are balanced with responsibility and propriety.

The terms *bàbá, ìyá, ègbón, àbúrò,* and *ọmọ* (father, mother, senior sibling, junior sibling, and offspring or child) are employed by Yorùbá Àyàn drummers when referring to persons to whom they are related, or to whom they relate. For example, after Chief Àyánlékè named several of his children, he identified some as his biological offspring and others as his professional offspring. He also referred to several individual males as *bàbá mi* (my father), *bùòdá mi* (my brother),[11] *ègbón mi* (my senior sibling), and *àbúrò mi* (my junior sibling). Female members of the family are referred to variously as *àwọn ìyá mi* (my mothers), *aya bàbá mi* (wife of my father), *aya ègbón mi* (wife of my senior sibling), *aya àbúrò mi* (wife of my junior sibling), or *aya ọmọ mi* (wife of my son). Other male relatives are referred to as *bàbá mi kékeré* (younger brother of one's father) or *bàbá mi àgbà* (elder brother of my father). At times when Chief Àyánlékè used the classificatory term *ìyá mi* (my mother), he may have in mind either a blood relation or an occupational relationship.

One of the most significant differences between *ọmọ* Àyàn in West Africa and *omo* Añá in Cuba is their respective emphasis on identity and inheritance through birth (*àjọbí*) on one hand, and initiation and occupational association (*àjọgbé*) on the other (Akìwọwọ 1983). If we apply a Yorùbá model that recognizes kinship through both birth (àjọbí) and ritual and occupational associations (àjọgbé) to ọmọ Àyàn, it becomes clear that the fundamental dynamics of family relations are essential to ọmọ Àyàn in both Yorùbáland and its diaspora. Although the kinship among ọmọ Àyàn in the diaspora is focused more closely on relationships formalized through initiation and occupation than the consanguinity that determines membership in West African Àyàn families, the initiation of omo Añá in the diaspora can be understood to establish analogous bonds between initiates and ancestral drummers that is the birthright of Àyàn families in West Africa.

The family unit is symbolized in the relationships between the drums of the bàtá and dùndún ensembles played by Àyàn drummers. The drums themselves are named and conceptualized as a family unit, and the various drums' specialized, yet interdependent, musical voices can also be likened to the functions of family members. According to Adégbìtẹ (1988, 22):

One interesting aspect of these drum ensembles is their hierarchical structure, which reflects the traditional Yorùbá family system in which the father is the head of the family while the other and the children are the members of the household. Thus, in every Yorùbá drum set there is always a "father" drum, and other drums which may be considered as the children. In the Dundun ensemble for example, the Gudugudu is considered the father of the ensemble while the master or lead drum is the mother of the drums, namely Iya'lu Dundun, Iya'lu Bata, Iya'nla Igbin, and so forth. In the Bata ensemble, there is the emele ako (male emele) and emele abo (female emele),[12] a pattern that further reflects a family system.

In most instances, the ensembles are a musical nuclear family unit comprising child, father, and mother drums. In the Yorùbá bàtá ensemble, the members of this family of instruments include the *omele akọ*, *omele abo*, and *ìyáàlù*. A clear analog is found in the Lucumí batá ensemble's *okónkolo* (also known as *omele*), *itótele*, and *iyá*. Likewise, the Yorùbá *dùndún* ensemble consists of the *omele* drums, *ìṣáájù* and *ìkẹhìn*, and *ìyáàlù*.

There is, however, another Àyàn drum whose role is often discreet or even private. In the Yorùbá tradition, this drum is typically the gúdúgúdú, which is cited by Chief Àyánlékè as the oldest and most senior of the drums in the ensemble. It is a small, kettle-shaped drum played with leather beaters. In a sense, the gúdúgúdú is a meta-drum that encompasses the metaphysical power of the entire drum ensemble. Chief Àyánlékè used the English word "family" to refer to the drum when he said, "Family *ni ìlù*" (the drum is family). To refer to the close-knit relationships among drummers and to the metaphorical relationship between the members of a drum ensemble, Chief Àyánlékè would repeat with a tone of respect: *"Gúdúgúdú ni bàbá àwọn ìlù!"* (Gúdúgúdú is the father of the drums!). The same is said of *Kútanyín*,[13] the mystical or metaphysical name for the gúdúgúdú, when Chief Àyánlékè repeats the adage, *"Kútanyín ni bàbá ìlù."*

In the Lucumí tradition, a drum called *elekoto* holds a similar ceremonial and metaphysical position in the Cuban batá ensemble. Although it is usually not played in public, it is essential to the initiation of drummers and most often remains at the home of the *olú batá* (owner or caretaker of Añá drums) when the other drums are taken out to perform. When newly initiated Añá drummers are first presented to the sacred drums and the community, they hold the elekoto under their arm or hung or around their neck as a symbol of their initiation. It seems wholly plausible that the Yorùbá gúdúgúdú and Lucumí elekoto play analogous ritual, symbolic, and metaphysical roles in Yorùbá Àyàn and Lucumí Añá ensembles. Both the gúdúgúdú and the elekoto are understood to be a focal point for Àyàn's spiritual energy, that is, the spirit of Àyàn, or the deified ancestor Àyàn Àgalú.[14]

Chief Àyánlékè posits that just as all humanity has its progenitor, so all drums have a common progenitor. From the cosmological perspective of Yorùbá Àyàn drummers, the progenitor of all drums is gúdúgúdú. In Chief Àyánlékè's view, *"Gúdúgúdú tàbí Kútanyín ni bàbá ìlù pátápátá"* (Gúdúgúdú or Kútanyín is the father of all of humanity's drums). The gúdúgúdú and elekoto drums can thus be understood as the earthly representation of òrìṣà Àyàn and ancestral drummers, the spiritual guides of all Àyàn drumming families.

Lílọ Ode Onílù (Going Out on a Gig)

By drumming, Àyàn devotees activate what Wenger calls "tremendous power, which like all preposterously intense forces moves the Yorùbá to seek a balance with ambivalent social precautions. The voice of the drum is the voice of the gods, and Ayọn [Àyàn] is the linguist and vocal emissary of Heaven" (1983, 203). In a complex network of relationships and communication, Àyàn endows drummers with the authority, technology, and inspiration to articulate its metaphysical voice through drumming; through Àyàn, drums address the community of devotees, the òrìṣà embodied in devotees, and heaven itself.

The texts of Yorùbá and Lucumí sacred music are often obscure in meaning, and knowledge of the textual and esoteric content of ritual music is highly regarded among devotees. Drummers and singers, like other ritual specialists, are reservoirs and mediators of Yorùbá *ìjinlẹ̀*, or "deep Yorùbá." While individual devotees may have very limited knowledge of specialized, ritual language, it is understood that òrìṣà respond to the "mystical potency" of words and music (Adégbìtẹ́ 1991, 50), especially if they flow from musicians' command of literal and symbolic meanings. Ritual musicians' esoteric knowledge of ceremonial repertories is generally regarded more highly than purely technical virtuosity, but this is not a static or abstract matter: the ability to execute—and thus embody—esoteric knowledge is the ideal, dynamic expression of àṣẹ. In this sense, Àyàn drummers' ability to perform sacred drum music is difficult to separate from their esoteric knowledge.[15] As an example, Euba (1990, 94) records a recitation of oríkì Àyàn performed by a drummer from the town of Òṣogbo named Làìsì Àyánṣọlá in his study of dùndún drummers:

Àyànàgalú, a tóó jẹ tóó tà	Àyànàgalú, provider of livelihood
Amúni wọ kòròkóró	He who leads one into
Ọlọ́jà mẹ̀rìndínógún	sixteen different corners of the market
Amúni wọ	He who leads
bí ténìà ò dé	one where ordinary human beings cannot go
Amúni wọ lé ọlá	He who gives access to influential homes
Amúni wọ lé	He who gives access
aláyé	to the owner of the world
Amúni wọ lé	He who gives access to
olówó	the homes of the affluent
Amúni wọ lé	He who gives access to
àwọn ènìà jànkàn jànkàn	the homes of powerful people
tí ń wọ́n tọjà	who are big enough
Ògún rà.	to buy merchandise from Ògún.

According to Euba (1990, 94), "Àyánṣọlá also likened the drum to *ìyá àfin* ('queen' or 'queen mother') for it gives the drummer the kind of freedom in an *ọba's* [king's] palace that only the royal wives enjoy. When the drummer carries his drum, he does not need to remove his hat or prostrate in the presence of the king (as would ordinary citizens, or even the highest-ranking chiefs), and when talking with the drum, he can call the king by his personal name." Thus master drummers enjoy a unique authority and privilege within Yorùbá sacred kingship through their ability to articulate the divine voice of the drum. In this way, sacred and royal drumming coalesce, just as ritual drummers address *òrìṣà* as revered royalty.[16] Like the familial relationships among ọmọ Àyàn, which balance privilege and independence with responsibility and propriety, the relationship between drummers and royal authority maintains a delicate balance between privilege and interdependence.

In a vivid cinematic allegory, the film *Ṣaworoidẹ: Brass Bells* (2001) fuses the mythic past and contemporary Nigerian politics through a dramatization of the metaphysical power of Àyàn.[17] The film's title character is a mystical drum belonging to Àyàn Àgalú. This drum, Ṣaworoidẹ, is named after the brass bells that decorate its body and sweeten its sound. The plot of the film revolves around a military coup: a brutish, greedy, and corrupt general named Làgàta attempts to usurp the throne of Jobo from the rightful heirs. The royal crown of Jobo, called Adé-idẹ (Brass Crown), shares an intimate relationship to Àyàn Àgalú's drum: only the legitimate ruler, initiated with the ritual incisions for the application of medicine, can wear the crown and hear the sound of Ṣaworoidẹ; if anyone other than the true, ritually prepared ruler heard Ṣaworoidẹ while wearing the crown, the drumming would drive them to madness and death. Àyàn Àgalú and his drum Ṣaworoidẹ thus pose a mortal threat to the scheme of the corrupt Làgàta, who stubbornly refused to undergo the initiation rituals after his coup d'état.

In the midst of intrigue and betrayal leading up to the illegitimate installation of Làgàta, Àyàn Àgalú is captured by Làgàta's henchmen. However, Àyàn Àgalú has hidden Ṣaworoidẹ and arranged for his son Àyáníyì to foil the plot by drumming Ṣaworoidẹ at the carnival-like installation of Làgàta. At the climax of the story, Àyáníyì is given Ṣaworoidẹ, and then manages to join the drum ensemble at the installation. Once the beaded crown—the symbolic and metaphysical authority of kingship—is placed on the general's head, a horrific sequence of events quickly unfolds. Àyàn Àgalú's son plays the following text on Ṣaworoidẹ:

Aṣọ funfun ni sọkún aró	White cloth cries for indigo dye
Ìkan sọkún ikejì tan tan tan.	The first part of a statement cries for the second part.

Làgàta is quickly seized by the combined metaphysical power of the crown on his head and the sound of Ṣaworoidẹ's poetic commentary on justice and retribution. To the soundtrack of spooky synthesizers and insistent dùndún drumming, Làgàta collapses to the ground and dies on the spot.

While this is a rather grave dramatization of the "preposterously intense" force of Àyàn described by Wenger, musicians in general and, more specifically, *àwọn ọmọ* Àyàn (children of Àyàn) are also referred to as *ọmọ amúlùúdùn* (those who make the town a sweet place). The late great *àpàlà* music maestro Haruna Ìṣọlá once commented upon this essence of the musical vocation. In one of his recordings, he sang:

Àti ìlù	Drums
Àti orin	And songs
Aládùn ni iṣẹ́ wa.	Making life sweet is our occupation.

According to Chief Àyánlékè, "A town in which there is no drumming will become a farmland. In a town, when we drum some wild animals will come to the town to experience the music. Even unseen energies of disease will return and [then] go elsewhere." Thus, drumming provides sweetness to life by creating stimulating dance rhythms and melodious citatory songs. This also implies that drumming is a therapeutic healing force that is both curative and preventative.

The common occupational objective of Àyàn drummers is *ìmúluúdùn*, making the community "sweet" to live in. Both drumming and songs are provided to serve that main objective. Through sound, Àyàn connects living humans to ancestors and òrìṣà, thus providing a stimulating energy that bridges visible and invisible worlds.

Notes

1. See, for example, Oyèlámì (1989, 1991), Euba (1990), Neeley (1994), Amira and Cornelius (1999), Coburg (2004a, 2004b), Moore and Sayre (2006), Villepastour (2010), and Schweitzer (2013). Recent scholarship that addresses some important metaphysical and esoteric dimensions of Àyàn includes Vélez (2000), Ramos (2000), Marcuzzi (2005), and Vincent (2006).

2. Traditional Yorùbá forms of orature include *odù* Ifá, *dínlógún, ìjúbà* (homage), *oríkì* (praise poetry), *òwe* (proverbs), and *ìjálá* (hunters' poetry). These forms can also be usefully understood as types of oral literature or oral composition (Lord 2000). See Payne (1992) for an assessment of Akìwọwọ's approach to Yorùbá orature.

3. Ifá is one of the central divination corpuses of Yorùbá traditional religion and consists of 256 odù (divinatory signs) an extensive body of orature. Every odù has its own identifying name (e.g., Ọ̀sá Ìrẹtè), each of which includes numerous ẹsẹ (frequently translated as "verses"). For more on Ifá, see Gleason (1973), Bascom (1991), and Epega and Niemark (1995).

4. All translations are by the authors unless indicated otherwise.

5. *Aláròfọ̀* can be translated as "one who thinks before he chants."

6. In particular, see Barber (1991).

7. Interview by Akínṣọlá Akìwọwọ with Chief Àyánlékè Adépòjù of Èruwà, Ọ̀yọ́ State, Nigeria, late 1990s in New York City, New York, USA.

8. Interview by Akínṣọlá Akìwọwọ with Ganiyù Ṣanùsi Àyánwálé Àyánlẹ́ye, Koito Compound, Modákẹ́dẹ́, near Ilé-Ifẹ̀, Ọ̀ṣun State, Nigeria, ca. 2003. Ọ̀ṣun State, Nigeria.

9. *Bí a ti ń kìí ba oun. Ni ma mumi òmí ràn sì wà lórí. Tá a bá ní ká máa sọ ọ́, ilẹ̀ á sú, oríkì Àyàn Àgalú pọ̀ repẹtẹ.*

10. *Mọ ọmọ ẹni tí ìwọ ṣe.*

11. *Bùọdá* comes from the English word brother, and—interestingly—does not denote a relationship in terms of seniority as do the Yorùbá terms *àbúrò* (junior sibling) and *ègbọ́n* (senior sibling).

12. *Emele* (or, *omele* in other dialects) is a generic term for a supporting drum.

13. Kútanyín is an oríkì (praise name), the etymology of which is *ikú ó tan eyin* (it is death that exposes the teeth).

14. The gúdúgúdú is relatively unusual as a temple drum/receptacle of Àyàn bàtá compounds. Although the gúdúgúdú is widely regarded as the senior drum among different kinds of Àyàn drummers, it is more common to find other kinds of equivalents to the Cuban elekoto in bàtá compounds, such as a kúdi, miniature drums, pots, and other variants.

15. Although drumming is clearly at the core of Àyàn worship, an ability to perform as a drummer is not the only expression of its spiritual energy. For example, in Cuba some Añá ritual specialists possess and embody esoteric knowledge in discreet, ceremonial settings that lies outside the realm of musical performance—and sometimes beyond the reach of highly skilled drummers.

16. For discussions of Yorùbá relationships between the sacred and royal, see Apter (1992); Matory (1994, 2008); and Pemberton and Afọláyan (1996).

17. Ṣaworoidẹ (2001) and its sequel Agogo Eèwọ̀ (2005) are both sociopolitical parables. For Nigerian audiences, these films by writer/director Túndé Kelani and co-writer Akínwùnmí Ìṣọ̀lá are clear, rather thinly veiled critiques of various contemporary political figures and regimes in Nigeria.

References Cited

Adégbìtẹ́, Adémọ́lá. 1988. "The Drum and Its Role in Yorùbá Religion." In *Journal of Religion in Africa* 18 (1): 15–26.

———. 1991. "The Concept of Sound in Traditional African Religious Music." In *Journal of Black Studies* 22 (1): 45–54.

Akìwọwọ, Akínṣọlá A. 1983. "Àjọbí and Àjọgbé: Variations on the Theme of Sociation." In *University of Ifẹ̀ Nigeria Inaugural Lecture Series*, 46. Ilé-Ifẹ̀, Nigeria: University Ifẹ̀ Press.

Amira, John, and Steven Cornelius. 1999. *The Music of Santería: Traditional Rhythms of the Batá Drums*. Gilsum, NH: White Cliffs Media.

Apter, Andrew. 1992. *Black Critics and Kings: The Hermeneutics of Power in Yorùbá Society*. Chicago: University of Chicago Press.

Awólàlú, J. Ọmọ́ṣadé. 1979. *Yorùbá Belief and Sacrificial Rites*. New York: Longman.

Barber, Karin. 1991. *I Could Speak until Tomorrow: Oríkì, Women, and the Past in a Yorùbá Town*. Edinburgh: Edinburgh University Press.

Bascom, William. 1991. *Ifá Divination: Communication between Gods and Men in West Africa*. Bloomington: Indiana University Press.

Coburg, Adrian. 2004a. *Batá Scores—Toques Especiales*. 5th Revised Edition. Bern, Switzerland: Self-published.

———. 2004b. *Cantos Especiales—Cantos Yorùbá, Iyesá y Arará*. Vol. 1. Bern, Switzerland: Self-published.

Epega, Afọlábí A., and Philip John Neimark. 1995. *The Sacred Ifá Oracle*. Brooklyn: Athelia Henrietta Press.

Euba, Akin. 1990. *Yorùbá Drumming: The Dùndún Tradition*. Bayreuth, W. Germany: E. Breitlinger, Bayreuth University.

Gleason, Judith, with Awótúndé Awórìndé and John Ọláníyì Ògúndípẹ̀. 1973. *A Recitation of Ifá, Oracle of the Yorùbá*. New York: Grossman.

Lord, Albert B. 2000 [1960]. *The Singer of Tales*. Cambridge, MA: Harvard University Press.

Marcuzzi, Michael David. 2005. *A Historical Study of the Ascendant Role of Bàtá Drumming in Cuban Òrìṣà Worship*. PhD diss., York University, Toronto.

Matory, J. Lorand. 1994. *Sex and the Empire That Is No More: Gender and the Politics of Metaphor in Ọ̀yọ́ Yorùbá Religion*. Minneapolis: University of Minnesota Press.

———. 2008. "Is There Gender in Yorùbá Culture?" In *Òrìṣà Devotion as World Religion: The Globalization of Yorùbá Religious Culture*, eds. K. Jacob Olúpọ̀nà and Terry Rey. Madison: University of Wisconsin Press. 513–58.

Moore, Robin, and Elizabeth Sayre. 2006. "An Afro-Cuban Batá Piece for Obatalá, King of the White Cloth." In *Analytical Studies in World Music*, ed. Michael Tenzer. New York: Oxford University Press. 120–60.

Neeley, Paul. 1994. "Discourse Peak and Poetic Closure in the Final Stanza of a Talking Drum Performance." In *Journal of West African Languages* 24 (1): 108–14.

Oyèlámì, Múráínà. 1989. *Yorùbá Dùndún Music: A New Notation with Basic Exercises & Five Yorùbá Drum Repertoires.* Bayreuth: Iwalewa-Haus.

———. 1991. *Yorùbá Bàtá Music: A New Notation with Basic Exercises and Ensemble Pieces.* Bayreuth, W. Germany: Iwalewa-Haus.

Payne, M. W. 1992. "Akiwowo, Orature, and Divination: Approaches to the Construction of an Emic Sociological Paradigm of Society." In *Sociological Analysis* 53 (2): 175–87.

Pemberton III, John, and Fúnṣọ́ S. Afọláyan. 1996. *Yorùbá Sacred Kinship: "A Power Like That of the Gods."* Washington: Smithsonian Institution Press.

Ramos, Miguel. 2000. *The Empire Beats On: Oyo, Bátá Drums and Hegemony in Nineteenth-Century Cuba.* MA thesis, Florida International University, Miami.

Schweitzer, Kenneth George. 2013. *The Artistry of Afro-Cuban Bátá Drumming: Aesthetics, Transmission, Bonding, and Creativity.* Jackson: University Press of Mississippi.

Vélez, María Teresa. 2000. *Drumming for the Gods: The Life and Times of Felipe García Villamil, Santero, Palero, and Abakuá.* Philadelphia: Temple University Press.

Villepastour, Amanda. 2010. *Ancient Text Messages of the Yorùbá Bàtá Drum: Cracking the Code.* Burlington: Ashgate.

Vincent [Villepastour], Amanda. 2006. *Bata Conversations: Guardianship and Entitlement Narratives about the Bata in Nigeria and Cuba.* PhD thesis, School of Oriental and African Studies, University of London.

Wenger, Susanne, and Gert Chesi. 1983. *A Life with the Gods in Their Yorùbá Homeland.* Wörgl, Austria: Perlinger Verlag.

Videography

Agogo Eèwọ̀. 2005 [2002]. By Túndé Kelani (dir.), Akínwùnmí Ìṣọ̀lá, Dejumo Lewis, Adébáyọ̀ Fálétí, and Lére Paimo. Nigeria: Mainframe Film and Television Productions. DVD.

Ṣaworoidẹ: Brass Bells. 2001 [1999]. By Túndé Kelani (dir.), Akínwùnmí Ìṣọ̀lá, Kolo Oyèwọ, Bukky Wright, and Lére Paimo. Mainframe Film and Television Productions. DVD.

2

Divining Àyàn: An Òrìṣà Priest from Ògbómọ̀ṣọ́ Speaks

Kawolẹ̀yin Àyángbẹ́kún, with Amanda Villepastour

• •

After undertaking my first three years of research in various areas of Yorùbáland (1999–2001), I was initially convinced that all bàtá drummers, and by association Àyàn priests, were Muslims.[1] It was not until my enquiries deepened beyond the most visible drummers at festivals, life cycle celebrations, and other parties that I was to encounter a handful of Àyàn priests whose families had never converted to Islam or, less commonly, Christianity. Such drummers appear to be concentrated in Ìjẹ̀bu where they play a different style of bàtá,[2] while Ọ̀yọ́-style players are almost all Muslims.

While working among the òrìṣà community in Òṣogbo, I heard about a man who was a master *dínlógún* (shell) diviner who was practicing bàtá and Àyàn traditions within an òrìṣà compound. In April 2002, Òṣogbo Ṣàngó priest Ṣàngódáre Gbádégẹsin Àjàlá generously drove me on the exceedingly dangerous road to Ògbómọ̀ṣọ́ to meet the man people had been talking about, Àyángbẹ́kún. My arrival turned out to be a rather major event in the Àyángbẹ́kún compound as they told me they had never received an *òyìnbó* (white person) before. I was welcomed with very formal prayers and libations.

I visited Àyángbẹ́kún on four further occasions in August 2003 and in August and September 2004.[3] I have yet to meet another Àyàn priest with Àyángbẹ́kún's depth of esoteric knowledge, for he was an initiate not only of Àyàn, but of Ṣàngó, Ẹgbẹ́, Ọ̀sun, and several other òrìṣà. Àyángbẹ́kún was also known and feared for his mastery of Ọ̀sanyìn, the òrìṣà of flora and medicine who is said to speak with a squeaky voice. Two years after my last meeting with Àyángbẹ́kún, I was shocked to learn from my research collaborator Rábíù Àyándòkun that this remarkable man, only in his late forties, died unexpectedly in 2007 from malaria. Àyángbẹ́kún and Àyándòkun used to play bàtá together thirty years previous. Àyándòkun told me that the last time he met Àyángbẹ́kún was shortly before his death at an Egúngún festival in Ẹdẹ, where Àyángbẹ́kún was carrying the full Egúngún (ancestral) body mask. Although the human identity of an Egúngún is publicly concealed, Àyángbẹ́kún made himself known to Àyándòkun in a covert manner in this last poignant, if not prophetic encounter (pers. comm., Àyándòkun, October 2008).

During my first meeting with Àyángbẹ́kún, he asked me to send people from abroad to his compound. He also told me that he would like to travel to my country. Sadly, this was an aspiration he did not live to fulfill. In August 2011, I went to find Àyángbẹ́kún's family in Ògbómọ̀sọ́ to ask for their permission to posthumously publish his interviews. The house I was taken to was not the same one I had visited in previous years. I was guided on foot through a winding back alley, surrounded by excited, curious children. A woman appeared and told us she was Àyángbẹ́kún's senior wife and led us to her house. She pulled up a chair for me and landed a pile of some two hundred photographs in my lap. Several were of African Americans who had heard about Àyángbẹ́kún since my first visit and arrived there for various initiations. After viewing a few dozen photographs, I encountered one of Àyángbẹ́kún and myself the last time we met each other in Ọ̀yọ́ in 2004.

Àyángbẹ́kún's family unreservedly granted me permission to share our conversations in print. This chapter comprises edited material from my several encounters with him. I have endeavored to maintain his voice with the least editorial intervention possible (in the smaller font). My own voice is included in the main text and endnotes where additional clarity is called for. In an endeavor to invert the traditional academic asymmetry of scholar-informant where the former unquestionably claims authorship, Àyángbẹ́kún is credited here as the primary writer, reflecting his intellectual authority as priest and my subordinate, less-informed status as consultant and student.

As a priest deeply steeped in divination and oral literature, Àyángbẹ́kún's communications about Àyàn and the bàtá were not conversational in the ordinary sense. Rather, he spoke in a declamatory manner, punctuating his speech with short phrases and sentences that he frequently repeated for emphasis and aesthetic effect. Heightening ordinary speech, Àyángbẹ́kún would interpolate divination chants and songs into his religious narratives (*ìtàn*). In an endeavor to capture his virtuoso oral performances, I have mostly maintained the Nigerian English vernacular of my translators—all òrìṣà priests rather than professional linguists—which I believe represents Àyángbẹ́kún's verbal artistry and ideas most faithfully.

AV

Receiving and Becoming Àyàn

Àyángbẹ́kún asserted his personal identity in opposition to the Muslim and Christian religious hegemony in contemporary Yorùbáland. As his traditionalist identity was inextricably linked with his lineage, and with his initiations and relationships with the òrìṣà, I open with his discussion of Àyàn rites.

Some [Àyàn drummers] are *dùndún* drummers, some are bàtá drummers. Yes, it is taboo for the Christians too. They are Muslims, they are bearing Muslim names. Àyángbẹ́kún is my name, and I have been initiated to Àyàn. My *odù* is Òtúúrúpọ̀n Méjì.[4] They will never know because they are Muslim. It is their profession. These people do not know about feeding Àyàn with blood because they are Muslims and they take Àyàn as a profession. If you are to be initiated to Àyàn, you and Àyàn will be bathed in *omi-ẹ̀rọ̀* [herbal potion]. Now that people tend to be Christians or Muslims, it is then that people do not want to perform the initiation of Àyàn as it is done deeply, but we still do the necessary and compulsory initiations for them. It is we who are the real Àyàn lineage, the real lineage sons of Àyàn. And anybody who beats [the drum], anybody who has come to learn about Àyàn, we must do the initiation tradition for that person too so that they can also initiate others.

We don't need a *babaláwo* [Ifá divining priest]; Àyàn is different. We perform all the necessary traditions at Àyàn's shrine for the person. We do it for women who are in traditional Àyàn families but now that people are Muslims, we do it for Muslims. The person will prosper; Àyàn will bless them, and the person will be rich. This is what we will give to the person (see Plate 2.1). We feed Àyàn with white bean cake, food, alcohol, kola nuts, and one can give a guinea fowl and a duiker for one's [annual] Àyàn festival.

Now that Christians play the drum and *alhajis*[5] are playing the bàtá, some of them just do it to get money, but we, we are born into it, so we must worship Àyàn. This is how we do it in Yorùbáland, this is how our forefathers handed over everything to us. We give the initiate a name. You should know that this thing has been taken from Nigeria to other places, they took it to Cuba.

The ceremony should be seven days. There are lots of things that we have to do during that period. We have to invite all of the head Àyàn priests, they must be there. We have to get some white clothes for you to be initiated in. You have to take a ritual bath. All of these things involve money. During this period, we give taboos. They have to consult Àyàn for the odù which will tell them exactly what to do for you.

Plate 2.1: Àyángbẹ́kún holding
his Àyàn. (photograph: Amanda
Villepastour, Ògbómọ̀ṣọ́, 19 July
2004)

After the ceremony, you have to take proper care of Àyàn and make
sure that you are maintaining her[6] properly. Whatever she eats, you give,
whatever she wears, you give. The more you do this, the better for you.
The moment you get the òrìṣà, if you have anything that is disturbing
you or giving you headaches, you just go directly to Àyàn and ask for
what you want.

The moment you are initiated, you too become Àyàn. You become a
messenger of the deity. You become a priestess. You are receiving and
at the same time you are becoming. When you hear the drum anywhere,
at times you may fall into trance. When bàtá possesses someone, all
the nerves in their head will rise, directed by their brain. It shows that
òrìṣà Àyàn has entered their brain. The whole body will be stimulated
by the sound of bàtá and both of their eyes will bulge out and turn red.
This is what happens when Àyàn possesses someone. When the rhythm
reaches the òrìṣà that belongs to someone, this time the rhythm of Àyàn,
it will send the òrìṣà into their body and they will be possessed by Àyàn.
Ah! Good god! She possesses someone like Ṣàngó does. One gets nervous. One's head starts making sounds. We would be saying [beating],

"sprinkle the wèrè [mad person] with water, the mad one is getting hot."
We would be beating this, stronger and stronger.

The [possession] rhythm is played during the period of the Àyàn festival or when an old bàtá drummer dies in order to dissociate the deceased
from the remaining drummers on earth; this rhythm will be played. The
process is called kunre and the rhythm is called faree Àyàn.[7]

No one can be initiated to Ṣàngó without the approval of Àyàn. That is
the interrelationship between Àyàn and Ṣàngó. If one wants to be initiated to Ṣàngó, bàtá must be interconnected. That is the main interrelationship between them. All bàtá drummers' families have Ṣàngó or Egúngún
in their compound or house. Even if the whole family is Muslim, they
must find someone to look after Ṣàngó in their compound. That is, there
must be at least one Ṣàngó priest in the family. I too had to go through
the same process with Ṣàngó, Ọya, Òrìṣà Oko, Ògún, Ifá, Ìbejì, Ọ̀sanyìn,
Eégún, Òrìṣàńlá, Ọ̀ṣun, they are there. I had to get initiated.

You can put Àyàn in a clay pot of any size. These are the things you
will be given after initiation (see Plate 2.1). It is the real Àyàn. You will
put it in a clay bowl. There are names for these small bàtá drums. But it
is only those who have been initiated who will know the name of these
sacrificial bàtá. When one does the Àyàn idóṣù, the name will come out
in Àyàn's odù.[8] For this reason, the name of small bàtá will be different
from one person to another.

There must be a reason for the small bàtá to be played. For example, if
a drummer hasn't been out to play for a while, he can offer these drums
some food, we can beat them, and then people will send for the client to
come and play. Also, if somebody is very sick, we can do a divination
and the oracle will direct them to feed Àyàn. As soon as they feed Àyàn
and beat the drum, the sickness will vanish.

It Is God Who Created Àyàn

When asked about the origins of Àyàn, Àyángbẹ́kún launched into a long and
winding story, virtuosically dramatizing his ìtàn with songs and chanted divination verses. Beginning with a scene in heaven, we are led through Àyàn's journey
to earth with the òrìṣà who is known to reside at the crossroad between this world
and the other, Èṣù. Àyángbẹ́kún's story uses Àyàn's name in the beginning but
then drifts seamlessly into using Bàtá, for the bàtá drum is the sacred vessel for
the òrìṣà Àyàn in Àyángbẹ́kún's lineage.[9] Àyàn and a humanized Bàtá become
interdependent and even fused with interchangeable names, but never confused.
Àyángbẹ́kún takes us through Àyàn/Bàtá's multiple conjugal relationships and
infidelities—all designed to elevate her status as a queen and as the desirable wife

of several powerful òrìṣà. Not only are many aspects of the narrative metaphors for making and caring for bàtá drums, but one sees a reflection of performance practice: bàtá is the preferred drum in Ṣàngó, Egúngún, and Èṣù rites.[10] In the ìtàn that follows, Àyángbẹ́kún humanizes the various òrìṣà and, through story, binds them irrevocably to Bàtá and Àyàn.

Àyàn was a woman, Àyàn was a queen. Ọ̀rányàn[11] was her husband, and Ọ̀rányàn was a king. They called him Ọ̀rányàn Agọ̀tún. The leopard (the fierce one) is Àyàngalú's husband.[12] Ọ̀rányàn was an enthusiastic warrior, a fierce one. Àyàn was one of the queens who chanted *rárà* for kings.[13] May Àyàn let them have money, bless them, support them, and make them prosperous:

Kí Àyàn kó jẹ́ kí àwọn ó lówó lọ́wọ́	May Àyàn bring them money
Kó kẹ́ àwọn, kó gbè àwọn	May Àyàn protect them
Kó jẹ́ kí àwọn lọ́là.	May Àyàn bring them wealth.

If we say it is a babaláwo, it is a babaláwo. If we say it is not a babaláwo, it is not a babaláwo. Because Ọ̀rúnmìlà[14] says exactly in one of his odù:

Níbi tí ó ti dífá fún Èṣù òhun Bàtá	When he divined for Èṣù and Bàtá
Èṣù nìyí òjiṣẹ́ Ọlọ́run ni	Èṣù is the messenger of God
Àyàn nìyí òjiṣẹ́ Ọlọ́run ni	Àyàn is the messenger of God
Àwọn méjèèjì	The two of them
wọ́n relé Èdùmàrè.	went to God's house.[15]

The two of them said that they were going to the world. They wanted to go there and become famous. Èṣù Láàlú[16] was the first to be married to Àyàngalú before she was taken away from him by Ọ̀rányàn. Èṣù said that they should take an oath before going to the world to ensure that he would not be betrayed by Àyàn.[17] Èṣù told Àyàn that if she would marry him, he would clothe her forever and she would be famous forever. Èṣù told Àyàn not to betray him after clothing her. That is the reason they needed to make an oath before getting to the world. Àyàn told Èṣù that if he clothed her, she would marry him and she would make him famous. He accepted and they made an oath.

Èṣù and Àyàn went to Elédùmarè's [God's] house and they told him to have a seat. They said they would like Elédùmarè to be their witness as that they were going to the world. They were going to live as husband and wife and they would not divorce each other. Elédùmarè encouraged them and told them to come and lay their hands on him. Bàtá laid her hand on Elédùmarè and Èṣù also laid down his hands. Elédùmarè laid his left hand over all of the hands and he told them that they would be famous and have many children when they got to the world. He said that there would be joy wherever they were invited, and the places they were not invited to would be boring. Elédùmarè made incisions on Èṣù and Àyàn and told them to taste it. He then told them to go.

When they arrived at the gate between heaven and earth, Àyàn told Èṣù that they were now at the boundary of heaven and earth. Àyàn said she was going back to heaven. Àyàn said that she was going back because she was naked and people would make fun of her. Èṣù told her to wait and he decided to go into the bush to look for Ẹtu [Maxwell's Duiker]. He looked for Ìgalà [Bushbuck], Èsúró [Redflanked Duiker], Ewúrẹ́ [She Goat], and Òrúkọ [He Goat].[18] Èṣù called the animals and told them that he had a gift for them from Elédùmarè. They said they were happy. He said,

"The main reason I am giving you this gift is so you can avoid being eaten by human beings. Don't you know that it was Elédùmarè who made the human beings kings over you so they could kill you?"

Èṣù called the animals and tricked them. He took a bean cake and dipped it into palm oil. *Eéran* leaves and other leaves grew.[19]

"Don't live among human beings. This is the bush where you should live and where you've been destined to live by Elédùmarè."

Èṣù went to look for Ògún. He said,

"Come!" but Ògún refused Èṣù's call. Èṣù said,

"Come! I have some food for you that Elédùmarè told me to give to you."

Èṣù told Ògún that when he heard a song on his arrival, he should come. Èṣù said,

"When you hear all of the animals responding '*yunyunyun*' you should come. Come, there is food. When there is not any response of '*yunyunyun*' kill them all. You will see food to eat."

All of the animals, Ẹtu, Èsúró, Ìgalà, Ewúrẹ́, and Òrúkọ started eating. While they grazed, Èṣù told Ògún to hide himself in the hut. Èṣù started singing to Ẹtu, Èsúró, Ìgalà, Ewúrẹ́, and Òrúkọ. They said,

"Let's walk in a group, let's walk in a group." The animals didn't respond to Èṣù's song. They said,

"If you don't respond, we'll die. Let's walk in a group, let's walk in a group."

They did not respond.

"Let's disperse, let's disperse." They responded to the song.

"Let's disperse, let's disperse."

Èṣù told Ògún to do his job and Ògún started shooting the animals, killing all of them. Ògún said he only needed the meat but he did not

need the skins. Èṣù said he needed the skins for his wife who was waiting naked at the boundary of heaven and earth. He said that she didn't
have any clothes to wear. Ògún told him to take the skins to her and Èṣù
took all of the animal skins and removed the fur from them. Èṣù has a
tricky character given to him by Elédùmarè. Èṣù removed the fur perfectly. Èṣù covered his wife with the skins, he covered his wife's body
with them. He gave her an *ọ̀já* [baby sling]. This is also the *ọ̀já* [points
to the antelope skin wound around the bàtá]. This [the small skin] is the
head. This [the large skin] is the bottom.[20]
    Èṣù covered Àyàn with the skins. After covering her, Èṣù became a
great man. After tying the ọ̀já on Àyàn's body, Àyàn praised him sweetly.
Àyàn started praising Èṣù with songs:

Baraànù Ẹlẹ́sẹ̀ Ọyán	Baraànù Ẹlẹ́sẹ̀ Ọyán (Èṣù praise name)
Baraànù alàmùlamu Bàtá	One-who-understands-the-language-
	of-Bàtá
Òfẹ́ Bàtá kìí jó	Bàtá's lover does not dance to
bamu bámú	*bamu bámú*[21]
Ẹlẹ́kún ń sunkún	The victim is weeping
Láaróyè náà ń sẹ̀jẹ̀	Láaróyè is bleeding
Ẹlẹ́kún kúúlé	The victim died inside
Láaróyè kú òde	Láaróyè died outside
Èṣù Látopa Èṣù gongo Èṣù	Èṣù Látopa with a pointed head
Èṣù Láàlú Baraàmi Ẹlẹ́sẹ̀ Ọyán	Èṣù Láàlú Baraàmi Ẹlẹ́sẹ̀ Ọyán

Èṣù was overwhelmed and he told Bàtá to lead them. When they got
to the world, his wife, Àyàngalú, was praising her husband with *arò* [a
lament]. Everybody in the world came to hear Àyàngalú's lamenting.
    Ọlófin was the king of Ifẹ̀, the original place of the Yorùbá people.
He was the first king. Ọlófin heard the sound of Bàtá and sent for them.
Ọlófin said he heard a sweet sound and said,
    "Are these people from earth or from heaven?" and he sent for them.
    "Lady and gentleman, where are you from? Are you from earth or
heaven?" They said they descended from heaven. He said,
    "Why don't you come and live with me?"
    Ọlófin told them he had a very big house where they could live. His
family and friends lived there. They were sitting down without anything
to do. He said,
    "Let your wife play for us in the morning as soon as we all wake up.
Let us wake up to the sweet sound of Bàtá. She should wake us up with
sweet songs."
    Wherever Èṣù's wife sat, he would sit beside her. Ọlófin said,

"There shall never be two kings on a single throne. He should live outside. This is the crossroad of earth, this is the crossroad of heaven, this is the crossroad of character." He said,

"He should live there."

Ọlọ́fin built a house for Èṣù. Èṣù left his wife to live with Ọlọ́fin.

Whenever he wanted to see Àyàn, he could visit her.[22] When his wife wanted to see Èṣù, she could see him in the morning. It was Èṣù who started it. When they wanted to make love they should have their own rooms. After the affair, each should go to their own room to avoid disrespect, because Èṣù is very hot-tempered. But his wife is a hedonist. She sang deeply arousing songs. Àyàn woke him up in the mornings. Àyàn praised the king and her husband every morning.

"I cannot disrespect my husband and the king. I have a deep respect for my husband. My husband is the head of the family."

That is how Elédùmarè created Bàtá and Èṣù. Bàtá is the leader of all drums.

Bàtá on the Warfront

War is a common theme across oral literature about Àyàn and the bàtá, reflecting the military might of the past Ọ̀yọ́ empire.[23] Accordingly, Àyàn/Bàtá's magical prowess is once again dramatized by Àyángbẹ́kún; in the following ìtàn, Àyàn is a sought-after powerhouse of war and politics.

Ìdin Gbégbé ń gbé	Ìdin Gbégbé,
Awo Ìdin Gbégbé ń gbé	The priest of Ìdin Gbè gbè ń gbé
Ìdin Gbégbé ń gbè	Ìdin Gbégbé,
Awo Ìdin Gbégbé ń gbè	The priest of Ìdin Gbègbè ń gbè
A dífá fún	Who performed Ifá divination for
Bàtá òun Ṣàngó	Bàtá and Ṣàngó
Tí wọ́n ń tì kòlé	when they were coming from
òrun bò wá sílé ayé.	heaven to earth.
Bàtá sọpé òun làgbà	Bàtá claimed to be the elder
Ṣàngó náà sọpé	Ṣàngó also claimed
òun làgbà	to be the elder
Bàtá ní "ẹfi sílẹ̀,"	Bàtá said, "leave it,"
yíò tẹ́ní gbà	and that she would disgrace him
ogun ni	during the war
Bí Ṣàngó se	That is how Ṣàngó
lọ ogun nìyìí	got into this war
Ṣàngó kò rí ogun ṣẹ.	Ṣàngó did not win the war.[24]

Ṣàngó went to Ọ̀rúnmìlà's house for divination. He said he was hungry because he didn't win the war. He didn't bring anything back from the war so he had nothing to eat. He lived on the loot from war. Ọ̀rúnmìlà said,

"The woman that you took along, go and beg her to help you win the war." Ṣàngó said that she doesn't speak to him anymore. Ọ̀rúnmìlà said the only way out left for him was to go and beg her, then he would win the war. Ṣàngó said to Ọ̀rúnmìlà,

"You are the only one who can appeal to Bàtá." She should forgive him so that she can help him to win the war. Elderly Ọ̀rúnmìlà went to Bàtá's house and started praising her. He said,

"Bàtá, the wife of Èṣù, the wife of Ṣàngó, the wife of Ògún, I have come to beg you. Please, just forgive him. I know that Ṣàngó, your brother-in-law, has already offended you."

Bàtá said that Ṣàngó should come in person and tender his apology because she had become worthless to him. She agreed to accompany Ṣàngó [to the warfront]. Ọ̀rúnmìlà said he should go home. Ọ̀rúnmìlà went to Ṣàngó's house, Ṣàngó also came to Ọ̀rúnmìlà's house. He came to hear Ọ̀rúnmìlà's reply as to whether Bàtá agreed to accompany him or not. Ọ̀rúnmìlà told him that she had forgiven him but she insisted that he should personally come and tender his apology. Ṣàngó agreed because he, himself, was already fed up and had lost his dignity. They regarded him as nothing in the war. Ọ̀rúnmìlà said he should go along. When Ọ̀rúnmìlà arrived, he started begging Bàtá for him. Bàtá kneeled down and Ṣàngó prostrated. Bàtá pleaded to him in the name of her husband. Ọ̀rúnmìlà said,

"Please, Bàtá has come to speak with you Ṣàngó, we are friends now. She has divorced her husband. Do you know where she came from? She divorced her husband, Ọlọ́fin. She won't accompany him anymore. You used to go to war together but now you're nothing." She accused him of keeping all of the war loot to himself.

"Continue, go on your own." She went her own way.

"The people love her, but you are greedy, you know I used to call you to the war front, but when it came to sharing loot you became greedy." Ṣàngó still pleaded with her [Bàtá] to forgive him. She requested *obì* [kola nut], *èkuru* [bean cake], *àmàlà* [yam porridge], and *ọtí* [alcohol]. He agreed to give her these things and said,

"Don't worry." Bàtá said she was ready. She asked for the things she had requested and Ṣàngó said he would give her everything when she agreed to accompany him to the war front. Ṣàngó agreed to prepare everything for her. Bàtá started to call all of her children.[25]

Bàtá went to Ṣàngó's house. Before she arrived, Ṣàngó prepared double of everything she had requested. Bàtá ate until she was full, then she went home. Ṣàngó dashed[26] Bàtá with all of the war loot, then she was ready to accompany him to the war front. Bàtá said,

"Let's go," and she started to chant to empower him. Ṣàngó did not rely on the traditional methods of survival, he has extraordinary powers.[27] Àrèmú[28] Ògún had now acquired the ability to turn the tide of war. He gave the glory to Bàtá, the warrior is short and kills tall.[29] It is Bàtá that kills both men and women, that is how Ṣàngó started to win the war.

When they finished the war, Ṣàngó put his *ìpònrí* on the ground.[30] He said Bàtá should continue living with him and that they should not separate. He said that she should not follow anybody else anymore. Bàtá agreed with him, but said he should not betray her. She said that she needed to go to her former husband to gain his permission. Ṣàngó said,

"Who?" and she said,

"Èṣù Láàlú." He asked what she needed in order to gain his permission, and she told him to provide salt, palm oil, shea butter, and other kinds of food. As long as Èṣù was satiated, then Bàtá would also be satisfied. She was given everything she asked for, Ṣàngó provided everything for Èṣù. Ṣàngó said,

"You, Èṣù, I want you to give me something." Èṣù said,

"What do you want?" He said,

"Your wife, the one you brought from heaven to earth." Èṣù said that Olófin had already taken her away from him. Ṣàngó said Olófin is a king, and that he was also a king, so it is a small matter. Èṣù said,

"Both of you belong to me (a vulture has authority over his eggs)." Èṣù said he released her for both of you. Ṣàngó asked whether he released her for him. Èṣù said he released her. Ṣàngó and Èṣù reached an agreement. They went to the war front together and won the war, that is why they can never separate. That is how Bàtá and Ṣàngó became one.

Bàtá, Eégún, and the Mortar

In Àyángbékún's family, the *ìyáàlù* (lead) bàtá drummer sits on a down-turned mortar to play, a practice I have not seen or heard of anywhere else (see Plate 2.3). The mortar is the vessel traditionally used for Ṣàngó in material form, just as the bàtá is a container for Àyàn. Not only does this performance practice illustrate the tight relationship between Ṣàngó and Bàtá, but it reminds us of Àyángbékún's own strong allegiance to Ṣàngó. Similarly, the following ìtàn expresses the mythological relationship between the ancestral òrìṣà Egúngún (Eégún) and his traditional drum, the bàtá. Remarkably, Àyángbékún was both a bàtá player and Egúngún masquerader. Plate 2.2 depicts a poster of the annual Egúngún festival undertaken by Àyángbékún's family.

Egúngún said,

"You Ṣàngó, you should know that Àyàn is your female friend. I won't snatch her." But he said she should also play for him to help him fight his own war so that he too could command respect. Ṣàngó said that he too would accompany her,

"Since you are my elder brother." Eégún now said that he should come along. Eégún went outside. He covered his head with his head covering. He then put on his socks.[31] Eégún said,

"Why don't you dance the dance of *alágàdàngbá*?[32] Perhaps, I can be emotionally moved. Start doing the alágàdàngbá dance, perhaps I can be moved. Let the *omele* [accompanying drum] resound, the fighting day has arrived." Bàtá also spoke lamenting words.

"We were in the open field when we put on trousers without a *bàntẹ́*, we are in the open field."[33] Eégún also sang, he played, he danced. He commanded respect beyond the applause he received. Formerly, Eégún didn't dance to drums. Whenever Eégún goes out in public, everybody applauds. He would say,

Báyìi láá se ìlú	This is how we do the city
Ìlú ì bá dùn	The city would have been so interesting
Báyìi láá se ìlú	This is how we do the city
Ìlú ì bá dùn.	The city would have been so interesting.

People applauded Egúngún. But when Bàtá went out with him, he [Eégún] was happy.

He did all of the things he needed to do that day. Ṣàngó was even advising him to perform his magical dance. Ṣàngó also performs his own magic. Eégún received his magic from Ṣàngó. That was how Eégún also started playing with magic. Because Ṣàngó came with his woman. Eégún was famous, maybe almost as famous as Ṣàngó. The king of Ìrèsé heard about this.[34] The king of Ìrèsé was surprised that someone like Ṣàngó still existed, someone who could go to war and be praised by a woman in this way.

"Call them for me." He said that they should come and perform what they are doing for him too. They now called Eégún. Eégún said,

"As you have called me, a woman who is a friend of my brother Ṣàngó is coming with me. Go and tell Ṣàngó to release his lady friend for me, we still have another outing." Ṣàngó said he didn't have any war to fight now and that she should go with Eégún. Eégún and Bàtá now went to Ònírèsé's palace. They reached Ònírèsé's palace, he's a king. They said,

"We are the ones you called for." He said,

Plate 2.2: Poster from the 2011 Egúngún festival of Àyángbẹ́kún's compound. From left, Àyángbẹ́kún's eldest son, Túndé, the family Egúngún mask, and Àyángbẹ́kún in ritual attire.

"I'm the one who called on you." He told them,

"Go back to the town's border and continue doing the things that are making you well-known. You should also do it so I can see." Eégún got dressed beside a bush.

Bàtá also dressed up. Eégún covered his head with his head coverings and his legs with socks.

Ó ní "o bá ta	He said, "why don't you dance
lágàdàṅgbá?"	lágàdàṅgbá?"
Bóyá o rí òun a dìde	Maybe he will rise up and dance
Bàtá bá ta lágàdàṅgbá.	Bàtá, dance to lágàdàṅgbá.

Bàtá also put on a singing voice.

"Bàtá says we are on an open field, since we didn't put on trousers without putting on bàṇtẹ́. That was how got we moved, and started playing to Ònírèsé's place. He took money from people from the right and from the left. He was performing acrobatics and he was dancing until he got to Ònírèsé's palace. Ònírèsé's had already sat down with his people, they sat down. Bàtá now sat down and she ordered someone to bring her

Plate 2.3: Àyángbẹkún's son Àyántópẹ plays the ìyáàlù seated on a down-turned mortar, accompanied by his brothers. (photograph: Amanda Villepastour, Ògbómòṣọ́, 2 August 2011)

husband's chair. She saw Ṣàngó coming as she looked back, Ṣàngó was coming with a *àpẹẹrẹ* which he would use to sit on. Ṣàngó asked his wife to sit down. That àpẹẹrẹ is called odó [mortar].[35] This is why Bàtá sits on a mortar whenever Eégún wants to dance. Ṣàngó was the one who gave the mortar to Bàtá so she could use it wherever she goes. This is why Bàtá sits on mortar from then until today, Ṣàngó was the one who gave it to her. This is what they use in praising the Bàtá people.

Metaphysical Àyàn Families

In Nigeria, most individual òrìṣà have numerous subcategories which Yorùbá-speaking devotees translate into English as "dimensions."[36] Each dimension has its own name, set of narratives (ìtàn) and imagined personalities. Multiple dimensions of a single òrìṣà can be diverse and contrasting within a unified whole.[37] Dimensions of an òrìṣà that is thought of as archetypally male or female may actually include opposite genders. For instance, Ṣàngó, who is considered to be the epitome of maleness, has a female dimension while Ọ̀ṣun, an òrìṣà of motherhood, female sexuality, and childbirth, has male, warrior dimensions. As òrìṣà dimensions are regionally diverse, a dimension that exists in one town can be unknown in another. Regarding these dynamic dimensions, Barber (1990, 314) deconstructs the myth of a fixed òrìṣà pantheon: "Fragmentation, multiplication and inconsistency have usually been overlooked, tidied away or acknowledged only in passing: put down sometimes to error and sometimes to regional cultural differences [. . .] the tendency to emphasise the orderly at the expense of the dynamic."

Though dimensions of major òrìṣà such as Ọ̀ṣun, Ṣàngó, and Èṣù are well-known and even commonplace in Nigeria and Cuba, Àyángbẹ́kún is the only person in Nigeria I have heard discussing dimensions of Àyàn.[38] As Àyángbẹ́kún paired different drums within a complicated web of Àyàn sub-identities, it is important that the reader understands the configuration of the Yorùbá bàtá ensemble. The two largest drums are the ìyáàlù (mother drum) that leads the ensemble, and the slightly smaller *omele abo* (female accompanying drum) that interlocks with the ìyáàlù to encode speech. In contemporary ensembles, a second ìyáàlù is employed to play an accompanying role and is called *èjìn*, mimetic of its simple musical part, often played by a child who slings the shoulder strap over his head. The considerably smaller accompanying drums are also conical but are only beaten on the larger, upturned head. These include the kúdi, the *omele akọ* (male accompanying drum comprising two small drums tied together), and the *omele mẹ́ta* (three small drums tied together). The *bílálà* is a flexible rawhide beater used on the larger skins of the ìyáàlù and omele abo and the accompanying drums. The *àgẹ̀rẹ̀* is used for Ògún worship and is not a part of the bàtá ensemble. (See Table 2.1.)[39]

There is a series of groups of Àyàn. We have Owólàákẹ́, Ajélànwá, Ajékù, Ajégbèmí, Ajéwùmí, Ajélànà, Àyándayépọ̀, Àyánlóríwù. Owólàákẹ́ is the head of all Àyàn. When you receive this òrìṣà, you can never lack anything in terms of money and wealth. The reason she is called Owólàákẹ́ is because she's a kind of Àyàn related to women. Her duty is to work towards getting money, wealth, property, and other things. The reason that women like money more than men is because of this Owólàákẹ́. Her function is to lead Àyàn to money. That is why you see women nowadays in love with money. Owólàákẹ́ was an òrìṣà when the drum was created as a woman. Owólàákẹ́ is a woman, and the ìyáàlù is a woman. God created the drum as a woman.

The *ṣaworo* [brass bells] are the earrings of the woman. Ìyáàlù is a respectable woman. She pays homage and takes care of her husband [omele akọ]. That is why she receives blessings. That is why you see this ṣaworo along her neck.[40] She has received the blessing from omele akọ. He gave her a lot of blessings so that she should prosper.

Table 2.1: Dimensions of Àyàn according to Àyángbẹ́kún.					
Dimension	**Etymology**	**Translation**	**Drum**	**Gender**	**Kin relationship**
Owólàákẹ́	*Owó ni à ń kẹ́*	It is money we take care of	ìyáàlù	F	1st wife of omele akọ
Àyánlóríwù	*Àyàn ni orí wù*	Orí* chooses Àyàn	omele abo	F	2nd wife of omele akọ & co-wife of ìyáàlù
Ajékù	*Ajé kù*	Ajé is remaining	omele akọ	M	Husband of Owólàákẹ́ (ìyáàlù) & Àyánlóríwù (omele abo)
Ajélàńwá	*Ajé ni à ń wá*	It is wealth (Ajé) we are looking for	omele mẹ́ta/ kúdi	M	The children
Ajélàńfẹ́	*Ajé ni à ń fẹ́*	It is wealth (Ajé) that we desire	2nd ìyáàlù (èjìn)	F	Young child of Owólàákẹ́ (ìyáàlù)
Ajéwùmí	*Ajé wù mí*	I love Ajé	kúdi (kónkóló)	M/F	1st son of Ajékù & Owólàákẹ́, older than Ajélàńfẹ́
Ajégbèmí	*Ajé gbè mí*	Ajé sides with me	omele akọ/ àgèrè	M	Initially was the husband of Owólàákẹ́ (ìyáàlù), senior to Ajélàńfẹ́
Ajélànà	*Ajé la ọ̀nà*	Ajé paves the way	bílálà	M	
Àyándayépọ̀	*Àyàn da ayé pọ̀*	Àyàn brings the world together	All bàtá drums	M/F	All bàtá drummers

* Orí is the òrìṣà of one's head or personal destiny.

Àyánlóríwù is a woman. Omele abo is the second wife of omele akọ. She doesn't have the ṣaworo like the ìyáàlù. The reason is that she can't hit too much. She is a lazy woman. She doesn't work too hard and she doesn't respect her husband. You see the difference between omele abo and ìyáàlù. Formerly omele akọ and omele abo were not together. Each of them stayed lonely but it was the drummers who joined them together.

Ajékù is a man. Ajékù doesn't really work for money, but money comes to him. He keeps the money hidden. He never likes spending money publicly. He is the husband of Owólàákẹ́. Ìyáàlù [Owólàákẹ́] and omele abo [Àyánlóríwù] are co-wives of omele akọ. When you see women working, they bring money back to their husband. This is the origin of that. Women work and earn money and they have to come back home and deliver the money to their husband. Without akọ bàtá, bàtá is incomplete. It is this omele akọ that Ṣàngó uses when he wants to fight.[41]

Ajélàṅwá is omele mẹ́ta, they are the male children. Ajélàṅfẹ́ supports Owólàáḳẹ́. Ajélàṅfẹ́ is the second ìyáàlù playing the supporting part. If bàtá drummers are many, just to keep them busy, that is why they introduced Ajélàṅfẹ́. She is a young female. She is a child to Owólàáḳẹ́.

Ajéwùmí [kúdi] is the first son of Ajékù [omele akọ] and Owólàáḳẹ́ [ìyáàlù]. Ajéwùmí lacked many things and was struggling to make ends meet. Whenever Owólàáḳẹ́ and Ajékù were going out he begged to follow them. He wanted to reach their standard.

"I want to be like you!" Ajéwùmí is the *kónkóló* beat. That is Ajéwùmí's voice. And when they [bàtá players] are on their outing and people are spraying the drummers, it is the function of Ajéwùmí to pick up this money and keep it for the entire set of drums. Ajéwùmí has a lesser [musical] function among the drums. It's only kónkóló [which is played] with one hand. While Ajékù is busy beating with two hands, and the others are beating with two hands, Ajéwùmí is only beating with more or less one, and that is why he has time to pick up money when there is spraying.

Ajégbèmí is àgèrè. Ajégbèmí is [also] omele akọ and is male. In the beginning, he [Ajégbèmí] was the husband of ìyáàlù. Formerly Ògún was dancing to bàtá drums. Ògún was seeking a drum and he went to Àyàn. Àyàn then gave him Ajégbèmí.

On its own, if you see a drummer coming with bílálà, he asks you to give him money. You ask of his drum. He will tell you his drum is coming, just bring money.

If bàtá drummers meet anywhere they become one. It is bàtá that makes them one. All bàtá drummers are Àyándayépọ̀.

Àyángbẹ́kún's complex mapping of Àyàn onto each drum of the bàtá ensemble (as well as Ògún's àgèrè drum) both reflects the musical roles of the ensemble and gendered stereotypes within Yorùbá culture. Owólàáḳẹ́ (ìyáàlù) is the "head of all Àyàn" as she is head of the bàtá ensemble, just as women head Yorùbá households. Owólàáḳẹ́ is a good wife who "pays homage and takes care of her husband," whereas Àyánlóríwù (omele abo) is a "lazy woman" who does not respect her husband, perhaps alluding to the second drum's relatively "lazy" musical role. Ajékù (omele akọ), who is the husband of Owólàáḳẹ́ and Àyánlóríwù, does not work for money but has his wives bring the money home to him, reflecting bàtá performance practice, whereby the omele akọ player is one of the least likely to be "sprayed" with cash as the drum plays a rhythmic accompaniment rather than the encoded praise poetry that attracts cash from onlookers. This gendering of labor also resonates with the traditional Yorùbá family structure whereby men and boys have more leisure time than women and girls, who endlessly toil in the domestic sphere and in the market. The omele akọ player too has leisure time as he stands in silence while the ìyáàlù player renders *oríkì* (praise poetry) in solo and attracts cash gifts.

The cohort of "children," Ajẹ́wùmí (kúdi), Ajẹ́lànwá (omele mẹ́ta), and Ajẹ́lànfẹ́ (the accompanying, "èjìn" ìyáàlù), reflects the propensity for these three drums to be played by drum apprentice children. The omele mẹ́ta and the second ìyáàlù are relatively recent additions—"offspring"—to the bàtá ensemble.

Bàtá came Directly from Heaven

All drums originate from Èṣù. Èṣù was an intellectual during his lifetime. There are bàtá drummers in Ìjèbu. So many of them are related to Ọ̀yọ́ in how they beat their drum. Some of them came to Ọ̀yọ́ to learn how to beat the drum; some just imitate Ọ̀yọ́ bàtá drummers. The sound their bàtá produces is not as good as the Ọ̀yọ́'s. Some bàtá drummers at Ìjèbu don't beat bàtá with bílálà, they use their fingers.

The thing inside the bàtá is called *oróhùn*, the thing that lives in the drum. It is the power [*àṣẹ*] inside of it that makes it to sound *kókororokokororo*. What is inside this one [ìyáàlù] is different from what is inside the other one [omele akọ]. What is inside this [ìyáàlù] is more powerful than what is inside the other one [omele akọ]. It [oróhùn] is only found inside the biggest drum [ìyáàlù] and the omele akọ [male accompanying drum]. It is not good for it be found inside the omele abo because a child cannot be more powerful than the mother. This [ìyáàlù] is the mother of all. This second one, the omele abo, is the younger sibling to the ìyáàlù.[42] The first one commands the second one to back her up by sounding *do do*, the second sounds *re re*.[43] The drum consecration can be done in one's presence but there is a need for one to be secretive. The drum would be damaged and one shall suffer a grave consequence.

We make a ritual before going out [to play] because we must feed [make a sacrifice to] Èṣù as he came to the world with Bàtá; so that we should see the good side of Ọlọ́run [God] and to return home in peace. After saying this [prayer], we go and hold Àyàn, we go and touch the Àyàn, where she is. Even if we do not go to Àyàn, when we are out of town or going, if we say, "Àyàngalú, don't let us encounter fights or evil spirits," Àyàn hears us.

• • •

The *kúsanrín* is just a ring.[44] Anything made of iron is kúsanrín. In Yorùbáland, we worship Ògún. This is Ògún's ìpọ̀nrí [symbol of spiritual essence]. If you put it in water and you lie, then you drink the water, you will die within seven days. That is why I don't want to lie. This is how they tie it on the bàtá's edge. It shows the interrelationship between Bàtá and Ògún. That is the purpose of kúsanrín. In the past, Ògún and Bàtá were very close and it was only Ògún who danced to Bàtá. But later Ṣàngó snatched Bàtá from Ògún.

When people are spraying money on Owólàáké with money, Ajékù collects and saves the money and keeps it safe. Ajékù stole some of this money. Owólàáké later challenged Ajékù, asking for the rest of the money. This was the genesis of their quarrel. Ajékù then refused to accompany them when they went on an outing. But without Ajékù, they were incomplete. Òrúnmìlà wanted to settle their quarrel. On getting to Òrúnmìlà's house, they refused and told him that nobody can settle this matter but Ògún. They went to Ògún. Ògún asked,

"What's the matter? Why are you fighting?" Owólàáké said that Ajékù stole some money. Ògún said that he would collect the money from Ajékù, but Ajékù refused. Ògún brought out kúsanrín. He gave it to Owólàáké and Ajékù and told them that it would serve as a witness between the two of them. Before the seventh day, Ajékù went mad. They were very surprised. They asked why Ajékù went mad. Ògún said that it was because Ajékù was lying. That is why she went mad. Owólàáké then said,

"If any Àyàn follower lies, kúsanrín will surely take his justice." This is the purpose of kúsanrín. From that time, kúsanrín has been a symbol of justice between Owólàáké and her followers. This is the reason why kúsanrín is usually tied at the edge of the bàtá. It is not medicine. It is there to control bàtá drummers' behavior. If there is a misunderstanding between or amongst bàtá drummers, they will be asked to swear on kúsanrín. They say to each other,

"Don't be like that! Kúsanrín is dangerous! You must not lie!"

Cowries are a symbol of money while the kúsanrín is Ògún's symbol, so they must be together to show that Owólàáké is receiving money from people. That is why the cowrie must be tied to the edge of the bàtá. Ṣàngó also has cowries tied on him. Also this cowrie can be used to swear. As it was money that caused Owólàáké and Ajékù's misunderstanding, that is why a cowrie is tied to bàtá's edge. The kúsanrín can be any iron or metal. This is a *kobo* [Nigerian coin]. There must be a kúsanrín on every ìyáàlù on the outside. But there are some ìyáàlù that don't have a kúsanrín. As we feed the drum, we are feeding kúsanrín. I have never heard of an *ẹṣẹ* [verse of] Ifá which talks about kúsanrín. The information was passed down from my forefathers.

Ìda [black tuning paste] is there just to soften the bàtá's voice. Without ìda on bàtá, it is not a good tone. Ìda is like the tongue. Without the tongue, it cannot talk properly. It does not have any spiritual significance.

Yes, they will come to the bàtá drummer's compound. Before you can take ìda from bàtá drummers for medicine, someone has to make offering to Àyàn. Without that offering, it will not work.

The ṣaworo are earrings intended to beautify the drums. All things that glitter belong to Ọ̀sun; women love glitter. Ọ̀sun was the one who gave the earrings to Bàtá when she was happy. Ọ̀sun gave earrings to Àyàn so that she should remember her forever.

Àyàn Owns All Òrìṣà

The bàtá is from Nigeria. The Cubans trained from Yorùbáland. My *ọga* [master] was from Ìbàdàn, Àyántáyọ Àyángunbùnmí. He had many apprentices from Cuba and my master also went to Cuba several times with Dúró Ládipọ̀.[45] All sons and daughters of Àyàngalú in Nigeria, America, all over the world, we are of the same mother and father. All òrìṣà beads, Iyemọja, Ṣàngó, all of them, are for Àyàn because they all love Àyàn. Àyàn owns all òrìṣà. Whenever the spirit of each òrìṣà hears Àyàn's voice, they will answer.

Editor's Notes

1. My appreciation goes to J. D. Y. Peel for comments on an earlier draft of this chapter.

2. See Ògúndùgbà with Amherd, this volume, and Vincent 2006.

3. My meetings with Àyángbẹ́kún took place on April 20, 2002; August 14 and 19, 2003; August 21 and September 1, 2004. I also visited his family after his death on August 2, 2011. Onsite field translations of Àyángbẹ́kún's interviews were done by Ṣàngódáre Gbádégẹsin Àjàlá (April 20, 2002), Àdìgún Davies Àjàní (August 14 and 19, 2003), and Kẹ́hìndé Oyètáyọ̀ (August 21 and September 1, 2003). Transcriptions and translation of recordings made in April 2002 were undertaken by Táíwò Abímbọ́lá, Abímbọ́lá Awóníran, Ògúnlékè Abímbọ́lá, and Kẹ́hìndé Abímbọ́lá and were financed by Michael Marcuzzi. In September 2003, Michael Marcuzzi and I commissioned a joint interview with Àyángbẹ́kún in Ògbómọ̀sọ́ that was conducted on our behalf and translated by Táíwò Oyètáyọ̀.

4. Òtúúrúpọ̀n Méjì is one of the 256 odù or "chapters" of the divination verses of Ifá. Àyángbẹ́kún's odù is one of the sixteen major signs.

5. Alhaji is the Yorùbá transliteration for those who have been on the pilgrimage to Mecca.

6. As pronouns are gender-neutral in Yorùbá and Àyángbẹ́kún viewed Àyàn as being unambiguously female, I use feminine pronouns in the English translation.

7. Tone marks uncertain.

8. The ìdóṣù is a seven-day ceremony to initiate one to a specific òrìṣà. The initiate's head is shaved, washed with herbs and blood, and painted, and divinations establish the initiate's new name and their religious taboos. In the case of an Àyàn ìdóṣù, Àyángbẹ́kún explained that the small bàtá drums one receives in his lineage will also be named through divination. This is

remarkably similar to current Cuban practice, whereby *fundamento* (consecrated) batá are named by divination during the seven-day consecration ceremony.

9. The dùndún and its bowl-shaped accompanying drum *gúdúgúdú* are the most common receptacles for Àyàn's medicines in contemporary times, though other kinds of sealed drums or a clay pot might be used. Open-ended drums are never used.

10. Dùndún is increasingly used due to the scarcity of bàtá drummers.

11. Ọ̀rànyàn is a son of Odùduwà, the mythological progenitor of the Yorùbá. Ọ̀rànyàn became the first king of Ọ̀yọ́.

12. Àyàngalú, Àgalú, and Àyàn are used interchangeably.

13. Rárà is a genre of oral literature that Barber (1991, 80) refers to as "royal bards' chant."

14. The òrìṣà of divination, interchangeably called Ifá.

15. Èdùmàrè and Èlédùmarè are interchangeable with Olódùmarè (god almighty), as is Ọlọ́run (literally, the owner of heaven).

16. Èṣù praise name.

17. Although the bàtá is best-known outside of Nigeria as Ṣàngó's drum, it is also the primary drum ensemble for Èṣù rites.

18. The skins of some of these animals may be used for making bàtá drums.

19. Eéran is a medicinal leaf. See Verger (1995, 539) for the different kinds of eéran (éran) leaves with their botanical names. Bàtá drums are washed with an herbal potion (omi-èrò) and presented with sacrificial food offerings such as bean cake (àkàrà).

20. Èṣù's clothing of Àyàn is a metaphor for the craft of making a bàtá drum. Male and female goat skins are dried, shaved, and then used for designated bàtá heads, although the gendering may vary from maker to maker (see Vincent 2006, 177–79). Antelope skin is wound around the body of the drum. The baby sling, òjá, which is also symbolically tied around the chests and waists of orixá priests in Brazil as in Nigeria, further humanizes the *iyáàlù* (mother drum that leads the ensemble).

21. *Bamu bámú* is probably drum vocables known as *ẹnà bàtá* for a bàtá rhythm.

22. Àyángbẹ́kún appeared to intentionally cast ambiguity on Àyàn's parallel erotic adventures by using only pronouns throughout this part of the story.

23. The Ọ̀yọ́ Empire dates from the fourteenth century but was at its strongest from the mid-seventeenth to late eighteenth centuries. Ṣàngó is said to be the third or fourth king of Ọ̀yọ́, and his drum was the bàtá.

24. Bàtá was once used as a war drum and was attached specifically to the Ọ̀yọ́ kingdom.

25. "Bàtá's children" refers to the smaller accompanying drums, *kúdi* and *omele akọ*.

26. "Dash" is Yorùbá English slang meaning "to give a gift."

27. *Ó ní àtàtà òràn, àtìjẹ, àtimu* (survive with food and drink), *sánánbọlé* (putting fire into the house), *Ọba kòso* (the king did not hang).

28. Oríkì (praise name) meaning "the ability to turn the tide of war."

29. This is a reference to the bílálà (rawhide beater used for some of the bàtá heads), which is short "but kills tall," i.e., makes a violent sound.

30. Ipọ̀nrí usually refers to an inner, spiritual essence, but may refer to a spiritually charged object in this context.

31. Àyángbẹ́kún is alluding to the full Egúngún body mask where no part of the masquerader's body is visible. Egúngún masqueraders are traditionally accompanied by the bàtá, although dùndún accompaniment has become more common as the number of bàtá players in Yorùbáland diminishes.

32. *Alágàdàngbá* is possibly vocables (ẹnà) for a bàtá rhythm that accompanies Eégún.

33. The bàntẹ́ (from the Hausa word for loincloth) is a scalloped, medicine-laden apron worn by Ṣàngó and his devotees. Bàntẹ́ also refers to the covering on bàtá drums, which may be constructed from brass and/or cloth and beads. See Thompson (1993, 170–71) for photographs. "The open field" alludes to a person's (or the bàtá's) vulnerability to be on the war front without medicinal protection sewn into the bàntẹ́.

34. Ìrèsẹ́ is a town in the province of Èkìtì.

35. Àpẹ̀ẹ̀rẹ̀ is a box decorated with antelope skin which is used as a footrest for kings. Ṣàngó's sacred medicines are housed in a mortar.

36. See Barber (1990) for information about *ibú* as dimensions of various water òrìṣà. Ibú is often translated as "whirlpool" in Nigeria and "river" in Cuba. Ibú has been explained to me by Òṣogbo Òṣun priestess Adédoyin Tàlàbí 'Fáníyì (pers. comm., Òṣogbo, August 2001) as "the swirling points of the river where there are white bubbles on top." Ibú are regarded as being high-energy points in the river. Indeed the Òṣogbo shrines of various dimensions of Òṣun are located along the riverbank at ibú points.

37. In Cuba, these sub-categories are generally known as *caminos* (roads). Writers often appropriate the Hindu term "avatar" when translating camino into English.

38. It is often the case that the dimensions of a particular orisha, such as those of Òṣun/Ochún, do not correlate across regions, be they intra-national or international. Nevertheless, there are numerous examples where transatlantic orisha dimensions do co-exist. Cuban artist Manuel Mendive discovered his own camino of Ochún, Ibú Yumú, in Òṣogbo, Nigeria. He told me that he saw the actual vessel (pers. comm., Havana, April 22, 2004). See Hagedorn, this volume, for information about Cuban caminos of the river goddess Ochún.

39. Linguist Túndé Adégbọlá assisted me with the etymologies presented in Table 2.1.

40. The ṣaworo are brass bells that are strung around the heads of the ìyáàlù and sometimes the second drum, omele abo.

41. Ṣàngó's spirit medium is called the ẹlẹ́gùn. Both in spiritual and public performance contexts, the omele akọ takes a lead role playing loud, dense and rapid "rolls" to accompany the drama of the ẹlẹ́gùn.

42. In the previous ìtàn, omele abo was a co-wife of ìyáàlù. Such kin-switching is typical in Yorùbá oral literature as the narrator shifts relationships to serve a larger metaphorical need.

43. *Do do* and *re re* refer to the colonial appropriation of *solfège* to communicate relative Yorùbá speech tones. Accordingly, *do do* prescribes two low tones, as in *bàtà* (shoe); *re re* prescribes two mid-tones, as in *kọrin* (sing a song); and for example, *do mi* designates low high, as in *bàtá*. An open tone on the large skin of the ìyáàlù mimics the low tone (*do*) while the omele abo open tone mimics the mid-tone (*re*).

44. The kúsanrín is a metal ring that is attached to the small head of *bàtá* drums. In Cuba, this ring is most often called *aro* or *agoya*. See Vincent (2006, 179–84) and Marcuzzi (2013) for a discussion of the kúsanrín.

45. Dúró Ládipọ̀ was a musician and actor who wrote and starred in a stage production about Ṣàngó titled *Ọba Kòso*. Premiering in Òṣogbo in 1963, the production toured in Africa, Europe, the Middle East, and the Americas in the 1960s and '70s, and perhaps facilitated the first appearances of bàtá drums outside of Nigeria. I have been unable to find any record of Ládipọ̀ or his production visiting Cuba, but he and his musicians would doubtlessly have encountered Cuban drummers in the Americas. With an estimated two thousand performances of Ọba Kòso alone, Ládipọ̀ earned an iconic status in Nigeria and among òrìṣà devotees in the United States. With this closing statement, Àyángbẹ́kún simultaneously aligned himself with Ọba Kòso's prestigious lineage of performers while placing Ládipọ̀ into a temporally compressed oral history that loosely overlaps with historical fact. By injecting Cuba and America into his personal history, I believe

Àyángbẹ́kún was reaching out to a new, international audience that my presence in his house promised. Àyángbẹ́kún's elaborate narratives both reflected and shaped his social world.

References Cited

Barber, Karen. 1990. "Oriki, Women and the Proliferation and Merging of Òrìṣà." In *Africa* 60 (3): 313–37.

————. 1991. *I Could Speak Until Tomorrow: Oríkì, Women and the Past in a Yorùbá Town.* Edinburgh: Edinburgh University Press.

Marcuzzi, Michael David. 2013. "Ring-around-the-rosie Atlantic: Transatlantic Uses of Rings among Bata Drummers, Caravan Guards and Muslim Insurgents." In *Journal of Religion in Africa* 43 (1): 29–52.

Thompson, Robert Farris. 1993. *Face of the Gods: Art and Altars of Africa and the African Americas.* Munich: Prestel.

Verger, Fátúmbí Pierre. 1995. *Ewé: The Use of Plants in Yoruba Society.* Rio de Janeiro: Odebrecht.

Vincent [Villepastour], Amanda. 2006. *Bata Conversations: Guardianship and Entitlement Narratives about the Bata in Nigeria and Cuba.* PhD thesis, School of Oriental and African Studies, University of London.

II

HISTORIES

3

My Life in the Bush of Drums: Àyàn in Ìjèbu-Rémọ

John Àyánṣọolá Abíọ́dún Ògúnlẹ́yẹ, with K. Noel Amherd

• •

The following chapter originates from conversations between friends, K. Noel Amherd and Chief John Àyánṣọolá Abíọ́dún Ògúnlẹ́yẹ from the town Òdè Rémọ in Ògún State, Nigeria. Coming from a long ancestral line of drummers, master drummer Àyánṣọolá and I have been discussing drums and traditional Ìjèbu-Rémọ culture since we first met in 1995. Out of these discussions came the idea to write a short autobiography of the chief, as one who was raised to be a keeper of traditions and a cultural authority.

The chapter title is a playful homage to modern Yorùbá literature, which is rooted in genres of storytelling and oral history. In 1954, Amos Tútùọlá published his famous novel, *My Life in the Bush of Ghosts*, which tells the story of a seven-year-old boy who inadvertently stumbles into the "bush," the West African forest, which is likened to stepping into the world of the spirits. Speaking in a Nigerian-English vernacular, the protagonist evocatively tells of his adventures meeting various "ghosts," their towns, and their magics and traditions, weaving a deliciously imaginative story rooted in Yorùbá mythology and oratures (oral genres). It is from this historically important novel that we pun and play to discuss the life of a contemporary young drummer navigating his world of local history, traditions, and responsibilities along with the "bush" of cultural and religious plurality, forces of globalization, diaspora, and competing religious traditions, both intra- and trans-nationally.

I have mostly performed an editorial role with Àyánṣọolá's manuscript and our many personal communications.[1] From the following section to the closing paragraph, the primary voice is that of Chief Olóòtú Ọdágbá Ifáníyì John Àyánṣọolá Abíọ́dún Ògúnlẹ́yẹ Ògúndùgbà, who speaks from a deep knowledge of his culture, history, and drums. My own voice (in the smaller font) is relegated to the editorial notes and captions, except where I make a short commentary before the final paragraph.

KNA

I Have Not Let the Job Die

I was born in Ìkaǹnán to the Ògúndùgbà and Làkóṣó Àyàn Àgbúlú family of Òdè Rẹ́mọ, Ìjẹbu-Rẹ́mọ, Ògún State, Nigeria on August 22, 1967. Because I was born in a very poor family, I used to follow my father to the farm. My mother and father's families were the poorest in my town, but they were popular families due to the work they were doing playing the drums. Sometimes we arrived home from the farm without any food and without any drinking water. I have been told that my mother gave birth to eight children before me but only four of them survived. When I was at the age of four years, there was a misunderstanding between my parents and my mother left me with my father and married another man. She lived in the nearby town of Ìpẹ́ru Àkẹ̀sàn in Ìjẹ̀bu-Rẹ́mọ. It was very hard for my father to meet our needs until the end of the year when we harvested what we planted in the farm.

Both my parents' family lineages were drummers of Òrìṣà Àyàn. Àyàn, when he was coming from heaven, arrived at a place called Ilé-Ifẹ̀.[2] He left there and he started his journey to Àtìbà in Ọ̀yọ́ Aláàfin.[3] From there he went to Ìbàdàn. When he left Ìbàdàn, he just came straight to Ògúnmógbó (near Òdè Rẹ́mọ). That is my father's home in Òdè Rẹ́mọ. During the Nigerian civil war my people moved to another area known as Ìkaǹnán and settled down there and Àyàn lived there until he decided to go back to heaven. He said before he would go back he must leave a symbol, which would represent him throughout the world. That is why he changed into a big tree that is called *igi àyàn* (the African satinwood tree). The tree is the one we cut to make drums. Goatskin is what we use to cover the surface of the drum. From that time the first shrine is still standing in my father's home in Òdè Rẹ́mọ.

Because of our family tradition as drummers, my father was teaching me how to play the drums and their rhythms. When I was young, I would see people come from the òrìṣà shrines to invite my father to play the drums for them. Because of the little money he would receive, we would rush to that place. Any amount we earned from drumming we would use to buy some food. A portion of the money would be shared with my father's apprentices. When the students finished their course under my father, each would go his own way, some going to Lagos, Ìbàdàn or some other part of the country. When they would return from seeking their fortunes as drummers (maybe every three months), they would bring something for my father to honor him as their teacher.

By then, my father was approaching old age, but I was always with him. One day, one of my elder brothers called my father and told him he was going to find a job in Lagos. I was about six years by then. My father prayed for him not to forget his younger brother (me) who was a very small boy.

Around this time, I told my father I wanted to go to school. The next thing my father did was to cry. "Why are you crying Baba?" I asked. He told me I should know only the children of the rich could go to school. I answered that God would provide for him on my account. "It will be okay," answered my father. "May God and Àyàn Àgalú bless me and provide for me to send this boy to school as he desires." To attend a school in my village was very expensive. This is true in Nigeria even today. So one day, my father took me to the Àyàn shrine to pray and he told Àyàn that this boy troubled him and wanted to go to school and he knew that he, Àyàn, would help him. He asked Àyàn to provide for him and I said, "Àṣẹ." That was in 1974. I continued to go to the farm with my father and to drum, especially during the Egúngún (ancestor masquerade) festival.[4] In the following year, 1975, I started primary school at Wesley Primary School, Òdè Rẹ́mọ.

Before admission, there was an interview for the prospective pupils, but the interview was not set for me because I was the first drummer to attend the school. The headmaster of the school was Mr. E. Osèsínà. I was very happy on that day. When we were in the assembly hall the day after my admission, I was asked to come up and play the drum set for the school because they were preparing for an inter-house sports event.[5] I first asked them to play it and let us see and hear. After this, I collected the sticks and played it better than they did. This made some of the teachers like me because it came as a surprise to them to see a small boy playing the drum like that.

One day while I was in primary six preparing for my school certificate examination, there was an installation of important chiefs in our town, Òdè Rẹ́mọ. Only my father and another drummer were in the town at that time and the Alaíyé Òdè (Òdè Rẹ́mọ's Ọba) asked my father, how was the day going to be made a success?[6] He answered that if he (the Alaíyé) could send somebody to my teacher in the school asking that I be allowed to come and play with them, things would be in good order. The Alaíyé Òdè sent his messenger to the headmaster and he released

Plate 3.1: Ìjẹ̀bu bàtá ensemble comprising ìyá ìlù (front left, ojú òjò head showing), ìyá ìlù (back left, ṣáṣá head showing), omele akọ (front left); omele abo (front right), omele abo (back right). (photograph: Wellington Bowler, Oakland, 21 May 2014)

me but told the messenger that there was going to be an examination and it meant that I was going to have to repeat the class. I had to repeat the class before I started secondary education in Òdè Rẹ́mọ. I passed my school certificate examination in the year 1987.

Throughout this time, I had never come across my mother. But one day, she came to her father's house in Òdè Rẹ́mọ. Her family's òrìṣà was called Òmólú (Nàná Bùrùkú)[7] and he was fighting her.[8] I did not know why she had come back, but Òrìṣà Òmólú had told her she needed to return to Òdè Rẹ́mọ and take care of her son. She had grown old by that time and when she made the offering to the òrìṣà, everything was good with her. She came to live with my father (her former husband). A short time later, I lost my father on December 7, 1993 and shortly after also my mother on February 23, 1994.

My second initiation in life (my first being my Àyàn initiation early in life by my father) came in 1998. I was invited to join the Òṣùgbó by Chief 'Fákúnò, Apènà Ilédì Òdùgbó Òdè Rẹ́mọ. So, on December 10, 1998, I was initiated into the Reformed Ògbóni Fraternity (R.O.F.) Lodge in Ilédì, Òdè Rẹ́mọ.[9] In 1999 I was further initiated into the society called Awo Imulẹ̀, where I was honored with the chieftaincy title Olóòtú Ọdágbá as the leader of the drummers in the society.[10]

The Ògún State bàtá drums are played differently from the way they are played in Ọ̀yọ́ State (see Plate 3.1).[11] I can play both of them due to the research I made, which enabled me to become a teacher of Àyàn. I learned *bàtá koto* in Ìsèyìn, Òyó State for nine months.[12]

After that, I moved with people playing *dùndún* and *sèkèrè* [beaded gourd idiophone] for six months. I thereafter crossed to another town called Ẹdẹ near Òsogbo, Òsun State, living with one of my friends and I played with him for a good year. I left there and came back to Abéòkúta in Ògún State where they play bàtá koto, dùndún, and *bèmbé* in that town. I played with them and gained more experience. That is also where I learned to build drums, even though I had some experience earlier on from my father. We made our own bàtá and dùndún. I have traveled all over Nigeria, especially in Yorùbáland, to learn more about Àyàn and gain more experience. As a result of this, I was installed as the Sèríkí Àyàn of Rémọland.[13]

In my family, my own generation is the seventeenth generation of full-time Àyàn drummers. I heard from [oral] history that this work has been done in our family since the eighteenth century. I cannot recite the history of all my forefathers, but I can write their names in chronological order: Lakọsọ Àyàn Àgbúlú, Ọládùnjoyè Ògúndípè Tembele, Samson Dìpèolú Fowódù, Ògúnwọlé Kalèjaiyá, Ògúndùgbà Ògúnléyẹ, Álímì Ọlárenwájú, Àìná Alábà Ògúnpè, and myself, John Àyánsọọlá Abíọdún Ògúnléyẹ Ògúndùgbà. I know that the spirits of all these ancestors move about with me and guide me because I have not let the job die in our family.

Ìtàn Àyàn (Àyàn's Story)

In the creation story according to the history of the Yorùbá people, Àyàn was the spirit of an entertainer sent by Èdùmàrè to the world at the beginning of time to make life enjoyable for the people, and to enable the various òrìsà and their worshippers to communicate.[14] When Àyàn left *òrun*,[15] he brought with him the *agogo*[16] to lead songs and to produce melodies for various kinds of music in the universe.

The first place of call Àyàn and his company made was Ilé-Ifè, the town of Odùduwà, who is the father of all Yorùbá people. Ilé-Ifè is now in Òsun State in the southern part of the Nigerian Republic. They stayed there for a while before Àyàn moved to the town of Òyó in Òyó State, which is also part of southern Nigeria. Àyàn was unable to produce a child of his own. The lack of children was a great concern to Àyàn; it made him very unhappy to worry about the need for a successor to sustain his legacy.

Plate 3.2: The aja (length 21.5 cm), made of iron. (photograph: Wellington Bowler, Oakland, 21 May 2014)

Àyàn eventually consulted an Ifá priest to inquire about the reason for this predicament. In West Africa, and especially in Nigeria, before any person ventures into anything, he or she must consult Ọ̀rúnmìlà.[17] Ifá consultation was the traditional practice even for an *irúnmọlẹ̀*.[18] The oracle advised Àyàn to leave the town of Ọ̀yọ́ and search for another place of abode. He moved with his company of musicians, passing by various towns in southern Nigeria before the oracle eventually told him to settle down at Ògúnmógbó village in the town of Òdè Rẹ́mọ.[19]

When Àyàn arrived in Òdè Rẹ́mọ he met many people in the town who were dancing, singing, and rejoicing without drums. Seeing them, he started beating his drum and producing music with the agogo. From that time, it was remembered well as a fantastic day. It was on this occasion that Àyàn saw a woman called Àgalú who was a namesake of his mother. He proposed marriage to her and Àgalú accepted. The couple fell in love and showed great affection for each other. By this time, Àyàn was advanced in age and his wife Àgalú gave birth to a child named Gúdúgúdú.[20]

Àyàn was an extraordinary creature and powerful person. When it was time for him to leave earth, according to the instruction given to him by the Edùmarè, he called his people and his only son Gúdúgúdú to announce the creation of a monument for his child and for the people of the community to be able to remember him well. He took his son

Plate 3.3: The odu (length 35.5 cm), made of small coconut-like shell. (photograph: Wellington Bowler, Oakland, 21 May 2014)

Gúdúgúdú back to Ògúnmógbó, Ògún State, and it grew to become a town near Òdè Rémọ. There, Àyàn gave words of encouragement to his son Gúdúgúdú telling him to continue the work of entertaining with music, which he has come to bring to mankind. Àyàn told his son to be trustworthy and multiply worldwide. After saying his final words, Àyàn went to a shed and immediately turned into a huge tree. Today the tree is called igi àyàn. This tree is used for making various drums in Yorùbáland.[21]

As history tells us, Gúdúgúdú, the son of Àyàn, also did not have children so, in time, he consulted an Ifá priest and offerings were made to appease the òrìṣà. After the offerings were made, Gúdúgúdú had children. His first child was named Gángan followed by Bàtá, Agbá, Gbèdu, Bèmbé, and Èṣì/Àpèṣì. Gúdúgúdú had many children, but these six named children were initiated into the society of sacred drums.[22] These children are the names of various sacred drums used in Yorùbá kingdoms and are worshipped as òrìṣà by those who play the drum.

Oríkì Àyàn

When communicating with Àyàn we will honor him with his names and history. This is an example of *oríkì* Àyàn that we will say or play on the drum.[23]

Àyàn ọmọ Àgalú	Àyàn, the offspring of Àgalú
Igi gbígbẹ tí ńso owó	The dry tree that produces money
Abọ́mọ bọ́yàá	The one who feeds children and mothers
Alèjẹlèsan	One who can eat and get paid
Igi jẹ́gẹ́dẹ́ onílù ọlá	The honorable, wealthy drummer, huge like an expansive forest tree
Ọmọ alùgi	One who first beats a tree
kótólù awọ	before beating a skin
Egbè lẹ́yìn ọmọ kàn	One who supports a child
egbè lẹ́yìn ẹni à ń dá láró	and supports anyone who is oppressed
Òkú ewúrẹ́	The dead goat
tí ń fọnun bí ènìyàn	who speaks like a human
Baba Ọláseéní	The father of Ọláscéní
Àṣá ò kú	As long as the hawk is not dead
aládìẹ kò sọmọ	the chicken cannot freely move around with its chicks,
yọyọ fún ọbàgbà lérù òun se ni	just as what frightens an elder is not worthy of having[24]
Òsìkà má yọ̀ mọ́	The wicked should stop rejoicing,
oun tó ń ṣeni kò lè pani	what troubles one cannot kill one
Òsìkà kò fẹ́ ká rẹrù kásọ̀	Wicked people do not want one to succeed in life
Orí ẹni ní ń sọ́ni	It is one's destiny that protects
Àgbàlagbà oyè tí ń yẹ́ni lọjọ aré	An elderly chief commands respect at a ceremony
Olójú lu kára	The one with eyes all over the body
Àyàn onílù	Àyàn, the sacred drummer
amú gboro dùn	who makes the city lively
Alówólodu	The owner of money so plentiful
bí ìyere	like the alligator pepper whose number of seeds are uncountable
Òrìṣà bí Àyàn kò sí	Àyàn is incomparable to other òrìṣà
Bí kò sí Àyàn lagbo,	If Àyàn is not present,
agbo kìí dùn	the gathering is not lively
Àyàn ọmọ Agbólú wòlú	Àyàn enters gatherings and cities
agbo kìí dùn	and makes people happy
Olówó ati tákàkà	Both the rich and the poor

wá ń sìn	come to worship [Àyàn]
Ọgbọgbà àga Àgalú	No one hears the sound of Àyàn
o dìdé mújó	without dancing
Tanílù baba baba tanílù	The one whose ancestors have the drum
Igi jẹ́gẹ́dẹ́ tanílù baba,	Àyàn, who is magnificent,
baba tanílù	is the owner of the drum
Àyàn ọmọ Àgalú ti dé	Àyàn of Àgalú has arrived
Omìgborojìgìjìgì	His presence shakes the whole city, he is here
Odé Àyàn Àgalú	Àyàn Àgalú,
ọmọ agbédè gbẹyò	one who speaks all languages
Alóyin lóhùn wun	The owner of sweetness/honey pleases people
Abi ṣaworo létí	One with bells for earrings
bí abo òrìṣà	like a female òrìṣà
Tó pé bí Àyàn báwo agbo	He said if Àyàn gets to the arena
ìbànújẹ́ wọn a wọ̀ gbẹ́	their sorrow will vanish
Òkú ewúrẹ́	The dead goat (skin)
tí ń fóhùn bí ènìyàn	sounds like a human
Àyàn ọmọ aṣawo	Àyàn, whose spirituality
gbọlá	begets wealth
Àyàn ọmọ aṣawo	Àyàn, whose spirituality
gbọmọ	begets children
Àyàn ọmọ aṣawo	Àyàn becomes rich
gba sẹ́sẹ́ fún	through spiritual practice
Ewúrẹ́ kò ní gbowó awọ rẹ̀ lọ́wọ́ mi.	The goat never receives money from me for its skin.

Awo Onílù: The Role and Function of the Onílù in Community

The *onílù* brings joy to the town and the community for both human beings and òrìṣà.[25] In Nigeria, we refer to the onílù as a man of great knowledge and honesty. That is why in my town of Òdè Rémọ, if the Alaíyé Òdè (the town's Ọba) is going somewhere, he usually goes with his onílù in order to seek advice from him because the Alaíyé Òdè knows he will get the real truth from him.

In a town, city, or even a village, if there is no onílù, it is just like when we cook a soup with no salt. The soup will not be sweet. The onílù makes the town and the community to develop and attract visitors to the town. After the day's work, people must have some time to enjoy life.

Without an onílù, there is nothing to do for fun. Also, the òrìṣà worship-pers need the onílù to properly praise their òrìṣà. For example, in the Ògbóni shrine, no one can go inside until after the onílù plays the drums. If the Aláíyé Òdè is inside his bedroom in the morning, the onílù must be there earlier in the morning to wake him up from bed. Onílù will an-nounce to the village when the Ọba is ready to receive visitors. The drum is used to set the day's agenda. If disputes are being settled, the drum will announce the final decision. That is why we say the onílù must be a man of patience, loyalty, and honesty in addition to being an accom-plished drummer.

The onílù must be a man of good character because he is a man that everybody should respect for his knowledge and whenever anybody comes to him either to learn from him or to invite him to come and play for him, he must take good care of the person and he must not be too mindful of his remuneration; being greedy can destroy his career. The onílù must not steal. This is a serious warning for all my people in awo Àyàn, because the onílù is a popular person. We all know that stealing destroys a man's good name and ruins his career in life. The spirit of Àyàn will leave the person who steals and he can never regain it. That is the end because Àyàn does not live in a place where people steal another person's property. So we must maintain our name and the spirit of Àyàn too.

The onílù must travel widely in order to get more knowledge on what he is doing, or learning how to beat other drums that he does not know about but has only heard about. For instance, I am a man born in Òdè Rémọ, Ìjẹbu-Rémọ, Ògún State, but I can cross to Ọyọ State to play for people there and go to other parts of the country to study and learn how to play the different types of drums, because when we call a person onílù, he must be able to stand before anybody and proudly affirm that he is an onílù by playing any drum he is asked to play.

For the sake of emphasis and the avoidance of doubt, I repeat here what I have already said about Àyàn himself. Àyàn was the entertainer that Edùmarè sent to *ilé ayé* (the world) at the beginning of time to make life enjoyable for people, the various òrìṣà, and their worshippers. It fol-lows, therefore, that an onílù is Àyàn's representative anywhere he goes throughout the world. An onílù must be conscious that he is producing sounds and that these sounds have an impact on people. The onílù is the society's most responsible observer; he pays close attention to the way people dance. The onílù is trained to note the significance of small ges-tures and tension as well as big movements, and thereby enters into con-tact with the visible aspects of the dance. So much of our dance reflects the movements and gestures performed in our daily lives because we use music/dancing to accompany our daily work. An onílù is trained to be an acute observer of all the work engaged in the town and community. The drummer must watch the workers he comes across with an alert and purposeful eye.

It means the better you play, the more nervously people behave. So if you see many people do not feel well, you must drum more sweetly. You do not need anyone to tell you about it if you are paying attention to what is happening. When you handle the drum, you need to be conscious of how you are affecting people. There are some drummers in Nigeria who want only to make a hit record regardless of the value of the drumming at deeper levels. They are not aware of the subtle effect of drumming on human well-being. But the onílù must be aware of the effects of what he does. The drum can build or destroy. The drum can produce tears, fatigue, excitement, or calm in people.

The drummer needs to know each person's character during community celebrations. When someone moves into the center of the circle, the drummer plays sounds of a friendly warning about his or her traits and temperament. When a drummer plays, his skill with his instrument must speak for itself. So by this, the drummer must be an extraordinary person because above all else, he is a healer. The onílù must know how to give therapy, to bring joy, to console people during the most difficult moments of grieving, to be disciplined and serious during rituals. This requires a mature person in all respects. In his maturity, the drummer must not be impressionable. He needs to stay calm and centered regardless of what is going on around him.

Genealogy is another branch of drumming studies. The onílù must learn the history of each family of the spirit beings, the trees, the animals, and different towns and countries. When we gather to sing and dance, we praise those who come before us and we praise those òrìṣà who support life around us. In order to praise these things, we must know their history very well. Drummers are also the keepers of the communal love of our people. The purpose of the drum is to create unity among those who dance.

Another aspect of the drummer's essential knowledge is self-protection from negative forces and evil spirits. Drumming facilitates communication between two worlds and an onílù needs to protect himself from the invisible world. The drummers can also protect each other.

The onílù is truly a psychologist in the midst of the people. His knowledge includes understanding the functioning of the different systems of the human body. Since he is sending sounds that affect people's bodies, he knows what effects can be beneficial.

The drummer must be a person with a good memory because drum rhythms are not written. We have some special herbal powders we use to facilitate memory and overcome performance anxiety. As guardians of the drum and our herbal legacy, we understand these things as being important to the welfare of the community. Onílù is a protector of morality. If we fail in our religious duties, we believe the whole community can suffer. This is an important responsibility.

Kíkọ́ Àyàn: Learning to Play Drums of Àyàn

We can classify drummers into two groups: the first is the heritage drummer and the other is the first-generation drummer who does not come from a family of drummers. The heritage drummer is one whose father and great-grandfather were drummers before him. It is very simple for him to know how to play the drum because drumming is his family's job. He would be initiated in the art before he is five years old. Do not forget that anybody who wants to play some of these drums must be initiated into the Àyàn society before he is entitled to be a drummer of any type of our sacred drums.

A first-generation drummer must apprentice with a master drummer. After demonstrating some skill, the newcomer is initiated into the *ẹgbẹ́ awo* Àyàn.[26] The initiate is given some traditional medicine to improve his memory so that he will retain all that he learns. Otherwise his apprenticeship will be useless. After all this, he is given a symbol/indicator that will make him known to everybody as an onílù.

The apprentice is supposed to respect his teacher, even if his teacher is younger than he. He must respect him and obey him because the teacher is sharing his knowledge and time with him during the apprenticeship. So he is supposed to ask his teacher from time to time what he needs to make him happy and to have a cool mind to teach him the ins and outs of the art of drumming. After all this, he will accompany his teacher on many occasions when the latter is invited to come and play for some people or an òrìṣà because on such occasions, there may be some rhythms which have not been played before. It is important for the apprentice to follow his teacher to every occasion because some rhythms may not come out more than once or twice in a year. Any apprentice who fails to be there will miss hearing and playing the rhythm for the whole year. That is why some apprentices who are supposed to spend about four or five years on their course of study spend many more years on it in order to finish in full and graduate.

The apprentice must serve his teacher in many ways. For example, he must follow his teacher to his farm and work for him, fetch water for him in his house, and do whatever else he is required to do. If the apprentice lacks the chance to do all these things, he must give some money to his teacher to hire a laborer to do all these things for him. This will give the onílù a chance to teach the apprentice better without any disturbances or obstacles.

Learning the mystery of playing the drum is very easy for an onílù born in an Àyàn family and also for an apprentice who puts his mind and time into it. In the olden days, our great grandfathers in Àyàn did not show people the mystery of playing the drum without long-term commitment from the apprentice. Today, we are now using modern methods (such as the tape recorder) to teach people by using techniques that help people to quickly understand what they are learning. Before being certified, a teacher would play many rhythms and record them on tape for the student to listen to every day for five weeks or more. Accordingly, if there was any error, the teacher would correct it for the student until he masters it. If the correction is not made, the student would be punished or pay a fine.

The first thing to do is take your apprentice to a very cool and convenient place, put down all the drums and introduce them to the apprentice. You will then play them for him by starting from *omele*, *omele akọ*, *omele abo*, and *iyá ìlù* Àyàn (see Plate 3.1). Then you give him the smallest one, the omele. You show him how to play it for a good thirty minutes and then you give the omele akọ to another person and do the same thing for the apprentice again, up to the abo.

The teacher plays the iyá ìlù. All of you will play together according to the instruction you give to them for a complete thirty minutes. Any who makes a mistake during the training must stand up and watch what the other people are playing for five minutes. The teacher will stop and show him how to play again and then continue once again with the others. After thirty minutes, the omele akọ, omele abo, and the smallest one (omele) will be exchanged amongst the apprentices. They will then play the rhythms accordingly. When we have done that for about four hours, everybody will put down his drum and take out his notebook and write down the rhythms that he has played on the different drums for that day.[27]

After four hours, if we still have more time, we stroll around for about an hour and come back to the spot and start again. The apprentices start with the rhythms they played before the break. The teacher will follow them until they master the rhythms. When they perfectly master the small drums, they will start to study the biggest one, the ìyá ìlù. In ẹgbẹ́ Àyàn, we learn drumming gradually, step by step.

When all these stages have been covered and the students are about to "graduate," their teacher gives them another medicinal herbal powder. This will sharpen their memory to remember what rhythms they played and what they are meant for, because the rhythms are meant for different outings.

Throughout a drummer's apprenticeship, he must be conscious he is emitting sounds that have an effect on people. You see this when you play a drum and people cry in response to some sounds and dance in response to others. If you beat a show-rhythm, people will say "oh no" and they will feel more nervous. As you play, you see many things like this. You do not need anyone to tell you about it if you pay attention to what is happening. In ẹgbẹ́ Àyàn, an apprentice drummer must be self-confident because a timid drummer would not be very useful to the society. Onílù might be called upon in the darkest hours of the night for his service. He does not learn to play the drum for himself but to help the town and community.

The apprentice must have patience and a good memory because each instrument, as I have observed before, is considered a universe to discover rather than master, and the apprentice needs to work with it patiently and to feel in no hurry. His teacher also must be patient in the sense that drumming is not just a thing that you can easily handle. It must be learned completely. It is not acceptable to say, "I forgot." For example, I have stated there are some rhythms played only once a year, like the drums played for òrìṣà Nàná Bùrùkú, Òmólú, and the Agẹmọ.[28] We have certain rhythms that are played only once every two or more years because there is no annual festival for some òrìṣà. So once the apprentice has learned a particular rhythm he must remember it. For instance, some drumming music involves short repeated phrases, and occasionally, these rhythmic combinations will be repeated over and over again.

The drumming must be nourished within the onílù, and he may practice by listening to it inwardly without touching an instrument or producing a sound. Later, at the appropriate moment, he plays it. In addition to drumming, the apprentice must learn the history of each family of the spirits, the trees, and the animals. The drummers are the keepers of the cosmological lore of our people.

The student needs to learn each person's character during social and religious dances. When someone moves into the center to dance, the drummers play the appropriate music. For example, when I come out in my own Egúngún masquerade, my people will continue to cheer me with the talking drums in order to wind me like the pepper grinder, due to my character.[29]

The apprentice must be an observer simply because a careful observer can read much in the way people dance. In Àyàn society and everywhere in Yorùbáland, we all understand and believe music is a bridge between the visible and invisible realms. The human voices and musical sounds produced on instruments arise from intentions interior to the performers affecting listeners as well as the surrounding invisible realm of spirits and ancestors. Drumming and music can be a potent force for maintaining and restoring human harmony with the cosmos. This is its ultimate purpose of life in Yorùbá traditional culture.

In the Àyàn society, the drummers are expected to live by high standards of morality and self-restraint. By their example, the drummer will influence the youth for better or worse. As the youth are the society's future, it is very important that their role models be good ones. The fundamental principle of Àyàn during training is devotion to drumming in service to the cosmos, the environment, and the community.

Drumming at Ceremonies for the Imalẹ̀ and Ènìyàn (People)

We all know the drum is important for ceremonies all over the world because ceremonies are something we create. We set aside a day or more to rejoice with one another to mark a special event. When we do this everybody will eat and drink, and after that they will dance together to enjoy themselves. But without the drum or music you know that any occasion will just seem dull, like when a sad thing happens. The effect the drum has on people and on the òrìṣà is to entertain them at occasions and to bring joy to the community. Nobody would like to stay in the darkness. People prefer to stay in the light. Drum and music brings light to the community and also to the òrìṣà.

Drumming makes life enjoyable to the òrìṣà and their worshippers when communicating with the creator, Èdùmàrè. It makes people enlightened. Also, the drum predisposes the òrìṣà to consider their worshippers with forgiveness and mercy when they trespass against them or when they are in want of anything from them when they pray. The òrìṣà worshippers play the drum when they are making offerings so they can pray with a happy mind.

The bàtá drum in Òdè Rémọ is the type beaten with two hands.[30] But there are others like the bàtá koto, the ones commonly used in Ọ̀yọ́ State, that are beaten with strips of leather.[31] For instance, sometimes we drummers are invited by other ẹgbẹ́ òrìṣà to play for them when they were expecting a spiritual visitation. They ask us to play strong and fertile rhythms for them so when their oracle hears this music, their spirits will come and rejoice with the worshippers. People in Nigeria believe that without drumming the deity will not come and receive their offerings.

With regard to drumming, human beings are strange animals. They go into a room, make some sound they call music and enjoy themselves moving around, which they call dancing. Just because of this, some of them spend their time planning what kind of sound to make while others become so attached to one particular kind of music they refuse to listen to any other sort. If such reactions to the drum are so evident to our eyes, there is power in music to affect our health and minds.

This is one example of the effect drumming has when we are doing or performing Egúngún festivals. An Egúngún who does not request drummers is a lazy one according to Yorùbá beliefs, but the one with a band of drummers will perform well on any occasion by listening to the drum. The onílù enlighten the medium with their rhythms, the drum tells them what to do and how to move. With all this, the Egúngún may build and destroy at the same spot, and this will have a good influence on the people of the community.

The family of a sick person may engage a drummer who will conduct close observation and interview. If, for instance, it is determined the disturbed individual is possessed by a spirit, a healing ritual involving drums and music is performed. The concerned family members, age-group members, and healers join in a circle to dance around the person being cleansed.[32] The first music played by the drummers is intended to calm the people and the spirits in the neighborhood and throughout the town. When the drummers feel they have accomplished this goal, they bring the person to be treated to the center of the town or to Àyàn's shrine. Usually, the patient must have slept the night before next to a sheep or a goat that is to be offered as part of the ritual, and also another ram will be offered. Each ceremony proceeds according to what the drummer in charge determines will be effective.

At this stage of the ritual, the drummer plays the rhythms known to be appropriate for the spirit that has been identified as possessing the patient. It may be Ṣàngó, Ọya, Ọbàtálá, or another òrìṣà; we have different rhythms for each deity. If the patient is not a Ṣàngó worshipper but they have Ṣàngó oracle in his family, the patient must learn Ṣàngó's dance. Performing the dance helps to free the patient of the spirit. Once the patient has been healed, they still dance to the spirit's rhythms at times of initiations, ceremonies, and offerings. Dancing to the spirit's rhythm helps to keep the patient free from unwanted possession. Once the right sounds are found, the rhythm is not changed. The drummer plays for as long as necessary using calming, stabilizing rhythms and proper sound combinations that help restore the disturbed individuals to inner balance. It serves no purpose for the drummer to vary the rhythm and music. In fact, if the drumming music is changed, the patient will not change. Through the monotony [repetition] of the drum [music], the day returns.

The drum is also played to bring a sense of well being to the entire human and spirit community. Beyond pleasing people with playing the drum, we need to communicate with the invisible world. Everybody can play drums generally, but to play certain drums like the *àgbá*, *ugbaji*, and *apedi*, one needs to be initiated into the drummers' society. Certain melodies and rhythms attract the spirits, and only a special category of initiated people may play such rhythms without risk. When we are talking of Àyàn and his followers, we are supposed to narrate a short story about the deities for whom we play, to describe the relation between them and Àyàn.

All these òrìṣà or *imalè* have a very tight relationship with Àyàn because they cannot do without song, and when there is song, there must be drum. Àyàn is an entertainer from Ọlọrun sent to the world to make life enjoyable for the people, especially the òrìṣà or imalè, and enable them and their worshippers to communicate. You see the importance of Àyàn and onílù because, for instance, in the olden days when Ọrúnmìlà himself was doing *ìtèfá* (Ifá initiation), there was nothing like aja (Plate 3.2), agogo, and odu (Plate 3.3). But, when Àyàn arrived, he brought along the agogo and other musical instruments that are necessary for initiations and are popular in the world now.[33]

Staying True to the Spirit: Creativity, Healing, and Community

In every tradition, there is a tension between the qualities of inspired innovation (which originally gave birth to what became the tradition in the first place) and conservative reiteration (solidifying what makes a tradition recognizable and nameable). Inheritors of Yorùbá culture, such as Àyánṣọọlá, live within this tension, both reiterating the past while adapting and innovating to the changes of the world around them. The varieties of gods, drums, and rhythms played across regions of southwestern Nigeria, eastern Benin, and their diasporas demonstrate the fertility of origins, exchange, adaptation, innovation, and replication. Inherent in their role as culture bearers, they recognize that innovation asserts itself in every ritual, initiation, and drumming event in order to achieve the ends to which the participants are aiming. Creativity and improvisation are what make tradition become art rather than static reproduction because the new enactment of an old ritual allows humans to find balance in this world and the other. Àyánṣọọlá's closing words that follow reveal his awareness of this tension; he alludes to the way that òrìṣà cultures survive by, in fact, making creativity traditional since the attention is on human and community wellbeing rather than rote reproduction.

The onílù who heals does not necessarily always fall back on a repertoire of established rhythms. To determine the right sounds of the drum in each case is a highly individual matter. There are certain rhythms especially created for each òrìṣà, but when all these are tried and they fail to work, no other predetermined formula may be available. The onílù needs to create a dialogue between the sounds he produces and the responses of the person he is treating. To put it more simply, music itself is a remedy. It gives joy. Even someone in good health can be lifted to a higher level of health through drumming and [other] music. Àyàn can calm or stimulate according to the needs of the person and the occasion.

Notes

1. My predilection is to leave texts by Yorùbá interlocutors with as little change as possible because, in the process of "cleaning it up," the rich and fascinating idiomatic transliteration of Yorùbá English disappears. The editor can inadvertently shift some of the meanings made possible by the original style. However, my predilections can also leave some texts obscure for readers not familiar with Nigeria and its modes of language and discourse, so, with this text, I have edited the original text with the hope that it flows more accessibly for readers.

2. In òrìṣà traditions, actors—both human and non-human—are perceived as coming into the world from another realm. Because entities can merge into or inhabit each other, even taking different shapes, all entities are seen as actors in the world who affect and effect outcomes. For this reason, non-humans are attributed with human-like qualities in narratives to reinforce the idea that they are more than they appear; they have histories, purposes, allegiances, even interests, and must be related to in this way.

3. The political head of the city of Ọ̀yọ́ is the Aláàfin. The àfin is the palace and symbolizes the corporate integrity of the city as a whole. The title, Aláàfin, translates as "owner of the palace." Because the Aláàfin title and palace define Ọ̀yọ́, Àyánṣọolá is identifying the historic settlement through its name cum ruling title. Also, as a characteristic play in Yorùbá narratives, his oral history temporally disperses Àyàn's primordial arrival on Earth through reference to towns such as Ilé-Ifẹ̀, Ọ̀yọ́, Ìbàdàn, and Ògúnmógbó, whose foundings and locations have occurred and shifted at different epochs. Rather than chronological linearity, importance is given to relational affinity in building up connections and authority. See K. Noel Amherd (2010, 203–83) for discussion of these issues of history and time in Yorùbá orature.

4. The Egúngún are masked performers who represent the ancestors and their presence in the community of living humans. The mask covers the dancer from head to toe and part of the lore says that no one knows who is inside the dancing attire.

5. Yorùbá drums exist in sets or "families" most often consisting of three or more instruments. Here, Àyánṣọolá is referring to one of these families of traditional drums though specifically which one is not mentioned.

6. The Ọba is the traditional ruler of a town, often translated as "king" in English. However, sometimes the Ọba may be a woman.

7. Nàná Bùrùkú is a primordial female òrìṣà of creation associated with water and her animal, the snake. Òmólú is one of her cognomina. In Òdè Rémọ, residents acknowledge that she originated in Dahomey (Benin), arrived with Àyánṣọolá's maternal great-great-grandfather, and now his descendants maintain the titled responsibilities of her worship.

8. Amongst people who worship òrìṣà in Nigeria, there is the idea that an ancestrally worshipped òrìṣà will make demands upon living descendants even though the person may not realize it nor want to fulfill the expectations. In this case, people will say that the òrìṣà "is fighting with the person," meaning that one is experiencing difficulties of various sorts in his/her life behind which lies the òrìṣà attempting to get attention and compel him/her to fulfill the òrìṣà's demands.

9. Òṣùgbó (òṣù: tufts of head hair; gbó: old/gray) is the Ìjèbu form of Ògbóni (ogbó: old age; ẹnì: person) comprised of town elders. The institution, acting at times as a judicial branch of town governance, is associated with the earth and the origin and perpetuation of a town. The Reformed Ògbóni Fraternity was formed in 1914 by Anglican priest Reverend Thomas Adéṣínà Jacobson Ògúnbìyìí, who changed the fraternity's rituals and symbolism to be acceptable to Christians, Muslims, and non-Yorùbá (Bíòbákú 1956; Lawal 1995; Nolte 1999).

10. Awo ìmulè is a ritual oath-taking act performed to bond traditional worshippers with each other and the gods through collectively drinking (ìmu) from a liquid-filled depression in the earth (ilè).

11. The Ìjèbu live in Ògún State, Nigeria, which lies in the southwestern region of Nigeria. The city of Ọ̀yọ́ lies further north.

12. Accepting that cultural heterogeneity manifests in multiple ways, the difference in bàtá drum families regionally should come as no surprise. The most well known of the bàtá come from the Ọ̀yọ́ regions of Yorùbá culture: the conical, double-headed drums wrapped in strips of indigo-dyed antelope skin and played on both heads. The smaller head is played with a leather cowskin strip (awọọ bàtá or bílálà) while the other is struck with the hand. Further south, the Ìjèbu play bàtá drums of slightly different construction and with a different ensemble composition. The two leading drums are conical and double-headed; the largest (ìyáàlù) is played on both heads with the hands (absent of any leather beaters) while the second drum (omele abo) is only played on the larger of the two heads with both hands. The smallest drum of the ensemble is a single-headed cylindrical drum which sits on the ground and is played with two wooden sticks (see Plate 3.1). This Ìjèbu ensemble configuration is very similar to some bàtá ensembles in Benin in areas such as Pobe, Kétu, and Ṣákétẹ (Branda-Lacerda 1996). The fact that Àyánṣọolá here refers to the Ọ̀yọ́-style bàtá drums as bàtá koto demonstrates his acknowledgment that the drum families differ but, at the same time, are each legitimate in their own right as bàtá. He has stated that his terminology for Ọ̀yọ́-style bàtá, bàtá koto, is what he learned growing up and is generally known, yet it is not used in Ọ̀yọ́ itself. Àyánṣọolá's designation should not be confused with an Ègbá instrument called bàtá koto, which is constructed from two large gourds and is skinned on one side where the gourd is cut out. To complicate things further, the Cuban batá koto appears to be unrelated to either Yorùbá predecessor, except by name.

13. Ṣẹríkí is a chieftaincy title that translates as "commander of young warriors" (Abraham 1958, 94).

14. Èdùmàrè is an alternate pronunciation and spelling for Olódùmarè and refers to the creator of the universe, historically also called Ọlórun.

15. *Ọ̀run* refers to the sky as an abode of some spirits (but not all), translated as "heaven" when Christian missionaries arrived. Often, the concept of a creator-god is referred to as Ọlọ́run, the owner of the sky.

16. Ìjèbu-Rémọ Ifá ritual employs the agogo, a conical iron bell with a clapper, a construction specific to this region. Most often the agogo is accompanied by the odu (see Plate 3.3), though each can be played solo. The odu (singular and plural) is particular to Ìjèbu's Ifá worship. It is constructed from two small coconut-like resonators, which are cut off at the bottom and hollowed (forming twin resonators). A hole is bored into the top of each coconut into which two sticks are inserted and act as clappers, making a resonant sound that accompanies Ifá songs along with the agogo. Clapperless bells that are struck with sticks are also called agogo. As seen in Plate 3.2, the aja is another kind of double metal bell with a clapper in each bulb. Used for prayers and songs to the òrìṣà, the person holds the middle bar and agitates the aja to activate the clappers.

17. Ọ̀rúnmìlà speaks through the divination system Ifá and is known as the "witness to creation," thereby knowing the beginnings and endings of all things—human lives, societies, animal and plant species, and so on. Therefore, in many narratives, when agents, whether human or non-human, are to begin a venture, they turn to an Ifá diviner (*babaláwo*) in order to know how to proceed effectively and successfully.

18. *Irúnmọlè* is a generic word for non-human entities including òrìṣà, which inhabit and maintain the earth. The word irúnmọlè is frequently redacted to imalè.

19. Òdè Rémọ, like many Yorùbá towns, is a composite of several earlier settlements that fused together to make the current single town. Ògúnmógbó was a separate town in the Remo district, whose residents migrated to Òdè Rémọ for safety during nineteenth-century wars in the region. They set up their own town quarter that still remains until now.

20. The *gúdúgúdú* is a small kettledrum that is suspended from the shoulders against the belly and played with two small leather beaters. The gúdúgúdú is often given as the first drum for new apprentices to learn to play (particularly in the dùndún ensemble) and is considered a pedagogical foundation of primary educational importance. Its pedagogical importance mirrors its cosmological importance as the first-born child of Àyàn, making it the most "senior" of all drums.

21. Like the òrìṣà themselves, the woods used to make drums vary and several species may be called *igi àyàn*. Abraham (1958, 86) notes it as the African satinwood, while Marcuzzi (2005, 246–57) and Vincent (2006, 169–72, 367–70) note several species under this same Yorùbá term.

22. For descriptions of various kinds of Yorùbá drums, see Thieme 1969; Láoyè 1959; Euba 1990; Vincent 2006.

23. Oríkì is a genre of orature (oral texts) recited at a target recipient, both human and non-human, designed to name, attribute, and construct a rich, aural montage of the recipient's character through collage-like panegyrics.

24. This line alludes to a story in the Ifá divination corpus explaining that hawks hunt chicks because the chicken had once betrayed her friend hawk. The line conveys the idea that Àyàn and his drummers become like hawk in their greatness and thereby provoking fear.

25. *Awo* means "secret" and refers to deep knowledge gained through initiation and work with the òrìṣà. An *onílù*, literally "owner of the drum," is an initiated drummer who may play for ritual events and purely social ones as well.

26. *Ẹgbẹ́* means "guild" or "association" and is used in this context to refer to the professional guild of inherited and initiated drummers.

27. In speaking with Àyánṣọolá, he says that he has found this to be the most expedient way for students to learn. When the student "writes down the rhythm," he will use *do re mi* notation which is a colonial adaptation of the solfège system to reproduce the three relative tones of spoken Yorùbá; *do* stands for low tone, *re* for mid, and *mi* for high. Therefore the name Àyàn

would be *do do* or the word babaláwo would be *re re mi re*. Learning the drums is learning their speech—each drum speaks its part and the different heads and ways of striking them reproduce the tones of spoken Yorùbá—and so writing down the rhythm is notating its tones and remembering how those are produced by the hands on each drum head.

28. Agẹmọ (chameleon) is a complex of òrìṣà particular to the Ìjèbu region. The aggregate òrìṣà appear publicly in a variety of masked forms utilizing raffia, woven mats, and head carvings. Among the Ìjèbu, Agẹmọ is a powerful creator-being whose autochthonous history gives it prominence amongst other òrìṣà, many of whom have arrived in Ìjèbu through migration of people from other regions.

29. "To dance to one's own Egúngún" is to reveal that masks are manmade and worn by humans. Revealed at the same time is the fact that people do inhabit the masks and enjoy the ceremony of representing the ancestors while the participating audience also enjoys the mysterious presence of these dancing cloths. In the scenario the author describes here, the drummers often know the dancer inside the cloth and will play according to that particular person's personality in order to inspire the dance.

30. In comparison, Ọ̀yọ́-style bàtá drummers use a leather beater (*bílálà*) on the smaller drum head (*ṣáṣá*) and their hand on the larger (*ojú òjò*).

31. One of the pitfalls of ethnographic research lies in expecting homogenous standards in cultural practice. A hallmark of Yorùbá cultural production is its ongoing fertility. Bàtá drums differ in construction, style of performance, and musical structure but people tend to acknowledge divergent sounds and sights as "the same," meaning that each variant has its legitimate history and function. I have seen this mirrored in the recitation of Ifá texts where babaláwo will state that differences of a shared theme in Ifá texts are legitimate expressions from Ifá, and therefore the recitations are "the same."

32. Often, people form associations based on being members of an age-grade or a generation. For example, the Rémọ Opẹrẹ̀ society was a warrior association comprised of young men. In Òdè Rémọ one finds the Ẹgbódò Babaláwo, which is an association of young Ifá diviners.

33. The aja is used when reciting oríkì, or singing and praying to òrìṣà. Devotees hold the instrument in the center and rhythmically agitate it to activate the clappers in each bulb. The odu (Plate 3.3) are used throughout Ìjèbu Ifá ceremonies together with the agogo. These two small coconut-like nuts are hollowed, then have twin sticks inserted into them to make handles used to knock them together to accompany songs and Ifá recitations. They have a beautiful ringing, resonant timbre.

References Cited

Abraham, R. C. 1958. *Dictionary of Modern Yorùbá*. London: University of London Press.

Amherd, K. Noel. 2010. *Reciting Ifá: Difference, Heterogeneity, and Identity*. Trenton: Africa World Press.

Bíòbákú, Saburi O. 1956. "The Problem of Traditional History, with Special Reference to Yorùbá Traditions." In *Journal of the Historical Society of Nigeria* 1 (1): 43–47.

Branda-Lacerda, Marcos. 1996. *Yoruba Drums from Benin, West Africa*. Sound recording liner notes. Washington: Smithsonian/Folkways Recordings.

Euba, Akin. 1990. *Yorùbá Drumming: The Dùndún Tradition*. Bayreuth: Bayreuth University.

Láoyè I, Tìmì of Ẹdẹ. 1959. "Yorùbá Drums." In *Odù* 7: 10–11.

Lawal, Babátúndé. 1995. "À yà Gbó, À yà Tọ́: New Perspectives on Ẹdan Ògbóni." In *African Arts* 28 (1): 36–49, 98–100.

Marcuzzi, Michael David. 2005. *A Historical Study of the Ascendant Role of Bàtá Drumming in Cuban Òrìṣà Worship*. PhD diss., Toronto: York University.

Nolte, Insa Margrit. 1999. *Ritualised Interaction and Civic Spirituality: Kingship and Politics in Ìjẹ̀bu-Rẹ́mọ, Nigeria*. PhD thesis, University of Birmingham.

Òjó, J. R. O. 1973. "Ògbóni Drums." In *African Arts* 6 (3): 50–52, 84.

Thieme, Darius L. 1969. *A Descriptive Catalogue of Yorùbá Musical Instruments*. PhD diss., Catholic University of America, Washington, DC.

Tútúọlá, Amos. 1954. *My Life in the Bush of Ghosts*. London: Faber and Faber.

Vincent [Villepastour], Amanda. 2006. *Bata Conversations: Guardianship and Entitlement Narratives about the Bata in Nigeria and Cuba*. PhD thesis, School of Oriental and African Studies, University of London.

4

Añá or Fundamento?
The Sacred Iyesá Drums of Matanzas, Cuba

Kevin M. Delgado

• •

This essay challenges beliefs regarding the Cuban drum deity Añá (Àyàn) that are so widespread in Cuba and its cultural diaspora as to be virtually universal. My proposition necessarily proceeds in a cautious and qualified manner, combining oral histories collected during fieldwork in the coastal Cuban city of Matanzas, citing some Cuban scholarly works while interrogating others, and reexamining Afro-Cuban religious practices by comparing mainstream accounts with both African and marginal Afro-Cuban traditions. In doing so, this essay also intersects with issues raised in this volume's introduction: the remarkable re-creation of African traditions in the Americas, the malleability of oral tradition and its reification through scholarly inscription, the plurality of histories undercutting notions of singular truth, and the manner in which dominant traditions marginalize alterative accounts and empower contemporary authority.

Followers of the Cuban religion known as Santería interact with *orichas* (*òrìṣà*), deified spiritual beings of West African origin brought to the island during the transatlantic slave trade.[1] As with their African counterparts, the orichas are anthropomorphically conceived and associated with domains of nature and human behavior. Believed to have once lived on earth, the orichas are thought to be closer to human beings than is God, and therefore more sympathetic to human plights. *Santeros* (Santería initiates) have a deeply personal connection with their tutelary oricha, whom they honor, worship, placate, and appeal to in several ways. While initiates may contact the orichas through rituals of divination or in communal instances of possession trance, a more everyday visceral presence of the orichas takes form in home altars containing oricha objects. Natural objects (such as stones) are ritually charged with oricha energy by religious specialists and "presented" to a devotee's head during his or her initiation, symbolically instilling within the initiate the partial essence of the oricha. Thereafter, the initiate salutes, maintains, and "feeds" these oricha objects as part of ordinary religious practice.

These objects, charged with the partial essence of the oricha, are often referred to by the Spanish word *fundamento* (literally, "foundation" or "basis") or, less commonly, *prenda* ("jewel" or "precious object"), identifying them as essential, consecrated living objects instilled with spiritual energy.[2] Consecrated drums used in Santería ceremonies house similar living objects and are also called fundamento, distinguishing them from less efficacious unconsecrated drums that lack a fundamento object.[3] In Cuba, consecrated double-headed *batá* drums are known as fundamento in Spanish, but only the fundamento batá are also known by the special term *ilú* Añá in Lucumí (a Cuban lexicon mostly derived from the Yorùbá language).[4] Ilú Añá (drum of Añá) identifies the sacred fundamento object within the batá as containing Añá, considered to be the oricha of batá drums in Cuba. Añá, then, is a special sub-category of fundamento, the only one instilled with the power and essence of the drum deity Añá.

In material form, Añá is housed within a medicinal packet attached to the inner shells of the batá drums in a weeklong consecration ceremony. Once sealed within the drum, Añá cannot be seen but is heard in drummed sounds and addressed tactilely through the batá's wooden shells and animal-hide drumheads, the drum a container made sacred by Añá's presence. Throughout Havana and Matanzas, Añá is a term widely restricted to exactly this context: the fundamento within consecrated batá drums. However, my research in Matanzas reveals a contested claim to the exclusive use of the term Añá. In a Matanzas *cabildo* (a lodge-type fraternal association) founded by nineteenth-century Cuban descendants of the West African Ìjèṣà (Iyesá) people, authorities claim that their *iyesá* drums, first built and consecrated in the mid-nineteenth century, also contain Añá. This paper examines the history of the Matanzas Iyesá cabildo, its rituals, and its sacred drums, critically exploring the case for referring to the cabildo's drums as Añá drums.

Because Añá batá drums are considered to be the most powerful, efficacious, and prestigious drums within Santería, a claim that Añá exists within other drum types challenges widely held beliefs regarding the exclusivity of the Añá batá lineage.[5] Exploring this claim involves reviewing the current oral history and traditions of the Cabildo Iyesá Moddu San Juan Bautista in Matanzas, as well as previous scholarship regarding both the cabildo and Añá.[6] My primary concern in this essay is the opening of a historical space for the existence of Añá in a specific set of non-batá drums, voicing the claims of a particular drum tradition. Using the cabildo's drums and its traditions as maintained by its current personnel, as well as the Cuban tradition of Añá as foci, I will present circumstantial evidence in support of the cabildo's assertion. It is my hope that this, in turn, might also suggest new ways of thinking about Afro-Cuban religious practices in both nineteenth-century and contemporary Cuba.

The Cuban Iyesá

The Iyesá are the Cuban descendants of the Ìjèsà people of Nigeria, an ethnic group whose territory lies within a forested area approximately seventy-five miles inland from the Bight of Benin. The Ìjèsà speak a dialect of Yorùbá and today are considered to be a subgroup of the Yorùbá people, linked not only by language but also through an ancient lineage of crowned kingships emanating from the city of Ilé-Ifè. In Cuba the ethnic groups descended from the Yorùbá became known as Lucumí (as did the language they spoke), a broad designation that included most, if not all Yorùbá ethnicities, as well as some neighboring non-Yorùbá culture groups. Santería is often called La Regla Lucumí (The Way/Rule of the Lucumí) or La Regla Ocha (The Way/Rule of the Orichas), acknowledging the cultural origin and focus of the religion and contrasting it with other African religions retained on the island.

Piecing together a history of the Iyesá in Cuba is difficult, as no statistics exist detailing the Iyesá population in colonial Cuba. Cuban scholars have collected a variety of mentions of the Iyesá, including numerous spelling variations, but the Iyesá seem to have always been classified among the broader category of Lucumí. The Iyesá were never a sizeable group in Cuba, though there were sufficient numbers in the nineteenth century to establish their own cabildos in several locales in the plantation-saturated sections of western and central Cuba, including the cities of Havana, Regla, Matanzas, Jovellanos, Trinidad, and Sancti Spíritus. One by one, nearly all of these Iyesá cabildos disappeared over time, with only the ones in Matanzas and Sancti Spíritus surviving to the present day.

In Cuba today, the Iyesá music and belief system is practically synonymous with the Cabildo Iyesá Moddu San Juan Bautista in Matanzas, which was founded in 1830 by men of Ìjèsà descent during the height of the Cuban slave trade and the sugar-plantation economy. It has existed for over a century and a half in a single house on Salamanca Street, near the border of the Simpson neighborhood. Oral history reports that its founders met in another Lucumí cabildo called Cabildo Santa Teresa that was dedicated to the oricha Ochún (Ọ̀ṣun—a female oricha of rivers, fresh water, motherhood, and beauty). According to past Iyesá cabildo president Ernesto Knight García (1941–2004), the Cabildo Santa Teresa sponsored the creation of the current Iyesá cabildo and "baptized" the cabildo's flag.[7] According to the cabildo's oral history, the creation of the new Iyesá cabildo was more than just the desire of the free men of Iyesá/ Ìjèsà descent to have a cabildo of their own; it was something demanded by the oricha Ogún (male oricha of war, iron, violent force, and mechanized technology), to whom the cabildo is dedicated.[8]

Current members emphasize that it was founded exclusively by men who were both of Ìjèsà descent and free. According to Ernesto Knight, among the founders who helped create the cabildo were twenty-one *babalaos* (or *babaláwo*—divination specialists, priests of the Ifá divination system and of Orula, the oricha of destiny and anthropomorphic personification of Ifá knowledge); this corresponds to information given to Cuban scholar Argeliers León in the 1970s (León 1981). Cuban scholar and folklorist Rogelio Martínez Furé, who described the Matanzas cabildo in the early 1960s as in "complete decline" (1979, 140), was told in the 1960s that the twenty-one founding men included fourteen babalaos and seven *osainistas* or *olósains* (priests of the oricha Osáin— an oricha whose domain is the forest/bush, plants, and their medicinal powers) (1965, 101–2).

Though 1830 was the year the cabildo was said to be founded, it was not independently established for at least an additional fifteen years. The reason for the delay between creation and full realization is not known, perhaps arising from some combination of internal cabildo logistics (such as lack of ritual resources, money, or physical space) and external forces (e.g., during this era Matanzas experienced cholera outbreaks, devastating hurricanes, and slave rebellions). The exact year of the cabildo's full, independent establishment is unclear according to both Cuban scholars and the cabildo's own sources, though it is certain that the initial celebration of the cabildo took place on June 24, the day of its patron Catholic saint, John the Baptist.[9] The cabildo was formally and independently established sometime between 1845 and 1854, probably in 1845, 1846, or 1848.[10] The creation dates will figure in a later comparison with the Cuban batá tradition. Having established the considerable age of the Matanzas cabildo, we now turn to its traditions.

Cabildo Divinities and Religious Practice

In a general sense, the Cabildo Iyesá Moddu San Juan Bautista is like most any Santería house of oricha worship. It is dedicated to a particular oricha (Ogún), whose sacred accoutrements are regularly maintained with "spiritual cleanings" and sustained through sacrificial offerings. Its primary annual ritual festival occurs on June 24, the feast day of St. John the Baptist, the saint associated with the oricha Ogún. Its most public celebration on the night of June 24 resembles those held in other Santería houses.[11] Called *tambor* or *toque de santo* in Spanish and *bembé* in Lucumí, these celebrations involve communal singing, drumming, and dancing that honor the orichas, who may make themselves physically present by "mounting" a devotee through possession trance.[12] While the focus of a tambor is a single oricha (in this case, Ogún), songs typically honor all orichas, though in the case of the Cabildo Iyesá Moddu San Juan Bautista, fourteen major orichas are honored (fewer than are honored in mainstream Santería celebrations).[13] Though reduced in number, the form and content of the cabildo's ritual repertoire are virtually identical to those performed in other Santería oricha houses.

Significant differences nonetheless exist between the traditions of the Iyesá cabildo and mainstream Santería, differences that, I believe, suggest a connection with an earlier era of Cuban cabildos and oricha religious practices. Santería did not coalesce into the generally unified and stabilized practice that exists today until well into the early decades of the twentieth century (Brown 2003). Variant practices have always existed in the religion, however, and even today religious practice is not without deviation and serious disagreement over ritual, procedure, and authority (Wirtz 2007b). I wish to propose here that the presence or absence of some ritual actions performed in the Cabildo Iyesá Moddu San Juan Bautista suggest antiquity rather than deficiency vis-à-vis mainstream Santería, which would imply that the cabildo's practices predate the creation of certain Santería rituals.

Among many distinct aspects of the cabildo's practices and artefacts are the unique drums, rhythms, and song-prayers it utilizes in its liturgy. Additionally, a unique ritual occurs at the close of their annual celebration honoring Ogún as the cabildo's men take turns dancing, one by one, before the iyesá drums (while songs are sung for Ogún), whether or not they are Santería initiates (typically only Santería initiates are permitted to dance directly in front of sacred drums). To my knowledge, this dance ritual is not practiced in any other cabildo in Cuba.

But the most striking difference between the Cabildo Iyesá Moddu San Juan Bautista and mainstream Santería practices is that in this particular cabildo, no one ever "makes *ocha*" (that is, becomes initiated into the oricha priesthood). During this Santería ceremony of making ocha, the oricha's vessel, which contains the deity's esoteric power in the form of stones and other materials, is reproduced or "birthed" in another vessel that is presented to the head of the new initiate (known as "seating the oricha"). The new vessel—understood as containing the essence of the newly born oricha—is then taken home and cared for by the new initiate. Interestingly, despite the fact that the consecrated vessel of Ogún has existed in the Cabildo Iyesá Moddu San Juan Bautista since its establishment, this oricha vessel has never been used to "birth" new oricha, and hence to initiate new oricha priests. Nonetheless, regardless of whether or not the men of the cabildo have been fully initiated into the Santería priesthood (and in fact most of its nonmusicians have not), through their very association and involvement with the cabildo the men have a special relationship with Ogún, the cabildo's spiritual "owner" (as is evidenced by the privilege of cabildo men to dance before the iyesá drums, as well as participate in certain rituals associated with June 24, celebrations). Interestingly, this collective relationship between cabildo men and their patron oricha resembles Nigerian òrìṣà traditions, where agnate household members may inherit an association with the family's patrilineal òrìṣà without the need for full initiation into the priesthood.

Though the Cabildo San Juan Bautista is first and foremost dedicated to Ogún and maintained by men, the cabildo has also always honored Ochún, the oricha of rivers and fresh water, strongly associated with femininity, beauty, love, and money. Cabildo Santa Teresa, the old cabildo that sponsored the formation of the Cabildo Iyesá Moddu San Juan Bautista, was itself dedicated to Ochún, and to the present day, Ochún also receives annual praise in the cabildo's rituals. Interestingly, despite the male-centered practices of the cabildo, its oral history maintains that it had a female founder, the only female member in the cabildo's history: Carmen García, an initiate of Ochún. When she passed away at some point during the nineteenth century, her fundamento oricha objects were cared for and maintained in the cabildo, a practice that continues to this day (though these oricha objects have never been used for any cabildo initiations either). When Ogún's fundamento objects and iron attributes are cared for and "fed" during annual activities surrounding June 24, Ochún's are as well. During some years a separate tambor celebration is held for Ochún on September 12, the day associated with Ochún's Catholic counterpart, La Virgen de la Caridad del Cobre (Our Lady of Charity of [the town of] Copper).[14] During other years a separate social gathering is held in honor of Ochún on June 25, the day after Ogún's ritual celebrations.

That both Ogún and Ochún exist as the primary oricha of the Matanzas Iyesá cabildo is not surprising, as both have a strong presence in the African territory of the Ìjèṣà people. Ogún is well known in Yorùbáland and beyond, while his legendary Yorùbá homeland is among the Oǹdó people, east of Ìjèṣà territory. Ogún festivals occur throughout the eastern forest regions of Yorùbáland, including the Ìjèṣà territories. The African worship of Òṣun is associated with the river bearing her name that flows from above the northern limits of Ìjèṣàland, southwest across what was northern Ìjèṣà territory during the era of the transatlantic slave trade, and south through Ìjèbu territory to the Lagos Lagoon. Òṣun worship was once restricted to this area, whereas Ogún worship is spread over a much larger territory. While men and male occupations, both traditional (e.g., hunters, soldiers, blacksmiths) and contemporary (e.g., drivers, railroad workers, mechanics), dominate the African worship of Ogún, African worship of Òṣun (Ochún) emphasizes femaleness. These gendered tendencies find correspondence in the oricha practices of Cuban Santería, while the exclusively male worship of Ogún in the Matanzas Iyesá cabildo suggestively echoes the male dominated sociooccupational worship of Ogún in Yorùbáland.[15]

The importance of Ogún and Ochún to the Matanzas Iyesá cabildo places their practices squarely within mainstream Santería. However, the anomalous absence of initiation rituals vis-à-vis most oricha houses removes the cabildo from mainstream religious practice, a point worth engaging in the interest of later discussions regarding the question of Añá. According to everyone in the cabildo with whom I spoke, no one has ever undergone a full initiation into the oricha priesthood ("making ocha") in the cabildo since its creation.[16] If someone affiliated with the cabildo desires to make ocha, they must go to a standard Santería house of worship to do so, even if the oricha to be initiated is Ogún or Ochún. Over time, very few men of the cabildo family have ever made ocha (perhaps their default relationship with Ogún provides less motivation for some to make ocha), while a great many of the women have.[17] Additionally, though the Añá/fundamento of the iyesá drums is of respected lineage and probably the oldest in Matanzas, no new Santería initiates have been ritually "presented" to the drums, as is commonly practiced throughout Santería today using Añá batá drums.[18]

Though confident in the consistency of their noninitiatory tradition, cabildo members generally could offer no explanation as to why no one made ocha in their particular house, and at times I sensed a bit of defensiveness in this regard, as the noninitiatory traditions of the cabildo stand in stark contrast to the numerous Santería houses in Matanzas. Cabildo president Ernesto Knight offered no historical rationale, though in one of our conversations he speculated that perhaps the reason no one makes ocha in the cabildo has to do with its founders, particularly the large group of babalaos. As specialized priests of the oricha Orula and the wisdom and divination system of Ifá, babalaos do not "make ocha" in the conventional sense. Though they "call down" Ifá for their ceremonies and important divination, they do not become "mounted" or "possessed" by Ifá/Orula. "And for this reason," said Knight, "[today] one doesn't 'make saint' or 'present' anyone. Why? Because at the time this cabildo was founded, the founders were twenty-one babalaos, and not one of those twenty-one babalaos was consecrated with any saint [oricha]."[19]

Knight's comment concerning "presenting" someone refers to the ritual presentation of a *yawó/yabó* (new oricha initiate) to the sacred drums containing Añá. Although santeros and particularly batá drummers state that this ritual has always existed in Santería, recent scholarship has questioned this claim (e.g., Marcuzzi 2005, 413–15). If in fact it is the case that the presentation ceremony is a twentieth-century innovation, the absence of this ceremony in the Iyesá cabildo is explained by the fact that their practices predate the creation of the presentation ritual. Viewed in this way, the lack of an Añá presentation ritual in the Iyesá cabildo does not represent the "loss" of an old ritual, but rather the resistance to adopting a more recent one.

Returning to Santería initiations, a visit I paid in 2005 to the Cabildo Santa Bárbara in the city of Sancti Spíritus (the only other extant Iyesá cabildo in Cuba and also founded in the mid-nineteenth century) revealed that its members also did not "make ocha" in their cabildo either.[20] Rather than suggesting a unity of Iyesá practices or retentions, I believe that the noninitiatory traditions of these cabildos may represent elements of nineteenth-century oricha cabildo practices, perhaps widespread ones. Recalling the mid-nineteenth-century dates of the Matanzas cabildo's founding and the early-twentieth-century standardization of Santería practices (Brown 2003), I interpret the distinct practices of the Cabildo Iyesá Moddu San Juan Bautista (vis-à-vis mainstream Santería) as signs of antiquity, ones that likely predate the aforementioned Santería rituals.

Cabildo Musical Instruments, Personnel, and Liturgy

Outside of the Matanzas Iyesá cabildo, "Iyesá music" is known primarily through ritual songs and drum rhythms that are found in the mainstream Santería repertoire performed in tambor celebrations and secondarily through folkloric reproductions modeled after the cabildo's liturgy and distinct music ensemble. Despite the existence of a second Iyesá cabildo

Plate 4.1 Iyesá drums in the Cabildo Iyesá Moddu San Juan Bautista. (photograph: Amanda Villepastour, Matanzas, 15 July 2013)

in Sancti Spíritus, Cuban iyesá drums are understood to be the type of drums used by the Cabildo Iyesá Moddu San Juan Bautista in Matanzas.[21] The Matanzas iyesá ensemble comprises four double-headed, cylindrical drums of differing sizes all carved from a single log of cedar (see Plate 4.1). Cabildo tradition states that the ensemble was originally a three-drum set in Africa, and that a fourth drum was added in Cuba when the drums were constructed for the cabildo (Martínez Furé 1965, 107; León 1981). The drums are painted green, each with a horizontal band of yellow circling the middle of the drum, a color scheme also found on the set of four nineteenth-century iyesá drums on display in the Museo Nacional de la Música in Havana. The colors are said to honor Ogún and Ochún, respectively.[22]

Unlike the Añá batá tradition, which requires a formal ritual initiation (known as the *juramento*) into a fraternity of "sworn" batá drummers before one is allowed to play the drums, the cabildo has no ceremonial ritual to initiate a member into a drumming fraternity. Likewise, Nigerian Àyàn traditions, which have a diversity of initiatory rituals pertaining to Àyàn priesthood, do not have rituals that specifically entitle the initiate to serve as a ceremonial drummer (see Vincent 2006, 84–88, 117–21). As with my argument about the "presentation to Añá," it is possible that the cabildo practice of not requiring an initiatory ritual for drummers predates the establishment of the initiatory juramento.

Little can be said with certainty regarding the creation of the cabildo's drums. According to cabildo sources, the drums currently used are the original set constructed for the cabildo in the first half of the nineteenth century, more than one hundred and fifty years ago. It is not unheard of for Afro-Cuban drums over a century old to be used on a regular basis today, especially if they are carefully maintained. In Matanzas alone, the two most prestigious sets of batá drums, currently belonging to the family of Estéban Vega "Cha Chá" (1925–2007) and Julio Marcos Suárez "Fantomas" (from his father Ricardo Suárez), are both said to date back well into the nineteenth century. The age of the iyesá drums is of relevance to the question of the drum's Añá, a topic to which we shall return shortly.

In terms of ritual performers, senior cabildo members have held many of the key positions for long periods of time. For decades during the twentieth century, the *agan* (ritual song leader) in the Matanzas cabildo was Adolfo Más Cartaya "Nene" who, according to one of his sons, never assumed song leader duties for other Santería houses, singing for Iyesá cabildo rituals exclusively.[23] By the time Cuban musicologists Argeliers León and María Teresa Linares organized in situ a recording session of the cabildo performing its traditional music in 1977, Nene had already been the principal singer for over thirty years.[24] He died in 1983, and his two sons, Luis Más Lamar "Titico" (1942–2004) and Bárbaro Más Lamar (b. 1952), took over the cabildo's song leader duties, which Bárbaro continues as of this writing.

The cabildo's principal drummer for many years during the mid-twentieth century was Lorenzo Urrútia, who played in the cabildo from at least the early 1950s (and probably much earlier) until his death in the 1980s. His sons, Moisés (b. 1946) and Reynolds (b. 1943) Urrútia Ruiz, have played drums in the cabildo for many years, with Moisés taking over duties as principal drummer from his father. Moisés cares for the iyesá drums when they need maintenance, as did his father. While Moisés plays numerous styles of Afro-Cuban religious drumming such as batá, iyesá, bembé, *arará* (a Matanzas tradition of Ewe-Fon origin), and *güiro* (beaded-gourd), his father only played for the Iyesá cabildo and for güiro ensembles.[25] Moisés's experience and expertise provide crucial support to the claim that the drums of the Cabildo Iyesá Moddu San Juan Bautista are Añá drums.

The cabildo uses only three distinct rhythms for its liturgical music: one each for Ogún and Ochún, and one as a special rhythm to close a tambor. For all rhythms, two iron bells struck with sticks accompany the drums (see Plate 4.1). Iyesá song-prayers typically consist of one or two brief phrases in call-and-response form. Of the approximately fifty songs used in the Matanzas Iyesá cabildo, roughly one-third are heard in the mainstream Santería liturgy in both Havana and Matanzas. Interestingly, many songs considered Iyesá in origin, which are regularly heard in Santería tambor gatherings, are not performed in the Matanzas Iyesá cabildo, suggesting, among other possibilities, long-extinct Iyesá cabildos as a source.

Añá or Fundamento?

Matanzas santeros in general, and Matanzas Añá batá drummers in particular, recognize the drums of the Cabildo Iyesá Moddu San Juan Bautista as being fundamento. That is, all agree that their drums are truly consecrated and sacred, containing secret objects instilled with spiritual power. However, all batá drummers with whom I spoke in Matanzas insisted that the cabildo's drums are fundamento but not Añá, because, in their opinion, Añá is a distinct entity whose fundamento objects are found exclusively in batá drums.[26] In other words, the conventional opinion given by batá drummers in Matanzas (and, for that matter, Havana) asserts that both the cabildo's iyesá drums and consecrated batá drums are fundamento (because both contain secret, spiritually charged objects), but only the objects of the batá should be called Añá because only these objects are instilled with the distinct and essential power of the oricha known as Añá. For nearly all batá drummers (and consequently, most santeros), Añá is not the oricha of sacred Lucumí drums in general but solely the oricha of the Lucumí batá drums. This notion is markedly different from Nigerian Àyàn practices, whereby Àyàn can be placed inside a variety of drums, including the bàtá (Yorùbá spelling).

In response to questions on the matter of Añá, the most knowledgeable Iyesá cabildo drummers and singers insisted that the cabildo's drums do possess Añá. I find Moisés Urrútia's opinion in this matter most important because not only is he the lead drummer of the Iyesá cabildo, but he also maintains and repairs the cabildo's drums (a great responsibility not only because of the age and uniqueness of the drums, but because one also must also be entrusted to safeguard the sacred objects inside the drums during such work). Significantly, Moisés serves as one of the lead drummers for the aforementioned prestigious batá drums of Fantomas, one of the primary sets of Añá batá in the city until the death of Ricardo Suárez. Moisés has also had the responsibility of tuning, repairing, and maintaining the Añá batá drums of Fantomas. In his duties as one who plays, tunes, repairs, disassembles, and examines both the interior and exterior of both sets of drums, which were both constructed and "loaded" with sacred objects during the 1800s, Moisés is uniquely positioned in his access and intimate physical knowledge of both drums. Moisés emphatically declares that both sets of fundamento drums possess Añá. His expertise and access to the drums in question strengthens the Matanzas cabildo's assertion that its drums are Añá drums, an assertion that corresponds with the cabildo's claim of Añá from an earlier generation, as collected in the 1960s research of Rogelio Martínez Furé (1965, 109).

Aside from the direct claims by cabildo authorities, additional practices and historical data indirectly suggest the possibility of Añá in the iyesá drums. One such example is found in a song. Included in the cabildo's regular liturgical corpus is a song for Elegbá (also known as Eleguá), the divine messenger. Known as both a warrior and a messenger oricha whose domain is the crossroads, Elegbá is saluted first in Santería tambor contexts to initiate communication between humans and the orichas. This song, however, is unusual in that it specifically mentions Añá.[27] Figure 4.1 is my transcription of how the song was taught to me in the year 2000 by Luís Más Lamar "Titico." Notice how the word "Añá" is sung on two consecutive pitches in both renderings of the word on the lowest notes in the melody's range. Though the Lucumí word "Añá" has an accent denoting a stress on the second syllable (as opposed to a rise in pitch, as would be indicated by a Yorùbá tone mark), these two low-melody pitches on the melody text "Añá" (bars 3–4 and 7–8) replicate the double low-tone speech contour of the Yorùbá word "Àyàn." Additionally, the melodic contours of Elegbá (mid-high-low) loosely correspond with the Yorùbá speech tone contour of the corresponding Yorùbá word Ẹlẹ́gba (mid-high-mid).[28]

Titico's brother, Bárbaro Más Lamar, sang the same melody but employed a slight variation in words (substituting "so mi 'Legbá" for Titico's "mi Elegbá" in measure six of the above example). In my individual work with each of the Más brothers, Bárbaro and Titico were very consistent in the liturgical usage of all cabildo song-prayers in terms of repertoire, sequence, and usage. However, despite their decades in the cabildo (and many years in La Regla Lucumí), neither brother could translate word for word all of the song-prayers, a common situation within the oricha religion in general.[29] Most often I would receive a general or "gist-like" description of the meaning of the songs, occasionally one that went no further than the name of the oricha whom the song honored. At times I would also receive more information from one brother or the other. The "Elegbá Añá" song, however, provided a case in which both

Figure 4.1: Iyesá "Elegbá Añá" song.

brothers independently gave virtually the same response, stating that the song in question refers to Elegbá preparing (or helping to prepare) the Añá of the cabildo's drums, as well as the other fundamento objects of the cabildo (for Ogún and Ochún).[30] While circumstantial at best, the inclusion of Echú-Elegbá with the preparation of Añá finds correspondence in some of the historical legends and divination texts pertaining to Ifá and Àyàn in Nigeria collected by Amanda Villepastour (Marcuzzi 2005, 153–61; Vincent 2006, 110, 122).[31]

An additional historical point in my argument concerns the age of the iyesá drums vis-à-vis the batá Añá tradition, which is generally regarded by santeros as not only being the only Añá tradition in Cuba but also one whose fundamento holds a status of chronological precedence over other drum fundamento objects on the island. Fernando Ortíz gives the most well-known and accepted account of the history of Añá in Cuba, citing 1830 as the approximate year in which Añá was established in Cuba (interestingly, the exact year that the Cabildo Iyesá Moddu San Juan Bautista was founded). According to Ortíz, two African-born men, Añabí (known as Ño Juan el Cojo, a drummer, babalao, and olósain) and Atandá (known as Ño Filomeno García, a drummer, babalao, and wood carver), used their combined knowledge to create the first Añá drums in Cuba. In 1866 Añabí and Atandá reportedly created a second set of Añá drums for a cabildo founded by renowned babalao Remigio Herrera "Adechina." Thereafter, several sets of Añá were created by this foundational duo, with these drums attaining an unparalleled level of authoritative authenticity in both the work of Ortíz (1955, 311, 315–18) and among the present-day Havana batá community.

Subsequent Cuban scholars have pointed out the lack of evidence of the earlier date (ca. 1830) and the qualified way it is presented by Ortíz in comparison to the second date (1866), which is triangulated with the participation of Adechina and the creation of a cabildo. Moreover, the widely quoted Ortíz account describes Añabí and Atandá as elderly (*viejo*) at the time of their initial meeting, meaning that they would have been "elderly plus thirty-six years" when a relative flurry of drum-making activity commenced in 1866 and continued until all sets attributed to these men were constructed. Noting the early date, the lengthy lapse of time between the reported construction of the first two sets, as well as the age of the men in question and timeline of activities attributed to them, Marcuzzi argues persuasively that 1866 is likely the more accurate of the two dates for the initial creation of Añá for batá drums, moving the establishment of the batá Añá tradition into the mid-nineteenth century (2005, 340–42). If correct, this would place the creation of the Añá of the batá *after* the appearance of the Matanzas iyesá drums, which occurred at some point between 1830 and 1854 (likely between 1845 and 1848). At the very least, it is clear these two Añá traditions were independent but contemporaneous, as the earliest possible date cited for the creation of each of the two traditions in question (the Añá batá in Havana and the iyesá drums in Matanzas) is the same (1830), and as the range of creation dates for both traditions falls between 1830 and the 1860s.

As for the creation of Añá in Cuba, I am unconcerned with which Añá set actually came first. (Indeed, the first Añá may have appeared and disappeared in Cuba well before 1830, only to be forgotten in the vicissitudes of Afro-Cuban colonial life.) While the centrality of Ortíz's work and the historical importance of Añabí and Atandá are well established, my interest here is in opening and exploring a historical space for Añá lineages outside of the conventional Ortíz-reported Añabí/Atandá orthodoxy. The fact remains that Añá, as with other fundamento objects in the Santería religion, was apparently (re)created on the island of Cuba, and in its Cuban incarnation it presented a reenacted and recontextualized tradition, one modified from its previous African existence.[32] A (re)creation by experts opens the possibility that other Añá creations were possible if the appropriate materials, knowledge, and motivation existed elsewhere on the island.

Moreover, the Cabildo Iyesá Moddu San Juan Bautista is far from the only challenge to the exclusive primacy of Añabí and Atandá's drums. Marcuzzi (2005) notes the Havana-centric nature of Ortíz's study of the batá, speculating that the Havana drummers Ortíz consulted took a proactive role in shaping the reputation of their own sets and Ortíz's predominantly negative evaluation of other lineages. In Matanzas additional lineages of nineteenth-century Añá batá are claimed, including the assertion by the batá authorities Amado Díaz Alfonso "Guantica" and the aforementioned "Cha Chá" Vega that the first Cuban Añá batá lineage was established in 1874 in the town of Cidra before spreading to the nearby city of Matanzas and Havana thereafter (Eli Rodríguez 1997, 339). Matanzas-born drummer and drum maker Felipe García Villamil cites a different lineage for his drums. Vélez (2000, 51–60) collected a narrative from García placing the creation of his drums at an unspecified point in the nineteenth century, while García has also claimed his Añá was brought from Yorùbáland during this time.[33] While far from conclusive (and without approaching the ca. 1830 date cited by Ortíz for batá in Havana), testimonies concerning the batá in Matanzas challenge the idea of a singular genesis of batá Añá in Cuba, revealing it to be a more constructed and less universally agreed-upon history. The narrative of a singular creation of Añá is further challenged by non-batá claims of Añá above and beyond the claims of the Matanzas Iyesá cabildo.

While the drums of the Cabildo Iyesá Moddu San Juan Bautista may or may not have been created before or at the same time as the first drums of Añabí and Atandá, their independent and contemporary creation, coupled with a claim of Añá, opens the possibility not only of multiple nineteenth-century Añá traditions, but also of non-batá ones. Again, the idea of re-creation is crucial. While Añabí's expertise in the West African practice of Ifá, Osáin, and Añá might have been extraordinary in a single individual, it would not have been impossible to locate multiple individuals with this knowledge, particularly during the height of the slave trade in the early nineteenth century and within the slave-saturated areas of Havana and Matanzas.[34] When considering the two oral histories regarding the personnel present at the creation of the Cabildo Iyesá Moddu San Juan Bautista—either the twenty-one babalaos account collected by myself and other scholars, or the fourteen babalaos and seven osainistas account collected by Martínez Furé—it is quite possible the ritual knowledge and capability to create Añá were present in the cabildo personnel at the time it was founded.

The Oricha of Drumming

In light of the cabildo's claims and the possibility that the ability to make Añá existed in the foundational personnel of the Iyesá cabildo, I propose viewing Añá as the oricha of Lucumí sacred drums (or select sacred Lucumí drum traditions) rather than the oricha solely of the Lucumí batá. This suggestion finds correspondence in select ethnographic evidence collected by Cuban researchers that documents the claims of Cuban non-batá Añá traditions in addition to those of the Cabildo Iyesá Moddu San Juan Bautista.[35] Scholarly research on two Cuban bembé drum traditions includes claims of Añá drums, though one is referred to in Cuban publications as a "*dundún*" ensemble.[36] The so-called dundún ensemble of the Cabildo La Divina Caridad in Cienfuegos is unusual in that it consists of four drums of three different shapes (cylindrical and double-headed, hourglass and double-headed, and hemispherical/single-headed). Cuban scholar Carmen Sáenz Coopat (1997, 361) uses the word "Añá" to describe the fundamento object of a drum in this ensemble, though her usage is slightly ambiguous by referring to the "Añá or secret prenda" that is put inside the lead drum, as not all secret objects referred to as "prenda" within consecrated drums are considered Añá by all drummers.

Cuban scholar Bárbara Balbuena Gutiérrez reports that the Sociedad Santa Bárbara de Guadalupe Stable in the town of Cruces (Cienfuegos Province) owns an additional set of fundamento bembé drums that contain Añá. Though the cabildo apparently incorporated a secular drum (a *tumbadora*) into its musical ensemble, Balbuena Gutiérrez notes that two of the cabildo's old drums resemble iyesá drums in shape and cordage. Importantly, she also specifically states that "these bembé drums are fundamento, they have Añá and receive offerings and sacrifices" (Balbuena Gutiérrez 2003, 95). However, in the glossary of the same publication Balbuena Gutiérrez defines Añá as the secret "oricha that resides in the fundamento batá drums," an inconsistency that draws her earlier Añá assertion into question (133).

Returning to Iyesá tradition, the less known of the two extant Iyesá cabildos is the Cabildo Santa Bárbara, located in the landlocked central Cuban city of Sancti Spíritus. Though it was not officially legalized until 1953, the cabildo was actually founded during the previous century, though the exact year is uncertain (Brizuela Quintanilla 1988, 32).[37] Cuban scholar Analeese Brizuela Quintanilla uses the word "Añá" to describe the drums of Sancti Spíritus (though, as with the previous bembé drum example, at least one of the original drums has been replaced by a manufactured drum suitable for secular music). In her 1997 article on the two extant Iyesá cabildos, Brizuela states that "both sets of iyesá drums are fundamento" and that the drums' owners "believe that inside [the drums] lives the deity Añá, who is the object of special rites" (355). In her 1988 bachelor's thesis devoted exclusively to the study of the Cabildo Santa Bárbara, she is more specific, implying that only the large *caja* (deep-pitched lead drum) is sacred, and stating that the drum's owners "affirm that inside it resides the deity Añá" (103).

These points, however, were complicated by a brief visit I paid to the Cabildo Santa Bárbara in late 2006, where contradictory claims regarding the drums also illustrated the malleability of historical tradition. Contrary to Brizuela's research, the then-current senior drummer of the cabildo, Raimundo Valle Pina "Nene" (1932–2009), stated that the cabildo's caja drum is fundamento but not Añá.[38] When I met scholar Analeese Brizuela, I specifically queried her regarding the exact claims she had collected in the 1980s. Responding without hesitation, she stated with certainty that the cabildo drummers with whom she worked decades earlier referred to their caja as an Añá drum.[39] Like the dundún and bembé traditions cited above, then, the earlier claim of Añá in the Cabildo Santa Bárbara as documented by Brizuela is suggestive but not conclusive. Taken collectively, however, these three drum traditions—dundún, bembé, and Sancti Spíritus Iyesá—do demonstrate that the Matanzas Iyesá cabildo is not alone in claiming a non-batá Añá tradition.

Significantly, while a claim that Añá exists in non-batá drums contradicts the accepted historical batá conventions in Cuba, there is no corresponding tradition of Àyàn exclusivity concerning bàtá drums in Africa. In Nigeria, the bàtá are but one of several drum types that house Àyàn objects. In addition to the Nigerian bàtá, the *dùndún* and *gúdúgúdú* drums all have a lengthy and well documented Àyàn tradition in Yorùbáland, while less common Àyàn vessels include miniature bàtá drums, large *sábétó* drums, and even a clay pot (Vincent 2006, 85, 96–97, 134). This suggests that Cuban claims that only batá drums possess Añá may represent a well-established (and perhaps elevated) Cuban innovation, rather than strictly "traditional" African retentions. As with my hypothesis regarding the absence of Santería initiations and initiatory presentations to the Añá drums in the Cabildo Iyesá Moddu San Juan Bautista, as well as requirement of sacred drummers to be sworn into a special drumming fraternity, the claim of Añá in the Matanzas Iyesá cabildo's drums (as well as the other cabildos named above) may represent the retention of old practices, remnants of a more heterogeneous Añá tradition that existed in nineteenth-century Cuba.

Summary and Conclusion

In this essay, I have argued for the claim that the drums of the Cabildo Iyesá Moddu San Juan Bautista in Matanzas possess Añá, an assertion that contradicts the accepted convention of Añá residing exclusively within batá drums as established by Fernando Ortíz, his esteemed informants, and present-day batá masters. At the core of my argument are the testimonies of cabildo authorities, which are reinforced by a previous generation of scholarship. These testimonies find exceptional support in the expert opinion of Moisés Urrútia, an individual with unique responsibility and interior access to both the Matanzas Iyesá cabildo drums and a set of batá Añá drums constructed in the nineteenth century. My argument has also relied on an analysis of historical dates for the creation of the Cuban batá Añá tradition and the Matanzas Iyesá cabildo,

which indicates that the Añá of Iyesá cabildo was contemporaneous to
the establishment of the batá Añá tradition, and perhaps even preceded it.
I have also proposed that expertise required to create Añá likely existed
among the cabildo's founders have and cited the cabildo's longstand-
ing inclusion of a song that mentions Añá (and the Más brothers' assertions regarding the song's meaning) as an additional reinforcement to the
Iyesá-Añá hypothesis. Collectively, these points make a compelling case
for arguing that the drums of the Cabildo Iyesá Moddu San Juan Bautista
are Añá drums.

In reviewing claims of additional non-batá Añá traditions in Cuba, as
well as the Matanzas-batá drum histories that exist outside the Havana-
batá narrative as established by Fernando Ortíz, I have reasoned that the
re-creation of Añá batá in Cuba likely did not have a singular genesis.
The possibility of multiple re-creations of Añá on the island leads me
to suggest recasting Añá as the oricha of Lucumí sacred drums (or select Lucumí sacred drum traditions) rather than the oricha of sacred batá
drums only. If the drums of the Cabildo Iyesá Moddu San Juan Bautista
are to be considered Añá, the existence of Iyesá Añá may be indicative
of a more heterogeneous nineteenth-century Añá tradition. Similarly,
by viewing the cabildo's unique traditions—the male focus, cabildo
men dancing before the drums (even if they are not Santería initiates),
not making ocha using the cabildo's oricha objects, and not presenting
Santería initiates to their drums—as signs of antiquity rather than mark-
ers of deficient absence, I have raised the possibility that the cabildo's
traditions predate the standardization and/or creation of certain Santería
practices. I view the case for referring to the Matanzas iyesá drums as
Añá drums as a persuasive one, though I acknowledge the data and historical hypotheses I have provided to bolster the cabildo's oral histories
and contemporary claim of Añá remain suggestive and not conclusive.

My primary interest in this essay has been to create a historical
space for the existence of Añá in a particular set of non-batá drums.
Nonetheless, for the vast majority of batá drummers and santeros, this
presents an admittedly controversial challenge to the established primacy
or exclusive centrality of batá drum Añá lineages. My intention has been
to voice the claims of a particular tradition and add to the narrative of the
Afro-Cuban past (and present), not to diminish the legacy and standing
of the Cuban batá drums. (Truthfully, given the extraordinary history,
international reputation, and virtuosic repertoire of the batá, I do not see
diminishment of its standing as either possible or desirable.) I acknowledge that questioning the batá's exclusive Añá status not only challenges
specific traditions or histories, but also has the potential to spill over
into realms of religious power and authority (and, in today's increasingly

capitalized Cuba, realms of economic authority as well). But the history of the Cabildo Iyesá Moddu San Juan Bautista is no less remarkable, and its drums and traditions provide us much to consider. It is my desire that these ideas stimulate discussion regarding the nature and overall history of Añá within the Santería milieu. It is also my hope that consideration of this single, local Afro-Cuban history can suggest new ways of thinking about Afro-Cuban religious practice in nineteenth-century Cuba and thus enrich our view of present-day Afro-Cuban culture.

Notes

1. In this essay, I privilege conventional Cuban spelling of Cuban deities, objects, and rituals rather than their Yorùbá cognates when speaking of a Cuban setting. This is admittedly an imperfect endeavor, as writing in English about Cuban usage of words of West African origin requires choosing between multiple conventions and arbitrary spellings. In general, I will choose a particular Cuban spelling (such as oricha) and provide a Yorùbá cognate in parentheses during the first instance (e.g., òrìṣà). I shall use Standard Yorùbá spellings when speaking of Yorùbá culture in a Nigerian setting (e.g., the African Ìjèṣà versus the Cuban Iyesá).

2. The word prenda has been appropriated from Palo (Reglas de Congo) spiritual practices in Cuba and is likely of western Central African origin.

3. Sacred drums in the Santería religion are double-headed rather than single-headed, sealing the drum's interior and providing a safe location for the fundamento object. The most common drums are the hourglass-shaped, double-headed *batá* drums, with the double-headed variety of bembé drums being very uncommon and iyesá drums quite rare. Unconsecrated batá drums known in Lucumí as *aberinkulá* are sometimes used in religious ceremonies (particularly outside of Cuba), but are not considered to be as efficacious in inducing spirit possession and tend to be used when consecrated fundamento batá are unaffordable or unavailable.

4. In Cuba today, Lucumí refers to a ritual language and cultural practices of Lucumí origin.

5. Regarding drum lineage, new Añá batá drums are "birthed" from existing sets of Añá drums. Thus, a significant portion of a particular set's legitimacy within the eyes of the religious community lies in its owner's claim to a respected drum lineage.

6. See, for example, Marcuzzi (2005), who presents evidence of variegated Yorùbá drums in Cuba, while describing the ascendancy of the batá and its ultimate hegemony in sacred Afro-Cuban drumming.

7. Ernesto Knight García, pers. comm., Matanzas, March 12, 2000 and September 12, 2000.

8. Ernesto Knight García, pers. comm., Matanzas, September 12, 2000.

9. Colonial cabildos were required to organize under the banner of a patron saint. Saints became a necessary link between the official Catholicism of the island and the unofficial African religion that persisted. The Catholic calendar also became important to Afro-Cubans because holy days were often the only time slaves were not required to work, or when free Afro-Cubans were allowed to parade with their cabildos. Now, as then, annual oricha celebrations are held on the day of the oricha's corresponding saint.

10. Ernesto Knight García cited the year 1846, while in 2007 the subsequent cabildo president, José de los Reyes Portillo García (b. 1932), cited 1848. Cuban musicologist Argeliers León, whose fieldwork at the cabildo included at least a visit in the early 1950s and in 1977, reported

the cabildo's year of establishment as 1854 (Lcón 1981), a date repeated by Brizuela Quintanilla (1997). Cuban ethnologist and folklorist Rogelio Martínez Furé gives 1845 as the cabildo's establishment date (1965; 1979). Martínez Furé is the only Cuban scholar who cites a second, separate date for the organization of the new Iyesá cabildo, which he lists as 1830 (ibid.). The cabildo possesses a commemorative banner of uncertain age marking the creation year as 1830 and the establishment date as 1848, supporting de los Reyes's date. Archival sources confirm the cabildo's existence in the nineteenth century. The Archivo Histórico Provincional de Matanzas contains letters from cabildo leaders requesting permission to conduct June cabildo activities in 1881, 1892, and 1893 (Fondo Religiones Africanas, Legajo 1, número 9 carpeta 1, número 10 carpeta 2, and número 41). In an unpublished manuscript on the Iyesá (2000), Matanzas scholar Israel Moliner Castañeda presents a brief report from the Matanzas archive written by a watchman in 1854 complaining of crowds and disorder when the cabildo members parade. I could not locate the original document Moliner Castañeda cites in the Matanzas provincial archive.

11. In contrast to the daytime practices in Havana, oricha celebrations in Matanzas are conducted at night.

12. The use of the word *bembé* for a drumming celebration should not be confused with the family of drums also known as bembé in Cuba.

13. The orichas honored in the cabildo songs are, in liturgical order: Echú/Elegbá, Ogún, Ochosi, Babalúayé/San Lázaro, Ibcyí, Agayú, Changó, Obatalá, Yewa, Oba, Oyá, Ochún, Yemayá, and Orula.

14. Affectionately known as "La Caridad," La Virgen de la Caridad del Cobre is the patron saint of Cuba. While the majority of the oricha houses in Cuba honor La Caridad on September 8, the cabildo maintains the practice of using September 12, a day formerly associated with La Caridad.

15. That these gendered tendencies find correspondence in Santcría does not mean that devotees are linked to particular orichas because of gender. To be clear, in both Nigeria and Cuba oricha devotees may become initiates to an oricha whose gendered identity is the opposite of the devotee's biological gender. For example, male devotees may become initiates to orichas identified as female, such as Ochún, and female initiates may become initiated to orichas identified as male, such as Ogún. The exclusively male focus of the Cabildo Iyesá Moddu San Juan Bautista is, however, atypical of Cuban Santería houses.

16. To clarify, "making ocha," *kariocha* in Lucumí or *asiento* in Spanish, involves a seven-day ceremony in which the initiate is inducted into the oricha priesthood.

17. Ernesto Knight García, pers. comm., Matanzas, July 6, 2000.

18. New initiates in Santcría are not recognized as fully fledged priests until they have undergone a ceremony known as "the presentation to Añá" (see Cornelius 1995 and Marcuzzi 2005, 411–21 for more detail).

19. Ernesto Knight García, pers. comm., Matanzas, 6 July 2000. Though Orula is considered an oricha, Knight's usage here refers to the majority of orichas of the religion, which may "mount" their initiated devotees through spirit possession. By "consecrated" Knight refers to those initiated to the common cohort of possession orichas, as opposed to babalaos who are consecrated in distinct rituals by the non-possession oricha of Ifá/Orula. Even if we take into account the slightly different composition of the cabildo founders collected in the early 1960s by Rogelio Martínez Furé—fourteen babalaos and seven osainistas—Knight's theory remains plausible, as osainistas do not "make ocha" in the conventional sense either because, like the babalaos, osainistas typically do not become mounted (possessed) by their oricha in Cuba. However, it should be noted that many Cuban babalaos do make ocha before becoming a babalao, thereby achieving both ocha and babalao status, but once an oricha initiate has been initiated into Ifá, they are no longer involved with initiating other oricha priests.

20. Olga Gutiérrez Valle, pers. comm., Sancti Spíritus, June 21, 2005.

21. Practically all discussions of Cuban iyesá drums and music refer exclusively to the traditions the Cabildo Iyesá Moddu San Juan Bautista in Matanzas. The cabildo in Sancti Spíritus is overlooked in the discussion of the Cuban Iyesá primarily because santeros in Matanzas and Havana are unaware of its existence. Also, because Havana and Matanzas expressions of Afro-Cuban culture dominate the national folklore industry's representations of Santería, disseminating the Matanzas Iyesá culture to a national and international audience has magnified the impression that the Matanzas cabildo is the only Iyesá cabildo in Cuba. See Delgado (2008).

22. Fernando Ortíz and his researchers were told that, contrary to the information collected by Martínez Furé in the 1960s, the color of the iyesá drums—which he described as blue-green—referred not to their patron oricha Ogún but was "in honor of Orúnla or Ifá" (Ortíz 1954, 370). If true, this assertion, which does not mention any stripe, might add weight to the notion of a deeper Iyesá connection with babalaos and Orula/Orúmila.

23. Bárbaro Más Lamar, pers. comm., Matanzas, July 3, 2000. The word *agan* is only used to refer to the song leader in the Cabildo Iyesá Moddu San Juan Bautista, mostly by the song leaders themselves. In all other houses of Lucumí-based oricha worship, the song leader is known as *akpon/akpwon*.

24. Argeliers León and María Teresa Linares conducted a recording session at the cabildo as part of a series of recordings documenting Cuban folkloric music. Released on LP in 1981, the recording remains the only commercially available recording of the cabildo's music.

25. Moisés Urrútia, pers. comm., Matanzas, September 17, 2000.

26. Among the drummers with whom I discussed this issue were Estéban Vega "Cha Chá," Pedro Tapanez González "Pello," Daniel Alfonso (1947–2010), as well as master song leader and drummer Francisco Zamora "Minini."

27. Intriguingly, Rogelio Martínez Furé's 1965 work contains mention of an additional cabildo song that mentions Añá, but unlike the Elegbá example, Martínez Furé lists this as an Añá song—a song solely for Añá and not related to another oricha. Though his article contains numerous musical transcriptions, the Añá song is not one of the examples rendered in notation. Martínez Furé lists only the song's text—"*Emó lemí, emo lemí, emo lemí, Añá güeregüé*"—and indicates that the song leader and chorus sing the same text in call-and-response form (118–19). This song appears to have disappeared from the cabildo repertoire. Neither of the Más brothers recognized these words, and in my attendance of cabildo tambor rituals, I have never heard this song performed.

28. I thank Amanda Villepastour for the insight regarding Yorùbá language usage.

29. See Wirtz (2005, 2007a) and Vincent (2006, 249–69) for discussion of Lucumí texts in Cuban Santería, including its intelligibility, exegesis, interpretation, translation, and comparisons to Yorùbá.

30. Interesting associations exist between Elegbá and Añá. Elegbá is associated with the Lucumí Añá batá drums, and in Matanzas (though not always in Havana) is said to be the owner of the smallest drum, the *okónkolo*. Also, both Elegbá and Añá have been described as messengers, empowering human prayers to reach divine spiritual beings.

31. While the double low-tone melody notes on the word "Añá" reinforce the case for viewing this song as pertaining to the drum oricha Añá, the uncertain process of determining past meanings or origins of contemporary Afro-Cuban sacred songs warrants comment. The Iyesá "Añá song" means what the Más brothers contend it means because that is its contemporary usage, and they may preserve its original intended meaning. However, while the retention of some West African songs and rhythms in Cuba over long spans of time and social change is often astonishingly stable and consistent (Vincent 2006, 194–271), it cannot be assumed that words critical to contemporary exegesis have not shifted to their current pronunciations from earlier ones. Such

shifts would occur through a combination of factors, including the loss of African languages as everyday vernacular and the Hispanicization of African words, particularly ones with consonant, vowel, and diphthong sounds that have no Spanish equivalent. In the "Añá song" example, the word "Añá" is crucial to the entire explication of the song. While it is unwise to dismiss the possibility of linguistic and musical change, the modern interpretation of the Lucumí text in this particular example seems well supported by the coherence of the Lucumí melody contour and the speech tones of transliteration of key words in modern Yorùbá.

32. It is important to note that not all oricha lineages in Cuba acknowledge the concept of re-creation. Some lineages established in the colonial era claim direct African origin. Oral traditions of certain Cuban house-temples or families contain stories of "swallowed stones": *fundamento* oricha objects that were brought to Cuba by slaves that took them aboard slave ships by swallowing them just prior to capture (Bascom 1950, 65; Brown 2003, 77–78; Felipe García Villamil, pers. comm., San Diego, 1996). Such histories subvert the disruption of the Middle Passage with a powerful narrative of purposeful agency and spiritual continuity with the African origins of Santería, lending greater historical authority and religious prestige to such lineages. Indeed, Matory's work in the Afro-Brazilian Candomblé religion (2005, 115–39) observes that Brazilian opinions regarding African "purity" and authenticity were often entangled in local efforts involving gaining and consolidating religious authority. Objects of African, rather than local Brazilian, creation were considered more efficacious (and therefore more valuable) because of their ostensibly "purer" origin, supposedly undiluted by the New World contaminants of miscegenation, syncretism, and forgetting.

33. Felipe García Villamil, pers. comm., San Diego, 1996.

34. Marcuzzi raises the possibility that Añabí's multiple talents may have been overstated, noting that Añabí's name is not recited in any of the detailed Ifá lineages he has encountered in his research (2005, 432). Vincent reports that in Nigeria, an individual with the combination of Àyàn lineage and *babaláwo* status is rare (2006, 130). Vincent (108–9, 132) also observes that the contemporary Àyàn tradition in Nigeria contains no association with the òrìṣà Ọsanyìn, a significant difference vis-à-vis the role of the osainista in Cuban Añá rites.

35. While these additional drum traditions bolster my argument, a note of caution is in order due to ambiguous terminology revolving around the words *fundamento* and Añá. Because all Añá objects are also considered fundamento objects—they are a specific category of the more generalized fundamento designation—the two terms are often employed interchangeably in certain contexts. While not a problem in everyday communication, this interchangeability has the potential to blur inquiry when introducing the notion of non-*batá* Añá. Accurate declarations depend upon the term usage, expectations, and knowledge of both the scholar and consultant. In my conversations with drumming authorities in the Cabildo Iyesá Moddu San Juan Bautista, I could directly inquire as to whether their drums were fundamento or Añá, a specificity I cannot presume in reviewing work by other scholars without firsthand quotes or declarations provided.

36. See Marcuzzi (2005, 361) for a discussion of how Sáenz apparently erroneously dubbed the tension drum of this cabildo "dundún" herself (Sáenz Coopat 1997, 357) and then applied this name to the entire drum ensemble.

37. Nearly all of the information concerning the Cabildo Santa Bárbara in Sancti Spíritus comes from the work of Cuban scholar Analeese Brizuela Quintanilla. I am grateful to Olavo Alén and the staff of Centro de Investigación y Desarrollo de la Música Cubana (CIDMUC) for allowing me the opportunity to review a copy of Brizuela Quintanilla's original 1988 thesis on the Cabildo Santa Bárbara.

38. Raimundo Valle Pina "Nene," pers. comm., Sancti Spíritus, December 1, 2006.

39. Analeese Brizuela Quintanilla, pers. comm., Sancti Spíritus, December 2, 2006.

References Cited

Balbuena Gutiérrez, Bárbara. 2003. *Las Celebraciones Rituales Festivas en la Regla de Ocha.* Havana: Centro de Investigación y Desarrollo de la Cultura Cubana Juan Marinello.

Bascom, William. 1950. "The Focus of Cuban Santería." In *Southwestern Journal of Anthropology* 6 (1): 64–68.

Brizuela Quintanilla, Analeese. 1988. *Presencia Iyesá en Sancti Spíritus. Cabildo Santa Bárbara.* Trabajo de diploma, Havana: Universidad de La Habana.

———. 1997. "Tambores Iyesá." In *Instrumentos de la Música Folclórico-Popular de Cuba,* Vol. II, ed. Victoria Eli Rodríguez et al. Havana: Editorial de Ciencias Sociales. 343–56.

Brown, David H. 2003. *Santería Enthroned: Art, Ritual, and Innovation in an Afro-Cuban Religion.* Chicago: University of Chicago Press.

Cornelius, Steven. 1995. "Personalizing Public Symbols through Music Ritual: Santería's Presentation to Aña." In *Latin American Music Review* 16 (1): 42–57.

Delgado, Kevin M. 2008. "Iyesá Complexes: Reexamining Perceptions of Tradition in Cuban Iyesá Music." In *Black Music Research Journal* 28 (2): 1–39.

Eli Rodríguez, Victoria. 1997. "Tambores Batá." In *Instrumentos de la Música Folclórico-Popular de Cuba,* Vol. 2, ed. Victoria Eli Rodríguez et al. Havana: Editorial de Ciencias Sociales. 319–43.

León, Argeliers. 1981. Liner notes to *Antología de la música afrocubana, v. 3: Música Iyesá.* Havana: Areito LD 3395. LP record.

Marcuzzi, Michael David. 2005. *A Historical Study of the Ascendant Role of Bàtá Drumming in Cuban Òrìṣà Worship.* PhD diss., York University, Toronto.

Martínez Furé, Rogelio. 1965. "Los Iyesás." In *Revista de la Biblioteca Nacional José Martí* 7 (3): 101–20.

———. 1979. *Diálogos Imaginarios.* Havana: Editorial Arte y Literatura.

Matory, J. Lorand. 2005. *Black Atlantic Religion: Tradition, Transnationalism, and Matriarchy in the Afro-Brazilian Candomblé.* Princeton, NJ: Princeton University Press.

Moliner Casteñeda, Israel. 2000. "Los Iyessa." Unpublished manuscript.

Ortíz, Fernando. 1954. *Los Instrumentos de la Música Afrocubana, vol. IV.* Havana: Editoriales Cárdenas y Cía.

Sáenz Coopat, Carmen María. 1997. "Tambores Dundún." In *Instrumentos de la Música Folclórico-Popular de Cuba,* Vol. 2, eds. Victoria Eli Rodríguez et al. Havana: Editorial de Ciencias Sociales. 357–62.

Vélez, María Teresa. 2000. *Drumming for the Gods the Life and Times of Felipe García Villamil, Santero, Palero, and Abakuá.* Philadelphia: Temple University Press.

Vincent [Villepastour], Amanda. 2006. *Bata Conversations: Guardianship and Entitlement Narratives about the Bata in Nigeria and Cuba.* PhD thesis, School of Oriental and African Studies, University of London.

Wirtz, Kristina. 2005. "'Where Obscurity Is a Virtue': The Mystique of Unintelligibility in Santería Ritual." In *Language and Communication* 25: 351–75.

———. 2007a. "How Diasporic Religious Communities Remember: Learning to Speak the 'Tongue of the Oricha' in Cuban Santería." In *American Ethnologist* 34 (1): 108–12.

———. 2007b. *Ritual, Discourse, and Community in Cuban Santería: Speaking a Sacred World.* Gainesville: University Press of Florida.

III

GENDERS

5

Anthropomorphizing Àyàn in Transatlantic Gender Narratives

Amanda Villepastour

. . . .

Aya aláàyàn ni mi o
Ọkọ mi ará Ògúnmọ̀nso
Àwọn ìmògún ará Ògúnmọ̀nso
Ọmọ aláàyàn ni
Ǹ máa bá aláàyàn rèlé
Èmi o bá aláàyàn rèlé
Owó ń só
Owó ń so lẹ́ẹ̀kunlé àwọn
Aya aláàyàn ni mi
I am the wife of the Àyàn drummer
My husband is from Ògúnmọ̀nso (Ògún's ancient town)
The Ògún families are from Ògúnmọ̀nso
Child of an Àyàn drummer
I will go home with the Àyàn drummer
I am the one who follows the drummer to his house
There is plenty of money
Money is buried at the back of the house
I am the wife of the Àyàn drummer.[1]

Songs for Àyàn reside in women's repertoires in Nigeria. Women and girls are not excluded from the broader matters of Àyàn in Yorùbáland, for they not only share the ritual responsibilities of this *òrìṣà* with men, they ensure the continuation of the Àyàn lineage through giving birth.[2] In traditional Yorùbá Àyàn compounds, whether Islamized or exclusively worshipping the òrìṣà, all youngsters—male and female—are given

Àyàn names through initiation or naming ceremonies. Such practices contrast sharply with the Añá brotherhood in Cuba, which is maintained through divination-ascribed initiation rather than lineage, and where the drumming cult is exclusively populated by males.

Based on fieldwork since 1999 in Nigeria, Cuba, and North America, this chapter approaches the complexities of humanizing and gendering the Yorùbá god of drumming in relation to the ritual and musical practices that gender and organize humans. In particular, the research highlights the general diversity of how the spirit of the drum is imagined and gendered, revealing major differences between Nigerian and Cuban practices in terms of gender imaginaries, hierarchies, prohibitions, and ritual practices. Just as the spirit becomes human, the human manifests the spirit through musical and ritual performance. Despite significant transatlantic coherence of the broader beliefs and practices surrounding the Yorùbá drumming spirit, gendering the orishas and their human devotees is historically and culturally informed, and therefore dynamic.

Theorizing Gender

Imagining an orisha as human—that habitual act of internal anthropomorphizing in Orisha Devotion—inevitably genders the spirit. Analyzing the process of human gendering, Judith Butler asserts that gender is a doing rather than a being and theorizes gender in terms of "performativity": a repeated, rather than singular act "which achieves its affects through its naturalization in the context of a body [. . .] The view that gender is performative sought to show that what we take to be an internal essence of gender is manufactured through a sustained set of acts, posited through the gendered stylization of the body" (Salih with Butler 2006, 94). Just as gender is humanly enacted through performance, Àyàn/Añá is anthropomorphized and gendered through culturally conditioned, repeated performative acts of drumming, initiation, and spirit possession.

Prior to the enactment of the drumming god through musical and ritual performance, the orisha is first revealed through utterance. Butler (2004, 102) reminds us that "the speech act is at once performed (and thus theatrical, presented to an audience, subject to interpretation) [. . .] speech itself is a bodily act with specific linguistic consequences." Since gender constructions in Yorùbá and Spanish are very different, so too are transatlantic social gender constructions. While Spanish and (to a lesser extent) English demand gender categories, Yorùbá has few gendered nouns, no articles, and no gendered pronouns or adjectives, partly accounting for the gender fluidity in the language, as heard in Àyángbékún's virtuosic Àyàn recitations (see Àyángbékún, this volume).[3] For him, Àyàn could be simultaneously man, woman, wife, husband, king, and queen. Fickle and unpredictable, Àyàn crossed social categories during Àyángbékún's oration, possibly confusing cultural outsiders accustomed to fixed identities in the storytelling realm. It is Yorùbá's lack of gender constraints that affords traditional poetic forms such entertaining creativity.

Lucumí, the Cuban vernacular that has now become a (rather unstable) lexicon of learned words and phrases, is only loosely related to modern Yorùbá. Assuming a closer relationship between Yorùbá and Lucumí, scholars, aficionados, and devotees frequently "translate" Lucumí utterances into European languages through highly imaginative processes. Trance language routinely involves improvised translation performance of an "interpreter" (Wirtz 2007), while those working with written texts (in a range of orthographies) back-translate Lucumí into modern Yorùbá and then into European languages using dictionaries. These speculative oral and written processes are frequently presented as fact, often producing fanciful or inscrutable glosses (see Mason 1992 for an example of etic dictionary excavation; Vincent 2006 and Wirtz 2007 for a critique of Lucumí-Yorùbá back-translation). Cubans often insert gendered, Spanish articles into Lucumí, such as *el añá* and *el iyá* (the mother [drum]), hence superimposing gender categories absent from or opposite to parallel Yorùbá words.[4] Gender is gleaned contextually in the Yorùbá language, yet the word Àyàn gives us no clues about this òrìsà, as does for example Iyemoja, a contraction of *iyá-yèyé-omo-eja* (great mother of fish). With the most likely etymology of Àyàn being the gender-neutral "one that chooses" deriving from *yàn* (choose), Àyàn's gender remains mysterious, flexible, and contested in different sites of Orisha Devotion, including within Yorùbáland.

Beyond the limitations of language analysis, cross-cultural gender theorizing opens one to bell hooks's charge that "Racism allows white women to construct feminist theory and praxis in such a way that it is far removed from anything resembling radical struggle" (1986, 132). Far from being a feminist intervention or call for social action, this chapter provides a comparative analysis of how gender is understood and performed in the utterances, ritual actions, and musical behaviors of Nigerian and Cuban priests in order to gain an understanding of how ritual insiders imagine their god. Butler's theory of performativity actually provides an ideal culture-neutral analytical framework for a performance-based tradition, while hooks (134) reminds us that "a behaviour pattern in one culture may be unacceptable in another [. . .] it may have different signification cross-culturally."

The God(dess) of the Drum

Àyàn's essence is embedded in sound, hence Àyàn is abstract and cannot be seen, touched, quantified, or qualified. Unlike most other òrìṣà that are depicted in human form with explicit, gendering physical features and symbols, Àyàn has not been traditionally represented in Yorùbá visual art, which is predominantly in the form of metal sculptures and plaques, pottery, and wood carvings.[5] In these media we frequently see depictions of òrìṣà such as Ṣàngó, Èṣù, Ògún, and Òṣun, whose genitals may even be on display.[6] The deities are each identified through their gender-specific coiffure, attire, and handheld items such as Ṣàngó's axe, Ògún's gun, and Òṣun's hair comb, each object further disambiguating their gender. Àyàn has no such visual representation. The drummer, whose lineage or initiation name will start with Àyàn, such as Àyándòkun (Àyàn is as mighty as the ocean) or Àyángbémiga (Àyàn lifts me high), is a living representation of an imagined deified drumming ancestor. It is the drummer, the one at Àyàn's service, who is depicted in Yorùbá artwork, while the òrìṣà him- or herself is believed to reside inside the drum vessel. Since Àyàn is heard and not seen, how does one imagine the gender of the drumming deity?

The Yorùbá god of drumming has many faces, communicated to us via vibrations in the air; the sound of music and uttered praise poetry and divination texts. Only when human bodies become involved (as in figurative art or humanizing text) is Àyàn envisaged as male or female, for it is the body that animates Àyàn's voice, the drum. Bodies also become crucially involved in the act of Àyàn initiation and possession, which both require human receptacles for the bodiless òrìṣà.

In Orisha Devotion systems, many different spiritual beings are placed in material form into sacred, sealed vessels. On both sides of the Atlantic, the most common receptacle for the god of drumming is, not surprisingly, a hermetically sealed drum. In Nigeria, the *dùndún* and *bàtá* are the most common vessels housing the god of drumming, while in Cuba, the *batá* is widely believed to be the only viable Añá vessel.[7] Oral narratives about the spiritual being that lives within the drum slip between male, female, husband, wife, child, friend, god, and goddess (see for example Àyángbékún, this volume).

The gendering of an òrìṣà is related to its imagined life on earth and is often connected to craft lineages derived from the òrìṣà, most of whom are believed to have been once human. The norms of how contemporary labor is gendered project the òrìṣà as male or female. So for example, Ìyámọòpó is the òrìṣà of pottery, and as pottery is a female craft among the Yorùbá, this deity is imagined as female (as inscribed by ìyá—"mother"). Likewise, the male-imagined Ọbàlùfọ̀n is the òrìṣà of cloth and weaving, which is traditionally a masculine craft in Yorùbáland. As an example of social framings recasting an òrìṣà's gender, Òrìṣà Oko is the Yorùbá deity of farming, so is widely regarded as being female in Yorùbáland, where women traditionally handled much of the agricultural labor. By contrast, Oricha Oko is unambiguously male in Cuba, as farm labor is predominantly undertaken by males. According to the same logic, drumming is regarded as a "man's business" in Yorùbáland and Cuba alike; Àyàn/Añá is known as the mythological drumming ancestor and first drum maker who once walked the earth around the fourteenth century. Since drummers are overwhelmingly male, it seems reasonable to cultural insiders to assert that Àyàn must also be male, but the fact that this òrìṣà is frequently gendered otherwise attests to a broader and more complex reasoning process among orisha priests.

Beyond the earthly consideration of gendered labor and social categories, in Nigeria, Àyàn's imagined gender appears to be largely shaped by the religious affiliation of the narrator. The overwhelming majority of Àyàn drummers are now Muslim, while Christian bàtá drummers are still quite rare. Within this Muslim hegemony, there are very few Àyàn drummers whose families never converted to the monotheistic religions. In the course of my research, all Muslim drummers I surveyed asserted that Àyàn is unequivocally male. Although these drummers may only be nominal Muslims, their primary relationship to Àyàn is through an allegiance to the mythological founder of their craft lineage.

While Muslim Àyàn drummers abstract Àyàn primarily as a male ancestor and drummer, two traditionalists (i.e., òrìṣà devotees) I have spoken with, Kawolẹyin Àyángbẹ́kún and Fúnmi Odúṣolú, have more esoteric views of Àyàn and apply more fluid conceptions of gender. Their imagining of a human Àyàn is less restricted by historical notions of a male ancestor drummer and is more informed by divination literature, which pairs Àyàn (often conjugally) with other òrìṣà such as Ṣàngó and Egúngún. Although Àyángbẹ́kún stated that Àyàn is female, he described both female and male dimensions (sub-identities) of this òrìṣà (see Àyángbẹ́kún, this volume). Similarly, Odúṣolú said that Àyàn is both male and female, so houses his òrìṣà in two large drums that enclose the gendered spirits separately. Òrìṣà priestess Susanne Wenger (1983, 203) also understood Àyàn to be female. Confirming this gender fluidity among traditionalists, Ifá divining priests (babaláwo) recite sacred literature that generates seemingly irreconcilable stories, personalities, genders, and kin relationships of the òrìṣà of drumming.

Religious identity has also shaped Añá's gender in Cuba, though not along the bifurcated terms found in Nigeria. In Cuba, it is very common

Table 5.1: Gender of Àyàn/Añá (primary sources).

Interviewee	Nigeria	Gender of Àyàn/Añá
Rábíù Àyándòkun	Èrìn-Òsun	male
Àlàbí Àyángbékún	Ògbómòsó	female
Adébáyò Àyánkósòó	Òyó	male
Jàre Àyánkósòó	Òyó	male
Àyánníyì Àyànlolá	Òyó	male
Àyánrìnólá Àyánkósòó	Òyó	male
Àyángbémiga Àyánwálé	Òyó	male
Àyánkójo Jimoh Àyánwolá	Lagos	male
Yemí Elébuìbon	Òsogbo	male
Fúnmi Odúsolú	Sàgámù	male female
Àyántúndé Sàlàkó	Sàgámù	male
Múráínà Oyèlámì	Ìrágbìjí	male
Alejandro Carvajal	Havana	male
Alfredo González	Havana	male
Regino Jiménez	Havana	male
Mario Jauregui	Havana	refused to answer
Fermín Nani	Havana	refused to answer
Armando Pedroso	Havana	male
Estéban Vega	Matanzas	male

for batá drummers to be concurrently members of the exclusively male Abakuá fraternity (said to derive from the east of Nigeria) and Freemason lodges. The Añá cult also has very strong ties with Ifá (whose priesthood was all-male in Cuba until 2000) and the Osáin cult, which stringently restricts female involvement.[8] On top of this plural involvement in all-male secret societies, most Añá priests are nominal Catholics. Given that this spiritual layering is normative among *oricha* devotees in Cuba, differing religious affiliations do not create contrasting genders of the god of drumming, as in Nigeria. No *omo* Añá (initiate) I interviewed in Cuba, several of whom are highly respected elders, said that Añá is female, yet Mason (1992) and Ramos (2000) authoritatively state that Añá is female without presenting supportive data. Almost all Nigerian drummers with whom I have spoken also deemed Àyàn male; Muslims imagine Àyàn as male while traditionalists cast this òrìsà as predominately female. Beyond my own fieldwork, most published sources also

Table 5.2: Gender of Àyàn/Añá (secondary sources).

Source	Informant	Gender of orisha
Abímbọ́lá (1997, 139–40)	Doesn't state	male
Bánkọ́lé et al. (1975, 49–50)	Doesn't state	female
Euba (1990, 90–93, 97, 103)	Jésúfù Àyánkúnlé, Ẹdẹ	male
Láoyè (1959, 10, 53–54, 56)	Doesn't state	male
Thieme (1969, 15, 17–19)	Àyánkósó Àǹkàmí, Ọ̀yọ́ Onílùúdé, Ìsúndùnrin	male
Wenger and Chesi (1983, 203)	Doesn't state	female
Hagedorn (pers. comm., Aug. 2006) (pers. comm., Oct. 2005)	Alberto Villarreal Francisco Aguabella	refused to answer male
Carlos Gómez (pers. comm., Aug. 2004)	Pedro Orta	male
Marcuzzi (2005, 180)	Maykel Villareal Ramiro Pedroso René Pedroso Antonio Urdaneta Osvaldo Urdaneta Yuleisy Ferrer Francisco Mora Pedro Alcántara	male male male male male male male male
Mason (1992, 6–7)	Doesn't state	female
Ortiz (1954, 305)	Doesn't state	male
Ramos (2000, 131–38)	Doesn't state	female
Vaughan and Aldama (2012, 28)	Carlos Aldama	male
Vélez (2000, 48–49; 117–18, 123–25)*	Felipe García Villamil	neutral

* Interestingly, García (as represented in Vélez 2000) does not regard Añá as an oricha but as a spirit. Consequently, throughout the text Añá is referred to as "it," denoting a genderless or ambiguously gendered spirit.

gender Àyàn and Añá as male (see Tables 5.1 and 5.2). As this data was collected from male drummers, babaláwo and drummer Ẹlébuìbọn suggests that the devotee's own gender may bias the view: "To my own knowledge and what Ifá says, Àyàn never appears as a female òrìṣà. There are some families, females might be the head of the worshippers. Maybe they think that the òrìṣà they worship is female. But the way it appears according Ifá, it is male" (pers. comm., Òṣogbo, April 2002).

In order to make sense of the varied descriptions of Àyàn and Añá, one might distinguish on one hand, contradictory material that primarily functions to elevate the òrìṣà and the narrator, and on the other, intersecting, repeated themes that serve to define Àyàn. Whether male or female, a native of Ọ̀yọ́ or Ìbàrìbá, on the warfront or standing naked between heaven and earth (see Àyángbékún, this volume), inside a bàtá or Iyesá vessel (see Delgado) or even a human cranium (see Introduction), Àyàn is never far from a drum.

Female Roles in Àyàn and Añá Traditions

Generally speaking, women in Nigeria are considered to be important members of drumming compounds as lineage provides the all-important relationship to Àyàn. Indeed, they may be the head of an Àyàn household, as stated above by Elébuìbon, so may be involved in the preparation and conduct of Àyàn ceremonies. By contrast, in Cuba Añá is considered to be an all-male business, and women are not involved in household ceremonies until they are needed in the kitchen to prepare and cook sacrificial animals during initiation rites.

Female drummers are not common in either transatlantic site, though for entirely different reasons. If the drums are consecrated with a hermetically sealed medicinal force, the issue of gender is theological. In both Nigeria and Cuba, the god of drumming is believed, on one hand, to have potential harmful physical and spiritual consequences for women who are in close proximity, and on the other, it is held that human bodies can have a negative effect on the medicinal force inside the drum. Both ideas limit the access of women to the god of drumming in Nigeria and Cuba, as menstrual blood is believed to be damaging to the spirit, and conversely, Àyàn/Añá is deemed to threaten women's fertility. But as I will explain below, the actual, physical boundaries are quite different in transatlantic sites.

In Cuba, *maricones* (a pejorative Spanish term for male homosexuals) are also forbidden from touching Añá drums. Maricones are considered to be feminized men, so taboos against female contact are collapsed into the exclusion of homosexuals, though without prohibitions justified by menstruation or any other biological discourse. In the absence of a biological argument, homosexuals are charged with the same disparaging social stereotypes as women. The late Estéban Vega "Cha Chá" succinctly stated, "In Abakuá we say that with a skirt, the secret gets out. Men wear trousers, so the secret stays in. Homosexuals are even worse [than women]." In the absence of anti-homosexual discourse in Yorùbá Òrìsà Tradition, the negative attitudes toward homosexuals within the Añá brotherhood may derive from the lateral influence of Abakuá, Ifá, and Osáin, each of which regard homosexuality as highly taboo.[9]

In Nigeria, there is little social motivation and no theological prohibition for a woman to pick up a consecrated drum, whereas in Cuba, there is increasing social aspiration for women to play bátá drums despite the strong theological deterrents against them playing. Hence, in some respects, one finds inverse situations in Nigeria and Cuba. There tend not to be unconsecrated bàtá and dùndún drums in Nigeria, and although women are not forbidden from touching or playing any drums, they exhibit little interest in drumming and gravitate to dancing and oral performance (where there is equal gender access). By contrast, in Cuba, *aberinkulá* (unconsecrated) and *fundamento* (consecrated) bátá drums are visually distinct, and while women are forbidden from touching and playing the fundamento, they have also been historically discouraged from playing aberinkulá. Attitudes toward Cuban women playing the unconsecrated drums have changed substantially since I began my research in the mid-1990s. While it was once shocking for Cubans to see women playing the drum, female bátá players have become increasingly visible and accepted in folkloric contexts (see Hagedorn 2001, and this volume). Indeed, some Añá drummers have now become involved with directing female folkloric groups in the secular realm.[10] Despite these transatlantic inversions in access and desire, changes in the demographic of drummers seems also to be heading in diametrically opposite directions in Nigeria and Cuba, whereby female drummers are becoming increasing rare in Yorùbáland and more common in Cuba.

Several of my Yorùbá research collaborators have told me that there were once more female drummers in Yorùbáland than there are now. Omíbíyìí (1975, 503) reported a case where a bàtá drummer did not have any sons and trained his daughters, although when I asked Omíbíyìí in August 1999 if she had ever seen or met any female bàtá players, she said no. Similar to Omíbíyìí's report, I have heard several firsthand accounts from people who have known or seen female bàtá players in various parts of Yorùbáland. Most of these stories reach into the remembered past, speak more recently of old women, or describe archaic and apparently superseded practices. Àyánwọlá[11] (pers. comm., London, October 2001) spoke of two very old women who played bàtá in his village in Ìdèrè, Ìbàràpá (Ìbàdàn), although I have not had the opportunity to meet these women and see them play. So rare is the sight of female bàtá players now that it is surprising or even shocking to the Yorùbá. Àyánwálé from Ọ̀yọ́ reported an event in the 1990s: "There is no religious reason [ẹ̀sìn] or culture [àṣà] prohibiting women to play bàtá. I remember one day in Awẹ́ [a town close to Ọ̀yọ́], one of my daughters accompanied me to a ceremony. She took the *omele* [accompanying] bàtá and started to beat it. The spectators were very surprised because they had never seen a girl playing bàtá before" (pers. comm., Ọ̀yọ́, August 5, 1999).

Such accounts of extreme surprise reach back into the nineteenth century. Collating journal accounts from the Church Missionary Society (CMS) archive, McKenzie (1997, 78) wrote:

If the gender of the drum could be female as well as male, the *gender of the drummer* was male in almost all references to drummers. There were, however, two exceptions to this rule, one at Ijaye in 1859, the other at Ondo in 1875. Gollmer, the pastor from Stuttgart, was in the market at Ijaye with his Yoruba Visitor when they "saw a woman beating a drum." It is known that women could "beat out a strange rhythm on *calabashes*" for instance at the Ṣàngó festival in Ẹdẹ (Beier 1959, 74). But beating a drum went further. According to the Yoruba Visitor, "such a thing was never seen before." He could find but one possible explanation, "they have had a new *òrìṣà* manifest to them." Only a new hierophany could justify this act of gender reversal.[12]

There was a second instance of women beating the drums, at Ondo in 1875. Charles Young, Yoruba catechist, reported that when, on the evening of April 13, "women turned out to worship the great goddess [not the god] Ọbàtálá [they] beat drums with great skill . . . All night the drums beat, with songs and dances around and over the goddess. In this case—it is now some years later and in another Yoruba kingdom—drumming does not seem to have been regarded as something unheard of for women meeting among themselves. (all italics and square brackets McKenzie's original)

McKenzie's closing sentence is pertinent here. It seems possible that instances of women drumming publicly were unusual events and were objects of surprise rather than taboo, as interpreted by Ramos (2000, 120).

Supporting the notion of a receding feminine tradition, Múráínà Oyèlámì described an antiquated Àyàn cult practice:

I have seen women folk who are originally from Àyàn families. But because they are female they had to go out and settle and make their own family. But then they have to inherit at least a drum from the parental home. So it's usually the *kúdi* that is given to them as a treasure from their birth place. In other places, you see women play only kúdi, never *omele akọ* and kúdi.[13] Some of the women are maybe as old as sixty. Listen to old bàtá from some parts of Dahomey [Benin]. It was only kúdi too. Only one kúdi. (Ìrágbìjí, pers. comm., September 3, 1999)

Àyándòkun reported a similar custom involving a miniature drum that was once ritually exchanged when an Àyàn girl married. In preparation for the nuptial ceremonies, the young woman's family would "feed" a miniature bàtá drum with chicken blood and strong alcohol (ọtí), then decorate it with cloth and drape the small, newly consecrated instrument onto the bride. Her family would take the bride to her future husband's compound, where she would ritually place one foot on the front doorstep. Her brothers would ask the groom's family for a live chicken and on receiving it, the bride's family would remove the small drum from her and pass the young woman over the threshold into her new home. A symbolic exchange was made between the woman and the chicken (used for feeding Àyàn) but the drums were not given to the bride's new family. Only the young woman, with her Àyàn lineage status and fertility potential, was formally presented to the new family across the threshold. Àyándòkun said that his father had one of these small drums but that he had not seen one for a long time, indicating that the above rite is a relic from the past (at least in Ẹ̀rìn-Ọ̀ṣun). Rábíù Àyándòkun also reported that he initiated a woman to Àyàn in his compound in the 1990s, saying that she "plays a little ìyáàlù [leading drum]."

There is, of course, a difference between a female drummer and a girl or woman who possesses a symbolic, miniature drum. But the intersection points of the above anecdotes are on one hand the medicine inside of the drum, and on the other the lineage status and fertility potential of girls and women who are born or marry into the Àyàn lineage. Not only are Yorùbá females permitted to hold a consecrated drum, they were once encouraged to do so.

One wonders if the Islamization of Àyàn compounds partly accounts for the increasing rarity of the female role as drummers in Àyàn lineages. Doubleday (1999) writes about previously female-dominated drumming traditions throughout the Arab region that were subsumed by a growing male hegemony among Muslim music professionals. She attributes this subordination of female musicians to the general social control of women introduced with Islam, the marginalization of women from communal worship, and the discouragement of all-female gatherings, which inhibited the possibilities of communal religious music making. Female professionals were usurped by men as "The legists' condemnation of music and restriction of women's freedom apparently went—and go—hand in hand" (113). The musical marginalization of Yorùbá Muslim females is only speculative, but the oppression of magical practices in which Àyàn women were clearly involved is rather more tangible. The Islamization of both ritual and musical Àyàn practices may largely account for the musical marginalization of women in Nigeria.

In conventional Añá households in Cuba, an aláña (caretaker of consecrated drums) would normally involve male members of the family in the various rituals that take place, including the hand washing ceremony (*lavada de manos* or *lavarse las manos*), the "swearing" (full initiation) of drummers to Añá (*juramento*), and the consecration of a new fundamento (*consagración* or *recibir* Añá/*el fundamento*). While male relatives are invited into the ritual space, women and girls in the house are relegated to the kitchen to prepare the sacrificial animals for oricha offerings and meals for those present. Generally, only a white curtain separates the females of the house (ritual outsiders) from the room where the ritual action takes place.

Aleida Nani is a woman born into a highly respected Añá household in Havana. Her late father, Fermín, was considered to be one of the foremost Añá ritual authorities and drummers in Havana, while her brother, Santiago, also held a very high status in the Añá fraternity before his untimely death in October 2008, and Aleida's son is now making his way up the Añá ranks. She started playing batá as a child and as a young adult was recruited by Amelia Pedroso as the *iyá* (leading drum) player in the all-female group Ibbu Okun.[14] Due to her interest in drumming, Aleida had an ambiguous status in Havana. While she was trusted to work in the family ceremonies, she described a fractious exchange with a young Añá drummer while she was working in her own family house during an Añá drum consecration (pers. comm., Havana, April 24, 2004): "The curtain was drawn where the consecrated drums were. I know that women are not allowed to look at the consecrated drums. He told me to be careful with the curtain. Then I responded, 'Eyes are indiscreet.' Then he answered back that women menstruate because it is God's punishment for curiosity. Then I replied back again, 'then that will always happen to me because I am very curious.'"[15] Aleida, a respected oricha priestess, was clearly indignant about the young aláña's accusation of indiscretion and non-observance. She felt that she was singled out from the other women working in the house by this drummer because, as a skilled and interested batá player, she poses an unusual threat in the ritual environment.[16] She may also be regarded with suspicion as an open lesbian, as gay women are regarded as subversive and perhaps not as responsive to the patriarchy (Villepastour 2012). The negative framing of menstruation as "punishment" in divination texts is indicative of a wider pejorative view of menstruation within the religious milieu. Furthermore, the ascription of curiosity as a negative female trait is but one of many socially constructed stereotypes that are projected onto women—and extended to homosexuals—to justify their exclusion from ritual spaces. In the course of my research, numerous female drummers have confided that they have received threats of punishment and even physical violence should they transgress the Añá boundary. It comes as no surprise that no one has heard of a woman playing a fundamento.

Initiation as a Gendered Act

In Nigeria there are many different kinds of Àyàn initiation, whereas in Cuba details of Añá initiation processes are variable but are generally cohesive in comparison to the diversity one finds in Nigerian Àyàn ceremonies. I have identified four primary elements that distinguish Nigerian Àyàn initiations from Cuban Añá initiations:

1) In Nigeria many Àyàn compounds consecrate the head of the Àyàn initiate in a ceremony known as the ìdósù.[17] While Cubans routinely do this ceremony for an array of orichas (as in Nigeria), they never do it for Añá, nor is there a cultural memory of Añá being "crowned."

2) In Nigeria Àyàn is a lineage that loosely overlaps with localized Àyàn cult practices. In Cuba the Añá cult is entered only through initiation, as opposed to lineage, although the two do cross over. If a son is born into a drumming family in Cuba, he is more is likely to be initiated to Añá than someone who is not.

3) In Nigeria, individuals are initiated to Àyàn for a range of reasons. Although involvement with drumming and membership in the Àyàn lineage are common motivations for initiation, people are also initiated to Àyàn for reasons of health and infertility. In Cuba, a propensity for drumming is the driving force behind Añá initiation. While it is common to be initiated into other oricha cults for health reasons, Añá is not an oricha devotees usually approach for health or fertility problems. Although there is a space for initiation into the Añá cult for non-drummers, primarily babalaos (Ifá divining priests), the incentive seems to revolve more around power management than healing. Babalaos initiated to Añá do not use their cult membership to heal people in the same way as in Nigeria, but rather, the initiation increases their spiritual and social power.

4) In Nigeria, an Àyàn initiate may be male or female, whereas in Cuba, Añá initiations are done exclusively for heterosexual males.

All four of the above distinctions have gender aspects. The ìdósù, which symbolically places the òrìsà into the human cranium, is undertaken for many orichas in Cuba and is believed to be a prerequisite for spirit possession. Those cults that do not involve the "crowning" and spirit possession on both sides of the Atlantic, such as Ifá and Ọsanyìn (Osáin in Cuba), exclude the initiation of women into the priesthood, whereas cults that involve the ìdóṣù and possession tend to be dominated by women and male homosexuals in Cuba. The hereditary aspect of Nigerian Àyàn facilitates the routine initiation of women, whereas the initiation-only entry into the Cuban Añá cult excludes them. In Nigeria, where Àyàn is believed to grant children to the barren, both male and female lineage outsiders seek Àyàn's child-giving powers. As one who has undertaken the ceremony, I asked senior aláña (Añá priest) Ángel Bolaños if he would "recognize" a woman with an Àyàn initiation from Nigeria.

> AV: If I were to come in here and say I am crowned [with Àyàn], what then?
> AB: Absolutely nothing. If you are crowned with Àyàn over there, I can't deny it, but here it doesn't hold any water because you are a woman. You can't touch the drums. Here women and Añá have nothing to do with each other.

With these differences in mind, let us now examine the "don'ts" of Àyàn practice.[18]

Taboo

The Yorùbá word èèwọ̀ and Lucumí word ewé are usually translated into English as "taboo," although in the context of Orisha Devotion, èèwọ̀/ewé should be viewed outside of the morally loaded implications of the English use of the word taboo, which marks something as breaching social custom or even implying something accursed. Èèwọ̀ (singular or plural) is sacrosanct and refers to ritual or religious contexts rather than social ones. An èèwọ̀ is something that may not be approached and that is prohibited, so has a morally neutral interpretation.

The taboo that is most relevant to the current transatlantic gender discussion is that of the prohibition against direct female contact with the god of drumming. The Cuban Añá ewé both limits female contact with the consecrated bátá and prohibits women from playing the drum. Male and female oricha initiates within the Cuban system routinely "salute" the Añá inside the bátá by crossing their arms across the chest and leaning forward to touch their forehead to the drums. Women are forbidden from touching the drums at any other time and are expected to keep their distance in ceremonial settings (see Schweitzer, this volume). Yet in my travels around òrìṣà and drumming communities in Nigeria I have yet to encounter restrictions from women touching or playing Àyàn drums. While nobody discouraged me from picking up a drum, and nobody I interviewed said that it is taboo for women to play the bàtá or other Àyàn drums, several of my research participants were more specific about the èèwò associated with Àyàn. I was told that while a woman can play Àyàn drums, it is prohibited for a menstruating woman to look inside of, or put her hand into an open Àyàn drum should the skin be damaged or removed. The way it was explained by Àyándòkun is as follows:

> Àyándòkun: You have had Àyàn initiation, but we don't let women look inside of the wood [. . .] This is the *awo* [restricted esoteric knowledge][. . .] You can hold it, you can play, but to look inside the wood, it is dangerous.
> AV: What about if the woman is menstruating, can she play the drum or pick the drum up? Is that O.K.?
> Àyándòkun: It's O.K, but to just want to look inside to look at what is happening, only this is taboo. Even for the man who doesn't have Àyàn initiation, it is not possible to look inside. The Cuba people think that the woman can't touch the drum. It's not like that. You can touch it but don't look [. . .] (pers. comm., Èrìn-Òsun, April 2002)

When I asked another drummer in a different region, Àyángbékún, if there are taboos around women and menstruation, he responded similarly:

> "Àyángbékún: It is not good for her to reach there, she especially must not use a hand. She must not touch there nor here. The reason why a menstruating woman should not use her hand to touch Àyàn is that she may not be able to give birth anymore, even if she has already delivered" (pers. comm., Ògbómòsó, April 2002).

Àyándòkun and Àyángbékún agree that a menstruating woman can destroy the Àyàn. These views are remarkably resonant with Cuban discourse, which also says that menstrual blood can harm Añá, and conversely, Añá can harm the woman. In environments where it is a grave tragedy to be childless and motherhood elevates one's status, threatening infertility appears to serve as an effective form of social control of women.[19]

The Nigerian and Cuban taboos are in some ways parallel. Since the Nigerian prohibition revolves around neither looking at the consecrated packet that is attached to the inner shell of the drum, nor touching it with the hands, the Cuban salute, in which the forehead is placed on the drum vessel with the arms crossed in front of the chest, resonates with the homeland taboo in that it both diverts the gaze and makes the hands unavailable. However, where the taboos are profoundly different is in their perceived boundary. The Yorùbá drum vessel is believed to protect the Àyàn. Hence, even a menstruating woman can hold and play an Àyàn drum. Cubans appear to believe that the vessel is as vulnerable as the consecrated packet (known as *la carga, el secreto, el añá,* or *afowobo* in Cuba) inside the drum. Therefore, the notion of a woman handling and playing the fundamento is inconceivable to all but radical, African revisionist thinkers.

Spirit Possession

Another important difference between transatlantic Àyàn and Añá practices is that in Nigeria, Àyàn can possess both initiates and cult outsiders, whereas Añá possession is unheard of in Cuba. To reiterate, while discourse in the diaspora tends to emphasize the role of installing the oricha in the head by way of the *asiento* ("seating") ceremony as a prerequisite for possession, it is not necessarily so in Nigeria. Every Àyàn drummer I asked said that Àyàn can and does possess and warned that such possessions can be intense, violent, or even life threatening. Àyándòkun described his one and only experience of Àyàn possession while still a teenager:

> I remember, this was maybe thirty years ago. I was fifteen to sixteen, and we went to Àró. Àró is about three kilometers to Èrìn-Òṣun. A *bàbá* there was a friend of my father and we ate and we drank and we did whatever, and only Àyàn people were there. When the Àyàn people die, we have to make a funeral ceremony. If I say the rhythm with my mouth now, I know my head will be coming off. It's a special rhythm. When somebody starts this drumming, everybody goes crazy. If you are a real Àyàn, if you hear this rhythm, everybody in the houses around the Àyàn funeral ceremony closes their doors. You can see everybody running into the house. They can play the rhythm on dùndún and bàtá, but not any drum. That day, when we did this ceremony I held the drum and I got on top of the roof. I don't know how I got there, maybe from the window. The people said "Aaaah!" When this thing happens, it's a problem for anybody who does [an Àyàn] funeral ceremony because I took the roof off. Somebody had to go to get *adìẹ* [chicken] and they threw the leg to me, and then I sucked the blood from the leg and then I started to calm down. They went to get a ladder to put water, plenty, not small, maybe ten buckets on my head. And after that I couldn't come down by

myself. They carried me. I just cried. I dreamt. I saw some old people making a ceremony like we were doing. But these people had died a long time ago. These people just smiled. I saw my [late] father in the dream. They took me to the inside of the house. Two people were sitting with me. There was a woman who just banged her head into the wall, bam! She kept the door shut, then bam! Blood came out from her head. We had to ask the drum to stop before they got the chicken. But the drummer played mad too. No one could stop him. People just held the drummer's hand and somebody took the stick off him and they took the drum from him, because he started to go mad too. Now, even if there is this thing [Àyàn funeral] happening, I don't go there. I have told everybody if this thing is happening and they ask me, I say, how much money will I contribute for this? But I don't want to go. We did the last [Àyàn funeral ceremony] ten years, maybe eight years ago, when somebody died. This is a totally dangerous rhythm.

As other research collaborators have told me and Àyándòkun's story illustrates, women, children, initiates, and non-initiates in the proximity may be possessed by Àyàn during a drummer's burial rite. Additionally, Àyàn drummers may also be possessed while playing, as in the above anecdote.[20]

There is no analogous space for Añá to possess people in Cuba. Aside from Añá's apparent inability to mount in the transatlantic tradition, batá drummers must not have a predisposition for spirit possession. Apart from the requirement that drummers remain in control, possession in Cuba is considered to be feminine and therefore within the domain of women and male homosexuals. Getting possessed, or "being mounted," is analogous to being mounted and penetrated in sexual intercourse. Drumming is considered to be a masculine occupation, and in order to be initiated, somebody in the Añá cult must vouch for the "masculinity"— the heterosexuality—of the initiate.

Spirit possession is the ultimate anthropomorphizing act. Àyàn becomes human by temporarily *being* human. Yet while both male and female bodies may be possessed by Àyàn, Añá possesses neither, perhaps rendering the Cuban manifestation less human and less accessible to men *and* women than Àyàn.

Conclusion

There are only a handful of deities whose genders are contested across orisha worship sites, and relative to other òrìṣà, Àyàn's gender is uncertain,

slippery, and elusive. Most orishas have very explicit genders related
to human activity: Yemọja and Ọ̀ṣun are female as women give birth,
Ògún is male as blacksmiths are men, Ìyámọòpó is female as women
are potters, while Ọbàlùfọ̀n is male as men weave. Although men drum
and make drums, it does not necessarily follow that Àyàn has to be male.
Àyàn/Añá is abstract and cannot be seen, touched, quantified, or qualified. Unlike babies, iron, pots, and cloth, Àyàn's product is abstract and
transitory—drums are the tool, not the product. Men drum, but Àyàn's
voice is vibrating skins, bells, and vessels that push around invisible air.
Sound is experienced in one moment and gone or recreated in the next.
Àyàn has an esoteric power that transcends that of other orishas, for it
is Àyàn's voice that calls all of the orishas into the bodies of humans. It
is especially difficult to gender this invisible, esoteric force, yet this orisha's gender is ultimately unimportant when endeavoring to understand
the gendered behaviors of the people around him/her/it.

As well as making drums, men make gods (Barber 1981). The orisha
of drumming is realized through repeated performative actions (Butler
1990): utterances, gestures, musicking, and ritual action. While these habitual and naturalized transatlantic performances bear some structural
and philosophical parallels, both the spirit's gendering and the construction of gender in the living clustered around this orisha vary significantly.
In Nigeria, girls and women share in Àyàn's creation and maintenance
as named lineage members, singers, and potential spirit mediums.
Moreover, if men make gods, then women make drummers, for Àyàn
women are responsible for the reproduction of Àyàn through childbirth
as wives and mothers of the lineage, as the opening song of this chapter
declaims. The male drummer *becomes* Àyàn by *performing* Àyàn. In
Cuba, the reproduction of Añá has been reduced to a metaphor that is
played out by an exclusively heterosexual male group that protects their
sacred space and ritual secrets with ferocity. Analogies of birthing per-
vade Añá ritual action and discourse in a manner I have not encountered
among the Yorùbá; Cuban drums are "born" and named through divination behind closed doors, as the consecrated packet referred to as el añá,
el secreto, or afowobo is ritually inserted into the drum away from the
female or homosexual gaze.

Might *el secreto* be the male mimicking of women's magical power
to create life? As African patriarchies lost their grip on female fertility
and reproduction within the social constraints of slavery in Cuba, could
it be that former social and biological control was dramatized in secret
rituals? Is a sense of control, male power, and self-esteem regained
through repeated performances that employ symbolic materials and the
language of human reproduction? Etymological speculation about the

mysterious word "afowobo"—a word not known in Nigeria among Àyàn priests—may provide some clues to el secreto, the añá. Its Yorùbá etymology may be *a fi owó bọ* (we worship money), alluding to the Àyàn/ Añá drummer's pursuit of cash, as indicated by the term *alágbe* (beggar) employed for drummers, as well as the claim that the sealed medicine in the drum attracts money. An alternative possibility, *a fi awọ bò* (we use leather to cover), may pertain to the leather pouch containing Añá's magical substances. Yet another feasible etymology, *àfi ọwọọ́ bò* (the one who uses their hand to cover), could refer to the very act of concealing and the highly secretive nature of Añá's reproduction in Cuba. When considering the metaphor of birthing in the ritual action and discourse of Añá, the following etymology captures the central power of conception and birth in Yorùbá Òrìṣà Tradition: *a fi ọwọ́ bọ òbò* (the one who puts the hand to the vagina) is both evocative and provocative.[21]

Notes

1. This song was performed by Ṣákìrat Àyándòkun, a wife of Rábíù Àyándòkun, in July 2011.

2. My thanks go to Debbie Klein, Jennifer Post, Katherine Hagedorn, and to the anonymous readers for their astute criticism of earlier versions of this chapter.

3. Oyěwùmí (1997) argued that the absence of gender in Yorùbá language provides proof that social gender categories among the Yorùbá are postcolonial constructs. See Peel (2002) and Matory (2008) for vigorous rebuttals to her proposition.

4. In reference to the male gendering of the "mother" drum, Ortíz (1954, 305) stated, "*Consciente del carácter varonil de ese ilú mayor, a pesar de ser llamado iyá o 'madre', el criollo siempre al citarlo en castellano dice 'el iyá', con el articulo masculino, y no 'la iyá' como correspondería por buena sintaxis si dicho instrumento fuese hembra*" (Conscious of the male character of this main *ilú* [drum], in spite of being called *iyá* or "mother," in citing it in Castilian, the Creole always says "el *iyá*" with a masculine article, and not "la *iyá*," as would correspond with good syntax if it was said that the instrument is female). The Lucumí word *iyá* derives from Yorùbá *ìyá* (mother). Not surprisingly, the Yorùbá unanimously regard the *ìyá ìlù* (mother drum) to be female.

5. See Willet (1977) for an archaeological approach to the representation of Yorùbá musicians and musical instruments in metal and pottery artefacts. Yorùbá musicians appear in wood sculptures in the form of doors, veranda posts, masks and headdresses, and religious accoutrements such as sacred vessels and divination objects. Consecrated items may include freestanding shrine sculptures.

6. Gender may also be ambiguated by including both male and female genitals in figurative art, as seen in, for example, Èṣù representations.

7. See Delgado, this volume, who presents a lesser-known practice of placing Añá in *iyesá* drums, which is a marginal tradition in Matanzas, Cuba.

8. Women have been initiated as *iyánífá* (the female equivalents of babaláwo) in Nigeria since the 1980s, though there is no archival evidence that they were initiated in the nineteenth century despite claims of the antiquity of female initiations. Acting on a revisionist philosophy, in 2000 Havana babalao Victor Betancourt "Omolófaoró" initiated two Cuban women, Nydia Alina de

León "Ifábiola" (his wife) and María Acuesta Conde "Ifáchina." Dozens of Cuban iyanifá initiations have since taken place led by Betancourt and now other babalaos, but the new practice remains controversial in the Ifá mainstream in Cuba.

9. In Boston, December 1999, I witnessed a conversation between a Cuban-American babaláwo (initiated in Nigeria) with religious leader 'Wándé Abímbọlá and his son Kọlá (both babaláwo) regarding the Cuban taboo against homosexuality in Ifá. The Nigerians both insisted that sexuality is a personal issue that is irrelevant to Ifá initiation, and one should not pry into the personal life or sexuality of an initiate.

10. One such example is Obini Aberikulá in Matanzas, a group Daniel Alfonso (1946–2010) is credited for forming and directing. Local drummer Luis Bran said that the group leader, Regla Mesa, the daughter of eminent drummer Enrique Mesa, is very skilled and knowledgeable and actually did most of the tuition (pers. comm., Matanzas, August 2012).

11. Àyánwọlá plays bàtá with the popular music star Lágbájá.

12. McKenzie was quoting from 066, 95, J. 9/2/59.

13. The *kúdi* is a small accompanying drum played with one or two rawhide beaters called *bílálà*, while the *omele akọ* is an accompanying drum comprising two small drums attached together.

14. Despite numerous counterclaims, Pedroso was probably the first Cuban woman to play the bàtá. See Villepastour (2012) for Pedroso's remarkable story.

15. The young drummer's reference to "God's punishment" for curiosity derives from the Cuban Ifá divination verse Ogunda Oche collected from an unpublished notebook (*libreta*): "*Había un cazador que le cazaba las palomas a Olofin para que éste se alimentará, después Olofin le regalaba la carne para que se la llevara a su casa, pero a la mujer del cazador le extrañaba que no tuvieran sangre, y le preguntaba, pero su marido nunca le decía, un dia es tanta su curiosidad, que decide seguirle y coge y le echa ceniza dentro del saco y le abre varios agujeros, para que le fuera indicando por donde iba, al llegar al monte se esconde, pero le sale al paso Olofin y le dice que saliera de allí y que por curiosa desde ese momento tendría su menstruación todos los meses.*" (There was a hunter who hunted pigeons for Olofin [God] so he could feed himself, then Olofin gave the meat to the hunter so he could take it home with him. But to the hunter's wife it seemed strange that the pigeons did not have blood, and she asked her husband, but he never explained. One day her curiosity is so intense that she decides to follow him and she goes and puts ashes into his bag and she opens various holes in it, so that it might indicate where he was going. Arriving in the forest she hides, but Olofin comes walking up and tells her to come out and that because of her curiosity, from that moment forward, she would have her menstruation every month.) Translation Michael Attwood Mason.

16. See the following chapter by Hagedorn, which points out that Afro-Cuban women are the group most prohibited from accessing bàtá drums.

17. This is the "crowning" ceremony where one receives their tutelary òrìṣà. The head is shaved, painted, washed with herbal medicine, and treated to "seat" the òrìṣà inside the initiate's head.

18. Nigerian babaláwo and writer Yẹmí Ẹlẹ́buìbọn translates *èèwọ̀* as "don'ts" (pers. comm., Òṣogbo, April 2002).

19. I have never heard that men may become infertile as a consequence of religious transgressions.

20. In Nigeria drummers may be possessed by other òrìṣà while playing. I witnessed a drummer being possessed by Èṣù while playing in Ìjẹbu in 2003.

21. I am grateful to linguists Akin Oyètádé and Clement Odòjé who discussed these possible etymologies with me. The full etymologies are as follows: 1) *a fi owó bọ̀* (we worship money): *a*

(we) *fi* (put) *owó* (money) *bọ̀* (to worship); 2) *a fi awọ bò* (we use leather to cover): *a* (we) *fi* (use) *awọ* (leather) *bò* (to cover); 3) *a fi ọwọ́ bò* (the one who uses their hand to cover): *a* (we) *fi* (use) *ọwọ́* (hand) *bò* (to cover); and 4) *a* (we/the one that) *fi* (put) *ọwọ́* (the hand) *òbò* (vagina). *A* can also mean "the one that" in this grammatical construction, as in *alubàtá* (bàtá player): *a* (the one that) *lù* (beats) bàtá.

References Cited

Abímbọ́lá, 'Wándé. 1997. *Ifá Will Mend our Broken World: Thoughts on Yorùbá Religion and Culture in Africa and the Diaspora.* Massachusetts: Aim Books.

Bánkọ́lé, Ayo, Judith Bush, and Sadek H. Samaan. 1975. "The Yorùbá Master Drummer." In *African Arts* 8 (2): 48–56, 77–78.

Barber, Karin. 1981. "How Man Makes God in West Africa: Yoruba Attitudes Toward the 'Orisa.'" In *Africa* 513: 724–45.

Beier, Ulli. 1959. *A Year of Sacred Festivals in One Yorùbá Town,* 3rd ed. Lagos: Nigeria Magazine Publications.

Butler, Judith. 1990. *Gender Trouble: Feminism and the Subversion of Identity.* New York: Routledge.

———. 2004. *Undoing Gender.* New York: Routledge.

Doubleday, Veronica. 1999. "The Frame Drum in the Middle East: Women, Musical Instruments and Power." In *Ethnomusicology* 43 (1): 101–34.

Euba, Akin. 1990. *Yorùbá Drumming: The Dùndún Tradition.* Bayreuth: Bayreuth African Studies.

Hagedorn, Katherine. 2001. *Divine Utterances: The Performance of Afro-Cuban Santería.* Washington: Smithsonian Institution Press.

hooks, bell. 1986. "Sisterhood: Political Solidarity between Women." In *Feminist Review* 23: 125–38.

Láoyè I, Tìmì of Ẹdẹ. 1959. "Yorùbá Drums." In *Odu* 7: 5–14.

Marcuzzi, Michael David. 2005. *A Historical Study of the Ascendant Role of Bàtá Drumming in Cuban Òrìṣà Worship.* PhD diss., York University, Toronto.

Mason, John. 1992. *Orin Òrìṣà: Songs for Selected Heads.* New York: Yorùbá Theological Archministry.

Matory, J. Lorand. 2008. "Is There Gender in Yorùbá Culture?" In *Òrìṣà Devotion as World Religion: The Globalization of Yorùbá Religious Culture.* Madison: University of Wisconsin Press. 513–58.

McKenzie, Peter. 1997. *Hail Orisha! A Phenomenology of a West African Religion in the Mid-nineteenth Century.* Leiden, New York, and Köln: Brill.

Omíbíyìí, Mosúnmọ́lá. 1978. "The Training of Yorùbá Traditional Musicians." In *Yorùbá Oral Tradition: Poetry in Music, Dance and Drama,* ed. 'Wándé Abímbọ́lá. Department of African Languages and Literatures, University of Ilé-Ifẹ̀ African Languages and Literatures Series no. 1. 489–515.

Ortíz, Fernando. 1954. *Los Instrumentos de la Música Afrocubana, vol. IV.* Havana: Editoriales Cárdenas y Cía.

Oyěwùmí, Oyèrónkẹ́. 1997. *The Invention of Women: Making an African Sense of Western Gender Discourses.* London and Minneapolis: University of Minnesota Press.

Peel, J. D. Y. 2002. "Yorùbá Religion and Gender." In *Journal of Religion in Africa* 32, Fasc. 2: 136–66.

Ramos, Miguel. 2000. *The Empire Beats On: Oyo, Batá Drums and Hegemony in Nineteenth-Century Cuba*. MA thesis, Florida International University.

Salih, Sarah, ed., with Judith Butler. 2006. *The Judith Butler Reader*. Massachusetts: Blackwell.

Thieme, Darius L. 1969. *A Descriptive Catalogue of Yorùbá Musical Instruments*. PhD diss., Catholic University of America, Washington, DC.

Vaughan, Umi, and Carlos Aldama. 2012. *Carlos Aldama's Life in Batá: Cuba, Diaspora, and the Drum*. Bloomington: Indiana University Press.

Vélez, María Teresa. 1996. *The Trade of an Afro-Cuban Religious Drummer: Felipe García Villamil*. PhD diss., Wesleyan University, Connecticut.

———. 2000. *Drumming for the Gods: The Life and Times of Felipe García Villamil, Santero, Palero and Abakuá*. Philadelphia: Temple University Press.

Villepastour, Amanda. 2013. "Amelia Pedroso: A Cuban Priestess Leads from the Inside." In *Women Singers in Global Contexts: Music, Biography, Identity*, ed. Ruth Hellier. Urbana: University of Illinois Press. 54–72.

Vincent [Villepastour], Amanda. 2006. *Bata Conversations: Guardianship and Entitlement Narratives about the Bata in Nigeria and Cuba*. PhD thesis, School of Oriental and African Studies, University of London.

Wenger, Susan, and Gert Chesi. 1983. *A Life with the Gods in their Yorùbá Homeland*. Wörgl, Austria: Perlinger Verlag.

Willet, Frank 1977. "A Contribution to the History of Musical Instruments Among the Yorùbá." In *Essays for a Humanist: An Offering to Klaus Wachsmann*. Spring Valley, NY: Town House Press. 350–93.

Wirtz, Kristina. 2007. *Ritual, Discourse, and Community in Cuban Santería: Speaking a Sacred World*. Gainesville: University Press of Florida.

6

Ochún and Añá: Engendering Spiritual Power and Empowering Gendered Spirits

Katherine J. Hagedorn

• •

During the past two decades that I have been studying Afro-Cuban religious music, I have been struck by the "provocative symmetries" (Wolf 1984) regarding gender roles in Afro-Cuban religious performance, particularly in the case of *batá* drumming within Regla de Ocha, also known as Santería.[1] The energy with which male drummers protest that women may not, should not, cannot play batá drums seems directly proportional to the energy women drummers put into to performing, and indeed mastering, this performance tradition. Since the early nineteenth century, Afro-Cuban batá drumming for religious ceremonies has been a male domain, with few female religious drummers attempting to enter the fray until the last two decades of the twentieth century. The male discourse of prohibitions against women playing consecrated batá drums has focused mainly on taboos about reproduction and menstruation (Pryor 1999; Sayre 2000; Hagedorn 2001; Marcuzzi 2005a; Vincent 2006; Villepastour 2010). In brief, women are not permitted to play the drums because their menstrual blood is said to offend the *orichas*, disempower the animating force of the drums (the dynamic energy called Añá in Cuba and Àyàn in Nigeria), or cause Añá to make them barren.[2] Añá, however, seems to have many descriptions—it is understood by some to be a road[3] of Changó (one of the most masculinized of the orichas in the pantheon), by others to be a road of Ochún (one of the most feminized of the orichas), and by still others as not an oricha at all, but rather a specialized form of *aché* (divine dynamic energy that animates everything in the world). A growing number of women who are learning to play the batá drums have begun to question the religious tradition within Ocha that prohibits women from playing consecrated batá drums in a religious context, particularly given the confusing rationale that surrounds the prohibition.

In this focused essay, I consider three central issues: 1) What is the significance of attributing gender to orichas, especially to Añá? 2) In a performance tradition that privileges "maleness," how do we interpret "femaleness"? 3) How does the gendering of spiritual attributes affect batá performance practice within the Cuban practice of Ocha and in secular contexts? I will draw on ethnographic research conducted by Fernando Ortíz, Lydia Cabrera, Natalia Bolívar Aróstegui, Michael Marcuzzi, Amanda Vincent [Villepastour], María Teresa Vélez, and others, as well my own field research with *olú batá* Alberto Villarreal (based in Havana) and the late olú batá Francisco Aguabella (based in Los Angeles for the last two decades of his life, originally from Matanzas), and other batá drummers with whom I have worked during my more than twenty years of fieldwork.[4]

Tambor, Batá, and Añá

The *tambor* (literally "drum," understood here as "drumming ceremony") is a primary performance practice within Regla de Ocha. It is a direct and communal way to communicate with the orichas—either in joyful appreciation for recent good fortune, as a means to mark the initiation of an *iyawó* (new priest or priestess of Ocha), as an offering and a request for help, or as a way to avoid tragedy in the future. In all of these cases, the tambor is an *ebó*, or a sacrifice. The drumming, singing, and dancing featured in a tambor, when successful, summon the orichas to earth, so that these deities may offer counsel. Rebukes, jokes, and other forms of ribald behavior are also likely to be manifested by orichas during tambores, depending on which oricha appears. If Eleguá, oricha of the crossroads, makes an appearance during a tambor, for example, one might expect mischief and disruption, as Eleguá is a trickster.

Possession performance—when an oricha possesses the body of a human adherent—is one of the most powerful phenomena in the practice of Regla de Ocha. This divine possession typically occurs within a musical context; indeed, many would argue that the music is the primary catalyst that enables divine possession to take place. The main instruments in this drumming ceremony are batá drums, and it is a combination of drumming and singing and dancing—as well as the receptiveness of the congregant—that entices an oricha to possess the body of a congregant. According to many practitioners of this religion, the batá drums must be

fundamento (consecrated) for them to have the spiritual power necessary to call the orichas to earth, and this consecrating power is known
in Cuba as Añá. Based on my fieldwork, many Cuban practitioners of
Regla de Ocha believe that batá drums without this sacred medicinal
aché (spiritual life force) are less powerful than consecrated batá drums,
and further, that such *aberikulá* (unconsecrated) drums should never be
used for ceremonial purposes because the use of unconsecrated objects
would insult both the orichas and the congregants.[5]

According to the male discourse surrounding this performance practice, women are not permitted to play these consecrated drums, nor are
gay or bisexual men. Although in theory anyone can play unconsecrated
(aberikulá) drums,[6] only heterosexual male drummers who have had
their hands ritually washed or are sworn to Añá in special ceremonies are
allowed to play consecrated batá drums.[7] This proscribed performance
realm creates an overdetermined male heterosexual imperative, which
has led practitioners and musicians to dismiss or ignore the feminine associations of these drums.[8]

Añá provides a compelling subject for analysis not only because of its
putative power, but also because of the various ways in which religious
practitioners have represented this power. At least since the early part of
the twentieth century and likely since the mid-nineteenth century, Cuba's
most famous batá drummers have characterized Añá as an oricha. The
best known documentation of Añá as an oricha and as an essential aspect
of sacred performance in Cuban Regla de Ocha was recorded by Cuban
ethnographer Fernando Ortíz in his five-volume work, *Los Instrumentos
de la Música Afrocubana* (1952–55), particularly in Volume 4 (1954).[9]
Ortíz's main informants for his research on Afro-Cuban batá drums were
olúbatá Pablo Roche (Okilákpa or "Brazo Fuerte"—Strong Arm), Raul
Díaz (Omó-Ológun or "Hijo del Amo de la Magia"—Son of He Who
Guards the Magic), and Trinidad Torregrosa (E Meta Lókan or "Tres en
Uno"—Three in One) (Ortíz 1954, 287–88, 310). Each of these drummers considered Añá to be an oricha, according to Ortíz (1954, 283), although it is also clear from Ortíz's account that Añá is treated differently
from the other orichas, as is discussed later in this essay.

At least one well-known living Cuban-American olú batá, Felipe
García Villamil, regards Añá not as an oricha but rather as a form of me-
dicinally potent aché, providing the dynamic spiritual life force essential to a successful tambor (see Vélez 2000, 48). García Villamil considers Añá to be a dynamic spiritual force, but not necessarily an oricha.
García Villamil appears to be alone in this understanding of Añá; all of
the other batá drummers on record not only consider Añá to be an oricha, but also describe the deity as having gendered attributes. Fernando

Ortíz's informants told him that Añá was a manifestation of Changó, the male oricha who in his human form was King of the Nigerian dynasty of Oyó, and whose ancestral form became a deity associated with thunder, lightning, virility, and the batá drums (see Ortíz 1954, 284, 305). Specifically, according to these drummers, Añá is a road of Changó known as Obbaña, translated by Ortíz in Volume 4 as "king of the drums." More recent Cuban ethnographers, such as Lydia Cabrera (1980, 70; 1986, 224, 280) and Natalia Bolívar Aróstegui (1994, 179), include references to both Obbañá and Ochún Añá as feminine orichas, which would indicate that the term Añá elicits associations with both male and female deities.

Gendering Añá: Dueling Divinities

In Volume 4 of his five-volume opus describing the instruments of Afro-Cuban music, Ortíz writes about "the secret" of Añá as the "fetish," the "magic" that enlivens and empowers the batá drums to speak and that protects the drummers and their congregants against the "evil eye of the enemy" (Ortíz 1954, 288). García Villamil in Vélez (2000, 120–27), Marcuzzi (2005, 429–472), and Ortíz (1954, *passim*) mention particular plant seeds, herbs, minerals, blood, shells, and other animal substances, as well as many other secret ingredients that go into the preparation of Añá before it is housed in the soon-to-be sacred batá drums. In Regla de Ocha, orichas are embodied in stones, and are activated by herbs and other organic and mineral substances, so in this context, Añá does not appear to be substantially different from other orichas (such as Osáin, for example) in its materiality.[10] Thus, it would seem reasonable to categorize Añá with the other orichas in Regla de Ocha.

One thing that does distinguish Añá from other orichas is that not all people who become initiated into Ocha are sworn to Añá. Only those drummers who are sworn to the drum in a separate initiation ceremony and who have been selected as the caretakers for a set of fundamento batá drums receive Añá (in the form of consecrated batá drums), and not all of these "sworn" drummers (*olú añá*) are initiated into Ocha. And the batá drums that are to be consecrated also must undergo an initiation process, much like that of humans who become priests and priestesses of Ocha. Receptacles for other orichas are ritually washed to purify and empower them, but they are not formally initiated, as are the drums for Añá. These differences are significant, and help make the case that Añá is more of an oricha rather than less of one, requiring that even its receptacle—the drum—be consecrated before entering it.

Whenever Ortíz mentions Añá, he goes to great lengths to discount any of the aspects that might indicate ambiguity regarding Añá's gender. Even after describing the "wombs" of the drums and the fact that the lead drum is called *iyá*, or mother, Ortíz emphasizes the maleness of the performance practice, telling his readers that the drums are made out of male goatskin and the players of these drums must be male, too (Ortíz 1954, 210–12, 266, 305–6). Nonetheless, he also writes about "El Ilú Batá Simbólico," the symbolic batá set, which is a diminutive set of batá drums given to Ochún in her road as "Ochún-ibú-Añá" (Ortíz 1954, 340). He adds, "This little drum of Ochún-ibú-Añá is only meant to symbolize the music or the poetic burbling of river water below. The goddess Ochún is the wife of the god Changó; she has her fluvial music in the same way that Changó has his thunder in the heavens" (Ortíz 1954, 340).[11] Earlier in the section, he writes about the *tambor elemú*, which is "like a set of batá, but with smaller dimensions" (Ortíz 1954, 338). This set of drums, according to Ortíz, featured the *chaguoró* (*chaworó*) with three little jingle bells on each one (Ortíz, 1954, 338). Not only that, but it was used in Jovellanos, Matanzas, for prayers to Chakpaná (also known as Babalú-Ayé), on the occasion of an epidemic (likely smallpox). Ortíz concludes that this elemú is perhaps a "prayer drum" used by the Lucumíes when they divine through *diloggún* (cowrie shells) (Ortíz 1954, 340). Toward the end of this section, Ortíz mentions the "*tamborcitos para Ochún*" (little batá drums for Ochún), but he emphasizes that "these little drums are never meant to be played [. . .] rather, they are meant to be hung at the altar of Ochún [. . .]" (Ortíz 1954, 338–40). These references indicate at least an association between Ochún and batá drums, if not Ochún as a guiding force within Añá.[12] In Cabrera (1986, 224), Obaña is described in the following way: "*Orisha, hermana mayor de Changó*," the first reference I have seen to Changó's older sister, much less an older sister with Añá in her name.[13] In both Cabrera (1986, 280; 1980, 70) and Bolívar Aróstegui (1994, 179) Ochún Añá is mentioned as "Ochún of the drums." None of the written sources leaves out Ochún Añá, but none abandons Changó (often in the form of Obbañá) as a primary owner of Añá. These references support the suggestion that there is a feminine quality, if not outright affiliation, with Añá, hyper-masculinized though it may have been in in conventional scholarship and in historical practice.

Cuban interpretations of Yorùbá characterizations of Añá are equally ambivalent about Añá's gender, as are Yorùbá characterizations themselves. Amanda Vincent's [Villepastour's] (2006) fieldwork revealed that although most of her Yorùbá and Cuban informants characterized Àyàn and Añá as male, several interpreted this powerful entity to be female, or, in one case "both" (Vincent 2006, 145). Vincent comes to the conclusion that "out in the world of work, commerce, and social organization, Àyàn/Añá is viewed as male," but that the "'inner' aspect of Àyàn/Añá [. . .] may be viewed as female" (Vincent 2006, 148). Michael Marcuzzi (2005) states that most of the Cuban drummers he has interviewed consider Añá to be a male oricha, but also reports that one Yorùbá batá drummer and shell diviner quoted an origin narrative for Añá (Àyàn in Yorùbá) as a "messenger of God" and the wife of Èṣù (see Àyángbẹ́kún with Villepastour, this volume). This narrative not only provides Àyàn with female attributes, but connects her with several more male orichas after Èṣù, including Ọ̀rányàn, Ògún, and Ṣàngó. Marcuzzi eventually concludes that Àyàn's relationships with these other òrìṣà as narrated in the orature signify the batá drum's necessary ability to communicate with all the orichas, highlighting "a plethora of lateral relationships between Àyàn and other òrìṣà" (Marcuzzi 2005a, 153–54, 161). He also supports Peel's view that attributing gender to òrìṣà, which are genderless, is simply an inevitable human projection.

Comparing Yorùbá *ìtàn* and Cuban *patakís* (sacred narratives about the deities), one cannot help but notice the similarity in the marriage narratives of Àyàn/Añá and Ọ̀ṣun/Ochún. Ochún, like Àyàn, was once married to Echú (Èṣù). And, like Bàtá, who is conflated in Yorùbá orature with Àyàn,[14] Ochún was Changó's preferred wife. Similarly, Ochún was the only oricha who was able to entice Ogún from his forest exile, and she did so by seducing him. And finally, Ochún's relationship with Orúnmila, discussed later in this essay, is reported to have been the origin of Ifá divination (Abímbọ́lá in Murphy and Sanford 2001). Where Marcuzzi sees Àyàn as òrìṣà communicating with all the deities, I see Àyàn as overlapping with the realm of Ochún for those particularly strong and productive relationships with male orichas.

The Ethnographic Project: The Personal is Political

We would do well to consider the positionality of scholars here. In this case, the personal is not only political, it is likely definitive. Two of the ethnographers who have emphasized the "Ochúnness" of Añá are Cuban women (Cabrera and Bolívar Aróstegui); one was gay and the other is a staunch feminist (Montero 1998, 161–74; Rodríguez-Mangual 2004, 90–93). I include sexual preference and gender politics here because to have been a gay Cuban woman (especially in the 1940s and 1950s, when Cabrera was doing her fieldwork) was to resist the particularly heavy burden of patriarchy and machismo so prevalent among Cubans at that time. This dynamic can create strong feminists who may notice and emphasize the clues pointing to Ochún as a guiding force and tutelary oricha for the batá drums more than a scholar from a different social milieu. In addition, a growing number of scholars have pointed to the fluid gender roles afforded by the ritual practices of Regla de Ocha (see Argüelles 1989; Conner 2004; and Clark 2005, for example), though none has explicitly mentioned the potential gender fluidity within the performance tradition of batá drumming.

More recently, female scholars Elizabeth Sayre (2000), myself (2001), and Amanda Vincent (2006) have written about our experiences playing batá drums in the United States, Cuba, Nigeria, and Britain, and these accounts will certainly refine our understanding of gender in batá performance. It is also relevant to note here that Lydia Cabrera wrote a book specifically on Ochún and Yemayá (*Yemayá y Ochún: Kariocha, Iyalorichas y Olorichas* [Colección del Chicherukú en Exilio, 2da edición, Miami: 1980]), thus highlighting further these two feminine/feminist water orichas. The main person who emphasized the maleness of Añá in writing was Fernando Ortíz, who was writing from a mid-twentieth-century Cuban paternalistic and patriarchal perspective in which the "femaleness" of a drum normally associated with the virility and machismo of male drummers as well as the masculine qualities of the oricha known as Changó might well have seemed so ludicrous as to obviate any further research in that direction (see María del Rosario Díaz 2004). It may be useful to include here J. Lorand Matory's observation that the ethnographic project greatly—and often unduly—influences oricha practitioners' representations of themselves, which then focuses the topic(s) of the ethnography (Matory 2005, 188–223), making the ethnographic project anything but "neutral." Considering the tremendous influence Fernando Ortíz's scholarship has had on Cuban ethnographic practice, even to the present day, his informants likely shaped their behavior in accordance with what he wrote and believed, and Ortíz's prolific output influenced and was influenced by these dynamics, as Marcuzzi has asserted (Marcuzzi 2005a, 32, 372–478). This is not to deny the importance of Ortíz's work, but rather to recognize the breadth and depth of his influence on the interpretation and practice of Regla de Ocha in Cuba.

Personal background is also relevant with regard to batá drummers and their understandings and interpretations of Añá. Cuban drummers speak with particular reference to lineage and geographical origin. Felipe García Villamil, who claims that Añá is not an oricha, comes from Matanzas and a lineage of drummers that began with his great-grandfather Iñoblá Cárdenas (see Vélez 2000, 50–55). Alberto Villarreal, who claims Añá is an oricha, comes from Havana and a different lineage of drummers, including Jesús Pérez, which leads back to Pablo Roche (see Hagedorn 2001). Francisco Aguabella, who was trained in Matanzas by Estéban Cha Chá Vega (who inherited his set of fundamento batá drums from Carlos Alfonso Díaz), believes Añá is a male oricha—a road of Changó—but also suggests that some batá drummers in Matanzas consider Añá to be a road of Ochún (Hagedorn 2001, 96). Alberto, who was trained in Havana, preferred not to comment on Añá's gender, but did state that he supported Natalia Bolívar Aróstegui's book (in which she states that Añá is a road of Ochún).

Supporting Ochún: Ifá, Odus (Divine Revelations), and Patakís (Sacred Narratives)

Ochún is a riverine deity within the pantheon of the Regla de Ocha. She is associated with all aspects of fresh water—from its sustaining potential and the life that teems within it, to the loss of life that can result from its velocity and overflow, to the audibly soothing sound of its journey over rocks and riverbeds. In her anthropomorphized form, Ochún is related to pregnancy and birth (sustenance of life), and in Cuba, she has become associated with the flirtatious and curvaceous *mulata* (abundance), a tempestuous shrew (velocity and flooding), and a deaf old woman (journey over rocks and riverbeds). These associations, perhaps not surprisingly, mark important milestones in a woman's life cycle. Ochún is also identified as an affiliative oricha for the *ajé*[15] (Yorùbá *àjé*), loosely translated as witches, who use menstrual blood—rich in the nutrients that may someday sustain a living being—as a powerful element in their mixtures. Menstrual blood is considered by Ocha practitioners to be so powerful that it can effectively disempower other medicines, including what Marcuzzi calls the "medicinal load" that activates Añá in consecrated batá drums (Marcuzzi 2005a, *passim*). The menstrual cycle is also directly associated with Ochún, on the grounds that new life could begin during this cycle. It is no coincidence that Ocha initiates travel to the river as the first step of their initiation. The river washes away the past, renews the present, and prepares one for a new future. All this is to say that Ochún is highlighted in the initiation—that is, the rebirth—of a person into the secrets of their oricha. Although she is the youngest and one of the last orichas to be saluted during prayers and musical invocations, Ochún holds a place of importance within the structure of the religion. This importance is echoed in her relationship to the batá drums in the tambor, one of the most significant performance practices of Regla de Ocha.

In the many patakís of Regla de Ocha, Ochún's ability to accomplish unlikely or seemingly impossible tasks is testament to her resourcefulness and wit. That her road should empower the sacred batá drums—indeed, allow them to speak the divine Lucumí phrases that change lives—seems to me to be uniquely appropriate. Some patakís maintain that Ochún learned the sacred art of divination—that is, the ability to speak the future and comment on the unknown present—from her lover Orúnmila; other narratives assert that Ochún herself "owns" this art and in fact taught it to Orúnmila (see 'Wande Abímbólá's article "The Bag of Wisdom" in Murphy and Sanford 2001, 141–54).[16] Regardless of who taught whom divination, Ochún is considered not only a good diviner, but "the best" diviner (Abímbólá in Murphy and Sanford 2001). She is referred to by priests and scholars alike as the orisha who alters "bad destinies" (see Rowland Abiodun, "Hidden Power: Os[h]un, the Seventeenth Odù," in Murphy and Sanford 2001, 10–33; David Ògúngbilé, "Ẹẹ̀rìndínlógún: The Seeing Eyes of Sacred Shells and Stones," in Murphy and Sanford 2001, 189–212, esp. 190). In another narrative, Ọ̀ṣun (Ochún) is the oricha who provides Ọbàtálá (the òrìṣà of creation) with the water to smooth the clay to make humans (between the three of them, they create humanity: Olódùmarè provides the breath, Ọ̀ṣun provides the water, while Ọbàtálá molds the fetus) (Ògúngbilé in Murphy and Sanford 2001, 190). It is Ochún's water, too, that is necessary to make the batá drums speak. The animal skins that become batá drumheads must be soaked in fresh water so that they may be stretched tightly enough to speak the divine wisdom of Añá.

At this point, let us move to a closer examination of Odu (Yorùbá Odù), which refers to Orúnmila's wife (Orúnmila is the deity of Ifá divination), and to the divinatory revelations known as *odus*. Ocha priest and scholar Michael Mason interprets odus as metaphoric vessels containing proverbs, *ebbós* (sacrifices), and generalized advice (2002, 15–25, esp. 19–20). The idea of a metaphoric vessel containing life-transforming information evokes the feminine, and, more specifically, the state of pregnancy. J. Lorand Matory connects the roundness of Yorùbá vessels and even the layout of palaces and compounds with the feminine in his discussion of the use of metaphors in engendering Yorùbá sacred and political power in Ọ̀yọ́ (Matory 1994, 144–78). Michael Marcuzzi strengthens this association, writing that Odu "is conceived of as a material/maternal calabash of existence, sustaining and impelling the words emanating from Orunmila's calculating divination complexes (*odu*)" (Marcuzzi 2005b, 184). Further, Margaret Drewal notes that in Yorùbá ritual, Odù is represented by a closed calabash, and that Odù's essential secret is "the knowledge of birth" (Drewal 1992, 73).

Ochún is also associated with the calabash in both Yorùbá and Cuban religious systems. In the Cuban cosmological system of Ocha, both Odu and Ochún play empowering roles in supporting Orúnmila. Ochún is referred to as Orúnmila's wife, and Ochún who is said to have taught Orúnmila the secrets of divination (see above). But Odu is the only feminine oricha who is present when Orúnmila is born (that is, during an Ifá initiation process—Ifá being the primary Nigerian and Cuban divination system, as well as a religious system unto itself). It should be noted that there is another important feminine presence at an Ifá initiation, and that is the *apetebí*. The apetebí is typically a priestess of Ochún and usually the wife of a *babalao* (priest of Ifá divination).[17] Odù's sole feminine presence at an Ifá initiation ceremony gives rise to the question of whether Odù gives birth to Orúnmila. The calabash represents the womb (in its literal and figurative senses) in Cuban Ocha, and Ochún is directly indicated in odus that refer to carrying a child in the womb, and childbirth. Odù is sometimes called Olofi (god-on-high) in the Cuban context of Ifá (Brown 2003, 79–80), which would seem to strengthen the position of the feminine in Ifá, if not in the overall cosmology of Ocha.

Drewal also writes about the àjẹ́, which she defines as "women with extraordinary powers," but which has been translated elsewhere in the scholarly literature as "witches." Drewal refers to the "concentration of vital force in women, their àṣẹ́, their power to bring things into existence, to make things happen, [which] creates the extraordinary potential that can manifest itself in both positive and negative ways" (Drewal 1992, 177). All elderly (that is, post-menopausal) women are àjẹ́, as are priestesses of the òrìsà, wealthy marketwomen, and female title-holders in prestigious organizations. Drewal also notes that these women are collectively and affectionately known as "our mothers" (Drewal 1992, 177–78). Several aspects of the àjẹ́ would seem to refer to Ochún: first, the association with birth, with bringing new life into existence, as mentioned above; second, the wealthy marketwomen—Ochún may be associated with wealth in Cuba even more than she is in Nigeria, and the wealthy Nigerian marketwoman's alter ego might well prove to be the Cuban *jinetera*, who exchanges sex for money and material goods; and third, the prestigious title-holder—Ochún is understood to be a status-seeker, climbing ever upward and gaining access to power in resourceful ways. Although Drewal does not mention Ochún as an affiliative òrìsà for the àjẹ́, Bádéjọ makes this link explicit (see Bádéjọ 1996, 1), and I find enough evidence to suggest that such a connection exists.

Cosmological Kinship and Musical Affinities

Even those few practitioners of Ocha (such as olúbatá Felipe García Villamil) who consider Añá to be not an oricha, but rather a potent form of aché (Vélez 2000, 48), assert that drummers must use consecrated drums for religious ceremonies because it is Añá that imbues the drums with their sacred potential. In this formulation, Ochún still looms large as an affiliate deity for the batá drums. Each of the three drums is associated with at least two orichas. Although these affiliations vary somewhat from drummer to drummer (and from Havana to Matanzas), the most common oricha associations with the lead drum (iyá) are Yemayá and Changó; the most common associations with the middle drum (itótele) are Ochún and Oyá; and the most common associations with the smallest drum (okónkolo) are Eleguá, Los Ibeyí (the sacred twins), and Changó (see Vincent 2006, 100, 107, 110).[18] If we look more closely at the affinities between batá drums and orichas, we see an interesting and interrelated series of kinship narratives. These relationships between the orichas and their affiliate drums become intensified when one considers the relationships among the orichas themselves.

Iyá, the lead drum, is associated with both Yemayá and Changó. Yemayá, the mother of all the orichas, would seem a natural candidate for iyá, the mother of the batá drums. Changó, son of Yemayá and owner of thunder, lightning, and the batá drums, is another understandable choice for affiliation with the lead drum. Ochún's role as vigilant and dynamic intermediary in the form of itótele will be discussed below. That she shares her affiliative ties to Oyá, who is the guardian of the cemetery,[19] is appropriate because Ochún has several roads that led her into intense contact with the spirits of the dead (roads such as Ochún Yumú and Ochún Awé, among others). Ochún, who presides over the beginnings of life (pregnancy and childbirth), is thus also intimately connected with death. (There are several patakís that characterize Ochún as being so coy that she flirts even with Ikú [death], making deals and changing fates wherever she goes.) In addition, both Oyá and Ochún are co-wives of Changó, according to Cuban and Yorùbá oral literature, which strengthens the argument that the itótele functions as a primary interlocutor for the iyá. Eleguá, one of the owners of the okónkolo, is the opener and closer of roads (also interpreted as the difference between life and death, the difference between moving forward and standing still). He is the messenger oricha, often portrayed as a hypersexed and childlike trickster, who is also a protector of Ochún because she saved him once when he was an infant. Los Ibeyí (the twins), also affiliated with okónkolo (the littlest drum), are said to be the offspring of Ochún and

Changó, but were raised by Yemayá (Bolívar Aróstegui 1994; Cabrera 1980). One of the Ibeyís' claims to fame is that they saved humanity from the Devil by playing the magical drums (given to them by their adoptive mother Yemayá) with such vivacity and flourish that the Devil was compelled to dance until he was too tired to plague humanity.[20]

Metaphors of Organology and Musical Interactions: The Response that Commands

First, and perhaps most obvious, consider the bells that encircle the drumheads of the iyá. These bells—called chaworó in Lucumí or *cascabeles* in Spanish—are most commonly associated with Ochún.[21] Her musical marker, as it were, is the ringing of bells. Brass bells are often employed to make Ochún hear one's pleas; even as she dances, she cups her hand over one ear, as if she cannot hear you over the sound of her rushing waters. All things brass belong to her, and brass bells and bracelets signify Ochún's presence. That these bells encircle the drum heads of the lead drum (and sometimes the drum heads of the other drums) is surely an indicator of Ochún as a guiding force, if not a primary affiliate of these drums. Further, when a congregant is on the verge of becoming possessed by an oricha, the lead drummer will often shake the iyá to make the bells sound more loudly and definitively, as if the ringing of these bells might be enough to push the devotee over the edge into the realm of possession.[22] Interestingly, the other female oricha with whom brass bells are associated is the female river oricha Yewa, who is the co-owner, with Ochún, of the itótele drum (see Ortíz 1954, 4).

Consider also that the lead drum is called "iyá," or mother, in Lucumí; *iyá ilù* (mother drum) in Yorùbá. "Itótele," the name of the middle drum, derives from the Yorùbá drum-naming system *itèlé*, meaning "the one that follows," and "okónkolo" means little one (also understood as a Yorùbá vocable for the ubiquitous compound meter sub-Saharan timeline, started on the second stroke, as in x.x.xx.x.x.x, or "[*-lo*]-*kon kolo kon kon ko-*"; see Kubik 1999, 55). This conjures up a family portrait of a mother and two children, referencing the matriarchal head of family so often represented in the patakís of the water deities Ochún and Yemayá. Consider also the fact that a consecrated (fundamento) set of batá drums must be "born" from another fundamento set of batá drums (Ortíz 1954, 285)—the birth metaphor is certainly a reference to a female experience (i.e., men do not give birth), and seems to be a specific reference to Ochún, who is the superlative protector of all pregnant and birthing women. Consider also the terminology that Ortíz uses when he is talking about the placement of the *resguardos* (protective objects representing Añá), which, after they have been fed, are enclosed forever in the respective "womb" of each batá drum (1954, 290). Ortíz's reference to the "wombs" of the drums is indicative of his gendered understanding of them.[23]

Consider also the musical function of the itótele, particularly in relation to the lead drum. The lead drum (iyá) initiates rhythmic calls to conversation, but it is itótele who needs to know how to respond in order to complete the conversation. Itótele gives meaning and rhythmic context to iyá's solo improvisatory forays by filling in the often wide spaces in between iyá's commanding phrases. While okónkolo keeps up a steady rhythm, iyá and itótele converse. In addition, if iyá is slow to "make a call," itótele pushes iyá—in an unorthodox though effective manner—by playing the response to a call before it is made (see, for example, García Villamil in Vélez 2000, 45). In this dialogic musical way, Ochún in her affiliative role as owner of the itótele is eminently responsive, so much so that she pushes iyá to make the call, to move forward along the musical road. Ochún-as-itótele responds to and in some cases determines the dynamics of the batá ensemble.

Obiní Batá: Romancing the Stone(s)

Relationships between masculine and feminine entities permeate all aspects of Ocha drumming ceremonies, and the "divine feminine" looms particularly large in batá performance, precisely because of its constructed absence. One group of women that has challenged the prohibition of women playing batá drums is Obiní Batá, an all-female musical ensemble that specializes in playing batá drums. Their name is a Lucumí phrase meaning "Women of the Batá"—already a signal to the male batá world that change is on the way. The group was founded in 1993 by Eva Despaigne Trujillo, Deborah C. Méndez Frontela, and Mirta Ocanto González. In its current configuration, it includes six members, all of whom sing, dance, and play percussion (batá, conga, bell, chekeré, and clave). In a 2003 interview for a DVD recorded by Luke Wassermann, John Randall, and Todd Brown, co-founder Despaigne Trujillo affirmed that she had graduated from the Escuela Nacional de Arte in folkloric and modern dance, and joined the Conjunto Folklórico Nacional de Cuba as a lead dancer.[24] It was there, she said, that she learned percussion, and in 1991 she raised the issue about women being discouraged from playing aberikulá drums, and prohibited from playing fundamento drums. Her reasoning was that "batá drums form a fundamental part of Cuba's cultural heritage, just like congas, maracas, and claves, so the drums should belong to all Cubans." Citing Cuban ethnographer Fernando Ortíz as an inspiration, Despaigne Trujillo asserted that Obiní Batá seeks to "bring batá drums out into the open, completely out of their religious context." She added that if foreigners can play batá drums "any old way," then Cuban women should be able to bring batá drums into the realm of popular music.

Despaigne Trujillo's linking of the rubrics "foreign" and "female" brings to light an internal logic that informs the prohibition of women playing consecrated batá drums. When Obiní Batá was formed, many of the leaders of Havana's religious drumming community were outraged, and voiced their disapproval loudly and openly about women playing batá drums. Obiní Batá had a standing weekly gig in summer 1994 at Don Giovanni, an Italian restaurant in Old Havana, popular with tourists. They had started one of their first public performances there with a plea for blessings from Añá. The male olú batá who were in attendance at this performance were shocked and angry, according to olúbatá Alberto Villarreal and olú batá Armando Pedroso. Their view was that women, who are prohibited from playing consecrated batá drums in a sacred context, and who were openly discouraged from playing any sort of batá drum (consecrated or not) until 1986, with the advent of FolkCuba (the Conjunto Folklórico's outreach program for tourists), should not even mention the word Añá, much less ask for blessings from the deity (see Hagedorn 2001, 91).

This made an impression on me because I was, at that time, studying batá drums with Alberto Villarreal, lead percussionist of Cuba's premier folkloric ensemble, the Conjunto Folklórico Nacional. In light of the negative comments made by Alberto and his colleagues about Obiní Batá, I asked Alberto whether he had a similarly negative reaction to teaching me batá. He said that in my case, it was different, because I was a foreigner (*extranjera*), and not only that, a white foreigner, so it was not the same thing. He and his colleagues at the Conjunto Folklórico Nacional had resisted teaching women until 1989, when they began to teach foreign women. What really upset him and his fellow drummers was the notion that Cuban women, especially Afro-Cuban women, would learn batá. They were "*atrevida*" (pushy), he said, and would not stop with simply learning how to play batá in folkloric contexts. His fear, and that of his fellow drummers, was that these women would learn enough and be "pushy," "assertive," and "aggressive" enough to attempt to play consecrated batá drums in a sacred context.

It is precisely in the realm of the olú batá that women are being left out of the conversation. If we imagine this conversation to take place in a

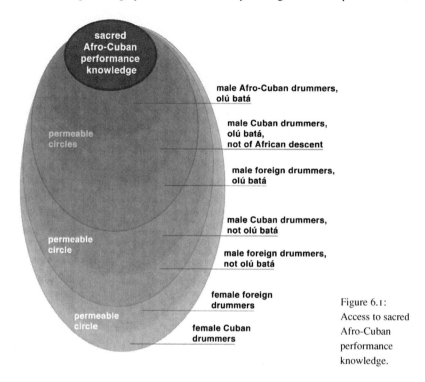

male Afro-Cuban drummers,
olú batá

male Cuban drummers,
olú batá,
not of African descent

male foreign drummers,
olú batá

male Cuban drummers,
not olú batá

male foreign drummers,
not olú batá

female foreign
drummers

female Cuban
drummers

Figure 6.1:
Access to sacred
Afro-Cuban
performance
knowledge.

series of concentric circles, the male Afro-Cuban olú batá are in the center, and Cuban olú batá not of African descent are just outside the center; the foreign olú batá exist in a permeable layer outside the Cuban olú batá; Cubans of all racial descriptions who would like to play batá but who have not done the appropriate ceremonies linger outside the foreign olú batá, and foreign men who are serious about learning to play batá but are not consecrated to the drums are left outside the Cuban secular drummers (see Fig. 6.1).

At the very periphery of this series of concentric circles are foreign and Cuban women who want to learn to play these drums. Access to the center depends on the more portable and public aspects of this performance tradition (a working set of batá drums, a series of notated or otherwise repeatable batá rhythms, and disciplined players and teachers), and on the knowledge of the secret and exclusive aspects of this sacred performance tradition. Afro-Cuban women who are Ocha priestesses and who play the batá drums represent an agitating and unstable combination of categories—they have some knowledge of the religious secrets of Santería (accessible only to those who have been initiated into the religion), they are members of the larger Afro-Cuban community, and they have extensive knowledge of the music. All of these factors move them close to the innermost circle; however, they are women, and Afro-Cuban, which blows them back to the outer edge of the periphery. Despaigne Trujillo stated in the same 2003 interview that, although she herself did not have *santo* (that is, she is not initiated as a priestess in Regla de Ocha), other members of her group do.[25] She emphasized that the religious knowledge shared by the group gives meaning to the content of the songs and beauty to their performances, because they understand what they are singing.

In the Wassermann-Randall-Brown DVD, Obiní Batá gives a breathless, riveting performance at the Yorùbá Cultural Association in June 2003. Their batá invocations for seven of the main orichas in what they call the "Orishas Suite" are well executed. The dancers for Eleguá and Ochún are playful and flirtatious; the dancers for Yemayá and Oyá are powerful and complex. The group has rehearsed exhaustively.

And yet two aspects of the performance are perplexing. First, what the group has chosen to wear: the musicians are dressed in black leotards with transparent black tulle miniskirts and black high heels, accessorized with silver metal belts (see Plate 6.1). In a typical Afro-Cuban folkloric performance, the musicians would wear white, symbolic of spiritual purity and the white clothing of an iyawó, or Ocha initiate. (The reference to the religious context is understood, even if the musicians are not "sworn to the drum," or "*omo añá.*") They might also wear red bandanas tied around their necks or over their shoulders, in homage to Changó, the oricha who protects the batá drums. And finally, each drummer would wear a cap—white (in honor of the religious context from which the performance is derived), or a color associated with their particular head oricha (e.g., yellow for Ochún, blue for Yemayá, red for Changó, etc.). No part of their outfit would be black, as black is considered to be a powerful and difficult color, unless the wearer is associated with Eleguá. By wearing black, the women disassociate themselves from the religious context, and move themselves much closer to the tourist context. This impression is heightened by the miniskirts and high heels, which could be interpreted as a surprising reference to *jineterismo*, or the exchange of sex for money.

At a religious ceremony, people are openly discouraged from wearing revealing clothing and shoes associated with profane activities and intent. Wearing white and covering oneself appropriately (legs, arms, midsection, feet) conveys modesty, humility, and purity before the orichas. The miniskirts and high heels represent the antithesis of appropriate clothing at a religious ceremony, and would be questionable attire even for a folkloric performance. The gray metal belts the group wears make a different sort of statement—iron and steel are associated primarily

Plate 6.1: Montage of Eva
Despaigne. (photograph
and artwork: Eduardo
Gálvez Cabalé, Havana, 19
November 2010)

with Ogún, but the batá drums are under the protection and patronage of
Changó. The only bit of metal used in a consecrated set of batá drums is
the tiny hoop affixed near the smaller head of each drum (the *aro*, associated with Ogún), to remind the drummers of their sacrofraternal obligations. The batá drums played by Obiní Batá are clearly factory-made,
with steel tuning lugs and rims, another reminder that we are outside of
the religion.

Second, I found myself taken aback by the strangely impassive audience. There is no audience participation (even in the form of shouts
of encouragement or applause) during Obiní Batá's performance at the
Yorùbá Cultural Association. The audience sits quietly while the young
women perform their carefully rehearsed repertoire. Twice—during the
rhythmically intense "Laro" played for Yemayá, and during an exciting
rhythmic invocation to Oyá meant to evoke her whirlwinds—the primarily Cuban audience claps spontaneously in recognition of the extraordinary effort involved in executing these complex rhythms with such acu-
ity and strength. The rest of the time, the audience seems unmoved. The
women put themselves on the line, performing a challenging repertoire
not normally associated with female performers, and the audience seems
not to support them. In a religious or folkloric performance context, with

male drummers, the audience would likely be freer and "competent" (see Hagedorn 2001, 57–58)—that is, secure in its expectations of the dynamics of the performance, joining in the chorus parts in some of the songs, swaying back and forth for certain rhythms, and showing a unity of performative intent. In this context, however, the audience acted more like people at a classical music concert, clapping politely at the end of each piece, and keeping quiet during the rest of the performance.

What gives the audience pause, perhaps, is not the fear of what these women are doing now, but what they might do in the future. For the time being, they perform in tourist restaurants and cultural centers, and they dress in black, wearing short skirts, high heels, and revealing clothing that refers to the streets of Havana's bustling tourist industry, which includes the venerable trade of jineterismo. For the time being, their conversation is mainly with each other. What this audience might fear, however, is that these women might extend their percussive voices to the religious arena, increasing their ritual power, that their musical expertise, religious knowledge, and Afro-Cuban heritage might propel them into the center of the very sacred space from which they have been excluded, thereby amplifying the feminine voice so that it must be heard alongside the masculine in fundamento batá performance.

Notes

1. I thank Amanda Villepastour, Michael Marcuzzi, and Michael Mason for their close reading and careful critique of this essay.

2. Because this essay focuses on concepts that are integral to oricha worship in Cuba, Nigeria, and the United States, I have chosen to use orthography that is most appropriate for the particular context. As a result (for example), Añá (Cuban Lucumí spelling), Àyàn (Nigerian spelling), and Anya (English spelling) may all appear in the same paragraph.

3. "Road" is a direct translation of the Cuban term *camino*, and refers to different aspects of an oricha's manifestation. In Cuban Regla de Ocha, most orichas have many roads.

4. Olú batá means one who not only has mastered the various patterns for all the batá drums and has comprehended the many rhythmic possibilities for each, but one who has been consecrated to the batá drums, and may have a set of sacred batá drums in his care.

5. It would appear, however, that even unconsecrated drums are ritually efficacious, judging from divine possessions that have taken place in secular venues using unconsecrated drums (see Hagedorn 2001; Vincent 2006).

6. Batá drummers began teaching women to play (unconsecrated) batá drums in Cuba in the early 1980s, but this was under duress, because many of the male batá drummers felt uncomfortable sharing this knowledge with women (see Sayre 2000; Hagedorn 2001).

7. A drummer's hands are washed with *omiero* (a purifying mixture of sacred herbs and water), he takes an oath to guard the secrets of Añá, and then a small cross is cut into his inside wrist. Although most of these drummers are heterosexual, even this rule is transgressed on occasion (pers. comm., Michael Marcuzzi, June 2006).

8. Ortíz writes that ritual names are given to fundamento batá drums (Ortíz 1954, 286) in the same way that initiates receive ritual names upon initiation into Ocha. He adds that the makers of unconsecrated batá drums (aberikulá) were also given Lucumí names by their makers, and that these names usually translated into insults or offensive phrases—as if to mark clearly the difference between fundamento ensembles and aberikulá ensembles. According to Ortíz's informant, the name considered most offensive for one of these unconsecrated ensembles was "Olomí Yobó," which translates as "vaginal menstrual flow" (Ortíz 1954, 326).

9. Two earlier works by Ortíz, *La Africanía de la música folklórica de Cuba* (1965 [1948]) and *Los bailes y el teatro de los negros en el folklore de Cuba* (1951), also mention Añá as an oricha, but in *Los instrumentos de la música afrocubana* (1952–1955), Añá is discussed frequently and given special attention.

10. Marcuzzi (2005, 429–77) draws attention to the similarities in the "medicinal technologies" that empower both Ọsanyìn (Yorùbá spelling) and Àyàn (Yorùbá spelling).

11. All translations by author, unless otherwise noted.

12. In her research with Chief Alhaji Rábíù Àyándòkun and Múráínà Oyèlámí in Èrìn-Ọṣun, Nigeria, Vincent found that Àyàn brides are ritually exchanged for a miniature bàtá drum (2006, 145–46), which echoes, if not amplifies, the feminine association with these drums. Villepastour has also noted that the Cuban miniature drums are used for Changó medicine, and Nigerian miniature drums are used for Àyàn medicine (Amanda Villepastour, pers. comm., August 2011).

13. Cabrera (1986, 54) provides two other entries of interest, which include the word "añá": "Añaga" is defined, in two separate entries, as both "drumming ceremony" and "prostitute." One of Ochún's most popular anthropomorphized roles in Cuba is that of a prostitute who enjoys dancing to the music of drums. This road of Ochún is known as Pansaga.

14. See Àyánṣọolá with Amherd and Àyángbékún with Villepastour, this volume.

15. A word that bears at least a phonetic resemblance to the Lucumí rendering ajé (witches) is the Yorùbá pronunciation and spelling, Ajé, the òrìṣà of wealth, signified by cowrie shells. In Cuban Ocha practice, Ochún and the Cuban Ajé share many of the same attributes, such as the colors gold and yellow, affinity for the number 5, and association with wealth. In 2003 I was told by my Cuban godmother that Ajé was "Ochún's secretary," and that Ajé's ritual vessel should reside next to that of Ochún on the altar. Although it is possible that the Nigerian words Àjẹ́ and Ajé might have been confused or even conflated in Cuba due to gradual language loss, the association of these two words and concepts with Ochún is understandable.

16. Abímbọ́lá is referring here to a narrative from within the corpus of ẹsẹ Ifá. At the heart of the Yorùbá Ifá divination system are divinatory revelations called odù, each of which is more fully explicated by verses called ẹsẹ. The ẹsẹ, chanted in poetic language by Ifá priests, contain important references to Yorùbá histories, cosmologies, and social issues that clarify the client's current situation and course of action. In this particular narrative, the òrìṣà Odù told her husband she would teach him how to divine if he treated her with respect and affection. Ọrúnmìlà agreed to do so, and together they had sixteen children (the sixteen major divination signs, or odù).

17. I thank Amanda Villepastour for reminding me of this crucial feminine presence. Villepastour also notes that in the *ìtẹfá* ceremony she witnessed in Ọ̀yọ́, the *apètèbí* was the Ifá priest's sister, who is a Methodist. Her family relationship and her status as woman apparently trumped her absent òrìṣà status (pers. comm., May 6, 2007).

18. Vincent provides a statistically significant set of drum-deity affiliations from her fieldwork in Havana and Matanzas (2006, 110). "[I]n Havana, Eleguá for the *okónkolo*, Ochún/Oyá for the *itótele* and Changó for the *iyá*; in Matanzas, Changó for the *okónkolo*, Ochún for the *itótele* and Yemayá for the *iyá*" (Vincent 2006, 110).

19. Ortíz (1954, 4) writes that Yewa, *la dueña de la entrada del cementerio* (guardian of the entrance to the cemetery), is the oricha most closely associated with itótclc. Both Oyá and Yewa are characterized as overseeing the journey from life to death, so I would interpret these two oricha-itótclc associations as being quite close.

20. This story is included in the odu Ifá titled Otura Odí. In this version of the story, however, what Bolívar Aróstcgui and Cabrera refer to as "the Devil" is called "Ẹbita." "Ẹbita" refers to an òrìṣà who knowingly and frequently entraps humans.

21. See Àyángbẹ́kún with Villepastour in this volume, in which Àyángbẹ́kún refers to the bàtá's ṣaworo (bells) as "Ọ̀ṣun's earrings."

22. It should be noted here that bells are also associated with other orichas, although less overtly so: Ochún (a warrior oricha who provides stability) features four tiny tin bells which are said to warn the initiate of destabilizing phenomena; bells associated with Osáin (a powerful healing oricha) are said to protect the initiate from witchcraft; and bells are left on the batá drums to prevent Egun (ancestral spirits) from entering them and diminishing or deterring the power of the orichas. Egun once had their own bells made from wood (Vincent [Villepastour], pers. comm., August 2006; from Armando Pedroso, pers. comm., September 2004).

23. Consider also Matory's references to feminine symbols within Yoruba sacred vessels and architecture (1994), and Marcuzzi's characterization of batá drums as "gynecomorphic vessels" (2005a, 43, 448–51).

24. Some of this material about Obiní Batá is excerpted from my 2007 review of this DVD in *Ethnomusicology* 51(1).

25. Despaigne has since been initiated to Ochún in December 2008.

References Cited

Argüelles, Lourdes, and B. Ruby Rich. 1989. "Homosexuality, Homophobia, and Revolution: Notes Toward an Understanding of the Cuban Lesbian and Gay Male Experience." In *Hidden from History: Reclaiming the Gay and Lesbian Past*, eds. Duberman, Vicinus, and Chauncey, Jr. New York: New American Library. 441–55.

Bádéjọ, Diedre. 1996. *Ọ̀ṣun Ṣẹ̀ẹ̀gẹ̀sí: The Elegant Deity of Wealth, Power and Femininity*. Trenton, NJ: Africa World Press.

Bolívar Aróstcgui, Natalia. 1994. *Los Orishas en Cuba*. Havana: PM Ediciones.

Brown, David. 2003. *Santería Enthroned: Art, Ritual and Innovation in an Afro-Cuban Religion*. Chicago: University of Chicago Press.

Cabrera, Lydia. 1980 [1974] *Yemayá y Ochún: Kariocha, Iyalorichas y Olorichas*. New York: Colección dc Chichcrukú en el exilio.

———. 1986. *Anagó: Vocabulario Lucumí*. Miami: Ediciones Universal.

Clark, Mary Ann. 2005. *Where Men Are Wives and Mothers Rule: Santería Ritual Practices and Their Gender Implications*. Gainesville: University Press of Florida.

Conner, Randy, with David Hatfield Sparks. 2004. *Queering Creole Spiritual Traditions: Lesbian Gay, Bisexual, and Transgender Participation in African-Inspired Traditions in the Americas*. New York: Harrington Park Press.

Díaz, María del Rosario. 2004. "Ethnography at the University of Havana." In *Cuban Counterpoints: The Legacy of Fernando Ortíz*, eds. Font and Quiroz. Lanham, MD: Lexington Books. 55–62.

Drewal, Margaret. 1992. *Yorùbá Ritual: Performers, Play, Agency*. Bloomington: Indiana University Press.

Duberman, Martin Bauml, Martha Vicinus, and George Chauncey Jr., eds. 1989. *Hidden from History: Reclaiming the Gay and Lesbian Past*. New York: New American Library.

Fálọlá, Tóyìn, and Anne Genova, eds. 2005. *Òrìṣà: Yorùbá God and Spiritual Identity*. Trenton, NJ: African World Press.

Font, Mauricio, and Alfonso W. Quiroz, eds. 2004. *Cuban Counterpoints: The Legacy of Fernando Ortíz*. Lanham, MD: Lexington Books.

Hagedorn, Katherine. 2001. *Divine Utterances: The Performance of Afro-Cuban Santería*. Washington: Smithsonian Institution Press.

————. 2007. Review essay of *Cajón Espiritual: Music Box of Cuba and Omí Iná and Obbara* (2004) by Luke Wassermann, Todd Brown, John Randall. Color DVD. Distributed by Earth CDs Partners. In *Ethnomusicology* 51 (1): 175–79.

Kubik, Gerhard. 1999. *Africa and the Blues*. Jackson: University Press of Mississippi.

Linenthal, Edward. 2006. "'Nothing Is Ever Escaped': Public History and the African American Historic Landscape." Lecture presented at the Center for the Study of World Religions, Harvard Divinity School. Cambridge, MA. April 11, 2006.

López-Valdés, Rafael L. 2002. *Africanos de Cuba*. San Juan, Puerto Rico: Centro de Estudios Avanzados de Puerto Rico y el Caribe con la colaboración del Instituto de Cultura Puertorriqueña.

Magrini, Tullia, ed. 2003. *Music and Gender: Perspectives from the Mediterranean*. Chicago: University of Chicago Press.

Marcuzzi, Michael David. 2005a. *A Historical Study of the Ascendant Role of Bàtá Drumming in Cuban Òrìṣà Worship*. PhD diss., York University, Toronto, Canada.

————. 2005b. "The Ipanodu Ceremony and the History of Orisa Worship in Nigeria and Cuba." In *Òrìṣà: Yorùbá God and Spiritual Identity*, eds. Tóyìn Fálọlá and Anne Genova. Trenton, NJ: African World Press. 183–207.

Mason, Michael. 2002. *Living Santería: Rituals and Experiences in an Afro-Cuban Religion*. Washington: Smithsonian Institution Press.

Matory, J. Lorand. 1994. *Sex and the Empire That Is No More: Gender and the Politics of Metaphor in Oyo Yorùbá Religion*. Minneapolis: University of Minnesota Press.

————. 2005. *Black Atlantic Religion: Tradition, Transnationalism, and Matriarchy in the Afro-Brazilian Candomblé*. Princeton and Oxford: Princeton University Press.

Montero, Oscar. 1998. "The Signifying Queen: Critical Notes from a Latino Queer." In *Hispanisms and Homosexualities*, eds. Sylvia Molloy and Robert McKee Irwin. Durham, NC: Duke University Press. 161–74.

Murphy, Joseph M., and Mei-Mei Sanford, eds. 2001. *Òṣun across the Waters*. Bloomington: Indiana University Press.

Ortíz, Fernando. 1954. *Los Instrumentos de la Música Afrocubana, vol. IV*. Havana: Editoriales Cárdenas y Cía.

Pryor, Andrea. 1999. "The House of Añá: Women and Batá." In *CBMR Digest* 12 (2): 6–8.

Rodríguez-Mangual, Edna. 2004. *Lydia Cabrera and the Construction of an Afro-Cuban Cultural Identity*. Chapel Hill: University of North Carolina Press.

Sayre, Elizabeth. 2000. "Cuban Batá Drumming and Women Musicians: An Open Question." In *CBMR Digest* 13 (1): 12–15.

Thomas, Hugh. 1997. *The Slave Trade: The Story of the Atlantic Slave Trade, 1440–1870*. New York: Simon & Schuster Paperbacks.

Vélez, María Teresa. 2000. *Drumming for the Gods: The Life and Times of Felipe García Villamil, Santero, Palero, and Abakuá*. Philadelphia: Temple University Press.

Villepastour, Amanda. 2010. *Ancient Text Messages of the Yorùbá Bàtá Drum: Cracking the Code*. Surrey: Ashgate Press.

Vincent [Villepastour], Amanda. 2006. *Bata Conversations: Guardianship and Entitlement Narratives about the Bata in Nigeria and Cuba*. PhD thesis, School of Oriental and African Studies, University of London.

Wasserman, Luke, Todd Brown, and John Randall. 2004. *Cajón Espiritual: Music Box of Cuba and Omí Iná and Obbara*. Color DVD. Distributed by Earth CDs Partners.

Wolf, Eric R., ed. 1984. *Religion, Power, Protest in Local Communities: The Northern Shore of the Mediterranean*. Berlin: Mouton.

IV

IDENTITIES

· ·

7

The Cuban Añá Fraternity: Strategies for Cohesion

Kenneth Schweitzer

• •

Forced to migrate to Cuba in the early nineteenth century as a by-product of the transatlantic slave trade, members of the Yorùbá Àyàn cult struggled to preserve their practices and beliefs in the face of a variety of cultural pressures. Historically, these included efforts from the Spanish government and Catholic religious leaders to repress African culture; influences from other African ethnic groups in Cuba; and, perhaps most significant for this study, the fragmentation of family and the interruption of kinship lines. In the latter half of the twentieth century, the cult has also responded to the dispersion of its members throughout the globe, a process that began with the emigration of practitioners in the 1950s and accelerated as non-Cubans began to seek initiation into the cult in the 1980s. Adapting to these many pressures, and in particular to the loss of the social cohesion inherent in the Àyàn kinship-lineage configuration of Yorùbáland, members of the Añá fraternity in Cuba and abroad have employed a variety of bonding strategies to establish and maintain their cohesiveness as a socioreligious entity.[1]

Membership in the Cuban Añá fraternity is potentially open to all heterosexual males.[2] Entry is obtained through a "swearing" ceremony (*juramento*) that bonds a new initiate to his godfathers,[3] to the community of drummers who assist the ceremony, to other members of the fraternity, and to the *oricha* Añá who inhabits *batá de fundamento* (consecrated *batá* drums).[4] While some *omo* Añá (Añá initiates) limit induction to their immediate family, many extend the opportunity to others regardless of kinship. In addition to welcoming Cubans of non-African descent, many highly respected omo Añá have expanded the fraternity beyond

Plate 7.1: Ken Schweitzer with godfather, Francisco "Pancho Quinto" Hernández Mora (1933-2005). The author (left) is playing the iyá and Pancho Quinto is playing the itótelc. (photograph: Kevin McRae, Havana, 2002)

Cuba by inducting godchildren (*ahijados*) from such distant places as North America, Mexico, Asia, South America, and Western Europe.

While entry into the fraternity formally begins with one's own rite of passage, bonds among members are continually reinforced and even redefined through participation in a variety of activities, including: 1) the induction of new members; 2) the creation of new sets of batá de fundamento; 3) the maintenance of drums (tuning, restringing, and replacing heads); and 4) public Lucumí music rituals, known as *toques de santo*.[5] After briefly addressing the potential impact of the first three rituals, the bulk of this essay focuses on the musical performances of toques de santo and the nature of bonding in these environments.

The conclusions in this chapter are based on ongoing research that began in 1997. They are developed from my experiences both as an objective observer and as an initiated performer of the Lucumí ritual music (sworn to Añá in 2004), and are a product of a comparative approach I have consistently employed. In addition to eight brief visits to Cuba between 1999 and 2013 (where I was permitted to both observe and perform in rituals in Havana, Matanzas, Trinidad, and Santiago), I have performed in Lucumí rituals in New York, New York; Union City, New Jersey; Baltimore, Maryland; Washington, District of Columbia;

Miami, Florida, and Mexico City, Mexico. From 2004 to 2008, I performed regularly with a professional ensemble that provided services for oricha communities in the mid-Atlantic region of the United States.[6]

The Induction of New Members

The induction of new members into the Añá fraternity is a common event that regularly occurs in Cuba, the United States, Mexico, Venezuela, and other parts of the world. The minimal requirements are a set of batá de fundamento and the presence of experienced drummers who have the knowledge to enact the ritual. While the essential elements of the ritual are standardized, the context surrounding them is highly variable. At one extreme, a father with the help of a friend may privately and quietly initiate his son. At the other extreme, a dozen drummers might be sworn with the aid of Añá initiates who have travelled from several cities or even countries. In an effort to illustrate some of the strategies employed to enhance cohesiveness, I examine the initiation of the first white Cuban into the fraternity. With the potential to generate a considerable amount of anxiety among the participants and the general Añá community, the organizers of this ritual employed a variety of strategies to facilitate this new member's broad acceptance and to mitigate any potential backlash.

While most Afro-Cuban religions and secret societies, including the Lucumí religion, have long accepted white initiates, the Añá fraternity has been slow to open its ranks to whites and/or foreigners. Even today, though countless numbers of whites and foreigners play the drums throughout the world, the Añá drumming community in Cuba remains a largely black-centric society. In fact, I have rarely encountered white Cuban drummers at the many toques de santo I have attended in Havana and Matanzas.[7]

On August 13, 1985, Ernesto Gatell "El Gato" became the first white man to be initiated into the Añá fraternity.[8] Though the event passed with little or no social tension, the potential for friction certainly existed. Whether or not the officiates thought strategically when they envisioned the framework for the ritual, the context surrounding Ernesto's initiation helped assuage any potential tensions or misgivings within the community.

Ernesto Gatell's milestone achievement resulted in part from the friendship he developed in 1978 with his neighbor, Juan Raymat "El Negro," a master batá drummer and skilled drum maker from Havana, Cuba. With El Negro, Ernesto learned to fabricate drums on a wood lathe and also received his first lessons on the batá. Through his friendship and experiences, Ernesto entered a world that was largely off limits to white Cubans.

A close friend of the late masters Pancho Quinto and Orlando Ríos "Puntilla," El Negro helped construct Pancho Quinto's first batá de fundamento, Obayé, in 1971.[9] Through El Negro, Ernesto developed a relationship with Pancho. When El Negro left Cuba for Miami during the Mariel Boatlift of 1980, Ernesto and Pancho's relationship deepened into a lifelong friendship.

Several years later, in August 1985,[10] Pancho and his cousin Enrique Ramírez Mora fabricated another set of batá de fundamento, named Babá Funké. Immediately upon completion of this set, Armando Pedroso "El Surdo" joined Pancho and Enrique in presiding over the swearing of thirteen drummers including Ernesto Gatell, Román Díaz, Humberto Rodriquez "Caballero Efó," Miguel Ríos, Augustin "Chinchila," Erick Romay, Orlando Laje "Palito," and several others (Gatell, pers. comm., 2007).

As a white man, Ernesto has had tremendous success in what traditionally has been exclusively a black man's career. As a ritual drummer, he regularly performs *okónkolo* in batá ensembles, and a variety of percussion in other types of Afro-Cuban religious ensembles. In addition, Ernesto excels as a singer of *rumba* and other Afro-Cuban folkloric genres and has recorded and toured with such groups as Clave y Guaguancó, Tata Güines, Conjunto Folklórico Nacional, and Los Rumberos de Cuba. His voice is familiar to all lovers of rumba. Through the years, I have had many opportunities to talk with Ernesto. On one occasion, I asked him specifically about the experience of being the first white man sworn to Añá. Our conversation focused on what he felt about his place in history and whether he felt any backlash or racism from others in the community. In his response, Ernesto conveyed the mixed feeling among his family members who were predictably concerned about Ernesto's involvement in artistic activities typically associated with blacks. He also shared with me the odd reaction he occasionally received from strangers. Ernesto reiterated that among the musicians with whom he worked, most of whom he still regards as his closest friends, he did not observe any type of discrimination:

Many people who don't know me think I am black because of my voice [on recordings], and do not believe that I am white! According to Armando "El Surdo" Pedroso,[11] my *padrino* [godfather] in Añá, I am the first white man to be sworn to the drum, something unusual, because in my time there were very few whites who played batá. Many whites are *abakuá, paleros, santeros,*[12] but drummers, very few. I did not have any problems with racism with respect to this. My padrino in Ifá,[13] Ricardo Carballo, was a drummer with Jesús Pérez.[14] Armando "El Surdo" has the seal of Añá. For these reasons, no one ever said anything to me during the drummings. (pers. comm., 2007)

Ernesto's final sentences illustrate the importance of the connections one makes during the swearing ritual, which are essential for establishing and reinforcing a sense of authenticity. The Añá community quickly accepted Ernesto because: 1) he was sworn to Babá Funké, that is, sworn to Pancho's drums; 2) Armando "El Surdo," a well-respected omo Añá, officiated the event; and 3) his padrino in Ifá was himself a widely respected batá drummer. Interestingly, Ernesto received his Ifá in a separate ritual prior to the swearing, and may have selected (or been advised) to work with Carballo because of his affiliation with Jesús Pérez. Of course, Ernesto did not actually tell anyone about all these important ritual relationships, as there were ample witnesses to the event. In addition to Pancho, Enrique, El Surdo, and the twelve others sworn on the same day, several other influential drummers were invited to work the ritual, including Luís Aspirina, Pedro Aspirina, and "El Largo."[15] Whether Pancho, Enrique, and/or Armando "El Surdo" truly grasped the gravity of the moment is unknown, but they certainly worked to ensure that it unfolded in such a way so as to ensure Ernesto's acceptance into a larger community. While Ernesto downplays any potential controversy and openly resists the idea that there might be any racist attitude among his peers, others were acutely aware of the prevailing resistance to white drummers being sworn. For example, Enrique, the proper caretaker of Obayé and Babá Funké, shared with me the prevailing view of his peers, contrasted with his own: "The only white drummer that was sworn in that time was Ernesto. There was an ignorant idea that whites wanted to take all of the information for themselves, but that was a lie. We are all Cubans and we have the same rights, both whites and blacks" (pers. comm., 2010).

In the swearing of a white drummer, Enrique and Pancho made a great leap toward permitting outsiders to join the fraternity. In the years following Ernesto's initiation, Pancho Quinto and Enrique would not only share the secrets of Añá with Cubans from diverse backgrounds, but would also openly initiate many foreigners. In the late 1980s, Pancho became one of the most important conduits for the spreading of the batá tradition throughout the world. In 1980 his close friend Orlando Ríos "Puntilla" had emigrated to the United States and begun nurturing a very successful career in New York City. Noting the insatiable curiosity of drummers in the New York area, Puntilla began to send U.S. American drummers to Cuba to learn how to play with Pancho and to be sworn to Añá with Pancho and Enrique. As a result, Pancho became one of the most internationally well-known Havana-based batá drummers. According to Enrique: "When Orlando 'Puntilla' Ríos went to the United States, he began to send people to be sworn to Añá. Over there, they'd say, 'Who taught you?' And he'd say, 'Pancho Quinto.' And many people came to see Pancho to be sworn. There have been more than two hundred sworn in Obayé and Babá Funké, among them fifteen Japanese, Americans, Canadians, Germans, and French."

In addition to opening the doors for whites and foreigners, Pancho, of course, enjoyed teaching in general. According to Juan de Dios, Pancho's lifelong friend and 1976 founder of the very successful group Conjunto Folklórico Raices Profundas, "Of the people I know, the one who has taught the most people was Pancho."

The development and subsequent refinement of the strategies employed in the initiation of Ernesto Gatell in turn promoted the further propagation of the fraternity by providing a framework for the initiation of non-Cubans. Though the initiations of foreigners originally required a pilgrimage to Cuba, many drummers are now being accepted into the fraternity without travelling. The resulting decentralization of the fraternity necessitates the continual need for strategies that help mitigate the anxiety and tension that results, and which augment the sense of cohesion among its increasingly diverse and dispersed members.

The Creation of New Sets of Batá de Fundamento

The consecration of a new set of batá de fundamento is an important event in the drumming community at large. Among other things, it provides extensive opportunities for the drummers of competing, and sometimes rival, ensembles to join in common cause and celebration, and to forge bonds. The intensity of the event, marked by its lengthy time commitment (seven days of actual ritual preceded by months of preparation) and the number of initiated drummers it draws (in some cases upwards of twenty-five), establishes the ritual as one of the strongest forces for maintaining cohesiveness between ensembles. In addition to connecting groups within Havana, who in the daily pursuit of their craft remain rather isolated from one another, the event also helps span vast generational and geographic distances. A brief examination of the ritual surrounding the consecration of a set of batá de fundamento illuminates the nature of this bonding, and the cohesion it generates.

Añá Cholá is a set of batá de fundamento owned by David Font-Navarrete, a resident of Miami and priest of Obatalá.[16] At the consecration of these drums in April 2004, no less than twenty-five Añá initiates, some of whom are well-known and widely admired for both their performance and ritual knowledge, participated in the lengthy ritual. Some of the more notable and central participants included: Ángel Bolaños, whose batá, named Añá Funmí, "gave voice" to Añá Cholá;[17] Cristóbal Guerra who, as a *babalao* (divining priest), oversaw the Ifá-related ritual proceedings, including the making of the medicines sealed within the body of the drums; Regino Jiménez, who led the *oro igbodú*, the drumming liturgy, on the final day of the ritual; and Amet Díaz, Fermín Nani, and José Pilar, who together performed Añá Funmí and then Añá Cholá during the ritual portion that gave the new set its "voice."[18] Clearly, in the context of the Añá fraternity, this ritual draws together drummers, who in daily life find little time to interact with each other. For members of the older generation, such as Regino Jiménez, Ángel Bolaños, and Fermín Nani, it is also an opportunity to pass on the ritual secrets of Añá.

Finally, the event serves as a testimonial to the pedigree of the newly consecrated set. To openly question the legitimacy of the batá set—as occasionally occurs between unfriendly rivals—disrespects not only the caretaker of the set, but also the large numbers of prestigious and revered initiates who witnessed and participated in the ceremony. Therefore, the ritual associated with consecrating a new batá de fundamento provides cohesion and continuity by mitigating some of the many forces that aim to fracture the socioreligious entity. These include generational differences, geographic separation, and antagonistic relationships between individuals and ensembles that are the natural outgrowth of human competitive nature, particularly in an environment as materially deprived as contemporary Cuba.

The Maintenance of Drums

The physical maintenance of batá drums includes tuning, restringing, and replacing heads. These arduous and time-consuming tasks require the combined skills of two or more people. As the drums comprise natural materials (primarily wood and leather), even the relatively simple act of tuning requires several hours of work for each drum.

The heads of the drums are held in place using one of two basic systems. In Matanzas, drumheads are commonly secured with rope or synthetic sailing cord. In Havana, they are commonly secured with leather straps, cut from the hide of a cow.[19] To tune a drum held together with leather, the woven leather strap that holds the two heads to the shell must first be soaked until pliable.[20] Typically this is achieved by wrapping the drum with wet towels and gently rubbing the straps with a wet rag. When the leather is saturated with water, the long leather strap that weaves the two opposing heads together must be forcefully pulled to remove all slack. Finally, these longitudinal straps are further tightened by weaving the remaining length of leather in transverse fashion around the mid-section of the drum shell six to eight times.

During these hours spent attending to the practical needs of the ensemble's accoutrements, drummers can develop and strengthen bonds, the particulars of which depend on interpersonal dynamics. For example, drummers who share close personal, ritual, and professional relationships utilize these moments to discuss deeper spiritual matters and engage in esoteric conversations about Añá, often considered inappropriate or impractical during regular daily interactions. Similarly, for members who perform together as an ensemble but do not yet share the strong bonds described above, these moments provide an opportunity for ensemble members to work together and further develop the unity, trust, and interdependence that will eventually allow them to enter into potentially deeper communications.

Musical Performance in Toques de Santo

Though several motivations for seeking membership into the Añá fraternity exist, most initiates have an interest in, and eventually develop an aptitude for, batá drumming.[21] While this aptitude begins with learning how to produce the proper tone and rhythms, mastery of the batá also requires the correlative knowledge of song repertoire and a comprehensive understanding of music's role in the drumming ritual. When Lucumí communities hire Añá priests to perform with batá de fundamento during toques de santo, these priests act as liturgical music-ritual specialists with considerable authority to shape the event.

Though the manifest goal of a toque de santo is to facilitate a community's worship of the orichas, and in many instances to help enact a spirit possession, drummers are also guided by their devotion to Añá and their desire to nurture and strengthen their own fraternal bonds through performance. As a result, the ability for an observer to interpret many of the behaviors of the musicians lies beyond simply understanding the ritual. Instead, the interpretive ability lies in also recognizing the complex set of interpersonal relationships among the drummers hired for an event, as well as between this drumming collective and the broader congregation.

To illustrate this point, I analyze several detailed observations made regarding the musical and social behavior of musician-members of the Añá fraternity during a three-week stay in Havana in January 2003. During this time, I was invited daily to accompany and occasionally perform with a vibrant professional ensemble.[22] The following edited excerpts from my personal field notes offer a simplified accounting of the events as they occurred. After each of these excerpts is a deeper analysis that strives to uncover some of the underlying motivations for many of the actions described therein.

Fieldnote Reflections

Vedado, Havana, January 8, 2003. With a toque de santo in full force, a young man walks into the performance space. He steps through the crowd, outwardly oblivious of its presence, and appears concerned only with the drums and the musicians. He offers salutations to both Añá and to the drummers. With his arms crossed in front of his chest, he bends to greet Añá by placing his forehead on the iyá, the largest drum. After repeating this gesture with the okónkolo, the smallest drum, and finally the itótelc, he passes again in front of the iyá and lightly places his fingers on the forehead of the lead drummer, an intimate greeting. This newcomer is a friend and a member of the Añá fraternity. He moves aside and takes a place next to the drummers where he can socialize with other musicians. Though he occasionally sings and claps, he neither dances nor plays the drums.

Judging by the combined facts that he neglected to greet any members of the congregation, arrived late, and was not invited to actually drum, the young man described in this passage appears to have been neither a member of the community that hosted this toque de santo, nor of the particular drumming ensemble hired for the event. His membership in the Añá fraternity was made clear when he touched the lead drummer, who he socialized with, and by his apparent knowledge of the rhythms, which he displayed by clapping. It is also notable that he positioned himself next to the drums, as only Añá initiates are permitted to stand next to or behind the ensemble. Since he left before I could speak with him, I can only speculate as to his intentions for attending the event. However, his actions were typical of a drummer-initiate.

Each night in January 2003, the ensemble I followed performed in a different part of the large city of Havana: Víbora, Santa Catalina, Santo Suarez, Cerro, Vedado, and Habana Vieja. Most evenings, I discovered that the musicians were not personally acquainted with the practitioners who hired them. As a result, they tended to socialize only among themselves, providing opportunities for the musicians to bond. On most evenings, one or more drummers from other ensembles would join us. Likewise, if we finished performing early, or had a night with no obligations, several of us would find another toque de santo to attend, where we would sometimes play but usually just socialize. Since drummers typically do not socialize with their clients, every toque de santo becomes an opportunity for Añá brothers to bond not only with those in their own professional ensemble, but to create a cohesiveness among various ensembles that might otherwise remain isolated within a large city like Havana.

> Lawton, Havana, January 4, 2003. Tonight the music rages, the room crackling with energy as the *akpwón* (officiating singer) and drummers entice an old *santera* (female Lucumí priestess) to temporarily release control of her body and allow the oricha Yemayá to "mount," or possess her. A smile grows on my face as the energy in the room grows to an excessive level. I am delighted that I have invited my two close North American friends to this ceremony to experience their first toque de santo.
>
> One of my friends, trying to be heard above the persistent drumming and singing, leans over and yells into my ear "Why are the drummers making so many mistakes?"
>
> "What?' I yell back, completely stunned by her take on the music.
>
> "The drummers seem to be making a lot of mistakes. It looks like that one [pointing to the drummer with the okónkolo, the smallest drum] needs a lot of help from the others."
>
> Caught off guard, I jump to the drummers' defense and chastise my friend for her lack of perception. Clearly this was a superior performance and she had no idea what she was looking at!

A variety of participants attend toques de santo, each person with their own perspectives, expectations, level of involvement, and level of understanding. Sponsors of the event (often a team consisting of godparent and godchild) determine the occasion, time, date, and place. The sponsors then contract up to three different types of professional performers: batá drummers, an akpwón, and perhaps a possession dancer.[23] Finally, the sponsors invite their associated religious community. These may include babalaos, santeros, other *creyentes* (believers who have had a variety of preliminary initiations and often dance and sing as well), and finally, non-initiates—likely to be family members, friends of the sponsors, or friends of the drummers—and others who might best be described as observers.

As one can see, my friend (an outside observer) and I had different perceptions of the same event. In the above scene, my friend noticed people assisting the okónkolo player by vocalizing rhythms, tapping his shoulders, and playing the drum for him by either facing him, or sitting on the top of the okónkolo and playing the drum behind their back. Indeed, the okónkolo player made mistakes, but the mistakes were actually subtle, unnoticed by most observers, and relatively minor.

The musicians' peculiar overt reactions to those "mistakes" drew my friend's attention. But, the interactive and constructive behavior surrounding these mistakes is such a common occurrence that I hardly noticed them and did not register them as a flaw in the performance. Instead, I understood this as the way drummers typically interact during a ritual; inexperienced drummers often sit and play, while more experienced players stand nearby and offer guidance. In this way, novice drummers learn by reaching beyond their current ability.[24] While from the perspective of the sponsor (who is paying for this service) and the santeros and other participants (who might be happiest when the drumming is clean and polished), it might be preferable for the older, more experienced drummers to play. But for the Añá fraternity, the musical and spiritual growth of young drummers often outweighs these other factors. Indeed, it is widely accepted that learning and teaching are integral components of the toque de santo, both for musicians and for the community of practitioners at large. This is where members of the Lucumí community first experience many of their songs and dances, and where santeros learn of, about, and from the orichas.[25] It is here that the meanings and uses of songs, dances, and rhythms are experientially apprehended through the body" (Mason 1994, 24–25).

My friend also observed a bit of competitive behavior between the two other drummers, playing the iyá and the itótele. In these competitive sequences, the iyá player initiated a series of musical calls, some of which were rather complex, and listened for the itótele player's responses.[26] As if judging one another's abilities, they shared questioning looks: it was a playful interaction, a sort of game or competition, and an integral component of the milieu. Neither of them made any fundamental mistakes. They were just sharing aesthetic critiques on an advanced level.

The drummers engaged in these playful drumming competitions to expand their individual abilities, to develop group musical cohesion, to foster an intimate connection among the drummers, and perhaps to create an elevated sense of excitement. But, to an outsider like my friend, these questioning looks and occasional minor slips that occur when musicians take risks may be interpreted as mistakes, and indicative of a poor performance. Trained as a vocalist in Western art music, my friend comes from a culture that values a well-rehearsed performance where mistakes (if there are any at all) are covered and masked.

How might insiders like babalaos, santeros, and other creyentes interpret these behaviors? Admittedly, I did not have the opportunity to interview them; however, their energetic participation through song and dance, the pleased expressions on their faces, the long length of the ritual (over six hours), and a number of successful possessions indicated to me that the community was more than satisfied with the performance. At this toque de santo, the drummers successfully nurtured their fraternal bonds while exceeding the expectations of the sponsors and the participants.

> Habana Vieja, Havana, January 6, 2003. Initially, I sensed that we must have arrived early this evening. Only a few people had gathered. Yet, the drumming had already begun in the *igbodú* (sacred room with an altar). Quickly we moved down the hall, made our way through the kitchen and the living room, and finally entered the room where the drummers were playing before the altar. Usually three musicians perform in the igbodú, one for each of the drums. But tonight, to my surprise, there was a fourth performer. An elderly gentleman was standing behind the okónkolo player and tapping on his shoulders, making no drum sounds, but very much shaping the performance.

This description refers to a portion of a toque de santo known as the oro igbodú, where the drummers face an altar, and perform a series of toques (rhythms), each a salute to one of twenty-two orichas. As prayers, the true audience for this performance is the orichas. Others are welcome to watch and listen, but they are expected to stand and not come between the drummers and the altar. During the oro igbodú, there is typically little of the socializing that often accompanies the *wemilere,* the public portion of the ceremony alluded to in the previous scenarios.

Therefore, I was surprised to find an elder drummer (who joined us only this one time in three weeks) tapping on the shoulders of the okónkolo player and uttering the syllables, "ki" and "la." At times, the teacher spoke to the okónkolo player, usually in a quiet and serious tone. Occasionally though, when the younger player made one of his many "mistakes," lighthearted joking and laughter were shared among all the drummers at his expense.

The elder teacher was not the only musician helping the young okónkolo player. The lead drummer, who played the iyá, made several interesting musical decisions that minimized the complexity of the music.

I believe these decisions were made to accommodate the okónkolo play-er's musical limitations. The first example of this occurred during the toque for the oricha Yemayá. This toque typically begins at a slow, com-fortable tempo with a simple pattern for the okónkolo. The speed gradu-ally increases until it is three or more times the original tempo. This may take several minutes and provides ample opportunities for the iyá to insert variations and improvisations. Following this segment, there is typically a transition into a section or toque known as "Taniboya," which requires the okónkolo player to modify his pattern. At the fast tempo, it can be difficult to execute. Rather than launch into the new section, the iyá player shortened the toque and cut it before the impending change. The second interesting musical decision occurred when the iyá player substituted the salute rhythm "Tuí-tuí" for the more common Oyá salute, both of which are suitable rhythms for the oricha Oyá. While the more common Oyá salute has many confusing changes for the okónkolo, "Tuí-tuí" consists of one simple pattern.

Because drummers have considerable discretion with regard to the rhythms they play during the oro igbodú, these musical decisions might not immediately appear to be significant. Indeed, one might be inclined to interpret these choices as purely aesthetic. However, by combining the actions of the teacher, who is not a regular member of the ensemble, with those of the lead drummer, we can see this as a well-coordinated strat-egy for ensuring cohesion by encouraging learning from outside the core ensemble. Essentially, the musicians adapted this portion of the ritual and blended their host's desires to fulfill an obligation to the orichas with their own need to transmit drumming ritual knowledge. However, a successful blending of desires is not always possible. As is illustrated in the next account, sometimes the fraternity's own needs conflict with the desires of the participants:

Vedado, Havana, January 8, 2003. In the middle of the room, the oricha Eleguá shows signs of his presence. A santero, wearing a black and red bracelet, begins to shake and shudder. As if satisfying a deep itch, he scratches and tears at his scalp. One moment he dances directly before the drums, the next he charges toward the exit, but is stopped by an impenetrable wall of practitioners eager to see, hear, and feel Eleguá's presence. From somewhere in the back of the room, the santero is show-ered with hard candy and sweets. From the other direction, he is sprayed with rum. Again, he dances, tries to escape, scratches his scalp, rubs his face. He is reluctant; the drums persist.

The practitioners stop dancing and form a semicircle to enclose the santero between themselves and the musicians who focus all their energy on the reluctant mount. The akpwon sings into the santero's ear and shakes a rattle. The semicircle begins to close. Trying to get a better view, several women move in and stand in front of the itótclc and the okónkolo. Two musicians quickly force themselves between the women and the drums, corralling the women away from obstructing the drummers. The excitement in the room continues to rise; the observers continue to close in. More women stand in front of the drummers to get a better view. Musicians continue to position themselves between the women and the drums. Finally, the iyá player has had enough: Eleguá is moments away from mounting his "child"; and yet the iyá stops the music!

In addition to clapping, singing, and helping the younger drummers, musicians have a role in "protecting" the drums (and by extension, the fraternity) by configuring themselves around the ensemble. In Figure 7.1 we see the musicians positioned around the okónkolo, iyá, and itótele. Sitting behind each of the three batá is a drummer. To the left of center, between the okónkolo and the iyá, another drummer sits and rests his legs on a short stool. Next to him, tucked into the corner, a musician stands. The akpwon stands in front of the drums, facing the practitioners. Practitioners occupy the open space of the room, singing, dancing, leaning against the wall, prostrating to the drums and to one another, and occasionally getting possessed. Over the course of the ritual, they continually rearrange themselves and adjust according the context. The two drummers standing on the left, nearest the okónkolo, and the two sitting on the right, nearest the window, provide a buffer between the practitioners and the drums. It is these musicians who had moved and forced themselves (as described above) between the female practitioners and the drums.

When asked directly why the non-drumming community (in particular women and homosexual men) should maintain a distance from the drums, most drummers provide vague, often contradictory responses that address the spiritual and physical safety of the non-drummers. Though I am more concerned here with ritual actions than with belief and theology, I have observed, in a variety of contexts, instances where the spatial delineation has broken down (e.g., participants having brushed up against the drums and/or managed to get behind the drums). To my knowledge, these individuals did not fall ill or have some misfortune befall them. (Of course, this does not suggest that there were not real repercussions, only that I did not witness them.)

The other reason given for the delineation of space is that the sacred medicine of Añá, which is housed inside the drums, might become

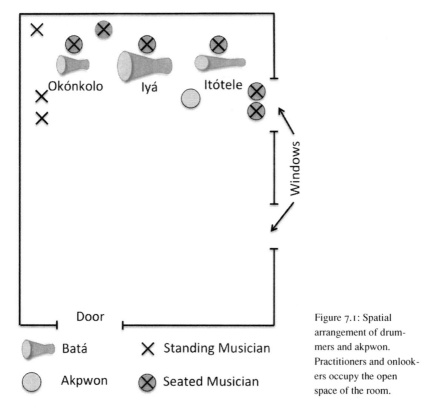

Figure 7.1: Spatial arrangement of drummers and akpwon. Practitioners and onlookers occupy the open space of the room.

contaminated by inappropriate contact—or the likelihood that the rumor mill might just as well avail itself of such violations of orthodoxy in order to disadvantage the group of drummers or their drums. For example, I could imagine a competing group of drummers spreading the rumor that the batá de fundamento of "so and so" are tainted because women, non-initiates, or homosexual men touched the drums. As a practical matter, this would be bad for business.

The prohibitions in the Añá fraternity against women and homosexual men are weakly justified. They appear to be Cuban inventions, with little precedent in the fraternity's African counterpart. Regardless of whether initiates invoke philosophical or ideological explanations for their perpetuation, they emerged within a culture widely identified for its misogynist and homophobic tendencies. They are most likely rooted within social culture and not intrinsic to religious doctrine. Nonetheless, the prohibitions remain largely unaffected by modern feminist influences and the increasing public acceptance of homosexuality. From this, I draw the tentative conclusion that maintaining the prohibitions are essential strategies for maintaining cohesion, as they permit initiates to engage in theatrical displays that demonstrate a sense of exclusivity. Women and men, both, are corralled away from the drums, women by virtue of their external identifier as female and men whose sexual orientation has not been investigated and is unconfirmed.[27] Therefore, when drummers stand guard around the batá, they believe they are protecting misguided practitioners, the spirit of the batá (Añá), and the reputation of their fraternity. The act of doing this helps augment established bonds, and for the youngest of drummers, secures the continued prestige of the fraternity.

While it is quite customary for the drummers to take an active role in demarcating a separation between the drumming space and the worshippers, it is extremely rare for the drummers to dramatically halt the ceremony when others violate their space. The unusual circumstance I witnessed at this event might further be explained by examining the lead drummer's more significant concern that practitioners had occupied the space between the santero and the batá. Repeatedly, the lead drummer motioned for everyone to move aside and create a clear line of sight between the drummers and the santero. But, when his requests remained unheard or unheeded, he eventually stopped the drums and the onset of possession. This may have been done out of concern for the practitioners but it may have also been triggered by concerns that the integrity of fraternity itself was being threatened by the broken line of sight. After all, if the lead drummer cannot see the impending possession, how can he claim that it is an essential component of the drummer's art to read the visual clues of the dancing santeros as he helps to encourage that possession? Furthermore, if visual contact is indeed essential for possession, the iyá player justifiably needs to see the action.

In an ideal setting, both the drummers and the practitioners benefit from the "arrival" of the oricha Eleguá (taking possession of the initiate) at the toque de santo. His presence rewards practitioners, who can touch, engage, and receive wisdom from the oricha. For the drummers, Eleguá's presence indicates an efficacious and successful ceremony. Therefore, one senses the reluctance with which the iyá player halted the music.

Though the arrival of an oricha is a sought-after event during a toque de santo, it does not necessarily indicate an effective ceremony. Had the possession been permitted to continue, the legitimacy of the drumming fraternity and the notion of "charged space" might tacitly have been brought into question. However, by making a spectacle of the incorrect behavior by stopping the ceremony, the community reflected upon the crucial role of Añá and the drummers in effecting the ritual. Soon after stopping, the music began again, apparently with a renewed sense of purpose and a higher level of excitement. The practitioners, likewise, seemed to be undaunted by the scolding they received and increased their involvement in the ceremony. Not long after the music restarted, Eleguá mounted the santero, perhaps an indication that expectations and needs only "appeared" to be in conflict.

Conclusions

During these three weeks in Havana (and throughout my other experiences) I found that, while the drummers typically balance their personal needs with those of the community, and keep their own needs transparent, there are notable moments when this is undesirable or impossible. Though I regard the way drummers balance multiple thematic acts as an essential component of their craft, overt expressions of the drummers' perspective (such as stopping a possession) can be a powerful strategy for establishing or maintaining cohesion within the fraternity.

Severed from the kinship-lineage configuration of Yorùbáland, the Añá fraternity that emerged in the Cuban context employs a variety of strategies to ensure cohesion at both the local and global levels. The challenge at the local level is to ensure that fraternity members within a ritual drumming ensemble develop a degree of intimacy. This is particularly important among those who do not have either the familial bonds of a father/uncle and son/nephew or the direct ritual bonds that exist between godparent and godson. This intimacy can be fostered in a variety of contexts.

During the initiations of new members and while engaged in the arduous maintenance of drums, experienced fraternity members work together toward a common cause. Both the physical element (working together toward a common end) and the spiritual element (working closely with Añá) establish and redefine these bonds.

During toques de santo, drummers employ a myriad of strategies with the same goal: these musical rituals provide opportunities for socializing, and for nurturing and developing individual musical ability. During these events, skilled musicians engage in amicable drumming rivalries where they become comfortable and familiar with each other's playing styles, and work to reduce musical response times to the point that the interaction feels seamless. This develops *communitas*, a condition where individuals lose direct consciousness of self, and experience a prevailing sense of sharing and intimacy with others (McNeill 1995; Turner 1967, 1969).

On the global level, many strategies develop continuity, and cohesion across generations, between competing groups within a single city, and across oceans and continents, as the fraternity continues to expand beyond Cuba's borders. With the initiation of new members, as in the aforementioned example of Ernesto Gatell, respected elders are often invited to attend or preside over the ritual. These elders provide ritual knowledge, a sense of authority and legitimacy, and may even help facilitate the acceptance of new members into the greater Añá community. When new batá de fundamento are created, fraternity members are invited, and expected to participate to varying degrees.

During toques de santo, there are also appropriate ways to greet and engage elders or any drumming guests. Though they may or may not be invited to actually play the drums, Añá initiates are invited to stand close to the drums where they can sing, clap, and most importantly, socialize with other members. Finally, as was the case in my last observation, Añá initiates take advantage of their role as ritual drumming specialists to ensure that the Lucumí community at large continues to both respect Añá and recognize the crucial role of the drummers in effecting the ritual.

Notes

1. The spelling "Añá" is adopted to reflect the Cuban pronunciation in Spanish. This term is derived from the original Yorùbá term "Àyàn."

2. A growing international interest in and affinity for the musical aspects of the Añá fraternity has contributed to the secularization of its musical components. As a result, much of the musical repertoire associated with the cult can now be enjoyed in a myriad of public venues. Accordingly, the lines between sacred and secular are increasingly blurred, especially among non-initiates. Increased access to the music has also fueled interest among fraternity outsiders who enjoy performing the music, predictably leading to challenges of the male-centered, heterosexual nature of the cult. While the sacred and secular dichotomy appears to generate a substantial amount of concern among initiates (see Schweitzer 2013), discourse regarding the lack of access permitted to women has been largely propagated by fraternity outsiders. In my personal fieldwork experience, I have witnessed only passing reference to the controversial nature of these restrictions. It is a topic that receives only a superficial treatment in this chapter, and one I would like to explore in depth in the future.

3. Several different terms may aptly describe the relationship between an Añá initiate and those who sponsored his initiation. In this text, I loosely employ the term "godfather" as a signifier of respect and ritual kinship. It is however, qualitatively different, and should not be confused with the godparent-godchild relationship that results from "making *ocha*" (the full oricha initiation).

4. The spelling of batá is adopted to reflect the Cuban pronunciation in Spanish. This term is derived from the original Yorùbá term, bàtá. The phrase batá de fundamento refers to a consecrated set of batá, which comprises three drums, from largest to smallest: iyá, itótele, and okónkolo.

5. In brief, the Lucumí religion is a Cuban religion that developed from the syncretism of Yorùbá and various other West African beliefs and practices with Catholicism. Though the Añá fraternity participates in a variety of Lucumí rituals, I will limit my discussion to those celebratory

events known alternately as toques de santo, toques de batá, *bembés, güemileres, or tambores.* The Lucumí religion is also known popularly as Santería, Regla de Ocha, and *el religión* Yoruba.

6. The period between 1997 and 2003 marks the time spent researching and writing my DMA dissertation. Many of the thoughts in this essay are derived from that work (Schweitzer 2003).

7. One notable exception to this is Rubén Bulnés, who I interviewed in 2003. At that time, Rubén was in high demand as an akpwon (officiating singer) and was performing nightly. During the three weeks that I worked with him, I noticed that he did occasionally play batá, though only for short periods of time. The relative absence of white drummers in Cuba is noticeable. It is a phenomenon that I have yet to carefully explore, and I am hesitant to speculate as to the significance of this observation without additional research. In this section, I examine the circumstances around the initiation of the first white drummer to the fraternity. I describe the potential friction not to examine race within the religion, but rather to demonstrate some of the strategies employed by the ritual coordinators to alleviate tension and to ensure the success of a controversial initiation.

8. The facts and quotes in this section stem from three interviews: the first with Ernesto Gatell in 2007, the second with Armando Pedroso "El Surdo" in 2007 (d. 2013), and the third with Enrique Ramírez Mora, cousin of Pancho Quinto, in 2010. Some scholars question whether Ernesto is, in fact, the "first" white to be sworn to Añá. For example, Amado de Jesús Dedeu Hernández, widely known as the director of the famous rumba group Clave y Guaguancó, was sworn before Ernesto. While Amado's skin is very light, and his official government ID indeed lists his race as "white," he was born of a white father and a black mother. Ernesto, by comparison, had two white parents. Or in his words, his race was "*blanco y blanco*" (white and white).

9. Strictly speaking, Obayé (as well the batá named Babá Funké) is cared for by Pancho Quinto's cousin Enrique Ramírez Mora. However, everyone refers to them as Pancho Quinto's.

10. The date of the initiation has been communicated to me as either August 10, 1985 or August 13, 1985 (Gatell, pers. comm., 2007).

11. Interestingly, Ernesto identified Armando Pedroso "El Surdo" as the first *mulatto*, with a black mother and white father, to be sworn to Añá. I have not been able to verify this.

12. Abakuá is an Afro-Cuban secret society with roots in southeastern Nigeria and southwestern Cameroon. Paleros and santeros are initiates of the Afro-Cuban Palo Monte and Lucumí religions, respectively. In Cuba it is common for an individual to maintain membership in multiple religions and societies.

13. In the Lucumí religion, practitioners often have several different padrinos and *madrinas* (godmothers). Drummers, for example, have a padrino in Añá. Most drummers also have a padrino in Ifá, who as a babalao is responsible for giving them the Hand of Ifá, or *mano* Orula (an entry-level initiation). Santeros, similarly, will have a padrino or madrina in *santo* (oricha), who is responsible for the "crowning" of their guardian oricha.

14. Jesús Pérez is among the most famous of all batá drummers. He was a primary informant of Fernando Ortíz and was a founding member of the Conjunto Folklórico Nacional de Cuba, as well as an international recording artist.

15. In Cuba, it is a common practice to be given a nickname. Their use is so pervasive that many people are known only by their nickname.

16. The facts in this section are derived from multiple communications with David Font-Navarrete between 2004 and 2012. David Font-Navarrete is also the co-author of an essay in this volume.

17. There are two types of batá drums, *fundamento* (consecrated) and *aberikulá* (unconsecrated). Whereas batá de aberikulá can be performed in any context by anyone regardless of initiation, gender, and sexual orientation, batá de fundamento must only be handled and played by omo Añá.

When a batá is consecrated with the spirit of Añá, it is said to have a "voice," which facilitates communication (in the form of drummed rhythms) between the drummers and the pantheon of orichas. Batá de fundamento are rarely performed outside the context of a Lucumí ritual.

18. Regino Jiménez Saez (1948–2005) and Fermín Nani Socarrás (d. 2007) passed away shortly after these drums were consecrated. This may have been their last collaboration.

19. The tradition of using leather straps seems to be shifting toward rope, as it is much easier to tune the drums using ropes.

20. Plate 7.1 shows two batá that are constructed with the leather strapping.

21. Non-drumming babalaos are regularly initiated into Añá because of their divination sign of Ifá, and not due to any desire to actually become a drummer.

22. During this three-week period, I worked with a variety of musicians. While I do not intend to connect any particular observation to a specific musician, I am comfortable sharing the names of a few key performers who were present at many of these toques de santo, including Amet Díaz on iyá, Jesús Lorenzo Peñalver "Cusito" also on iyá and performing as akpwon, and Rubén Bulnés as akpwon.

23. A possession dancer, known as a *caballo* (horse or mount), is sometimes hired for a toque de santo. The caballo is a santero/a who is highly regarded for the depth with which he/she enters into the possession state. This is a valuable quality when there is an exceptionally strong desire on behalf of the sponsors to witness a particular possession during the toque de santo.

24. Though it is increasingly common in the present-day to engage in lessons and conduct rehearsals, especially among foreigners, much of the training required to master batá occurs during ceremonial performances. To facilitate this, the batá drumming tradition has evolved in such a way so as to allow developing players to learn in situ.

25. When orichas possess their mounts, they may communicate with the congregation in a variety of ways. This can be accomplished with general statements directed to all those in attendance, or they may be conveyed more intimately. Sometimes the orichas leave the performance space and sit near the altar where they entertain inquiries and personal requests for assistance and knowledge.

26. An essential feature of batá drumming involves a type of interaction best described as call and response. During these types of interactions, the iyá player indicates a call by deviating from a pre-established pattern. These calls can be simple or complex, bold or subtle. It is the responsibility of the itótele player to respond to these calls by also deviating from his pre-established pattern in a stylistically appropriate way. Many calls and responses are highly codified, while others provide the drummers with a tremendous amount of latitude.

27. In 2000 I participated in a ritual known as "hand-washing," which transpired in the Havana home of Pancho Quinto. Compelled to investigate my sexual orientation prior to allowing me access to his Añá drums, Pancho phoned a mutual acquaintance in Miami to inquire about my personal life. Only after satisfying his concerns did Pancho proceed with the ritual.

References Cited

Mason, Michael Atwood. 1994. "'I Bow My Head to the Ground': The Creation of Bodily Experience in Cuban-American Santería Initiation." In *Journal of American Folklore* 107 (423): 23–39.

McNeill, William. 1995. *Keeping Together in Time: Dance and Drill in Human History.* Cambridge, MA: Harvard University Press.

Schweitzer, Kenneth. 2003. "Afro-Cuban Batá Drum Aesthetics: Developing Individual and Group Technique, Sound, and Identity." DMA dissertation, University of Maryland, College Park.

———. 2013. *The Artistry of Afro-Cuban Batá Drumming: Aesthetics, Transmission, Bonding, and Creativity*. Jackson: University Press of Mississippi.

Turner, Victor. 1967. *The Forest of Symbols*. Ithaca, NY: Cornell University Press.

———. 1969. *The Ritual Process: Structure and Anti-Structure*. Chicago: Aldine.

Interviews

Juan De Dios Ramos "El Colo," 2010. Juan de Dios is a professional singer and was a good friend and colleague of Pancho Quinto. Recorded conversation in his home, August 2010, Havana, Cuba. Transcribed by Ernesto Gatell, and translated by the author.

Rogelio Ernesto Gatell Cotó "Gato," June 2007. Ernesto is a professional singer and percussionist, including batá de fundamento. Recorded conversation in his Havana home. Transcribed by Ernesto Gatell, and translated by the author.

Enrique Ramírez Mora, August 2010. Enrique is the cousin and close friend of the late Pancho Quinto. Recorded conversation between Enrique, Ernesto Gatell, and the author in Havana, Cuba. Transcribed by Ernesto Gatell, and translated by the author.

Quintín Armando Pedroso "El Surdo," June 2007. Armando is a professional percussionist, including batá de fundamento. A conversation between Pedroso, Ernesto Gatell, and the author was recorded in his Havana home. Transcribed by Ernesto Gatell, and translated by the author.

8

Being Àyàn in a Modernizing Nigeria:
A Multigenerational Perspective

Debra L. Klein

• •

My family is the most important thing to me. I know how valuable they
are to me. They are my roots—where I learned the art of drumming and
skills I will never forget. And now I must pass this knowledge along.
That's how it is. (Àyánníyì, pers. comm., July 24, 1997)

A medium-sized, semi-rural town in Ọ̀ṣun State renowned for its traditional culture, Èrìn-Ọ̀ṣun is home to a multigenerational family of
practicing *bàtá* and *dùndún* drummers from a compound called Ìyálọ́jà.[1]
Training their children in the art and profession of bàtá and dùndún
drumming, the past three generations have inherited a common thread
of Àyàn identity, or "Àyàn-ness" as expressed by the young Àyàn drummer quoted above; they are rooted in the Àyàn drumming profession and
work hard to keep bàtá and dùndún performance traditions alive by performing for local and global audiences in secular, ritual, and educational
settings and by teaching their knowledge and skills to family members
and students from Nigeria and all parts of the world.[2]
  Yorùbá drumming families in Nigeria identify with Òrìṣà Àyànàgalú
(also known as Àyàn), the spirit of the drum. While Èrìn-Ọ̀ṣun artists
do not directly incorporate the *òrìṣà* Àyàn into their everyday or ritual
lives, they acknowledge Àyàn's spiritual role in their family's history.
This chapter will illustrate that "being Àyàn," for three generations of
drummers, revolves around an inherited and professional identity rather
than religious beliefs or ritual practices. Yet each generation has crafted
its Àyàn identity within local, national, and international contexts characterized by intense juxtapositions between the national devaluation of

the òrìṣà, shaped by Nigeria's modernizing discourses, and worldwide demand for the òrìṣà, shaped by global and diasporic discourses of culture preservation. Each generation has performed its Àyàn-ness differently; in an effort to understand what it has meant to "be Àyàn," I turn to the words and experiences of the past three generations of Ìyálójà's Àyàn drummers.

Since the 1960s, the past three generations have contributed to and been shaped by their participation in a Yorùbá culture movement, a global network of artists, students, scholars, and òrìṣà worshippers who participate in and perpetuate aspects of traditional Yorùbá culture. The idea of a Yorùbá culture movement emerged from my everyday conversations with the artists and their apprentices from Germany and the United States. Èrìn-Òṣun artist "discourse"[3] about the meaning of Yorùbá traditional culture was thus produced in dialogue with German and US collaborators. Èrìn-Òṣun artist discourse often hinged on their networks of concrete relationships—real people from real places navigating real relationships. Greg Urban's (1996) juxtaposition of "intelligible" with "sensible" aspects of discourse lends further clarification to the concept of a Yorùbá culture movement. The sensible side is discourse about lived experience, actual people narrating their experiences. The intelligible side is "discourse about meaningful discourse" (Urban 1996, 22), metadiscourses such as a culture movement about the production of culture. In this sense, a Yorùbá culture movement has become a metaculture that has self-consciously and collaboratively produced its forms of tradition and culture.

Within the global community of òrìṣà devotees, there appears to be a prevailing assumption about Yorùbá identity that also holds true for Àyàn identity: being Yorùbá and Àyàn hinges around belief in and worship of the òrìṣà. I suggest that, in a global discourse about Yorùbá identity, "performances"[4] of Àyàn identity have become naturalized as "òrìṣà belief and worship," leaving little room for the notion of Àyàn-ness as a professional lineage-based identity that changes over time and does not privilege the òrìṣà. Arguing against the assumption that "being Àyàn" equals Àyàn worship, I examine how the "performativity"[5] of Àyàn-ness has changed within Èrìn-Òṣun from the 1950s to the present. By looking at "being Àyàn" as a performative process, this chapter tracks how Àyàn-identified artists have historically, institutionally, and discursively redefined and recreated the social category of "Àyàn."

It is worth noting that the discourse of Àyàn-ness revolving around the worship of the òrìṣà Àyàn began, at least in part, in New York in the 1950s, when Cuban drummers introduced bàtá to the United States. Cornelius describes the context in which bàtá grew:

New York's drummers understood the relentless power of sinew and drum to move the body and free the mind. These, after all, were the currencies of America's African-rooted musical experience . . . of slave-era ring shouts, of the tonal slides and rhythmic grooves of Louis Armstrong, of the dance bands of Machito and Mario Bauza, and the ferocious rhythmic drive of jazz drummer Elvin Jones. These were the sources of authenticity from which New York musicians drew as they ventured outward into the rhythmic styles and sonic efficacy of bata drumming. (Cornelius 2008, 11)

Associating some sort of authentic or natural experience with the Yorùbá drumming tradition of bàtá, US-based practitioners helped shape the discourse that naturalized Yorùbá drumming as religious and spiritual versus lineage-based and professional. Thus, the tendency to naturalize Àyàn-ness as òrìṣà-centered is variously rooted in diasporic contexts and histories.

This discourse of Yorùbáness rooted in òrìṣà worship also emerged during the project of Nigerian nation building, from the 1950s through the 1970s. During this time, Nigerian politicians, scholars, and artists became invested in defining a Yorùbá identity that predated and stood in opposition to Islam and Christianity. Many scholars have documented the collaborative movement to revive Yorùbá òrìṣà and artistic cultures in Òṣogbo as an example of a successful and multi-valenced commitment to reinvent a Yorùbáness rooted in the òrìṣà (see Beier 1991; Klein 2007; Probst 2011). This intellectualization and folkloricization of òrìṣà culture has been and continues to be part of a Yorùbá nationalist movement.

Since the conversion of Nigeria to Islam and Christianity, òrìṣà worship has seriously declined in Nigeria; many òrìṣà scholars and remaining practitioners are alarmed that òrìṣà-related traditions, including those around the òrìṣà Àyàn, are endangered (Vincent 2006; Klein 2007). When I began my fieldwork with Èrìn-Òṣun's most prolific Àyàn lineage in the early nineties, the artists had been enmeshed in overseas networks of sponsors, researchers, and fans for over thirty years. Without these networks, these artists' Àyàn identities would have been very different, perhaps nonexistent. These artists' senses of "being Àyàn" were crafted within their town and in collaboration with their overseas interlocutors.

While the oldest of three generations of Àyàn artists in my study did not have much contact with overseas collaborators, the next two generations have come of age in a global culture movement.[6] While I show how "being Àyàn" revolves around family identity and professionalization of drumming for all generations, I also illustrate that the past two generations have incorporated the popular diasporic discourse about Àyàn-ness into their performances of Àyàn identity. I argue that Nigeria-based Àyàn artists have become inspired to re-embrace the òrìṣà, challenging the discourse of Nigerian modernity that excludes the òrìṣà yet performing a Yorùbá modernity defined by such strategies of incorporating old and new cultural elements.

As an anthropologist with a long-term commitment to an Àyàn lineage in Èrìn-Òṣun, I challenge the dominance of the òrìṣà-based notion of being Àyàn by paying attention to multiple and emergent meanings of Àyàn-ness in Nigeria. Though that is my central concern in this chapter, it is significant that the òrìṣà-based notion of Àyàn-ness has influenced and empowered Nigeria-based Àyàn artists. But I caution us against the assumption that Àyàn-ness is endangered if the òrìṣà are not at the center.

Àyàn Artists of Èrìn-Òṣun

According to oral and written primary and secondary historical sources (Johnson 1976; Peel 2000; Villepastour 2010), Èrìn-Òṣun was founded by Yorùbá refugees from Èrìnlé (close to Ìlọrin in today's Kwara State) who fled the violence of the Fulani invasions during the mid-nineteenth century. Èrìnlé is storied to have been founded by Ọbàlùfọn (òrìṣà of cloth and weaving), who walked north from Ilé-Ifẹ̀, the reputed birthplace of Yorùbá people (Villepastour 2010, 29). In 1817 Àfọ̀njá, the ruler of Ìlọrin, wanted to enhance his power (after having lost his bid to become the next king of Ọ̀yọ́) and thus invited a prominent Fulani priest known as Álímì to support him in Ìlọrin. Significantly, Àfọ̀njá was not a Muslim himself but a believer in the òrìṣà. Álímì and his army of Hausa slaves turned against Àfọ̀njá and carried out a jihad against "pagan" Yorùbá people (Peel 2000, 33). According to Àyándòkun of Èrìn-Òṣun, the people of Èrìnlé supported Àfọ̀njá and ended up fleeing their town on the fateful night when the Fulani invaded. The ancestors of the Àyàn family of Èrìn-Òṣun with whom I work were responsible for warning the king, Ọba Ọyágbọ́dùn, and waking up the town so that they could escape. This was when they fled and founded Èrìn-Òṣun. When the war ended in Ìlọrin, the king returned but left one of his sons to continue the kingship in Èrìn-Òṣun (Villepastour 2010, 31).

Today's king of Èrìn-Òṣun, Ẹlérìn Ọba Yusuf Ọmọloyè Ọyágbọ́dùn II, is a descendent of Ọyágbọ́dùn. Though he is a Muslim, the Ẹlérìn hosts an annual festival in honor of Òrìṣà Ọbàlùfọn during the harvest in June or July. In the late nineties, the king estimated the number of Muslims in Èrìn-Òṣun to be about 65 percent and the number of Christians to be about 35 percent of Èrìn-Òṣun's total population of about 100,000. In our interview, he said that a small percentage (less than 5 percent), including practitioners of Islam and Christianity, also continue to worship the òrìṣà.[7]

Analyzing linguistic and archival evidence, J. D. Y. Peel argues that Songhai people from the northwest, rather than Hausa people, initially brought Islam to Yorùbá people as early as the late sixteenth century. But by the eighteenth century, predominantly Hausa and other Nigerians were converting Yorùbá people. And by the 1810s, a substantial number of Yorùbá people had already converted to Islam. When the founders of Èrìn-Òṣun fled south, it is likely that many of them had already converted to Islam. As Peel states, however, the Islamization of Yorùbá people "varied from town to town according to local circumstances" (2000, 191). Given the two-hundred-year history of the mutual constitution and coexistence of òrìṣà worship and Islam, coupled with the Yorùbá ethos of incorporation, I suggest that the Àyàn artists' ways of being Muslim are historically and specifically flexible and even incorporative of the òrìṣà.

My long-term ethnographic research with Àyàn artists, beginning in 1990, has revolved around the extended family of Làmídì Àyánkúnlé in Èrìn-Òṣun. One of the few compounds that continues to school its children in the art of traditional drumming, the Ìyálójà compound consists of about two hundred members, spanning five generations and five different towns in Òṣun and Kwara states. There are Ìyálójà compounds in the towns of Èrìn-Òṣun (Òṣun State) and Èrìnlé (Kwara State). Over the course of three years of fieldwork in the nineties and during subsequent research trips in 2005 and 2010, I lived with the Àyàn drummers in their compound and attended about one hundred Àyàn and Òjè[8] performances as a participant-observer. Òrìṣà ceremonies comprised about twenty-nine of these performances: three for Ṣàngó, three for Òṣun, two for Ògún, and twenty-one for Egúngún.[9] Though it was not a topic of everyday conversation, I was able to engage the artists in dialogue about their identities as members of Àyàn and Òjè lineages and their relationships to the òrìṣà during formal interviews, which I recorded and transcribed with the help of my research assistants, Ràṣídì Àyándélé and Tájù Àyánbísí. Throughout the nineties, we conducted series of formal interviews with about thirty members of three different Àyàn and Òjè generations.

In order to understand and articulate generational shifts in Àyàn family members' identities, I have differentiated among the three generations of artists. After listening to, reviewing, and analyzing my interviews with the artists, I came up with the following phrases, from direct quotations during interviews and conversations, to help characterize each generation's relationship with the òrìṣà: the "No More Òrìṣà" generation, the "Reviving Òrìṣà" generation, and the "Grasping for Òrìṣà" generation.

Those of the No More Òrìṣà generation were born between 1925 and 1940 during British colonialism: they were mostly in their sixties and early seventies when I lived with and interviewed them. Most members of this generation were not formally educated in Western or Koranic schools and were second-generation Muslims in their families. Their Àyàn heritage signified an inherited drumming profession and family identity as drummers for traditional leaders and òrìṣà worshippers. During the 1950s and 1960s, many members of this generation bought kola nut or cocoa farms in nearby towns in order to supplement their incomes from drumming. At the time of this writing, the artists I interviewed from this generation have all passed away and are sorely missed.

Members of the Reviving Òrìṣà generation were born between 1945 and 1960 during a Nigeria on the edge of independence: they were mostly in their forties and fifties when I lived with them. I spent most of my time with members of this generation, particularly Làmídì Àyánkúnlé and his family, with whom I have collaborated on documenting the history and culture of Yorùbá bàtá. Làmídì and I maintain regular correspondence via email and mutual friends. Like their fathers, most members of this generation were not formally educated in Western or Koranic schools. In addition to drumming professionally, most of them apprenticed in and mastered another trade, such as carpentry, barbering, or sewing. They were raised as third-generation Muslims. This generation came of age during Nigeria's nation-building decades and its members have traveled extensively within and outside Nigeria as representatives of Yorùbá culture. Their Àyàn heritage signifies pride in and a desire to revive their culture's traditional roots, àṣà ìbílẹ̀ (literally "deep culture").

The Grasping for Òrìṣà generation incorporates those born between 1965 and 1980 during a modernizing Nigeria: they were mostly in their late teens and twenties in the late nineties. Most members of this generation attended Western-modeled elementary school and then studied a trade to supplement their incomes from drumming. They were raised as fourth-generation Muslims and identify with and perform the Muslim-inspired, Nigerian popular music known as fújì.[10] Like their fathers, they are proud of their Àyàn heritage, yet they have come to realize that they have been steadily losing touch with their àṣà ìbílẹ̀, Yorùbá roots. Several members of this generation have since become interested in understanding and documenting their cultural roots. During our interviews,

for example, they expressed goals of publishing their own family histories. Many of my collaborators[11] from this generation have performed
overseas, following in their fathers' footsteps, and several have moved to
the United States.

No More Òrìṣà

The Àyàn forefathers of Ìyálójà's compound had not yet converted to
Islam during the Fulani invasions; they continued to worship the òrìṣà
until the early 1900s. During our interviews, I learned that the parents
of the No More Òrìṣà generation converted to Islam during their per-
formance- and business-related travels around Nigeria and West Africa.
Once converted, this generation raised their children as second-generation Muslims in Èrìn-Òṣun.

Despite being second-generation Muslims, the primary profession of
this generation was to play bàtá and dùndún for year-round òrìṣà and
secular rituals.[12] When the careers of musicians in this generation were at
their height, the daily, year-round ritual calendar, a series of two-week or
monthlong celebrations for different òrìṣà, was still intact. These drummers had plenty of work during the peak of their professional lives. Even
though most of these drummers also owned kola nut or cocoa farms to
supplement their incomes, their identities revolved around their occupations as traditional drummers. Members of this generation raised their
sons to follow in their professional footsteps and remained rooted in
their roles as husbands, fathers, and drummers for their town and the
Yorùbá region.

As Nigeria transitioned into an independent nation-state in the 1960s
and the economy went through cycles of boom and bust, the drummers'
work schedules, which once followed the yearly ritual calendar, were
largely consolidated to weekends, when families celebrated naming ceremonies, funerals, and weddings. Òrìṣà festivals also dwindled as Islam
and Christianity continued to dominate the religious and ritual landscape;
thus, the drummers were unemployed on weekdays and were forced to
turn to other kinds of work for wages. As it became increasingly difficult to depend on drumming as a sustainable profession, many Àyàn
families stopped drumming and stopped passing their inherited profession down to future generations. The No More generation witnessed
this transition: their profession became less relevant in a modernizing
Nigeria. Significantly, however, they became the first generation of their
family to become active players in the emergent global Yorùbá culture
movement of the 1960s. While members of other Èrìn-Òṣun drumming

Plate 8.1: Bàba Ràṣídì was a member of the No More Òrìṣà generation. (photograph: Debra Klein, Èrìn-Òṣun, 10 June 2005)

families began to leave town to pursue other forms of work or education in Nigerian or West African cities, the Àyàn drummers of the Ìyálójà compound were discovered by and began to collaborate with Ìbàdàn- and Òṣogbo-based artists and scholars who were founding members of the movement for the revival of traditional Yorùbá culture.[13]

In the 1950s, for example, German scholar and culture broker Ulli Beier began to work closely with Ìgè Àyánṣínà, a member of the No More generation and father of Làmídì. Beier's academic interest in and sponsorship of Àyánṣínà's profession contributed to Àyánṣínà's desire to pass his skills and passion for bàtá down to his sons. At the same time, Austrian artist (and eventual resident Ọbàtálá priestess) Susanne Wenger (1915–2009) became enamored with the artistry and skills of Àyánbísí, another member of the No More generation: Wenger asked Àyánbísí to become her personal drummer for her weekly òrìṣà ceremonies in Òṣogbo. Àyánbísí played for Wenger's ceremonies, working as her personal drummer for about thirty years until his death.

Another member of this generation, Bàba Làtí, remarked on his family's unique success: "Since our family has passed down our profession to the next generations and we have become well known throughout the world, our success will continue into the future. We can say, 'This is the drummers' compound,' and people from all over the world will come to us to learn the art of drumming" (Bàba Làtí, pers. comm., December 10, 1997). As these drummers became more involved with local, national and international networks of Yorùbá culture enthusiasts, they began to spearhead a significant shift away from the negative perceptions of traditional drummers. The perception of drummers as irrelevant and uneducated grew out of a dominant nationalist discourse about what it means to be a modern Nigerian citizen: someone with a formal education who practices Islam or Christianity is modern, while someone who trained in a traditional "craft" with no school certificate is not. As opportunities for work waned, drummers began to rely more heavily on small sums of money from individual patrons. The success of Ìyálójà's drummers countered negative perceptions of drummers as uneducated beggars. These drummers garnered national and international work and respect precisely because they were lineage-based professional drummers.

Members of this generation were not only successful participants in a burgeoning global culture industry, but they were also active in local and national politics. One of the traditional roles of a talking drummer is a spokesperson and critic of local and national affairs. I had the honor and pleasure of knowing one of the most gifted and understated artist-activists of southwestern Nigeria, Alhaji[14] Dúrólù. Alhaji's instrument was the *iyáàlù* dùndún drum. Following his father's advice, the young Alhaji studied dùndún drumming at another compound and was responsible for bringing the art of dùndún to Ìyálójà's compound. More so than the other drummers, Alhaji wanted to tell me what it was like for drummers during Nigeria's tumultuous early days as a nation.

> During our independence wars, politicians used to invite me to drum for them. I played for my [political] party, "Ẹgbẹ́ Awólọ́wọ̀" Action Group. I would be sitting on the roof of a vehicle, and we would be campaigning all around the Ọ̀sun area—Òṣogbo, Ifọ́n, Ìlóòbú, Òkínní. On the day we won the election, our political opponents told the police to arrest me. They accused me of using my drum to incite people against the opposing side. I asked the police why I was arrested, and they said it was because I was the drummer for the opposing side. My family paid my bail so I was not imprisoned. I have experienced both positive and negative things as a member of the Àyàn lineage. We all witnessed the effects of the civil war. We were running helter-skelter. There were no ceremonies because of the war. It was during that time that we formed the Drummer's Union, "Ẹgbẹ́ Onílù." We formed this union when the military government passed an edict that there shouldn't be drumming or ceremonies because of the war. The edict did not allow us to do our

work. A highly educated man came to Ẹrìn-Ọ̀sun from the lineage of
drummers from Ògbómọ̀ṣọ́. He helped us to repeal the edict. (Dúrólù,
pers. comm., September 7, 1997)

Today, most drummers claim to belong to all political parties and religions so that they can perform at any political or religious event. In
fact, drummers are particularly accepting of multiple religions and political parties: they cultivate such open-mindedness as part of their pro-
fessionalism. However, during Nigeria's first election, most drummers
from Ìyálójà's supported the Action Group, Ọbáfẹ́mi Awólọ́wọ̀'s party.
Taking seriously his role as spokesman for political issues affecting his
community, Alhaji risked getting caught by members of the opposition
party. Such a risk, he knew, came with the territory of doing his job
well. In the 1970s, the traditional drummers formed their union, Ẹgbẹ́
Onílù, in the face of the Biafran war. This new level of organization
helped validate traditional drumming as a professional career. In 1997
the Drummer's Union elected Alhaji as their chairman. He was honored
by this title and considered it one of his life's crowning achievements.
Alhaji's passing has left a hole in the drumming community and the social fabric of Ẹrìn-Ọ̀sun. With the passing of the No More generation,
the role of the drummer as spokesperson and critic has been steadily
disappearing.

With the passing of the No More generation, many rhythms and songs
for the òrìṣà have also been disappearing since they are played less and
less. However, communities who continue to worship the òrìṣà have
been working with Ìyálójà's drummers to record, preserve, and learn
their drum texts. Even though the No More generation had the most exposure to òrìṣà ceremonies and were the most familiar with a wide range
of òrìṣà rhythms, they were the most adamant in their anti-òrìṣà worldview, at least publicly: they had been raised as Muslims. In the following
quotations, note how the drummers emphasized that they were not òrìṣà
worshippers and that their work as drummers in no way conflicted with
their religion.

People know quite well that the art of drumming is our occupation. The
same drums that we play for a Muslim or a Christian are the same drums
that we play for Ṣàngó worshippers and Egúngún devotees. The only
differences are the rhythms. There is a clear distinction between one's
religion and drumming. (Àyándélé, pers. comm., September 30, 1997)
  My father converted to Islam. Before that, he worshipped Òrìṣà Oko.
When someone was born, the family consulted with the òrìṣà to find out
what type of religion that child would follow. The òrìṣà might divine

that a child would become an Ifá devotee. But in the case of my father, the òrìṣà divined that he would become a Muslim. When my father grew up, he was totally involved with Islamic affairs. He never worshipped the òrìṣà. (Alhaji Ẹ̀rìnlé, pers. comm., October 24, 1997)

Due to the advent of Islam and Christianity, the children of òrìṣà worshippers did not get involved with òrìṣà initiations. Worshipping the òrìṣà is not our religion. Drumming is our work, and worshipping the òrìṣà is their religion. I am a Muslim. I have been a Muslim since my childhood days. There is no conflict when we play for different ceremonies because people know that we are doing our work by playing the drums. They know that we are not òrìṣà devotees. (Àyánbísí, pers. comm., October 30, 1997)

Having been disciplined by their society, this generation publicly embraced their Muslim religious identities; however, most members also maintained private relationships with town, family, and personal òrìṣà. While Nigerian society by and large rejected the òrìṣà, the global community was seeking to revive them. Members of this generation thus walked the line of this contradiction: how could the "civilized" world embrace the òrìṣà while Nigeria had abandoned the òrìṣà? While this generation, no doubt, lost touch with the òrìṣà through public ritual, their relationships with the òrìṣà were complex and are largely unknown due to the lack of representation of this generation of Àyàn artists in anthropological and historical records.

During the fifties and sixties, members of the No More Generation crafted their Àyàn-ness during times of contradiction and tension. As they witnessed Nigeria gain its independence, they experienced unrest due to local struggles for resource control. While their local communities were continuing to reject the òrìṣà, global demand for the òrìṣà was on the rise. And while they experienced a steady decline of professional opportunity locally, possibilities for professional opportunity were increasing overseas. This generation's Àyàn performativity was characterized by their changing roles as professional drummers; their continuing roles as community spokesmen; and their up-and-coming roles as representatives of Yorùbá culture at home and overseas.

Reviving Òrìṣà

I want to tell the story of my birth. My parents went to the shrine of Òrìṣà Oko to pray for my birth. My mother gave birth to me there. My father was Ìgè Àyánṣínà. My mother was Àwèrò. My mother had two husbands before getting married to my father. Whenever she gave birth, she kept losing her child. None of her children had survived before she met my father and married him. When they married each other, her children kept dying. Later, she went to the shrine of Òrìṣà Oko. My father had accepted Islam. Before, he was not a Muslim. He accepted Islam when he grew old.

Women are not at peace without a child. They prayed to Òrìṣà Oko at the Ìdí-Ọ̀ṣun shrine. My parents consulted Òrìṣà Oko. They prayed for my life and that I would not die. They gave birth to me. During the Òrìṣà Oko festival, they named me. My mother became a worshipper of Òrìṣà Oko. But she also claimed to be a Muslim for me not to die. I grew up knowing Òrìṣà Oko. I would always go to Òrìṣà Oko festivals with my father as a child. (Àyánkúnlé, pers. comm., October 10, 1996)

It was a clear, moist night in Ẹ̀rìn-Ọ̀ṣun when Làmídì Àyánkúnlé began to unravel the story of his life in my presence. We set up metal chairs in the unfinished, empty cement house next door to Làmídì's compound. The evening air and dim moonlight flooded into the empty space through the two large openings intended for windows. A certain wave of inspiration and urgency shaped the session that ensued. Làmídì and I knew that this meeting, if successful, would spark the formal opening of a lifelong dialogue between us: about his life story, the collaborative production of Yorùbá culture, and our mutual stakes in making the world a better place through the search for cross-cultural understanding.

While Làmídì neither identifies as a Muslim nor formally worships the òrìṣà, he believes in and gives thanks to Òrìṣà Oko for bringing him into the world safely and for protecting him throughout his life. Làmídì also believes in the power of the òrìṣà as part of his heritage. Faith in àṣà ìbílè, traditional culture inherited from his ancestors, drives Làmídì's life story. As he narrated the story of his birth, Làmídì repeated the point that although his parents converted to Islam, they continued to worship the òrìṣà. The fact that Làmídì and his parents inherited the òrìṣà, not Islam, continues to define Làmídì's identity. Làmídì identifies as a practitioner of àṣà ìbílè, cultural traditions that preceded Islam or Christianity. I would characterize Làmídì's experience of his parents' conversion to Islam as one of surprise and loss. Over time, Làmídì has developed his critique of Islamic influences in Yorùbá culture: Yorùbá traditional culture existed before Islam and has been threatened by Islamic beliefs and culture. According to Làmídì, the presence of Islam has not allowed àṣà ìbílè to breathe, grow, and change in Nigeria.

In his late teens and early twenties during the late sixties, Làmídì was coming into his own as a master drummer. The No More generation,

Plate 8.2: Làmídì Àyánkúnlé (front), of the Reviving Òrìṣà generation, with his sons. (photograph: Debra Klein, Èrìn-Òṣun, 19 June 2005)

including Làmídì's father, had become involved in the revival movement based in Òṣogbo and Ìbàdàn. Scouted by theater groups looking for local talent, Làmídì was approached by several of the Yorùbá popular theater directors and playwrights, including Kọlá Ògúnmọlá and Dúró Ládíípọ. At a moment in Nigeria's history when Yorùbá traditional culture was going through a revival, Làmídì was coveted for his knowledge, skills, and ability to perform them. While the unsolicited opportunity to perform with such well-respected theater troupes appealed to Làmídì, his father exercised much ambivalence and caution around his son's participation in popular, non-traditional art. Despite his conversion to Islam, Làmídì's father continued to practice, teach, and respect the òrìṣà drum texts and ceremonies—cultural material he expected his son to carry on. As Làmídì recounted his entry into the popular theater scene, he always acknowledged his father's skepticism:

> I have been a very skillful drummer since my childhood days. When I was discovered, I was playing drums for the masquerade festivals in 1969. Dúró Ládíípọ invited me to play bàtá in his theater group, but my father did not allow me to play for him then. He told me that if I followed a theater group, I would no longer be an expert in the rhythms for

the different gods and goddesses. My friend from Lagos, who had been playing for Dúró Ládiípọ̀'s theater group, did not know how to play different rhythms for the òrìṣà. If I played for theater, I would forget how to play traditional drums. So we did not accept the invitation then. (Àyánkúnlé, pers. comm., February 1, 1997)

While Làmídì eventually accepted Dúró Ládiípọ̀'s invitation, he heeded his father's advice: he did not rehearse with the group every day so that he could spend the majority of his week playing for local celebrations. As other professional artists asked Làmídì to participate in their projects, Làmídì continued to limit his commitment to stage work. Like his father, Làmídì was more compelled by opportunities to play a wide range of drum music for various local audiences as opposed to repeating the same songs on stage.

Làmídì's understanding of àṣà ìbílẹ̀ emerged from his childhood training in the òrìṣà and the local traveling theater (alárìnjó) tradition. Though Làmídì had witnessed his father's conversion, he also knew that his father still valued, practiced, and taught Yorùbá traditional culture, self-consciously passing along the Àyàn legacy. Làmídì's father, Ìgè Àyánṣínà, was a purist when it came to bàtá: he was unwilling to fuse other musical genres or styles with bàtá. When it came to his profession, Àyánṣínà strived to keep the classic bàtá repertoire alive by teaching his son to become a bàtá master as opposed to a popular theatre musician. Following in his father's footsteps, Làmídì's sense of being Àyàn revolves around his inherited notion of àṣà ìbílẹ̀: traditional culture rooted in an inherited body of drumming knowledge and skills. Influenced by his own faith in the òrìṣà and the culture movement's metadiscourse about authenticity, Làmídì's sense of being Àyàn is grounded in an òrìṣà-centered worldview.

In addition to their participation in the Òṣogbo- and Ìbàdàn-based revival movement, the Reviving generation also began to represent Yorùbá drumming in state and national festivals and competitions, including FESTAC '77 (Festival of Black Arts and Culture) and NAFEST (National Festival of Arts and Culture). In order to enter the competitions, artists were required to be affiliated with a state-sponsored cultural center. Thus, the Ọ̀yọ́ or Òṣun State cultural centers hired the Àyàn drummers of Ìyálójà's compound to compete alongside their artists in residence. While cultural center artists had school certificates in the performing arts, most did not inherit their performance knowledge and skills within an extended family context. In order to win competitions, cultural centers relied heavily on the performance skills and experience of the Èrìn-Òṣun artists.

The irony was not lost on the Reviving generation: how could their nation condemn as anti-modern their lifestyle and practices while rewarding them for their professional knowledge and skills? Làmídì's junior brother, Rábíù Àyándòkun, told me the following proverb about having to confront people's prejudice around Àyàn drummers' lack of Western education:

> *Ó lé mi ò kàwé. Ó lé mi ò kàwé. Alákòwé ń ṣe lébìrà ní Ìkẹjà. Ó lé mi ò kàwé o. Iṣẹ́ ọwọ́ọ̀ mi mò ń ṣe. Ọ̀rọ̀ ìwé kọ́ la ń wí.* (He despises me for my illiteracy. He despises me for my illiteracy. Meanwhile many educated people are engaged in laboring jobs in Ìkẹjà. Yet he despises me for my illiteracy. I profit from the work of my hand. Literacy is not the issue here.) (translation from Villepastour 2010, 145)

When I ran into someone who wanted to give me a hard time for not going to school, I would play this proverb on my drum. When I played the proverb, I was happy. If that person understood my drum's message, he would stop bothering me. Back then, a drummer might also play a message about something going on in our society. If I observed something going on, I would comment on it with my drum. Today, things have changed drastically because modern drummers play the rhythms but may not know the meaning of what they're saying. My son's generation had not been born when we were playing such rhythms. It is quite different today. They can play the percussion, but it's not easy for modern children to play the proverbs because they are very difficult sayings. (Àyándòkun, pers. comm., September 27, 1997)

When he played the proverb, Rábíù challenged his audiences to consider how other forms of knowledge—proverbs, rhythms, and professional musicianship—are just as valuable as book-based education. In our discussion, Rábíù expressed one of the defining tensions that members of his generation have negotiated throughout their professional lives. While his generation participated in the drumming profession when it had a significant cultural relevance in Nigeria, his children's generation did not participate in their inherited profession as an invaluable aesthetic art and commodity in Nigeria. Rábíù and Làmídì often commiserate that their children will never experience their own culture's support and celebration of the Àyàn profession in the same career-defining ways that they had.

In contrast to the modernizing Nigerian nation-state, the Yorùbá culture movement values the Àyàn drummers' inherited knowledge and skills. When members of the Reviving Òrìṣà generation began to tap into this movement by performing overseas, they were truly liberated from disparaging stereotypes of their profession and hence reinvigorated. Another member of the Reviving generation, masquerade dancer Ọ̀jẹ́yẹmí, described his first time performing in Germany in the nineties: "What surprised me about performing in Germany and the U.S. was how much they loved our performances! People do not like us as much here in Nigeria. This is because we are the owners of Egúngún performance. Nigerians look down on us for our association with the òrìṣà and for our lack of education" (Ọ̀jẹ́yẹmí, pers. comm., January 3, 1997).

When members of the Reviving generation return home after touring overseas, they bring back stories about their performance successes. Incorporating their overseas experiences into their local performances, these artists have been re-educating their communities about the cultural value of their inherited profession. While most members of the Reviving generation have not publicly embraced an òrìṣà-based worldview, they have come to appreciate, value, and identify with the òrìṣà as central to Yorùbá culture and their identities as Àyàn drummers and Ọ̀jẹ̀ masqueraders.

For the Reviving Òrìṣà generation, Àyàn performativity revolves around their commitments to sustaining their inherited drumming profession; roles as representatives of Yorùbá culture; and inheritance of the òrìṣà. Coming of age during the seventies and eighties, the Reviving generation negotiated a different set of contradictions. Their own nation at once embraced and rejected their Àyàn-ness. Yet while the global community embraced their Àyàn-ness, it expected them to be even more òrìṣà-centered than they were. Members of this generation learned to perform their Àyàn-ness by straddling their own culture of modernization and a burgeoning global market for the Àyàn brand. The global discourse that naturalized Yorùbá Àyàn-ness as òrìṣà-centered challenged this generation to question their religious beliefs and identities and to thus redefine their Àyàn-ness in conversation with global culture and market demands.

Grasping for Òrìṣà

Today, drumming has modernized. In the old days, we had real traditional rhythms for our gods and goddesses, the òrìṣà. But the young drummers do not know those rhythms. When I went to America for the first time, everyone asked me about those traditional rhythms. So, when I came back to Nigeria, I tried to learn them. While most people with the traditional knowledge in my family have died, a few are still alive. If you don't ask, they won't teach you the traditional songs. So, I wrote down the music in my book. I worked with Alhaji Bàba Alágbàfộ and Bàba Múdà. They are all dead now, but I wrote down their songs in my book. That's the only place you can learn the real thing. The only people you can ask now are Làmídì, Bàba Làtí, Alhaji, or Bàba Tájù. There are no other drummers alive with this knowledge. (Àyánníyì, pers. comm., July 24, 1997)

I am older, I have had opportunities that my younger siblings do not have. In the old days when there were many ceremonies, like Egúngún festivals in Ìwó, we would travel there to perform. There, we would meet different performers, and we would learn by watching their performances and listening to their songs. But today, we can hardly find traditional ceremonies. (Òjéyẹmí, pers. comm., October 1, 1997)

Of the ten members of the Grasping for Òrìṣà generation I interviewed, Akeem Àyánníyì was the only one who had left Nigeria to settle in the United States. Akeem had married an American woman from Santa Fe, New Mexico, where they shared a home and had a child together. He still lives in Santa Fe, now with a Yorùbá wife, where he teaches and performs Yorùbá drumming. Túndé Òjéyẹmí is a well-respected, well-traveled and gifted masquerade dancer who continues to perform locally, nationally, and overseas whenever possible. The other members of this generation who are still based in Èrìn-Òṣun have learned òrìṣà songs during annual òrìṣà festivals (viz., Ṣàngó, Òṣun, Ògún, and Egúngún) and during their fathers' workshops with foreign students.

While members of the Grasping generation have begun to appreciate the relevance of the òrìṣà to their heritage and to the broader Yorùbá culture movement, they grew up either as Muslims or òrìṣà worshippers who are comfortable with cultural fusions. For example, many members of this generation practice Islam and òrìṣà worship and easily incorporate fújì music and bàtá-fújì fusions into their Àyàn identity and repertoire. Inspired by the global interest in Yorùbá culture, members of the Grasping generation have been making efforts to embrace and/or rediscover their cultural heritage that once revolved around the òrìṣà.

Though the members of the Grasping generation were raised as fourth-generation Muslims, they have also been raised to represent their Yorùbá heritage at home and abroad. Coming of age in an era of increasing international respect for an òrìṣà-centered worldview, some members of this generation have been reinventing a belief system and ritual lifestyle that revolves around the òrìṣà. During our interviews, the members of this generation who identified with the òrìṣà were the Òjè masqueraders. The

Plate 8.3: Àyánkúnlé's sons, Saheed, Musiliyu, Kabiru, and Muidini, are members of the Grasping for Òrìṣà generation. (photograph: Debra Klein, Èrìn-Òṣun, 19 June 2005)

Àyàn drummers, on the other hand, identified as Muslims who embraced the òrìṣà predominantly as their cultural and professional heritage.

Cousins Túndé Òjéyẹmí and Kójèdé Òjééwọyè were born into a powerful family of Egúngún worshippers. While Túndé and Kójèdé were raised both as Muslims and Egúngún worshippers, they have chosen to follow the path of the Egúngún.

I am not a Muslim. My parents are Egúngún worshippers. My grandfather was a Muslim, but his mother was an Egúngún devotee. My parents and I are Egúngún worshippers. An Egúngún worshipper needs to know how to chant ewì very well—that's number one. Secondly, he must know how to dance to traditional rhythms. Thirdly, he must know how to change in and out of Egúngún costumes while dancing. He must be able to handle the masks very well. It is not compulsory for one to be able to do acrobatic tricks, but today, acrobatic tricks are becoming more important in the art of performance. (Òjéyẹmí, pers. comm., October 1, 1997)

My parents initiated me into the Egúngún cult. And that's why they named me Akójèdé—that I would be an Egúngún worshipper and performer, right from creation. I give thanks to God that our Egúngún

heritage has been a blessing for our family. (Ọ̀jẹ́ẹ̀wọyè, pers. comm.,
May 3, 1997)

Túndé explained what it means to be an Egúngún worshipper by defining the body of knowledge and skills of a masquerade performer. Both
cousins have been performing overseas since the mid-nineties, so they
have been participating in the global market for Àyàn and Òjè performance. In addition to their commitment to practicing and perpetuat-
ing Òjè performance, however, both cousins also pray to and honor the
Egúngún during rituals with close family members, particularly during
annual outings of the Egúngún masquerades.

The Àyàn drummers of the of the Grasping generation based in Èrìn-
Òṣun play for òrìṣà ceremonies and have made an effort to learn òrìṣà
rhythms; yet being Àyàn, for them, is mostly about their inherited profession. During a recent interview with half-brothers Múìdínì Àyánkúnlé
and Wàìdì Àyàn, Múìdínì could hardly contain his enthusiasm when I
asked him what it meant to him to have been born into an Àyàn family:
"That is an important question. Our ancestors gave us a great opportunity. I am very grateful. Our fathers were serious about the work of
Àyàn. If they didn't enjoy and excel at drumming, they would not have
continued to play. Today, all of Africa knows us. And we love what we
do. Today, we tour all over the world" (Àyánkúnlé, pers. comm., June
12, 2005). When I asked how they saw their future careers unfold, they
said they would like to incorporate more bàtá and dùndún drumming into
fújì, highlife, and jùjú music. For this generation, bringing their instruments and musicianship into pop music styles represents a rebirth and a
recontextualization of Àyàn drumming in a modern Nigeria.

Following in the footsteps of the preceding generations, these Àyàn
drummers identify first and foremost with their inherited knowledge and
skills. While their fathers and grandfathers have been forced to negotiate the tensions between local culture loss and global culture revival,
members of this generation came of age after this tension had begun to
dissipate, at least locally. For the Àyàn and Òjè artists of this generation,
popular culture dominated their landscape of culture production; they
sought to bring their inherited knowledge and skills into the pop culture
arena. On the other hand, they apprenticed to their fathers by hosting students and traveling overseas as representatives of "traditional" Yorùbá
culture. Thus, this generation rides the tension between their identities
as pop culture fusion artists and as heirs to an Àyàn legacy. Even though
this generation is stepping into their fathers' roles, they are furthest

from fulfilling the expectations of the global community that naturalizes
Àyàn-ness as òrìṣà worship.

Being Àyàn

Multiple generations of Àyàn-identified artists in Èrìn-Òṣun have been
performing and continue to redefine and recreate what it means to be
Àyàn in Nigeria. While I have illustrated how all three generations'
Àyàn identities are rooted in: 1) their inherited and learned drumming
knowledge and skills; 2) the Èrìn-Òṣun lifestyle; and 3) their roles as local and global representatives of Yorùbá culture, I have also revealed the
complexity of each generation's relationship to Òrìṣà Àyàn.

Because members of the No More Òrìṣà generation were raised as
Muslims, they did not publicly identify with an òrìṣà-centered worldview. Before the decline of òrìṣà worship in Nigeria, this generation
played regularly for òrìṣà ceremonies. When they were discovered by
the scholars and artists of the Ìbàdàn- and Òṣogbo-based culture revival
movements, members of this generation continued to play òrìṣà rhythms
and texts in new venues: Wenger's rituals, popular theater, popular òrìṣà
festivals, university music programs, etc. Members of this generation
were also the founders of the Nigerian drummer's union that protected
and legitimized the profession of drumming. I have illustrated how this
generation navigated the tensions between a modernizing Nigeria that
declared the òrìṣà irrelevant and a local/global culture revival movement
that supported the òrìṣà. While many members of this generation maintained private relationships with the òrìṣà, their Àyàn performativity did
not include the òrìṣà or Islam. The No More generation's Àyàn-ness was
about the journey of their professionalization as Àyàn drummers in local, national, and transnational contexts.

Members of the Reviving Òrìṣà generation came of age during
Nigeria's nationalist efforts to "unify through diversity" and thus embrace and support, at least rhetorically and symbolically, Àyàn cultural
expression. While these artists were encouraged to perform and teach
their repertoire of drumming knowledge and skills within national and
global contexts, they were discouraged, on local fronts, from incorporating the òrìṣà into their lives and performances. Resisting societal pressures and inspired by global market demands, this generation began to
explore and reclaim the òrìṣà culture of their grandfathers.

Most members of this generation, trained by their fathers, were artisti-
cally inspired by òrìṣà rhythms and song texts—to the point of making it
a lifelong goal to preserve òrìṣà music through recording and teaching it

to their children and foreign students. In the case of Làmídì Àyánkúnlé, the òrìṣà became important to his spiritual and cultural identity. Even though they do not publicly worship the òrìṣà, members of this generation began to redefine and perform Àyàn-ness through òrìṣà rhythms and song texts. For members of this generation, being Àyàn came to exclude Islamic beliefs and cultural forms. Shaped in dialogue with foreign members of the global community, the Reviving generation has contributed significantly to living, transmitting, and reinventing an Àyàn-ness that began to identify with and privilege a repertoire of òrìṣà music and dances.

The Grasping for Òrìṣà generation came of age when their inherited skills and knowledge made more sense in the realm of popular culture than in the arena of òrìṣà worship; unlike their fathers and grandfathers, this generation never knew the òrìṣà outside of a community dominated by secular and Islamic culture. The Òjè artists of this generation were raised both as Muslims and Egúngún worshippers, while the Àyàn drummers were raised as Muslims. Perhaps ironically, members of the Grasping generation are stepping into their fathers' shoes as representatives of Àyàn culture at a moment when the global discourse of Àyàn-ness centering on òrìṣà worship has never been so dominant. If they want to claim relevance and status within the global community, this generation is under pressure to demonstrate its dedication to and knowledge of the òrìṣà.

All three generations have redefined their Àyàn identities within tensions among local, national, and global communities. While Nigeria was gaining its independence, it was also at war; Àyàn drummers became legitimate professionals but were forced to leave the òrìṣà behind and claim identities as Muslims. While Nigeria was celebrating its diverse traditional cultural roots, it was modernizing; Àyàn drummers represented their nation in spectacles but were condemned for being uneducated. Thus, they sought refuge and community in the global movement for Yorùbá culture. While Nigerian national discourse continued to disparage the lifestyle and profession of Àyàn artists, the global community became interested in Nigeria-based Àyàn artists as representatives of an òrìṣà-centered Àyàn-ness.

Àyàn culture is emergent and contested in Nigeria. In an everyday way, Àyàn drummers are constantly struggling (like the rest of us) to keep their profession alive and relevant in shifting local and global markets. For the artists of Èrìn-Òṣun, what it means to be Àyàn has and will continue to mean playing the juxtaposition between local and global culture and market demands. By re-embracing the òrìṣà, the Reviving and Grasping generations are performing a Yorùbá modernity that flexibly incorporates cultural forms relevant to changing political and economic contexts. But the òrìṣà are not equivalent to any other cultural form: the òrìṣà are spiritually and symbolically emblematic of Yorùbáness. Gods and goddesses, the òrìṣà are feared and loathed by many Nigerian Christians and Muslims; they are taken very seriously. By reclaiming the òrìṣà in Nigeria, the Àyàn drummers risk alienation in their own communities. Documenting exactly how the Àyàn generations reincorporate the òrìṣà into their lives and professions merits further research in order to deepen our understanding of Àyàn-ness in Nigeria.

Notes

1. Meaning "mother of market," Ìyálójà is one of the few important leadership positions and titles for women in traditional government. Not only is this compound reputed for housing the town's traditional drummers, it is also known for being the family of the town's market head.

2. Many thanks to the late Katherine Hagedorn, Jami Weinstein, the late Michael Marcuzzi, and Amanda Villepastour for their substantive comments on versions of this chapter.

3. By "discourse," I mean the poststructuralist idea that people narrate, make sense of, and frame their worlds. These discursive frameworks vary from place to place and over time. Within a culture, there are always hegemonic and competing discourses.

4. According to an expressive theory of gender, when you read someone's gender (or identity), you assume that that person is expressing something natural (i.e., biology, anatomy, etc.). A performative theory of gender (Butler 1988, 1990, 1993) includes the expressive theory but recognizes that gender begins as random performances; the actor is disciplined; the actor starts to internalize gender; and gender gets naturalized and thus read as expressive. Borrowing from Butler, I am arguing that Àyàn-ness has become naturalized through a similar process. While most Yorùbá people do know that Àyàn artists tend to be Muslims, they still naturalize Àyàn-ness as backwardness due to Àyàn artists' association with òrìṣà culture as well as the fact that most lineage-based Àyàn artists have little or no formal education past the secondary school level.

5. Performativity refers to the production of performative acts (of identity) that are taken as real yet have been historically and culturally produced.

6. Although issues of cultural and religious identity among Àyàn drummers are in some ways unique, the wider contexts of colonial interventions, independence movements, modernizing nations, and the burgeoning global world music industry since the 1980s, have had loosely parallel impacts on musicians throughout Africa. See, for example, Berliner (1978); Tang (2007); Counsel (2009); and White (2012).

7. Pers. comm., Ẹlẹ́rìn Ọba Yusuf Ọmọloyè Ọyágbọ́dùn II, Ẹ̀rìn-Ọ̀ṣun, October 2, 1997.

8. In addition to their roles as worshippers and bearers of the sacred masks for the Egúngún (òrìsà of the ancestors), Òjẹ̀ families or ẹlẹ́gùn Òjẹ̀ are entertainment masqueraders—also known as agbégijó, alárìnjo, and apidán. Children born into an Òjẹ̀ lineage are thus given names starting with the Òjẹ̀ prefix. Òjẹ̀ families work closely with and at times marry into Àyàn families: Òjẹ̀ performers dance, praise-sing, and perform acrobatic and masquerade displays, while Àyàn drummers provide the accompanying drum rhythms and texts.

9. The òrìṣà of lightning, femininity and fertility, iron and war, and the ancestors, respectively.

10. For discussion of how Àyàn drummers incorporate fújì music into their performance repertoire, see Klein (2007).

11. While I listened to the daily reflections and stories of Èrìn-Òṣun artists, it became clear to me that the artists had found meaning and sustainable resources in their local and international networks of collaborators, sponsors, friends, students, and fans. Becoming an active participant in the artists' local performances and networks, I began to understand the significance of these collaborative relationships in artists' everyday lives. When referring to the artists with whom I have been working over the years, I thus use the term "collaborator."

12. During our interviews, the Àyàn elders mentioned drumming for the following òrìṣà: Ẹgbẹ́, Ẹlẹ́gùn Fópomọyọ, Ẹlẹ́gùn Olojojo, Ẹlẹ́gùun Másóràntán, Erinlẹ̀, Òrìṣà Oko, Olóde, Òrìṣàńlá, Ọya, Ṣàngó, and Ṣòpọ̀nnọ́. Secular rituals include naming ceremonies, graduations, weddings, and funerals.

13. Prominent Nigerian playwrights, novelists, artists, and scholars (e.g., Wọlé Ṣọyínká, J. P. Clark, D. O. Fágúnwà, Demas Nwoko, Uche Okeke, et al.) collaborated with an array of international scholars and artists—Susanne Wenger, Ulli Beier, and Georgina Beier—in the production of a cultural revivalist movement that centered around the legendary Mbari Mbayo Club (signifying "creation") (Klein 2007). While the movement proper was short-lived, no more than ten years, it paved the way for today's internationally renowned Òṣogbo Arts style and has put Òṣogbo on the map as a tourist destination.

14. Though Alhaji did not actually make the pilgrimage, he is respected for being an exemplary Muslim and elder in his community.

References Cited

Beier, Ulli. 1991. *Thirty Years of Osogbo Art*. Bayreuth: Iwalewa.

Berliner, Paul. 1978. *The Soul of Mbira: Music and Traditions of the Shona People of Zimbabwe*. Berkeley: University of California Press.

Butler, Judith. 1988. "Performative Acts and Gender Constitution: An Essay in Phenomenology and Feminist Theory." In *Theatre Journal* 40 (4): 519–31.

———. 1990. *Gender Trouble: Feminism and the Subversion of Identity*. New York: Routledge.

———. 1993. "Imitation and Gender Insubordination." In *The Lesbian and Gay Studies Reader*, eds. Henry Abelove, Michele Aina Barale, and David M. Halperin. New York: Routledge. 307–20.

Cornelius, Steven. 2008. "Straying from the House of the Ancestors?: Traditional and Folkloric Music Initiatives in Contemporary Ghana." Unpublished paper.

Counsel, Graeme. 2009. *Mande Popular Music and Cultural Policies in West Africa: Griots and Government Policy since Independence*. Saabrucken: VDM Verlag.

Johnson, Rev. Samuel. 1976 [1921]. *The History of the Yorubas: From the Earliest Times to the Beginning of the British Protectorate*. Lagos: C.S.S. Bookshops.

Klein, Debra L. 2007. *Yorùbá Bàtá Goes Global: Artists, Culture Brokers, and Fans*. Chicago: University of Chicago Press.

Peel, J. D. Y. 2000. *Religious Encounter and the Making of the Yoruba*. Bloomington: Indiana University Press.

Probst, Peter. 2011. *Osogbo and the Art of Heritage: Monuments, Deities, and Money*. Bloomington: Indiana University Press.

Tang, Patricia. 2007. *Masters of the Sabar Wolof Griot Percussionists of Senegal*. Philadelphia: Temple University Press.

Urban, Greg. 1996. *Metaphysical Community: The Interplay of the Senses and the Intellect.* Austin: University of Texas Press.

Villepastour, Amanda. 2010. *Ancient Text Messages of the Yorùbá Bàtá Drum: Cracking the Code.* Burlington: Ashgate.

Vincent [Villepastour], Amanda. 2006. *Bata Conversations: Guardianship and Entitlement Narratives about the Bata in Nigeria and Cuba.* PhD thesis, School of Oriental and African Studies, University of London.

White, Bob W., ed. 2012. *Music and Globalization: Critical Encounters.* Bloomington: Indiana University Press.

V

SECONDARY DIASPORAS

9

Añátivity: A Personal Account of the Early Batá Community in New York City

John Amira

• •

For at least the past twenty-five years, consecrated *batá* drums, or Añá, have been regularly played in the USA. There was, however, approximately a twenty-year period leading up to the arrival of Añá batá drums to the USA in which the unconsecrated batá, or *aberikulá,* were played in New York City. In many respects these earlier decades paved the road for the arrival of Añá. I was both a witness to and participant in this development, and this chapter documents the history to the best of my ability. Other than briefly in 1953 when the Cuban boxer Kid Gavilan brought a Havana nightclub revue to Las Vegas, the batá did not officially arrive in the USA until the 1960s. The seeds for their arrival were planted in the 1950s with the coming of batá drummers Julio Collazo "Julito" and Francisco Aguabella to the United States.[1] The initiation of Christopher Oliana into Santería, the first U.S. American to do so, also came to have a profound impact on the history of Añá in New York. However, for organizational purposes alone, I will reserve any discussion of Oliana's contributions to a later part in this chapter.

Dunham, Collazo, and Aguabella

It was on a trip to Cuba in 1953 that Katherine Dunham, the famous African American dancer and anthropologist, was first taken with the drumming of Julito and Francisco, and from this meeting invited them to join her company. The drumming duo toured with her, eventually coming to land in New York City. That Julito and Francisco actually played batá drums in her company is clear, but what happened to those drums when they left the company is not. In all likelihood the drums did not belong to either of the drummers but to Dunham herself, and probably remained in her possession. According to Marta Vega (1995, 202), when Julito and Francisco arrived in 1955 there was already a sizeable Cuban community in New York, including many practitioners of Santería.[2] Shortly thereafter they learned about what was probably the first *bembé* (drumming ceremony for the *orichas*) given in New York, or for that matter the USA. Not only did Julito and Francisco attend the event, but also they greatly impressed all who were there with their knowledge of the ceremonial songs. To my knowledge, there is no documentation of any bembés between 1955 and 1961, but they undoubtedly did occur.

According to John Mason (1992, 19), in 1961 the Cuban *babalao* (divining priest) Pancho Mora gave the first major public bembé, which took place at Casa Carmen, a Bronx dancehall. The ceremony was for the oricha Changó and Julito led the drumming and singing. Mason stated that the drummers played on a set of unconsecrated batá, but with Francisco now living on the West Coast and no one with the knowledge to drum with him, it seems unlikely that even an aberikulá ceremony could have been performed in its entirety. The most I ever saw Julito do in this early period to approximate batá was to play the *iyá* (lead drum) part from Chachálekpafuñ[3] over the standard conga and *agbe* (beaded gourd) rhythms. Julito would play on a double-headed drum from Kenya, which sounded nothing like a batá drum.

I first met Julito in 1961 while I was still in high school and playing in a Latin band. At that time I had heard only one recording of batá, *Santero* (n.d.),[4] which featured various artists, and I had virtually no knowledge of Cuban folkloric rhythms, so to me Julito was solely a band drummer. As I began to associate and practice with more drummers, my exposure to the recordings of various repertoires necessarily increased and I saw Julito's name appear over and over again on the LP jackets. My learning in those years was a relatively slow and difficult process given that none of us had any real insight into how these complex rhythms were actually played.

My own connection to Santería and bembés actively began in 1963. By this time, I had been playing congas for about four years and lived in a section of the South Bronx that was home to a number of luminaries of Cuban music, the best-known of whom was Arsenio Rodríguez. The neighborhood also produced many of the New York musicians such as Willie Colón and Orlando Marín, who were crucial in the creation of the derivative dance music form we now know as salsa.

My Early Years of Study

A neighbor of mine, knowing my musical interests, introduced me to his co-worker Tommy Jagar, who also played congas. We got together and jammed one afternoon, and at the end of our session he invited me to a rehearsal of the Makeda Mayorba African Dance Company, where he had been drumming. Needless to say I was more than interested. A week later I was at the rehearsal as an observer, or so I assumed. As luck would have it none of the drummers, other than my new friend, showed up. Tommy suggested to the head of the dance company that I would be able to help out by playing along with him. Not only did she agree, but when the rehearsal was finished, she asked me if I would like to be in the company. Being neither Hispanic nor African American, it was the last thing I expected to hear. Naturally I jumped at the opportunity; I had just learned half a dozen new rhythms and was in heaven!

The next rehearsal brought me in contact with some of the other drummers in the company. Although they all deserve recognition, I will just focus on those who were involved with the batá drumming. Had it not been for three people—Carl Vail, Ray McKethan, and Rudy Wright—there might never have been any attempt to arrive at an "authentic" batá drumming in New York until the arrival of the Marielitos in 1980.[5]

These three individuals, all highly talented drummers and singers, had been interested in learning batá. They would often work from copies of the batá records available at that time, such as *Santero* (n.d.), *Mongo in Havana* (1960), and *Rituales Afrocubanos Lucumí.*[6] In those early years, it is possible that Carl, Ray, and Rudy had already approached Julito about studying with him and were turned down, or maybe they felt that being indirect would yield better results. Whatever the reason, they chose to build a homemade set of batá drums, bring them to a bembé where Julito was playing, and offer to let him use them.[7]

The temptation was perhaps too much for Julito to refuse, but in order to play them he had to quickly teach the two other parts of the rhythm Chachálekpafuñ to the other drummers. I do not know if he also taught them Rumba Yesa (another generic dance rhythm) at that time, but after the bembé they went home and, using the recording of *Rituales Afrocubanos Lucumí* for its clarity, located the Chachálekpafuñ rhythm and proceeded to identify the sounds of each drum. With this newfound knowledge they systematically went through the entire recording, dissecting and learning every rhythm. It is possible that they repeated the offer to Julito; but access to their set of homemade batá nonetheless did not give Julito the incentive to form a batá group.

Somewhere around that same time, another homemade set of batá made its appearance. Carlito and Ángel Gómez, two relatives of the Changó priest Juan Candela, who often sang at and presided over bembés, along with Onelio Scull made and played this set.[8] Whereas the set made by Carl, Ray, and Rudy consisted of one conical drum and two truncated congas with skins tacked on both ends, this other set went one step further in making the drums tunable. Yet neither of these two sets sounded like the real thing: the sizes and shapes just were not right. Although Julito played occasionally on this second set on some of the early Santería records made in New York (*Fuerza Santera* and *Santería Cubana*), he was content to play bembés with congas and agbes with all of the aforementioned drummers and others assisting him. This was the scene as I found it.

The Drummers Congregate in New York

Carl Vail first introduced me to playing batá. He and Ray McKethan came to the second rehearsal of Makeda's dance company, and afterwards, without any explanation, taught me the *itótele* (middle drum) part for a Yemayá rhythm. When I learned later who these drummers were and what I had just been shown, I felt that a great opportunity had been given to me. Carl did not return to the company rehearsals for a few weeks, but the next time I saw Ray I asked him if he would teach me. Unfortunately, Ray was not interested at that time, and I assumed that Carl would not be either, so I felt quite frustrated.

Since I could not get any formal instruction, my next option was to observe as much as possible. With that goal in mind, I organized a jam session and invited Carl, Ray, Rudy, and others including Marcus Gordon, a drummer who had just returned from a trip to Cuba. At some point Carl's group played a batá rhythm on congas. I taped the session so I could try to study all of it later, but before I even had the chance, Marcus called me and asked if I was interested in being part of a batá group. Marcus had seen batá played in Cuba and wanted to learn. On returning to New York he was told that there were two books by Fernando Ortíz (*La Africania De La Música Folklórica De Cuba and Los Bailes Y El Teatro De Los Negros En El Folklore De Cuba*) with many of the batá rhythms notated. Not only did he obtain one of them, but he too had approached Carl about lessons. Carl, it turned out, was quite willing to teach. Marcus and another drummer named Johnny Montalvo were part of this group, and when a third person did not work out I filled the open slot. I suppose it was meant to be.

Plate 9.1: From left, John Montalvo, Marcus Gordon, Carl Vail, and John Amira performing at the Village Gate. (photograph: William Cherry, New York City, May 1964)

At first we played on congas, but before long we felt compelled to have our own set of batá. The iyá was made from a drum carved in Kenya. The *okónkolo* (smallest accompanying drum) and itótele were made from conical drums made in Mexico. We used adhesive tape as an early substitute for *idá*, the paste applied to the skins to modulate the tonal quality. Instead of tacking the skins on, or using tuning lugs, we tried to duplicate the traditional method of tying the skins on with rawhide (see Plate 9.1). It worked moderately well, but we were only guessing at how to tie the skins and the shape of the drums still did not quite give us the right sound.

Christopher Oliana: Seeing the Need for Añá in New York

Marcus Gordon had also met Chris Oliana, who in 1959 became the first U.S. American to be initiated into Santería. Oliana was determined to create a consecrated set of batá in the USA, particularly for the New York community. Using information obtained in Cuba, as well as from one of the Ortíz books (*Los Instrumentos De La Música Afrocubana Vol. IV*), Oliana, along with a few drummers such as Teddy Holliday, Manny Ramos, and others, carved the shells of this batá set out of solid

Plate 9.2: From left, John Amira, Marcus Gordon, and John Montalvo sitting down to play a ceremony for Babalúayé. (photograph: Joseph Dankowski, Tom's River, NJ, June 1966)

mahogany. Before the skins were put on, Chris placed certain materials inside the drums that were part of his consecration process. This was done without the assistance of any babalaos or priests of Añá (initiated drummers), which was at odds with the traditional procedure in Cuba. It is unclear whether Oliana did this by consciously choosing not to involve anyone else, or by necessity, being unable to find anyone willing or able to assist him.

Oliana's drums were completed in 1962 or 1963, but they were never played. Chris had hoped to oversee the training of three drummers to play his set of batá, but with only a partial knowledge of the rhythms, this proved to be an insurmountable obstacle. After Chris's death in 1993, the woman who was taking care of him took possession of all his belongings, including the batá. Their whereabouts are unknown, as is the spiritual force they might have contained.

Inspired by Chris Oliana's vision, Marcus bought a large block of mahogany so that we could carve our own shells. He also obtained a huge, hand-turned drill and bit that looked like a giant corkscrew, and we began the rather arduous job of carving out the largest drum, the iyá. One night, Marcus overzealously continued drilling long after the rest of us

had gone home. Marcus was so focused on finishing the drum that he neglected to periodically remove the sawdust as it formed around the drill
bit. The heat from the friction, in combination with the moisture and oil
of the wood, melted the sawdust back into a paste and basically turned it
back into solid wood, leaving the drill bit permanently stuck: we could
not bore in or out, and after various, failed attempts at removing the bit,
we scrapped the project.

At this point, I personally was even more desperate to make a set of
batá with the right shapes so they would sound authentic. I devised a
method of taking both curved and conical drums (congas and bongos),
cutting them to various lengths, and then conjoining the pieces together
to achieve the desired shapes. With a minimum amount of filing and
sanding we had a near-perfect set of shells. By that time we had learned
how to make idá, and with the traditional method of attaching the skins
learned from various photos, we finally achieved a set of batá that looked
and sounded authentic (see Plate 9.2).

Early Oricha Drumming in New York City

Our batá group eventually broke up. Marcus Gordon moved to San
Francisco, where he formed a new group and became a key figure in the
Cuban music scene there. I formed a new group with Manny Ramos and
Teddy Holliday, and we started getting called for a few ceremonies. A
santera (priestess) I knew, who was a godchild of Juan Candela, hired us
to play for her oricha. This was the first time Candela heard us playing
batá, and he was so impressed that we really knew the correct rhythms
that he began hiring us rather than his own family members to perform
at the musical ceremonies. With this type of recognition, our work increased until we often played several bembés in one weekend. In all honesty the drums, or perhaps our drumming, rarely failed to invoke possession by the orichas among the devotees, and the oricha would always
salute the drums when they appeared. At one point, a devotee possessed
by the oricha Oyá told us that even though they were not consecrated
drums, the time had come that we should "feed" them because they had
achieved an energy of their own.[9]

Although Julito Collazo had not been motivated to make his own
group before, our success probably convinced him that there was every reason to do so. In 1969 he started teaching Gene Golden, Sonny
Morgan, Babafemi Akinlana, and Richie Landrum "Pablo." They used
a set of batá drums made by Richie that was similar to, but less elaborate than ours in terms of their fundamental construction. Each of these

drums was made from two truncated cones conjoined to approximate the shape of a batá. For whatever reason, Collazo's group did not last very long, and it would be at least five years before Julito was to form another one. In the meantime, this idea of conjoining truncated cones to one another to construct the batá drums caught on, and companies such as Gon Bops and Skin On Skin eventually made a number of tunable sets, relying on their own conga and bongo hardware to affix and tune the skins.

Many of the bembés we played were given for new initiates, or *iyawós*, and this seemed to function for some time as a substitution for the presentation of the iyawós to Añá. As can be imagined, there was an ever-increasing number of santeros who had yet to be presented, and this could not really be alleviated given the absence of a consecrated set of Añá drums in New York. Among the many iyawós for whom we had played was Hector Hernández "El Flaco." Hector approached me about learning batá, and not only did he become one of my best students, his playing prowess became renowned in the New York scene. He played with us for several years and eventually left when Julito, recognizing his skill, decided to form another group and asked him to join.

Over the years a number of singers worked with us. It was a common event to see singers such as Juan Candela, Domingo Gómez, and Máximo Texidor at most bembés, but that was not always a guarantee. If none of them were in attendance, then I sang and played. It became obvious that we needed a singer who would be a part of our group. Russell Burroughs, Reynaud Simmons, and Caridad Torres all filled that role, but Caridad often got possessed and the singing duties reverted to myself or Hector in later years. We also had the fortune to work with Olympia Alfaro, the sister of the Cuban popular singer Xiomara Alfaro. Though Olympia was a ceremonial singer for the orichas, she was as great a singer as Xiomara in every aspect. She learned her craft under José Antonio Zubiadur and Luis Santamaría and sang with the very best batá groups in Havana; we had the privilege of working with her when she first moved to New York. The other singer who worked with our ensemble, Domiciano Valdez, began with us on a regular basis soon after Olympia.

The period when Hector left our group and Domiciano replaced Olympia as our principal singer also coincided with a proliferation of drumming ceremonies in New York and a noticeable increase in the number of groups that played them. By 1973 we had so much work that we were adding extra people to our ensemble in order to do two and even three bembés at the same time. The inevitable downside was that those who did not work with our ensemble on any given occasions, such as when we only had one ceremony to perform, then became available to work with any of the other groups who were in need of players.

Eventually many of these drummers worked so regularly with other groups that they were no longer available to work with us. In trying to accommodate all our clients we spread ourselves too thin, and our group collapsed. The breakup of our core group and the resultant reconfiguration of other groups left me without drummers and singers, and although I wanted to create another group, there were just too many obstacles at the time to move forward with such a plan. It seemed to me at the time as if I had reached a dead end, but another road was about to open for me.

The First Añá and Final Thoughts

I had stopped playing Latin dance music in order to concentrate on traditional ceremonial drumming; the idea of returning to the Latin club dance scene had not even really occurred to me. Nonetheless, when I coincidently was asked to play in a new Latin band I jumped at the opportunity. One opportunity led to another, and before long I was working full time with several Latin dance bands. Not playing at bembés left me out of touch with the batá scene, which made it all the more surprising when I received a call in 1976 telling me about an historic event soon to take place: the presentation of two santeros to Añá drums in New York City. Hector Hernández and Domiciano Valdez were to be presented to Añá, and this was to take place at Olympia's apartment in upper Manhattan. This first set of Añá batá to come to the USA was owned by the Miami babalao Reinaldo Peña "Pipo," and was being brought to New York for the presentation ceremony. Julito Collazo was to lead the drumming, and though I never asked, nor did I learn, who was responsible for coordinating this event, it was readily apparent to me that I simply had to be there. It was possible that many of the batá drums used in the recordings I had been studying might have been Añá, but to see and hear an Añá set in person would by definition have to be an experience of an entirely different order.

On the designated Sunday I arrived at Olympia's apartment as early as possible in order to see the ceremony from the beginning. I was disappointed to learn that the *oru igbodú*, or instrumental drum salutes, had already been played. The room was not as crowded as I anticipated; because the majority of priests in attendance had not been presented to consecrated drums, they could not be in the same room with them. The ceremony began without Julito. Olympia sang, "Pipo" Peña played iyá, while the itótele and okónkolo chairs were taken up by his sons, both in their early to mid-teens. The drums were a bit out of tune, due to the change of climate I suppose, and the playing seemed somewhat incomplete and lackluster.

After what felt like an unbearable wait, Julito finally showed up. He sat down in the center and took the iyá and Pipo moved to the itótele. They played a variety of rhythms, and at a number of junctures it seemed that the itótele was either not answering properly, or that the okónkolo was displaced. Of course, in some cases more than one rhythm can be used for the same song, and this was possibly what accounted for some of what I was hearing. Nonetheless, Julito never seemed disturbed by the other two drummers as they continued to play. Finally the presentations began, and I was going into uncharted territory; I had never heard or seen this main initiation rhythm before. (I have to admit I was even more interested in memorizing the individual patterns than in witnessing the event, and I transcribed them as soon as I got home.) Years later, when this rhythm became common knowledge among New York drummers, I realized that there were several different interpretations of it. What Julito and Pipo played that day was a hybrid of two of those many versions, and in all likelihood they tacked on one more version for good measure.

Hector Hernández's presentation preceded that of Domiciano Valdez, but since they were both priests of Obatalá, the ritual sequence of their presentations was fundamentally identical. Each of the initiates was brought in front of the batá by their godparents once the presentation rhythms had started. After the songs of presentation were finished, they each danced for their oricha, Obatalá. They now had the authority to be "in the presence of Añá," and since Hector and Domiciano were both actively involved in playing bembés, this was of great importance for both of them as well as the larger religious community.

• • •

Julito played for a little while longer and then left. I stayed until the end of the bembé, leaving with mixed feelings about what had transpired. If I had expected the drums to deliver some discernible magical force, I did not feel or hear it. Instead, I found myself leaving without the experience of an extraordinary "happening." In retrospect, however, I realized that my expectations were unrealistic.

In the first place, no matter how great the spiritual forces within a set of drums or the skill of the drummers playing them, if those drums are out of tune they will not sound good. Second, even if the drummers are all initiated to Añá, their levels of skill as well as their styles of playing can vary widely, limiting the composite sound of the group. In other words, the voice of Añá can be affected by various factors.

I was eventually initiated into the Cuban line of Añá as well as Adya Hounto, the Haitian equivalent, and I know what it feels like to have the energy flow through my arms and out my hands. This does not mean, however, that my playing is always at a consistent level day in and day out. Nor does it mean that I can make another drummer sound better than they are capable of sounding.

I now understand that even if I didn't feel the intensity of Añá that I was looking for, it did speak and I was very fortunate to have been there as a witness.

Notes

1. Julito Collazo passed on March 5, 2004, at the age of seventy-eight years; Francisco Aguabella passed on May 7, 2010, aged eighty-four.

2. Although at odds with the date given in the DVD *Sworn to the Drum* (2007), which states that 1957 was the year that Collazo and Aquabella moved to the USA, I defer to Vega, who collected her information directly from Collazo.

3. Chachálekpafuñ (also known as Chachálokefuñ) is one of the common generic dance rhythms that accompanies many songs in the repertoire.

4. There is no date is listed on the LP jacket, but this was released around 1957–59.

5. Marielitos is the name used for the Cubans who came to the USA by way of the Mariel Boatlift.

6. *Rituales Afrocubanos Lucumí* is the original title for *Ritmos Afrocubanos con los Auténticos Tambores Batá* by Giraldo Rodríguez.

7. I propose that the ceremony to which Carl, Ray, and Rudy brought their homemade batá drums was the 1961 bembé that John Mason reported (1992, 9), discussed earlier.

8. *Editor's note:* see Quintero, this volume, to learn of Scull's key role in the instigation of batá and Añá in Venezuela.

9. By "feeding" I refer to ritual sacrifice made to an oricha. When the oricha Añá is fed, blood from a sacrificed animal is put directly onto the drums.

References Cited

Cornelius, Steven. 1989. *The Convergence of Power: An Investigation into the Music Liturgy of Santería in New York City*. PhD diss., University of California, Los Angeles.

Mason, John. 1992. *Orin Òrìṣà: Songs for Selected Heads*. New York: Yorùbá Theological Archministry.

Ortíz, Fernando. 1996 [1954]. *Los Instrumentos De La Música Afrocubana vol. IV*. Madrid: Música Mundana.

———. 1998a [1950]. *La Africanía de la Música Folclorica de Cuba*. Madrid: Música Mundana.

———. 1998b [1951]. *Los Bailes y el Teatro de los Negros en el Folklore de Cuba*. Madrid: Música Mundana.

Vega, Marta Moreno. 1995. "The Yoruba Orisha Tradition Comes to New York City." In *African American Review* 29 (2): 201–6.

Discography

Conjunto Obaoso. Nd. *Fuerza Santera.* LP *Santero*-17.

Conjunto Obaoso. Nd. *Santería Cubana (Toques y Cantos) Santeros Lucumí.* LP Santero-135.

Rodríguez, Giraldo. 1980. *Ritmos Afrocubanos con los Auténticos Tambores Batá de Giraldo Rodríguez [Rituales Afrocubanos Lucumí* (n.d.)]. Orfeon LP-LAB-08, or LP-12-38008, or LPO-33.

Santamaría, Mongo. 1993. *Mongo Santamaría: Our Man In Havana [Mongo in Havana* 1960]. Fantasy FCD-24729-2.

Various artists. N.d. *Santero (Toques de Santo).* Panart CD-1A-501-00416A.

10

The Making of Añá in Venezuela

Alberto Quintero, with Michael Marcuzzi

• •

Though the arrival of Añá in Caracas remains of critical importance in this chapter, this study also stands in as a firsthand look at the larger history of orisha worship in Venezuela.[1] As is the case in numerous parts of the world where orisha worship is found, many religious communities in places like Caracas do not overtly demonstrate any direct historical connection to Yorùbáland, from where orisha worship came to the Americas, but rather indirectly through one of two principal sites, Cuba or Brazil, which represent (along with Trinidad and Tobago) the main territories of the orisha diaspora in the Americas.[2] Compared with the history of these major orisha traditions in the Americas, that of orisha worship in Venezuela is of a different order; it is in effect part of a secondary diaspora, having emerged and been predominantly shaped by the traditions of orisha worship that coalesced in Cuba, and to a certain degree Puerto Rico, where Cuban orisha worship also took hold.

What is constructed for the reader here is a narrative from a set of notes that have been gathered from: 1) personal observation on the part of the principal investigator, Alberto Quintero, and 2) various drumming colleagues and informants in and around Caracas with whom he has worked. In a sense, this is an attempt to disseminate what has up until now been a de facto oral history of orisha drumming in Venezuela, albeit a personalized one insofar as it is a narrative which has been received by Alberto, one in which he acts as a principal player, and one in which he now appears as author. Any first-person narrative or reference made to the "author" in the chapter that follows is meant to indicate Alberto himself, while my own commentary is relegated to the endnotes. In a larger sense, this chapter is a record of some of the critical events and key players in the establishment of *batá* drumming in Venezuela that eventually led first to the arrival, and then to the consecration, of sacred Añá drums in Venezuela: it is a record of how the drumming *oricha* Añá came to be constituted within the larger Venezuelan religious community.

Alberto's narrative, which immediately follows this brief introduction, begins from the perspective of a performing musician's oral history, the narrative bits and pieces of musical contexts and personal accounts that come to frame the ways in which we as musicians enter into the performing world. In the narrative that ensues, the reader will find that the nicknames, epithets, and initiation names of oricha peoples often stand in for the complete names of these players in the religious and/or musical scene, a trend that is characteristic of orisha cultures in the Americas in general. So, many of the individuals referenced in Alberto's account are simply remembered by their first names, nicknames, or the name of the oricha that they worshipped, such as "Sara, the daughter of Obatalá" (Sara, the Obatalá devotee), or "La China Agayú" (the Chinese devotee of Agayú). Likewise, one finds that in Cuba many early prominent oricha figures are also referred to in similar fashion, and this is particularly so in the recitation of religious lineages. Perhaps this is indicative of the fact that what is of primary importance to practitioners, and even musical performers, is an active lineage of ritual connectedness, less than the matter of reifying an accurate record of names.

Beyond the scope of this chapter, I briefly present here some details concerning what seem to be the earliest recordings of Afrocuban drumming in Venezuela. Included in a plethora of archival recordings of Venezuelan folk music produced by Venezuelan poet and folklorist Juan Liscano (1914–2001) are three sixteen-inch LPs that document a variety of Cuban and Venezuelan instrumental and song recordings made in Venezuela before 1950. This three-disc collection can be found in the American Folklife Center of the Library of Congress and is titled *Juan Liscano Collection of Cuban and Venezuelan Folk Music*. Most recently, a commercial release of one of the tracks from this three-disc collection appeared on *The Yoruba/Dahomean Collection: Orishas across the Ocean* (1998). The track, "Song for Eleguá," features the Cuban ensemble Conjunto El Niño, led by the Cuban percussionist Guillermo Rigueiro, with Afrocuban batá drumming accompanying the song. No exact date is provided on the jacket materials, except to say that the recording was made by Juan Liscano prior to 1950.

These sound documents appear to have existed somewhat in the periphery of the dominant oral history among the Venezuelan musicians—musical details that have remained outside the confines of the stories musicians tell of the early days of batá drumming in Venezuela. It also suggests that there is a rather glaring disconnect between the "official" ethnological work that has been undertaken by Venezuelan musicologists and that which has been made available to the larger musical community. (In this chapter, Alberto only makes mention of some early recordings of oricha music made in New York, which came to hold certain sway among Venezuelan drummers.) Nonetheless, vis-à-vis ethnology in other parts of Latin America and the Caribbean, Venezuela has continually demonstrated one of the more stable traditions of a national musicology. Certainly the tireless years of study, publication, and institutional initiatives generated by the husband-and-wife team of Luis Felipe Ramón y Rivera (1913–1993) and Isabel Aretz (1909–2005) have been the most obvious example of such work in Venezuela.[3] And it was the earlier work of Juan Liscano, first director of the Servicio de Investigaciónes Folklóricas Nacionales created in 1946, that was of primary importance in terms of documenting the earliest examples of Afrocuban drumming in Venezuela. This organization, which was constituted on October 30, 1946,[4] helped support Liscano's seminal work before the 1950s, and by all indications provided the first documented performances of Afrocuban music making in Venezuela. However, for Alberto (and I imagine this to be true for many oricha musicians in Venezuela), the story of oricha drumming nonetheless begins in 1952 with the arrival of Cuban drummer Jesús Pérez "Oba Ilú" in Caracas, Venezuela.

MM

This chapter is a set of reflections and historical narratives designed to give insight into what our oricha drumming community in Venezuela says about itself. Undoubtedly there are numerous events that are missing from my account and other moments I narrate that might be considered lacking in detail. Nevertheless, the important currents in this story demonstrate the continuing efforts of our community in its early years to seek out information, share expertise, and collectively cobble together the makings of a fraternity that gradually arrived at a religious orthodoxy and performance expertise that is now internationally recognized beyond our own narrow self-evaluation.

I begin this story in 1952 with the arrival in Venezuela of the renowned Havana drummer Jesús Pérez. Jesús was a monumental figure in Cuban batá drumming as a founding member of two of Cuba's major state-funded groups, the Conjunto Folklórico Nacional de Cuba (National Folkloric Ensemble of Cuba) and Danza Moderna.[5] Pérez's arrival in Caracas was the spark that started the fire within, culminating in a watershed moment within the Venezuelan drumming community in 1995. Not only was this the year that another renowned Havana drummer and *babalao* (divining priest) Marino Angarica "Papo" first came to Venezuela, but his work here beginning in 1995 brought about the first consecrations of Añá drums in our country. So I chose 1995 as the closing point in this story not because it represents any real end, but rather the beginning of an entirely new chapter in oricha drumming in Venezuela.

Up until 1995, the fledgling Venezuelan oricha drumming community had been dependent upon foreign expertise, relying on intermittent transnational interchanges with drummers from abroad. After Papo Angarica's first visit in 1995, our drumming community could proceed on its own. By then we had a community of ritual drummers with sufficient religious expertise and our own consecrated sets of Añá batá drums to continue the drumming legacy and consecration rites without the need for outside help. The year 1995 in effect marked the moment in which we had been given the proverbial keys to our own car: the years of guidance under such masters as Jesús Pérez, Felipe Alfonso, Regino Jiménez, Ángel Bolaños, Papo Angarica (all from Cuba), and Onelio Scull (from Puerto Rico) had resulted in the maturation of our community and its ability to step out alone.

Foreign Pioneers in Venezuela

While in Caracas for the first time, the Cuban percussionist Jesús Pérez was working as the bongo player for local group La Sonora Caracas under the directorship of Carlos Emilio Landaeta "Pan Con Queso," who founded the ensemble in 1948. While with Landaeta's ensemble, Pérez supplemented his income by contracting additional work as a carpenter during the day, a trade he had acquired in Cuba. It was Pérez who first introduced the concepts of Afrocuban drumming to many younger Venezuelan aficionados in Caracas's barrio Marin, San Agustín, and his occasional presence continued in Venezuela over the course of many years. On one of his other trips in 1955, Pérez traveled to Venezuela with legendary Cuban conga player Tata Güines, as part of the Havana cabaret Montmarte.

Eventually a young Venezuelan percussionist by the name of Jesús Quintero "Chu"[6] came to establish himself as the Venezuelan most knowledgeable of Afrocuban drumming, which seems to have meant at this time that he was Pérez's most dedicated disciple.[7] His continued efforts to distill Pérez's musical musings during his years in Caracas were decisive in establishing his own expertise as well as leaving an indelible mark on the Cuban master Pérez, who would later take on Chu as his student.

When the Fania Records U.S. American star musician and producer Larry Harlow came with his group to Venezuela, at least one of his percussionists, Frankie Malabe, also played batá, though again the drums that would have been used were not consecrated. Harlow's drummers were joined by the singer Domingo Gómez "Changó Miguá," who was in Caracas at the time.[8] Gómez had recorded an LP of oricha songs in New York and Puerto Rico, one of the earliest to be made commercially available, which set off an initial period of interest among the Venezuelan community in the ritual repertoire of oricha worship. This seminal recording, *Fuerza Santera: Toques y Cantos Santeros*, featured the ensemble Conjunto Obaoso[9] of Puerto Rican musician Onelio Scull, who played *okónkolo* (smallest batá drum) on this recording. The lineup included some of the most important percussionists on the New York scene at the time: Julito Collazo, Ángel Gómez, and Carlos Valdés "Patato."[10]

A growing interest in the Cuban oricha tradition among Venezuelan percussionists and devotees alike inevitably led to a desire to have batá drums and drumming experts brought from abroad to perform musical rituals. The earliest *santeros* and *santeras* (male and female oricha priests) in Caracas, such as Virginia Borroto (Cuban priestess of Changó), her son Pedro Alonso "Olochundé," Sara (the daughter of Obatalá), and "La China Agayú," all made efforts to bring ritual batá drummers to Venezuela to enliven their oricha festivities. It was also a time in the history of oricha drumming when traveling with the sacred batá drums outside of Cuba was simply not commonplace, and the idea itself would likely have met with some initial hesitation among batá drummers. Though drummers in the USA and Puerto Rico may have been more liberal in their views on such matters at the time, those individuals who had been traveling to Caracas to perform in this era had yet to acquire their own sets of consecrated Añá drums. Hence, none of them were in a position to provide any other type of religious services other than musical accompaniment and direction using *aberinkulá* (unconsecrated) drums.[11]

In 1972 the Conjunto Folklórico Nacional de Cuba visited Venezuela, performing at the Universidad Central (Central University). Included among the many performers on this tour were percussionists Carlos Aldama (who now lives in California),[12] Felipe Alfonso Pérez, Jesús Pérez and his wife Nancy, and vocalist Candido Zayas. Though access to the musicians was not easily achieved, Chu Quintero managed to make contact with some of them,[13] and it was from his efforts to meet with these Cubans that Chu was invited to Havana by Jesús Pérez to study with him. It was not until 1974, however, that Chu was able to travel to Havana, almost ten years after his first meeting with Pérez. Being a member of the Juventud Comunista de Venezuela (Communist Youth Party of Venezuela), Chu was able to secure a one-month visa to study in Cuba. Alongside his political science courses in Havana, Chu began his percussion lessons with Jesús Pérez.

Venezuela's First Batá Drums

When Chu visited Cuba in 1976, batá drums were not commercially available there, so while in Havana, Jesús and Chu began making templates for a set of batá drums using sheets of *Granma*, the official newspaper of the Cuban Communist Party. Upon returning to Venezuela, Chu contacted Carlos Gutiérrez, a conga maker as well as baseball player for Cervecería Caracas (Caracas Brewery). With the newspaper patterns in hand, Chu convinced Gutiérrez to construct the first batá drums in Venezuela. It could be said that Gutiérrez did so "in the dark." Not having seen batá drums before, Gutiérrez had only Chu's recommendations and some newspaper cutouts to guide him. In the end, these drums were constructed larger than the actual newspaper templates. Nonetheless, metal lugs were attached to the drums to secure the rims and drumheads, probably taken from the odds and ends of Gutiérrez's inventory of conga drum parts, and these became the first batá drums made in Venezuela.

Chu returned home to the Marin quarter in San Agustín del Sur, Caracas, and it was from this neighborhood that many of Venezuela's first batá drummers were recruited: Felipe Rengifo "Mandingo" (now living in Germany), Farides Mijares, Omar Oliveros, and Ricardo Quintero, among others. Immediately after his return in 1974, Chu founded the Grupo Madera (the Wood Ensemble), and with this collective as the nexus, the study of batá drumming in Venezuela truly began. A study group was organized by the renowned percussionist Orlando Poleo (currently residing in Paris), along with Mijares and Oliveros, and members met twice a week at the Taller de Cultura de San Agustín, Tucusan (The Tucusan Culture Workshop of San Agustín).

Religious and Musical Consolidation

In 1975, as part of an exposition of Cuban culture realized in Caracas, a delegation of Cuban artists descended upon the cultural scene, including *rumba* group Los Papines, vocal ensemble Quarteto Las D'Aida of which Omara Portuondo (of Buena Vista Social Club fame) was a member, plus a cohort of performers from the Conjunto Folklórico de Cuba among others. As part of the mandate of programmed events, the Cuban musicians delivered classes and workshops on Cuban music styles such as *güiro*[14] along with more advanced studies of religious drumming in general.

As the oricha religious community became larger and ritual knowledge became more widespread, oricha initiations were a far more frequent event in Caracas, as were religious musical events. Another of the important drummers in the fledgling 1970s scene was the Cuban *batalero* Alfredo Vidaux "Coyude." He was a frequent player in the early days of batá drumming in Caracas but did not have his own set of Añá at that point. I remember Vidaux performing in 1976 (not his first visit) with *akpwon* (ritual singer) Franklin Rodríguez, though I do not recall who the other drummers were.

By 1978 it had become common to have aberinkulá performing at oricha initiations. The actual initiation occurs on the first day, while these musical events for the most part took place during the *día del medio* (middle day), which is in fact the second day of the seven-day oricha initiation. During this festive break in the initiation, drummers are hired for what is a semi-public celebration, attended by friends and family of the initiate along with the wider oricha community. With the musicians present, the community has the opportunity to sing and dance in honor of the oricha. In late-1970s Venezuela it also became the custom that similar song-and-dance events would be organized for the initiation anniversaries of devotees, who would hire drummers to play for their oricha.[15]

In 1980 the Danza Nacional de Cuba, under the musical direction of Jesús Pérez, came to Venezuela for a series of performances. This particular tour was extremely influential in the history of batá drumming in Venezuela because it also introduced to the Venezuelan community the renowned Havana drummers Regino Jiménez "Omi Saidé" and Ángel Bolaños "El Muerto,"[16] both of whom were protégés of Jesús Pérez and major contributors to the development of both batá drumming and religious orthodoxy (including initiation rites) in Havana. It was this famed trio of drummers from the Danza Nacional de Cuba —Pérez, Jiménez, and Bolaños—that was the first to record the *oro seco*[17] for the Venezuelan community of drummers.[18]

Death and Renewal

On August 15, 1980, tragedy descended upon the Venezuelan drumming community. A boat carrying the Grupo Madera across the Orinoco River near Puerto Ayacucho in Amazonas State, Venezuela, sank, claiming the lives of Chu Quintero and ten other members of the ensemble.[19] Percussionist Felipe Rengifo "Mangindo" was one of the few survivors, able to save himself by floating to safety on the *iyá*, the largest of the batá drums that the ensemble had brought aboard the vessel. Though the loss of so many talented musicians was a grave tragedy for the music and oricha community, the year 1981 brought with it a celebrated development in the history of oricha drumming in Venezuela. Drummer Pedro Alonso "Olochundé," along with the ritual singer and *oriaté*[20] Roque Duarte "Jimagua," brought a set of consecrated drums to Venezuela, apparently the first *fundamento* to be played in the country. During the fundamento's "stay" in Venezuela, numerous *tambores* (drumming celebrations) took place, including one in the city of Calabozo. There were also numerous "presentations to the drums," the formal, public recognition of a devotee's initiation in the presence of Añá.[21]

Soon after this important event, Puerto Rican drummer Onelio Scull came to Venezuela in 1983 with his fundamento "Añá Ilú Addé," which had been consecrated in Havana in 1979. With his drums he performed a tambor for the oricha Obatalá in the home of Juana María Montes de Oca "La Niña." To my knowledge, this is the first time that Scull's Añá drums appeared in Venezuela.[22] In November 1984 Scull returned to Caracas with his drums to play a tambor for the santero Noraida Rodríguez Hernández "Ofún Dolá," though this time he was joined by the ritual singer Caridad, who came with him from Puerto Rico. In the case of this second appearance by Scull, the principal motivation seems to have been to facilitate a series of presentations of new initiates that had been "accumulating" in Ofún Dolá's religious home over the years. By this time, Ofún Dolá would have likely initiated many *iyawós* (neophytes) to the religion, all of whom were in need of presenting themselves to the Añá drums.

For batá drummers, the presentation of new initiates is a potentially lucrative affair, depending on the number of iyawós at any given event. When drummers are required to travel with a fundamento to an event, it is quite often necessary to procure a critical number of presentations at the ceremony so as to offset the costs of travel, accommodation, and fees for the performers. This was also the case during the early years of Añá drumming in Venezuela, and though the organization of these musical events had the advantage of proceeding because of so many initiates awaiting presentations, they also served to strengthen the musical confidence of the developing drumming community and generally move the religious community forward in its own self-realization.[23] Throughout 1988 and 1989 there was a steady increase in the overall number of tambores organized in and around Caracas. To summarize:

1) On January 24, 1988, Onelio Scull came to Caracas to play for Obatalá, which in fact turned out to be more of a "*tambor de presentaciones*" than simply a tambor.[24] On this particular date, forty-two new initiates were presented in a single ceremony held in the home of Ofún Dolá;

2) In March 1988 the Cuban Ogún priest Juan Raymat "El Negro" brought his drums, "Añá Obayé," from Miami to Venezuela with an impressive group of musicians, which included the drummers Orlando Ríos "Puntilla" (originally from Havana but by this time resident in New York City),[25] Ángel Maldonado "Chachete" (a New York-based Puerto Rican), Skip Burney "Brinquito" (an African American percussionist initiated by Puntilla), and the singer Máximo Texidor "Changó Laddé."[26] They performed in a tambor in the home of "Sara, *omo* Obatalá";

3) In December 1989 Johnny Angarica arrived from Puerto Rico with his Añá drums and stayed with me until August 1990. During this time, Angarica's drums were contracted to play to the Obatalá of Ofún Dolá;

4) During this same period, Angarica performed a tambor in honor of Yemayá (oricha of the ocean) for Gloria Díaz "Omileí," during which time thirty-four iyawós were presented to the drums; and

5) Soon after, Angarica played in the town of Los Teques to the Yemayá of Bebo Moré. During these tambores with Angarica's drums, the Puerto Rican drummers Ángel Maldonado "Chachete," Tempo Alomar, and Papo Cadenas performed with the late Venezuelan singer Eddie Chacoa and alongside the Venezuelan drummers Miguel Ángel Urbina, Orlando Poleo, Johnny Rudas, and this author.

In spite of this increased activity, the absence of a consecrated set of batá drums permanently residing in Venezuela held back our development as a religious community, particularly in terms of the importance of the presentation ceremonies, which were accumulating within some of the more prolific oricha houses. It was not until 1989 that Scull made his move to Venezuela permanent, bringing with him his drums, "Añá Ilú Addé" and thus establishing a presence of Añá in Venezuela.

"In the Land of the Blind, a One-Eyed Man Makes Himself King"[27]

Though many details about the unfolding of events in Venezuela's oricha community between December 1989 and the first half of 1990 remain obscure, a certain sense of religious urgency characterized this period for those of us interested in batá drumming. In hindsight, this era merits particular attention to illustrate how this period of flux led to greater religious stability for the drumming community soon after. It also resulted in the eventual involvement of Cuban batá masters with Venezuelan drummers, displacing the earlier dominance of Puerto Rican drummers in Caracas.

In 1989 a group of Puerto Ricans arrived with a fundamento to present a large group of initiates. At this point in time I had still not made my own oricha—some twenty to twenty-five years in the waiting—and I was still very much a novice in terms of any religious authority within the larger Venezuelan community. There was a long lineup of religious work that was to follow the arrival of fundamento drums, and yet there were no consecrated drummers in Caracas available to perform on these drums. That is, the Venezuelan drummers were not ritually authorized to perform on the sacred batá drums, as they had not been initiated. The Puerto Rican drummers took it upon themselves to set about establishing their unique corrective to this situation. They decided to prepare a hand-washing initiation ceremony that would officially sanction the Venezuelan drummers-in-waiting to participate in the drumming ceremonies and allow the elders to avoid any admonition from the larger religious community for not having used initiated drummers. Like my Venezuelan colleagues such as Miguito Benigno, Farides Mijares, and Orlando Poleo, among others, I was eager to become a member of the wider Añá community.

One of the greatest difficulties that all oricha novitiates face in their religious development is the ability to assess the ritual competence of elders who will either stand in as their sponsors or participate in religious ceremonies. This competence is based on a complex set of factors that is often masked or compromised by the financial, social, and personal interests of all those involved in the ritual activity. Ultimately, the new initiates are at a disadvantage because of their inexperience, and at times, outright collusion can occur among the religious community in order to control the material and personal stakes of an initiation. Sadly, this type of manipulation can continue to undermine the autonomy of the initiate throughout his or her religious development.

In some parts of Cuba, the hand-washing ceremony (*lavarse las manos*) authorizes the new drummer to fully access the Añá fraternity; in other parts, particularly Havana, it only permits the drummer to perform on the consecrated drums, but bars him from the larger consecratory rites of Añá until they undergo the ritual of being "sworn" (*jurado*) to the drums. In either instance, however, the hand-washing ceremony would have offset any criticism from the larger religious community about the participation of the Venezuelan drummers. The Puerto Ricans who undertook our "initiation" had supposedly been sworn by Julio Collazo and Alfredo Vidaux, two individuals of decided repute in the U.S. American batá drumming scene.[28] This was a sufficient criterion for those of us in

Caracas. We would undertake the ceremony being planned by the Puerto Rican drummers, though in retrospect, given our enthusiasm not much could have prevented us from proceeding with our initiations. We were filled with faith, emotion, and excitement; yet the Puerto Ricans gave us the worst treatment of the century.

The elders set about making an *omiero*, a ritual bath made primarily from a variety of crushed herbs in water, which is used as part of any oricha consecration ritual. Of course, that any of these elder drummers understood the nuances of which particular flora would be both effective and required in such an herbal concoction for a drumming consecration was clearly wishful thinking on our part. This was only confirmed by the inventiveness of the remainder of the "ceremony" that we were required to endure. Though the Havana initiation ceremony for drummers is recognized for its rather arduous test of physical discomfort, we were forced to endure a series of physical onslaughts at the hands of our Puerto Rican initiators that are unheard of in Cuba—blows with the divination tappers of Ifá,[29] swipes with switches on the bare back, and hits with wet leather straps! Knowing what I know now, little in the ceremony had any basis in preparing a drummer for ritual work or had much resemblance to Cuban Añá initiations, though we were in no position to assess the proceedings at the time. We truly believed in and wanted Añá in our lives, and our preparedness to deliver ourselves unto anything that was asked of us in the name of Añá became the primary motivating factor in our endurance of the hand-washing "ceremony" that we underwent.

As time went on, we approached our Boricua elders on numerous occasions to provide us with religious guidance and knowledge. The religious information they provided always seemed suspect, even backwards at times, and we as a community constantly found ourselves increasingly dependent on them for answers and clarifications that never seemed to be forthcoming. These Puerto Ricans repeatedly returned to Venezuela to avail themselves of the lion's share of the religious work, all the while keeping the Venezuelan drummers ritually and monetarily under thumb. On one particular occasion they came to perform four tambores over the course of fifteen days, but paid the Venezuelans a lump sum of approximately one hundred US dollars in total for the four tambores. (This translated to approximately fifteen dollars US per Venezuelan drummer for all four musical events!) By my calculations, the Puerto Ricans amassed around three thousand US dollars; I was privy in part to the fees that had been negotiated with them because my wife at the time, an oricha initiate, was at the center of many of these transactions.

The asymmetry in the payment was rationalized by way of the hand-washing ceremony: because the Puerto Ricans had sponsored us as Añá initiates, our financial indebtedness, according to them, was in perpetuity. The monies that were given to the Venezuelan drummers were not taken from the fees procured by the Puerto Rican drummers, but rather extracted from the *jícara*, the large gourd set down in front of the drummers into which devotees "splash" additional monies for the musicians when they play for their own oricha.

Re-initiation in Cuba

Significantly, of the group of Venezuelan drummers who were initiated with the Puerto Ricans as described above, nearly all of us later went on to receive our own fundamentos. We did so in spite of events that took place in that first "initiation." Our realization about the real nature of the betrayal by the Boricua elders helped us to persevere: our resolve was still strong, and we believed we had earned a moral high ground that inspired us to continue down the religious path. Due to the ritual events we endured and the exploitation that followed, we began to look elsewhere for religious guidance. This search led us to the Cuban drummers Ángel Bolaños and Regino Jiménez, who became crucial players in rectifying the religious orthodoxy of Añá in Venezuela.

In August 1990 I traveled to Havana with Farides Mijares, Orlando Poleo, and Benigno Medinas to meet with the renowned Havana batá drummer Regino Jiménez. As one would expect, during the first half of 1990 it became increasingly clear to us that our earlier experience as Añá initiates had been compromised by the Boricua contingent that had landed in Caracas, and so, on this trip to Havana, we approached Regino with the idea of overseeing another initiation to Añá. Regino responded positively to our request and insisted that we also involve the renowned drummer and Añá priest Ángel Bolaños. On August 23, 1990 in Regla (an area of Havana), we were sworn to the drums of Alejandro Adofó, "Ida Ilú," which were in the custody of Lázaro Zambian Calderón "Papaíto," a Yemayá priest and stepson of Adofó himself.[30] Three days later, on August 26, we presented ourselves to the drums during a tambor held in the home of Pedro Valdez "Aspirina" on Calle No. 1, Guanabacoa, a neighborhood of Havana.[31] We became the first Venezuelan drummers to be initiated in the Añá fraternity (at least in the form recognized by the larger batá community). In attendance at our presentations were Carlos Aldama, Nury Torres (wife of Ángel Bolaños at the time), Eusebia Eloina, Carmen Ascoy (wife of "Papaito"), Julio Guerra, Alejandro Carvajal, Pedro Lugo "El Nene," Fermín Nani, and Pedro Ramos "Pepe Calabaza," among other renowned drummers.[32]

Following our return from Cuba, our Venezuelan drumming circle gained greater access to playing consecrated drums. Scull had already been living in Caracas since 1989 with his drums, and during the early 1990s many more Venezuelans traveled to Havana to be sworn to Añá. Included among this second wave of drummers were Gustavo Ovallés, Tomás Fajardo, Gerson Ruiz, Fidel González,[33] and William Hernández, who were all initiated in Havana. They were "sworn" to the drums "Ewerikan," "Acobiaña," and "Eweaddé."[34]

New Cuban Connections: Matanzas and Oriente

Not until 1993 was the Venezuelan drumming community able to welcome a new group of musicians from outside the Havana scene.[35] In August of that year, musicians from the Conjunto Folklórico de Santiago de Cuba arrived in Caracas, and included among them as a guest artist was the famed religious drummer, Estéban "Cha Chá" Vega.[36] Armed with a delegation of musicians, dancers, and representatives—all of whom were religious initiates—the group traveled with the newly consecrated drums "Añá Bí Ará Odo Melli," which Vega had prepared for his godchild, Melián Galí Rivero, in the Matanzas style of construction.[37]

According to conversations that I had with Galí and other ensemble members while in Caracas and Havana, it seemed that the ensemble agreed to a series of financial conditions during this trip that were less than adequate for their needs, no doubt a direct result of the desperate economic situation facing all Cubans during the crisis years known as the *periodo especial* (special period) in 1990s Cuba.[38] During this difficult time, Cuban artists often found themselves accepting even the most one-sided contracts abroad in their attempts to gain access to foreign currency and weather the economic hardships at home.

The ensemble agreed to a per diem of twenty-five dollars and a weekly salary of seventy-five dollars, which was to include any and all performances to be negotiated by the representatives and the musical leadership of the ensemble. These remunerations were never forthcoming. The ensemble stayed for an entire month in a hotel, which had agreed to donate its rooms; their meals would be brought to the members in boxes. Conditions severely strained the cohesiveness of the group, and some members began to disperse from the scene, while others looking for pickup work began to make contacts with Venezuelan musicians. Given these difficult conditions, one of the representatives decided to perform a tambor, first honoring the ancestors (Egún) and then the oricha Changó, with the hope of procuring the help of the orichas so as to return to Cuba.[39]

Along with the participation of the Caracas oricha community, the Cubans set up shop in a central locale and began the tambor to the ancestors at 10:00 a.m. and continued until midnight. In fact, it was a *tambor doble*,[40] organized with the drums of Galí, "Añá Bí Ará Odo Melli," and those of Onelio Scull, "Añá Ilú Addé," who was still living in Venezuela. Soon after the tambor to the ancestors was finished, the musicians played in honor of Changó. Four days later, the Cubans received an invitation to perform in Colombia!

The ensemble accepted the contract, which resulted in a preferable performing opportunity and a few square meals of "meat and bread" each day. Given the months of food scarcity experienced in Havana during this period, the comparatively robust diet turned out to be, for the performers, as important as their newfound performing opportunities. Returning from the Columbian trip, they remained in Caracas for a brief stint, hoping to procure any similar contracts that might be available. When none were forthcoming, the ensemble returned soon after to Cuba with little to show for their time abroad.

Consecrating Añá in Venezuela

The year 1995 was a particularly historic year for batá drumming in Venezuela. For the first time, Papo Angarica arrived with his consecrated drums, "Ilú Ará." From his set of batá drums were "born" two other sets of Añá batá that year: the drums of the babalao Marito Abreu, named "Añá Bí Lerí," and those of Ricardo González, which were named "Añá Okan Ilú." This consecration took place on December 19, 1995 and was the first to be undertaken in Venezuela. In October of the same year, Angarica had already initiated the Venezuelan drummers Miguel Ángel Urbina, Johnny Rudas, Luis Díaz, César Pérez, Richard Ávila, and Maurice Melo in the home of Juanita Martínez "Laddé Oyá"; it was a move that ensured that there would be sufficient initiates to work in future consecration ceremonies, like those of the aforementioned sets of drums.

On November 29, 1996, another set of consecrated drums was prepared, this time for Miguel Ángel Urbina under the direction of Papo Angarica and the author. The ceremony took place in the town of Camatagua, Edo Aragua, Venezuela. I started building the drums late in the day, and when we were about to sacrifice a goat for Eleguá, the lights went out and we had to work by candlelight under heavy rain. In the moment that Orunla was eating his goat,[41] the rain stopped and suddenly a clear and starry sky appeared with a beautiful full moon. Accordingly,

Plate 10.1. Añá drummers during a consecration ceremony of two sets of Añá. From left to right: Ricardo Rivera, Marino Angarica "Papo," César Argenis Tovar, and Alberto Quintero, the author. (photographer unknown, Caracas)

Papo suggested calling the drums "Añá Ilú Okan Irawo" (Añá drum heart of the star). The drums were placed in the custody of Miguel Ángel Urbina, Johnny Rudas (an Ochún initiate), and Fidel González "Baba Loyú" (a babalao and Obatalá priest), as well as under the matronage of Gloria Díaz "Omilcí," godmother of Urbina. These drums were "given voice"[42] on December 2, 1996 in the home of Ofún Dolá.

Onelio Scull

Few individuals have had more of a continuous and influential presence in the life of Añá outside of Cuba than Onelio Scull. For the early drumming community in Venezuela, that influence was tangible from Scull's early contributions on the recordings *Fuerza Santería* and *Santería Cubana*, both of which featured his ensemble Conjunto Obaoso. By the time that Cha Chá Vega and later Papo Angarica had made their appearances among the Venezuelan community in 1993 and 1995 respectively, Scull had been living in Venezuela for many years and had been traveling between San Juan and Caracas for many more, bringing his *fundamento* in and out of the country. After arriving permanently in Caracas in 1989, he had been operated on for appendicitis, and the ordeal had not been an easy one to assimilate. Many of the drummers in Caracas had taken up his cause to varying degrees, as though he were a bachelor uncle living alone among us. Unfortunately, Scull was not in the best financial situation and the daily demands of life in Caracas limited the degree to which even those of us in the drumming community were able to devote our time and resources to supporting Scull through this period. He had been living in the Parque Central region of the city, in a pension that was, by anyone's standards, unacceptable. It was here that he spent some of his roughest moments.

Scull was first and foremost a craftsman. Though already recognized in Puerto Rico as a great drummer, Scull was also renowned for his work making oricha tools and ritual objects there. He had been convinced to leave Puerto Rico by many in the Venezuelan religious community, enticed by the idea of great prospects for a future in Caracas that in the end fell utterly short of its promise. He arrived in Venezuela in 1989 with his tools, his machines, and his orichas. He arrived with his Añá drums, "Añá Ilú Addé," with great hope for lucrative opportunities that never came to fruition. And unfortunately for Scull, his move also left an indelible sacrifice in his personal life: his separation from Carmen, a renowned Yemayá priestess whose religious reputation extended well beyond Puerto Rico.[43]

Scull's set of drums became the first focal point for the religious drumming community in Caracas, and eventually all the early musicians came to sing or play with his drums at one time or another. On September 8, 1989, I was initiated into the secrets of the oricha Ochún, and one month later I was presented to the drums of Onelio, just as so many had been up to that point in Caracas. We all remain indebted to Scull.

A few years after the tambor doble in Caracas in 1993, the United States consulate apparently contacted Scull. He was informed that, in order to continue drawing his Medicare benefits, he would have to take up official residence in a US territory. Given his declining health, Scull's options were few, and he made the choice to return home. It was with Miguel Ángel Urbina that he chose to leave his drums; by this time Miguel had been initiated as an Eleguá priest and was perhaps the most "orthodox" of the drummers. Though there were elder oricha initiates, myself among them, Miguel also represented one of the most advanced apprentices among us.

My Añá

"Añá Bí Ará" is the name given to my own set of Añá. I received these drums on April 24, 2004 under the direction of my godfather, Ángel Bolaños "Echú Bi Okan," with Regino Jiménez. The attendant accoutrements of Ifá[44] were prepared by Cristóbal Guerra "Echú Tolu," and the ceremony took place in the home of the renowned batá drummer Fermín Nani "Ochún Leti," in the neighborhood of Luyano, Havana. Both Fermín and Regino have passed away since this ceremony. They will be sadly missed by all of us who worked with them in the consecration of my Añá during the spring of 2004.

Though the ceremonies were realized with perhaps one of the most prestigious gatherings of Añá drummers that could have been united under one roof at that time in Havana, I would be amiss in not mentioning the gracious efforts of Michael Marcuzzi, my godchild David Font-Navarrete, and William Pettit, whose particular ritual expertise, support, and skills were crucial in the preparation of these drums. There was, however, one man who opened the way for me who was not with us in that Havana consecration.

Jesús Quintero "Chu"

It is somewhat ironic that, in the final summation, the most influential individual in the development of Afrocuban music in Venezuela, Chu Quintero, had not received even a single consecrated bead around his neck at the time of his passing.[45] It was Chu who followed Jesús Pérez into the *barrio* Marin de San Agustín del Sur, one of Caracas's oldest colonial neighborhoods, and it was Chu by Pérez's side as he spoke to the aspiring musicians and offered those earliest musical orientations on Cuban percussion. Yet no one really taught Chu to play during these early years. He sat by, patiently collecting what information he could until he was able to reunite with Pérez in Havana many years later through the Communist Youth Party. It was then that, for the very first time, a Venezuelan began to assimilate the familiar "*ki-ha*" of the okónkolo.[46] It was by way of the seminal work that Chu had undertaken in Havana and the now famous *Granma* newspaper patterns that the batá began their journey south, across the Caribbean to Caracas. It has been a half century since Chu sowed the first seeds of Afrocuban percussion, and we have all been able to reap the benefits of his endeavors.

Chu Quintero's untimely death in 1980, along with other members of the Grupo Madera, remains one of the deepest ironies of all. His life in

many respects was marked by a profound personal sacrifice that facilitated the path for many others to travel on, not only to perform oricha
music on the sacred batá, but also undertake their own personal journey
through the world of the orichas—experiences that Chu would never realize for himself. For this reason, I feel it is only apropos to mention Chu
in this final paragraph on Añá in Venezuela. I believe there are lessons
to be learned from his story. This history began because of the efforts
of a single individual with no standing in the religious community, who
nevertheless left behind a legacy that in many respects supersedes the
influence of some of Venezuela's most renowned oricha devotees.

Notes

1. Special thanks go to David Font-Navarrete, Larry Harlow, Bernardo Padrón, Ken
Schweitzer, and Michael Spiro for their help in clarifying many crucial details in this chapter.

2. This is of course not meant in any way to lessen the importance of other communities in the
Americas that partake in forms of orisha worship claiming a linear connection to Yorùbáland. One
of the more obvious examples would be Trinidad and Tobago, which, in spite of the importance of
orisha practices that came from nearby Grenada, has been influenced by concerted reconnections
with òrìṣà practitioners in Nigeria since the 1980s. Nonetheless, it is clear that Cuba's oricha tradition has been most influential in establishing orisha practices throughout the Americas since the
end of the transatlantic separation, with Brazil also bringing its influence to bear in many locales
(e.g., New York City).

3. He was the director of the National Institute of Folklore for twenty years where Aretz set
up the music section. In 1988 they founded the International Foundation of Ethnomusicology and
Folklore (now Centro de La Diversidad Cultural).

4. In 1953 the Service was renamed the Instituto de Folklore, and the directorship passed on
to Luis Felipe Ramón y Rivera (Aretz 1962, n.a.).

5. Founded in 1962, the ensemble was initially called the Conjunto Nacional de Danza
Moderna and later named Danza Nacional de Cuba. The same ensemble is now known as Danza
Contemporánea.

6. Not related to the author.

7. The author has stated that Chu Quintero was approximately eighteen years old when he met
Pérez for the first time. Their meeting then would have taken place in the mid-1960s, suggesting
that Pérez had been traveling to Venezuela repeatedly after his initial 1952 trip.

8. Domingo Gómez initiated Harlow, an Ochún devotee. Harlow was unsure of the dates for
this tour; however, he informed me that in the early 1970s his percussionists were Tony Jiménez,
Pablito Rosario, and Frankie Malabe. Of the three, Harlow says that "Frankie Malabe played
batá, so it was probably him" who performed at these events (pers. comm., August 4, 2009).
Whether the other percussionists who performed were Harlow's drummers is not clear, though
Tony Jiménez, Frank Rodríguez, and Gene Golden are listed as batá drummers on his brother
Andy Harlow's 1976 LP *Latin Fever*, which Larry produced. To complicate matters, there is
no indication that the ritual drumming mentioned here took place in the early 1970s, as the author's original chronology suggests, or during a subsequent tour that Larry Harlow undertook
in Venezuela. The degree to which these religious events would have conformed to orthodox

religious ceremonies is not entirely clear. It is likely that, at this early juncture in Venezuela's oricha history, they were less formal musical events that engaged the community in a general participatory environment of oricha music making, as opposed to the very structured unfolding of a more orthodox *tambor* (drumming ceremony).

9. The name of this ensemble also appears throughout the literature, and at times on various LP liner notes, as "Obaso." The name appears to be intended as a homage to the oricha Changó, whose epithet is "*Oba-(k)o-so*" (the King did not hang).

10. In addition to these percussionists and the lead voice of Domingo Gómez, the ensemble also featured the lead singer Máximo Texidor and the chorus of Julia Valdés, Juan Candela, Merceditas Rojas, Nicolás Hernández, and one "Papito." A subsequent LP, *Santería Cubana* (*Toques y Cantos*) *Santeros Lucumí*, soon followed, featuring more oricha musical selections with the exact same musical personnel.

11. The author says that 1981 marked the first Añá in Venezuela, a date that seems to be in accordance with the emergence of consecrated drums in the USA. For example, it was in 1979 that Onelio Scull, a prominent figure in Venezuela's early drumming history, had his set of drums, "Añá Ilú Addé," consecrated in Havana. Scull did not begin performing in Venezuela with his consecrated drums until 1983. US-based Cuban Alfredo Vidaux "Coyude," who often performed in Caracas, did not have his set of Añá, "Añá Ire Owantolokun," consecrated until the 1980s. This set appear to have been the first consecrated on US soil. Coyude's set was "born" from Scull's drums in a ceremony in Los Angeles. Scull's drums were preceded by the Añá drums of "Pipo" Piña, the first brought to the USA in 1976. Both Piña and Scull had their drums consecrated in Havana (Capone, 2006).

12. See Vaughan and Aldama, 2012.

13. Cuban ensembles traveled during this time with "facilitators" or representatives who, often with the excuse of state concerns over the security of the group in foreign territories, invariably restricted the independence of the performers to move about or associate with individuals from without. Members of the group were permitted to move about while on tour, but only in pairs so as to "look out" for one another.

14. Güiro refers both to the beaded gourd (also called *chekeré*) and the musical rite in Cuban oricha worship, which makes use of an ensemble of güiros.

15. This gradual unfolding of drumming events—formal and informal musical gatherings—has also played out in many other sites of oricha worship where Añá drums were not available to the religious community in its early stages. The organization of these more social musical events is indicative of the importance of drumming in the establishment of the religious community and an overall desire among the oricha communities to see their own musical evolution progress. Toronto (Canada) and London (UK) are but two examples where this same dynamic has been unfolding for some time now.

16. Jiménez passed away in 2005; Bolaños continues to reside in Havana and work with the Danza Nacional de Cuba.

17. The oro seco (also known as the *oro igbodú*) is an instrumental rite and is the foundational corpus of repertoire for Cuban batá drumming. It comprises approximately twenty to forty-five minutes of continuous drumming in a collection of salutes to the major orichas of the Yorùbá pantheon. It is performed to begin every communal ritual where the sacred batá perform (see Amira and Cornelius, 1992).

18. Significantly, this trio of drummers also traveled to Nigeria in 1977 to play for the king of Ọ̀yọ́, the Aláàfin, who is believed to be the living descendent of the *òrìṣà* Ṣàngó (Changó).

19. The other band members who died were Nilda Ramos, Tibisay Ramos, Alejandrina Ramos, Ricardo Quintero, Luis Orta, Carlos Orta, Jesús Sanoja, Héctor Romero, Lesby Hernández, and Juan Ramon Castro.

20. The oriaté is a master shell diviner and lead priest in oricha initiation ceremonies. Duarte is considered one of the most senior and prestigious oriatés in the USA.

21. Prior to the arrival of the consecrated batá—that is, Añá-laden batá drums—the presentation ceremonies could not be observed. For more on the subject, see Cornelius (1995) and Marcuzzi (2005, 370–71).

22. It is impossible to attest to Scull's intentions here. Perhaps this was in direct response to the appearance of Pedro Alonso's Añá drums in 1981, since it seems that up to this juncture: 1) the use of unconsecrated drums had been the norm in Venezuela, even by foreign musicians, and 2) the transnational movement of Añá drums would have likely been viewed as a rather contentious venture by many orthodox drummers during this period, irrespective of its commonplace nature today.

23. The presentation of the iyawó is also a crucial ritual step for those religious families who work actively within the larger religious community. Without undergoing the presentation ceremony, neophytes can find themselves unable to proceed as functioning *santeros* and *santeras* (male and female priests, respectively) until such time that their initiations are rendered complete by the presentation ceremony. And until such time, the elders in the initiatory family have a reduced cohort of fully functioning initiates, often severely limiting their ability to continue initiations and function with their own self-contained team of dependable religious experts.

24. A *tambor de presentaciones* is an event focused on presenting initiates to Añá, whereas a tambor is a drumming celebration with another focus, such as placating an oricha or celebrating an initiation anniversary.

25. Orlando Ríos passed away on August 12, 2008 in New York City as a result of complications arising from heart surgery.

26. One of the lead singers on the two seminal recordings, *Fuerza Santera and Santería Cubana*, that were mentioned earlier in this chapter.

27. This proverb appears in the divination texts of Ifá in Nigeria and Cuba.

28. Julio Collazo and Francisco Aquabella arrived in the USA in the 1950s at the invitation of the renowned African American dancer Katherine Dunham and her troupe (see Capone, 2006).

29. Ifá tappers (*iró̟ké̟* Ifá) are made of wood (or ivory in former times) and are slightly curved and tapered into a point, approximately nine to eleven inches long.

30. Jesús Pérez took on a rather proactive role in moving Papaito to the forefront of Adofó's drums. Upon Adofó's passing, his drums were passed onto the younger Papaito given the family connection. Papaito, however, never demonstrated any real interest in either taking over Adofó's instruments or becoming an accomplished drummer in his own right. It was Nicolás Angarica's crew of drummers, most prominent among them Jesús Pérez, who began to instruct Papaito and insist on his continued attention to the drums. Though by all indications Papaito never progressed musically beyond an adequate okónkolo player, he remained at the forefront of these drums for thirty years until his death a few years ago.

31. The presentation of new Añá initiates is different from the iyawó presentations for new oricha initiates and involves the new *omo* Añá dancing in front of the drums with an *elekoto* (fourth consecrated batá that is not taken out to play) under arm. They then play all three drums in succession. Not all omo Añá have done this ceremony; it is not obligatory for the recognition of their Añá initiation, as with other oricha initiates.

32. Reciting a list of priests who witnessed a ceremony, particularly one of historical significance as in this case, is important in establishing the authority and prestige of the event.

33. In 2005 González received his fundamento from Ángel Bolaños.

34. There remains some confusion here as to the ownership of these drums, and if in fact more than one set was present on any single occasion or whether there were various ceremonies in

which any one of these sets may have been used. Acobiañá is likely the set made by Pablo Roche for Gregorio Torregrosa (pers. comm., Armando Pedroso, December 10, 2009), and Fernando Ortíz suggests these were used in the old *cabildo* of Yemayá in Regla (Marcuzzi 2005, 397; Ortíz 1952–55, 4:319). The drums Ewerikan are likely those also made by Roche for Trinidad Torregrosa (pers. comm., Armando Pedroso, December 10, 2009), though I have not been able to find any details concerning the drums named Eweaddé.

35. The Puerto Rican drummers who had appeared in Venezuela up until this point had all trained in the Havana style of playing.

36. Vega passed away in July 2007.

37. Minor construction differences and consecratory practices can be found between Havana and Matanzas traditions, though these distinctions do not affect the universal recognition of the Añá's efficacy among the two batá traditions. Fundamentally, however, the drums prepared by Vega for Galí, like those in the Matanzas construction style, generally make use of a traverse binding made from hemp or any appropriate type of rope (synthetic sailing rope is now common). This system allows for greater ease in applying tension to the drumheads (including additive cross-bindings) than does the use of strips of animal hide typically used in the Havana region.

38. The *periodo especial* refers to a temporary peacetime policy instigated by Castro when the Soviet Union broke up and withdrew financial aid to Cuba. Cuba's citizens suffered devastating material deprivation during the initial phase of the periodo especial in particular.

39. The orichas can be petitioned through playing batá drums and making other offerings at a tambor.

40. The tambor doble is as it suggests: two batá ensembles performing simultaneously.

41. Alberto refers to the sacrificial offerings made to Eleguá (the divine messenger) and Orunla (Ifá) during the consecration rite.

42. From the Spanish *dar voz al tambor*. This ceremony is also known as the transmission. This takes place on the seventh day of the consecration ceremony. This is open to community members who are excluded from the ritual space during the first six days. In this ceremony, the fundamento that gave birth to the newly consecrated batá is played first and the new set quietly begins to play along and gradually takes over as the first fundamento diminishes in volume and eventually fades out (see Marcuzzi 2005, 411–21).

43. Stefania Capone (2006) perhaps best contextualizes the links established by Scull, his drums, and the principal icons of Añá drumming inside and outside Cuba during this period.

44. Havana batá consecrations require the involvement of babalaos (priests of Ifá, the divination cult). They not only conduct the divination for the drums, name them, and predict their "life," but they are involved in preparing the drum shells and skins along with consecrating some of the ritual objects associated with the drums (see Marcuzzi 2005, ch. 7).

45. Santería and Ifá initiations are usually marked by consecrated neck and wrist beads, though not Añá initiations.

46. Batá drummers communicate with vocables, and "*ki-ha*" represents the okónkolo's (smallest batá) most ubiquitous rhythmic pattern.

References Cited

Amira, John, and Steven Cornelius. 1992. *The Music of Santería: Traditional Rhythms of the Batá Drums*. Crown Point, IN: White Cliffs Media.

Aretz, Isabel. 1962. *The Folklore and Folk Music Archivist* 5 (1): n.a. Venezuelan Institute of Folklore.

Capone, Stefania. 2006. "Des batá à New York: le rôle joué par la musique dans la diffusion de la santería aux États-Unis." In *Nuevo Mundo, Mundos Nuevos, Debates*. http://nuevomundo. revues.org/index2258.html.

Cornelius, Steven. 1995. "Personalizing Public Symbols through Music Ritual: Santería's Presentation to Añá." In *Latin American Music Review* 16 (1): 42–57.

Marcuzzi, Michael David. 2005. *A Historical Study of the Ascendant Role of Bàtá Drumming in Cuban Òrìṣà Worship*. PhD diss., York University, Toronto.

Ortíz, Fernando. 1952–55. *Los Instrumentos de la Música Afrocubana, vols. I–V*. Havana: Ministerio de Educación, Dirección de Cultura (vols. 1–3). Havana: Editoriales Cárdenas y Cía.

Vaughan, Umi, and Carlos Aldama. 2012. *Carlos Aldama's Life in Batá: Cuba, Diaspora and the Drum*. Bloomington: Indiana University Press.

Discography

Fuerza Santera. N.a. Conjunto Obaoso. LP Santero–17.

Santería Cubana (Toques y Cantos) Santeros Lucumí. N.a. Conjunto Obaoso. LP Santero–135.

The Yoruba/Dahomean Collection: Orisha across the Ocean. 1998. Library of Congress Series/ Endangered Music Project. Ryko RCD 10405 CD.

Latin Fever. Andy Harlow. 1976. Fania VS-59 LP.

11

An Ogã Alabê's Añá

Fernando Leobons

● ●

What follows is a description of the liturgical aspects of drumming in Afro-Brazilian Candomblé, a religious system that developed from West and Central African traditions brought to Brazil by enslaved populations. I write this account of Candomblé drumming against the background of the *batá* drum and *omo* Añá brotherhood in Cuba.[1] As I am an initiated drummer and orisha devotee in both traditions, I offer a personal view of how these religious and musical worlds are related. In this chapter I present a comparative description of ritual drumming practices within Candomblé and the Afro-Cuban religion Santería, drawing on my experience across national boundaries as a devotee and ritual drummer. My narrative is not that of a scholar; this chapter is authored by one who has a lifetime religious relationship with the drum, with Añá, and with the international orisha community. Crucially, I conclude with my story about bringing Cuban drumming, its repertoire, and its *oricha*, Añá, to Brazil.

Entry into the Drumming

My maternal grandfather was a practicing *espírita*, a follower of the Brazilian version of Allan Kardec's spiritism, which started in France in the nineteenth century and spread through Latin America. In what came to be seen as a natural evolution of these spiritual practices in Brazil, as a child my mother began to attend *terreiros de* Umbanda (temples of Umbanda), a Brazilian religion that brings together African, Christian, and Native American elements and has been developing since the 1930s. She eventually joined a terreiro of Candomblé where she was "made" (initiated) to Iemanjá, the *orixá* of the ocean. It was my mother who took me to this same house of Candomblé when I was still a child.

My religious direction was decided at an early age when I was *suspenso* (literally "suspended"), the act by which a male member of a Candomblé community is chosen by an orixá to be in his or her service. As a child I was chosen by the orixá Xangô to be an *ogã de* Xangô (devotee of the orixá of thunder, lightning, and justice).[2] I was later "crowned" or "made *santo*" (translated English terms for full orixá initiation) with Omolu Azoane, an avatar or "road" of Omolu, the orixá of smallpox known as Obaluayê in Brazil and Babalú Ayé in Cuba.[3] I have also received Azojano (the Arará equivalent of Omolu) from priest Pedro Abreu in Havana, Cuba.[4]

As a young adult I moved to Washington, D.C., in the United States in 1970; by 1973 I had met the Cuban drummer Julito Collazo, who introduced me to batá drumming and became my first batá teacher.[5] While in D.C., I co-founded the *rumba*[6] and batá group Kubatá with Roberto Borrell, Pepe Calabaza (now passed), and Ernesto Guerra. After seventeen years in the United States, I returned to Brazil in 1987.

After twenty-four years of study, I took my first ritual step in the Cuban batá tradition in 1997 when I was "sworn to Añá" (initiated to Añá) in Havana by renowned drummer Armando "El Surdo" Pedroso.[7] In the following year, I received my own *fundamento* (consecrated batá drums), which were named Ako Bí Añá. My drums were consecrated by Alberto Villareal and were born from the famous fundamento named Añá Bí Oyó (known as "La Atómica"), built by Pablo Roche for José "Moñito" Calazán Frías.[8]

Through the years, I have had the opportunity to meet, play, and study with many accomplished *bataleros* (batá players) and omo Añás (initiated drummers) in and outside of Cuba, and I am grateful to them all, for each of these drummers added something to my own playing and knowledge. Although I consider all of them to be my teachers, I would like to acknowledge my true and primary Cuban *mestre* (maestro), my late friend and brother Fermín Nani Socarrás. He was a man I was privileged to have known for years, who both taught me new rhythms and polished all I knew about the batá, and more importantly, about Añá.

Candomblé

Apart from giving some general historical background, I will not attempt to fully describe Candomblé, which has much written material by authoritative scholars.[9] Rather, I will focus on the aspects most directly related to my own experience as a ritual drummer.

There are three major branches or *nações* (nations) of Candomblé: Angola, Nagô, and Jeje, titles deriving from their antecedents in Central and West Africa. Accordingly, Angola derives from mainland African peoples in Angola, while the Nagô and Jeje nações have evolved from the Yorùbá and Fon peoples in West Africa respectively. Other nations and fusions of these three major nations have developed over the twentieth century; my own branch is the Ketu, a subgroup of Nagô I will refer to as Ketu-Nagô through this chapter. In its contemporary form and structure, Candomblé dates back to the 1930s, at which time significant changes took place. One of these developments has led to the predominance—both in numbers and in the public perception—of terreiros affiliated to the Nagô (Yorùbá) nation and its subgroups.[10]

I have chosen to limit my observations in this chapter to the ceremonies and accompanying drumming within Ketu-Nagô for two reasons. The first is that I was initiated in a terreiro that observes the Ketu-Nagô ritual, the Ilê Fi Orô Sakapata terreiro in Juscelino, Nova Iguaçu, in the state of Rio de Janeiro. I severed my ties to this particular terreiro several years ago, but Ketu-Nagô remains my spiritual home of "birth in santo," and it is the Brazilian ritual style with which I am most acquainted. The second reason I will only discuss Ketu-Nagô rituals is my close association with the ceremonies and drummers of one of the oldest and most traditional terreiros in Salvador in the northern state of Bahia, the Ilê Oxumarê, the House of Oxumarê.[11] The *elemaxó* (head drummer and singer) of the Ilê Oxumarê, Erenilton Bispo dos Santos, and his son, the *otun alabê* (the second in the hierarchy) Erisvaldo dos Santos (see Plate 11.1), are my longtime personal friends and mestres of Candomblé drumming.

Although the Ilê Oxumarê claims to be a terreiro of Jeje (Fon) origins, it observes the Ketu-Nagô (Yorùbá-derived) ritual. Therefore, all facts and assertions contained herein pertain to the Ketu-Nagô ritual in general, and to the Ilê Oxumarê in particular.

Religious Houses

One of the characteristics of Candomblé, which explains much of its internal structure and indeed its diversity, is the fact that the wider cult is organized, structured, and developed around temples, interchangeably called *terreiros, casas de santo*, or *roças*. This organization into localized communities recalls the Afro-Cuban *cabildos* of past times and loosely corresponds to contemporary house temples in Cuba referred to as *ilés*.[12] From my personal experience, the closest thing I have seen in Cuba to a Brazilian terreiro is the Cabildo Arará in the neighborhood of La Marina in Matanzas. The first terreiros of Candomblé were populated by extended

Plate 11.1: Erisvaldo "Nei de Oxóssi" dos Santos and Fernando "Léo" Leobons (right) in front of the atabaque drums at Ilê Oxumarê. (photograph: Jean Dumas, Salvador, 23 January 2012)

families. Some, at their core, are still constituted by brothers and sisters, uncles and aunts, cousins, relatives, neighbors, and friends of these relatives and neighbors who naturally formed the community that grew around local terreiros. Some temples became famous, others notorious. Many terreiros expanded, branching out and moving south from Salvador during the 1940s and 1950s mainly into the largest southern cities, Rio de Janeiro (the capital of Brazil at the time) and São Paulo (the financial center of the country). These ties to the "mother houses" in Salvador are cultivated to differing extents. Some terreiros perpetuate their links to northern antecedents, while others became increasingly independent.

In many respects, the "birth" of a new terreiro is synonymous with the "birth" of a new *tambor de fundamento* (consecrated set of Cuban batá drums). All true *casas de nação* (orthodox terreiros) have a consecrated object, referred to as the *axé*, buried in the center of the *barracão* (the main structure of the terreiro).[13] This axé is "born" out of the axé of the "mother" terreiro. The axé in the architectural foundations of a terreiro might be compared to the *aché* inside a batá drum, called the *carga* (load).[14] In both the context of the founding of a new terreiro and the consecration of a new fundamento batá, the axé/aché is "born" from a predecessor. Both "births" involve a "transmission" ceremony that legitimates the new terreiro or fundamento, while establishing and re-asserting the religious lineage that created it. Along with the terms terreiro and casa de santo to designate cult houses, one often refers to his or her own house as "the axé."

One of the major differences between Brazilian and Cuban festivals is that the Brazilian *festa de santo* is a prescribed community affair in a terreiro, whereas a Cuban tambor is more often a private, individual event situated in a devotee's home. Brazilian festas de santo are communal events for one particular orixá at a time (following a pre-established yearly calendar, which may vary slightly from house to house). All the "sons" and "daughters" (initiates) of the orixá being celebrated are expected to provide monetary and labor resources for the event. In observing the calendar of a particular terreiro, those devotees deemed to be financially better off may end up contributing considerably more money to the ceremony than anybody else. In practice, nearly every terreiro has devotees who act as sponsors by contributing funding for the general upkeep of the buildings and grounds. They may also finance festivals with all of their expenses such as sacrificial animals, other food, and decorative garments for the santos who descend and possess initiates during the proceedings. These sponsoring individuals, when male, often receive the honorary title of *ogã*, and may be suspended and confirmed even though they will never be assigned any specific function or task beyond providing funding. (Female sponsors are normally already initiates.) The festa is never an individual affair offered by one person.

In Cuba, festivals are a much more personal affair. There is frequently a sole sponsor who is responsible for the tambor and personally finances the event. In such circumstances, the aché of the fundamento within consecrated batá drums may be called upon by an individual to honor his or her own oricha on an initiation anniversary or to procure a favor or blessing from their oricha. A drumming might also be a response to a divination that prescribes a tambor as an *ebó* (sacrificial offering), designed to placate the oricha and achieve a specific result or objective.

Candomblé Priests and Drummers

Up to the early and mid-fifties, men were not allowed to make santo in traditional terreiros of Candomblé in Bahia where the religion originates. To this day, in the more traditional terreiros, men who do make santo are not allowed to participate in the *xirê*. This is a section of the festa de santo (festival dedicated to one or more orixás) in which devotees dance in the *roda* (circle). The only occasion when a male initiate is allowed to take part in the roda is once he is possessed by his orixá, since in that instance it is no longer the individual, but the deity who is present and taking part in the festivities. As soon as an orixá manifests him- or herself, the spirit possessing the body of an initiate is temporarily attired with an *atacá*, a piece of cloth tied across his chest in the case of a male orixá, or a *pano da costa*, a longer piece of cloth, tied at the front, for female orixás.[15]

Before men were allowed to make santo and become an *iaô* (new initiate), they could assume several other positions of different *postos* (signification and rank) designated by the term ogã. With the exception of men who make santo, all other male initiates in Candomblé are ogãs. They may move up in the hierarchy and assume titled positions that bring specific duties and attributions, but all of them are ogãs. Of peripheral interest here is the pronunciation of the term ogã, which is remarkably similar to *houngan*, the Haitian designation for male *vodou* priests; within the Jeje nation the drummer is called *huntor*, and in the Angola nation he is called *xicarangoma*.[16]

Terminology aside, what ultimately unites all ogãs is the first stage of initiation into Candomblé. For a man, the traditional entry into the cult is to be *suspenso* (suspended), whereby one is chosen by an orixá to be his or her ogã. "Suspending" usually involves the possessing orixá approaching the chosen individual and embracing him with both arms and literally lifting him off the floor and suspending him. After this action, which expresses the wish of the orixá to have that individual brought into his or her service, two older ogãs create a *cadeirinha* (little chair) by interlocking and gripping arms. The newly chosen ogã is seated into the human chair, lifted up, and paraded in front of the congregants where he is congratulated for this great honor. Later, the selected person will be "confirmed" as a full-fledged ogã for that particular orixá in a rather elaborate ceremony. I was "suspended" by Xangô at age eight and was confirmed as an ogã de Xangô.

There are several types of ogãs such as *ogã perdigã*, who takes care of welcoming people into the barracão for the festa, and *ogã reré*, who is charged with overseeing the ceremony of the *padê*, a section of the festa de santo described below. Although it is the orixá who honors an individual by choosing him to be an ogã, it will be up to the new initiate and his *pai de santo* or *mãe de santo* (male or female head of the terreiro or cult) to steer him according to needs of the religious community and the personal inclinations of the individual. For example, if the initiate shows an interest and ability in butchering, cleaning, and skinning animals, he will probably become an *ogã axogun* (or simply *axogun*), the ogã who takes charge of ceremonial sacrifices and their related accoutrements and tasks. Each category of ogã has its own internal hierarchy with ranks of "right" (*opá-otun*, second in command) and "left" (*opá-osí*, third in command).[17] These ranks act as the lieutenants of the head ogã. If the initiate is a person with social skills who likes to deal and interact with people, he may become an *ogã de salão,* whose duties include receiving visiting elders, members from other terreiros, and the general public at the barracão (the space where the festivities take place) and directing them to their designated chairs. As I showed an interest in drumming, I became an *ogã alabê*, the Brazilian equivalent to the Cuban omo Añá.[18] As with other kinds of ogãs, there is a well-structured internal hierarchy among ogã alabês that serves to establish who occupies the main position and who discharges the duties pertinent to each position.

At the Ilê Oxumarê, the highest-ranking ogã alabê is the elemaxó, an elite musician and priest who is responsible for leading the drumming and singing in the terreiro's ceremonies. As a master drummer and singer, the elemaxó has the combined skills and status of the dual Cuban roles of the omo Añá, who generally specializes in drumming, and the *akpwon,* the dedicated ritual singer who leads parts of Cuban ceremonies. At the time of writing, the elemaxó at the Ilê Oxumarê is Erenilton Bispo dos Santos, a man much respected in the community at large for his profound knowledge of the drumming, chants, and rituals of Candomblé.

In contrast to their Cuban counterparts, who may eventually attain a fundamento set of batá and are routinely paid for their musical services, alabês never own their drums, nor do they get paid for performing in their own terreiro. In Candomblé, alabês are attached to the religious community and center themselves around the particular terreiro where they were chosen as ogãs by the resident orixás.[19] This is because drummers are regarded to be fulfilling their duty to their own orixás, their pai de santo or mãe de santo (head of the house), and to the terreiro rather than providing commercial services. There are, however, contexts in which drummers are paid, such as when alabês from Salvador, in the northern state of Bahia are called upon to play and sing at festas de santo in Rio de Janeiro, São Paulo, Belo Horizonte, and other cities around the country.

The Making of Drummers

In this section I touch on the rituals that consecrate Brazilians and Cubans as ceremonial drummers, being careful to respect that which should remain concealed. The ceremony of consecrating a Brazilian ogã is more involved and takes considerably longer than the *juramento* (initiation) of a Cuban omo Añá. On the surface these two ceremonies seem similar in many aspects and have points in common with the ceremonies of making santo in Brazil and Cuba, which are much more complex and detailed than either drumming initiation. In comparison to these elaborate santo consecrations, the initiation of an ogã is relatively simple.

After a child or man has been suspended, or chosen by a particular orixá for the priesthood, he is not a full-fledged ogã until he undergoes the ceremony called the *confirmação* (confirmation), thus confirming his position in the religious hierarchy. The process consists of having the individual "interned," meaning that he is placed in seclusion in the terreiro near the axé—the central point where the medicine is buried—for a total of twenty-one days. This internment within the grounds of the compound brings him closer to the magical and sacred energies of the terreiro, preparing him spiritually for his consecration under the watchful eye of his pai de santo, who oversees the ogã's initiation. The structure of his seclusion is as follows:

1) five days of general ceremonies whereby the candidate is pretty much free to move about within the grounds;
2) three days within the *roncó* (ceremonial room) awaiting the confirmation ceremony proper;
3) three more days in the roncó undergoing the confirmation ceremony; and
4) ten days where he can go outside to work or run his personal errands and businesses but must return to the house in the evening.

The first step of the actual initiation commences with a spiritual bath called *banho de fôlha*, which is an herbal mixture similar to the Cuban *omiero/osáin* (also used to bathe the omo Añá at the end of the swearing ceremony). Propitiatory *ebós* (sacrifices) are made to Egún (the spirit of the ancestors) and to Exú (the divine messenger), to ensure prosperity and to guarantee that the initiation runs in a smooth and positive manner. At the end of five days, the initiate is confined to the roncó, the space reserved for the iaôs when making santo. On the eve of his confirmation proper—the eighth day being the confirmation—the neophyte undergoes a *borí*, a ceremony where the head is fed through *eyebale* (sacrifice). After the borí, the *matança* (ceremonial sacrifice) is made both for the initiate's own orixá and for the orixá who suspended him. For instance, if the initiate is a child of Xangô and he was suspended by Ogún (the orixá of iron, blacksmiths, and war), sacrifices are made to both of these orixás. When ceremonial incisions called *curas* are made to various parts of the drummer's body, his confirmation ceremony is complete.

In the evening of the same day, the initiate dresses formally in a suit and tie as if he were attending a wedding, symbolizing his symbolic marriage to the orixá. In preparation for his *saída* ("coming out"), the new initiate also dons the *faixa*, a sash with his honorific title embroidered in it. This is the celebration of his confirmation as an ogã. Accompanied by drumming, various chants are intoned, followed by two or three songs for him to dance. The dancing is followed by specific chants that signal the section of the ceremony where the initiate is made to sit down three times in his cadeira de ogã, his own drummer's chair. The third time he is seated, the initiate remains in the chair, marking the completion of the confirmation ceremony.

Figures 11.1 and 11.2 depict two chants that derive from the private, insiders' repertoire of alabês. The repertoire, which includes these two songs, is usually intoned at confirmation ceremonies. They are not exclusively accompanied by the atabaques but may also be sung a cappella.

Figure 11.1: Alabê's chant used at confirmation.

Figure 11.2: Alabê's chant used at confirmation.

As well as appearing in confirmation ceremonies, they can be performed after the drums have been fed.

The next morning, the newly initiated drummer is taken to a church in his confirmation clothing. The church of choice is usually the Church of Our Lord of the Bonfim, the patron saint of Bahia who is syncretized with Oxalá (the orixá of white cloth) in this region of Brazil. After being taken back to the terreiro, the initiate remains there for three more days within the *sabagi* (inner sanctum) in the roncó, the same place where iaôs are confirmed after being initiated. After these three days, he can now walk freely inside the terreiro and access places that were forbidden prior to his confirmation, for he is now a full-fledged ogã and a full member of the religious community of his terreiro.

After having completed the initiation, the ogã is obliged to feed his head (bori) at least once a year and to perform his regular offerings to his orixá or to the residing orixá (*assentados*) within the terreiro. The ogã must repeat several of the rituals that he performed for his own orixá during the consecration after one, three, and seven years.

Ritual Drums

The Candomblé orchestra is comprised of three atabaque drums. Even though contemporary atabaques are built from wood slats and are regarded as traditional, the drums were likely carved out of one piece of wood in earlier times. The Ilê Axé Iyá Nassô Oká, also known as Casa Branca do Engenho Velho, is generally accepted as being the oldest and one of the most revered terreiros in Bahia. It seems to be the only terreiro left with drums carved from whole tree trunks.

The smallest drum in the atabaque orchestra is called *lé*, the middle one *rumpi* (both played with two sticks), and the tallest and largest drum, usually (though not always) played with a hand and stick, is the *rum*. (There are a few rhythms that are played with both hands on all drums, such as *ijexá* and *agabi*. In the *alujá* for Xangô, the rum is played with both hands while the other drums are played with sticks called *aguidavís*.) The drums may be ordered from a particular maker or purchased at a specialized shop and brought to the terreiro where they will be fed and consecrated. The atabaque sticks, aguidavís, are usually made from guava tree branches, and although they can be found around the drums of any ilê, many alabês will prepare their own. The branches are cut to size and scraped of the bark and sometimes rubbed with *azeite de dendê* (palm oil) and placed over a flame in order to straighten and harden them. The hides utilized for atabaques usually come from animals that have been sacrificed; goatskin is the first choice for the drum heads, although it is also common to use cowhide.

Unlike in Cuba where Añá is associated with drumming, there is no single, specific orixá associated with drumming in Brazil. Brazilian drummers do not discuss or argue about the drum genders or which orixá may be associated with each drum as happens in Cuba, where there may be disagreement about which oricha "owns" particular batá drums.[20] In Candomblé, the smallest atabaque, the lé, is unanimously believed to belong to the orixá Oxum, the rumpi belongs to Oxóssi, and the rum is Ogún's drum. (An exception to this formula comes when a trio of atabaques are donated to a terreiro. In this scenario, the orixá of the donor will also "own" the drums.) Oxum, Oxóssi, and Ogún (or a donor's orixá) are fed alongside each of their drums, which are laid down and covered with a white cloth for the feeding ritual. Oxum's chicken is killed over the lé and the drum is then crossed (*cruzado*) by smearing the blood over the hide. The feeding of a drum resembles the regular matança (ritual sacrifice) for the corresponding orixá. In the case of the lé, one sings the same chants used when sacrifices are made to Oxum. The drum is decorated with some feathers from the sacrificed bird and it is then offered the prepared axé, the ritual food prepared with the meat from the sacrificial animal. Accordingly, Oxóssi's drum, the rumpi, receives a rooster and the rum receives Ogún's rooster.

After the sacrifices are complete, the officiating priest intones chants to *didê* (literally "bring the drums up"), that is, to "lift" drums into their upright position, although these chants are not specific to the drums. Chants for Oxum, Oxóssi, and Ogún are used for didê. Chants for the orixá who owns the drum are intoned: Oxum chants will lift up the lé, Oxóssi's chants raise the rumpi, and Ogún's chants bring up the rum. In the Ilê Oxumarê, although the chants (see Figs. 11.3 and 11.4) are particular to Oxumarê, they are used for lifting the drums and may be used for lifting any orixá. To my knowledge they are not performed in any other terreiro.

Despite undisputed ties of the Ketu-Nagô to the Yorùbá people, the design, performance practice, and repertoire of the atabaques do not suggest Yorùbá precedents in the same way that the chants do, as the latter use a lexicon largely derived from Yorùbá. Rather, contemporary Candomblé seems to have subsumed some elements of the Jeje nation, even though these are not always explicit. To acknowledge this fusion, the term "Jeje-Nagô complex" is often employed. The utilization of hand-stick performance techniques, the style of rhythms, and the structure of the atabaque drums do not immediately recall Yorùbá drumming but all seem to point toward Jeje (Fon) drumming antecedents. More

Figure 11.3: Chant to lift up Oxumarê, which can also be intoned for lifting the drums.

Figure 11.4: Chant to lift up Oxumarê and lift the drums.

research about the musical roots of both Jeje-Nagô drumming is needed to draw firm conclusions.

Thus far, I have limited this study to the rituals and ceremonies as practiced by the Ketu-Nagô in Salvador in the state of Bahia in relationship to Cuban Lucumí practices. But outside of Bahia, in the northeastern states of Maranhão and Pernambuco and in the southernmost state of Rio Grande do Sul, one finds other interesting drumming traditions that may be related to Yorùbá antecedents and the Cuban batá.

In Maranhão one finds the Tambor de Mina (literally, "Mina Drum"), a spiritual tradition of the Mina (Ewe and Fon) peoples, so called because they were identified as being originally from the coastal regions situated east of the Castelo de São Jorge da Mina in Benin.[21] They were subdivided by slave traders as being either Mina-Jeje or Mina-Nagô. Having established a particular and unique form of the Jeje and Nagô traditions, their liturgy utilizes two drums called *abatás*, which have a cylindrical shape with two heads tensioned by metal rods and are played horizontally like the batá. Surprisingly, these drums can be manufactured from either plywood or from a sheet of zinc, unlike Cuban consecrated batá, which demand a hollowed shell carved from a tree trunk.

In the capital of the state of Pernambuco, Recife, one finds the religious branch known as Xangô do Recife, which aligns its traditions with the Nagô nation. At the time of writing, it appears that only the oldest Xangô do Recife terreiro, the Sítio de Pai Adão, or Ilê Obá Ogunté, still utilizes three drums called batá. With the hourglass shape and two heads tensioned by rope, they are the closest thing in Brazil in name, shape, and religious context to the Yorùbá bàtá and Cuban batá. The names given to the Recife drums are *melê* for the smallest instrument, *meleunkó* for the middle-sized, and *yán* for the largest. These three terms appear to relate to the Yorùbá *omele* (generic term for accompanying), *omele ako* (male accompanying drum), and *ìyá ìlù* (literally "mother drum"), generic for lead drum in Yorùbá ensembles. All three terms are employed in Yorùbá bàtá ensembles, while the words *omele* and *iyá* are used for the second and first drums respectively in the Cuban batá ensemble.[22]

Still another manifestation of Afro-Brazilian religious traditions, the *batuque*, in the southern state of Rio Grande do Sul, utilizes drums with a cylindrical shape and two heads tensioned by rope, called simply *tambor* (drum). The tambor can be played either in the vertical or horizontal position. In some houses of batuque one finds a large drum excavated from a tree trunk and also with two heads tensioned by rope. This drum is called *inhã*, which may derive from *ìyá*, or even Àyàn (Añá), though this remains speculative.

In spite of striking similarities in nomenclature and aspects of the structure and performance practice of these drumming traditions, there appears to be no close affinity in the music of these liturgies with the music of the batá/bàtá as played in Cuba or Africa. Nor is there any mention or record of an orixá exclusively associated with drums or drummers in any of the above traditions. Speculations about the relationships between these drums in Brazil as vestiges or descendants of the tradition of the Yorùbá bàtá and Àyàn must remain just that—speculation—until a scholar, with the tools and abilities that I as a drummer do not possess, decides to tackle the issue.

Introducing Cuban Repertoire to the Ketu-Nagô

Through performing Afro-Cuban batá drumming and chants in *güemileres* in Brazil, it has become evident to me that Brazilians are aware of the similarities and common elements in Cuban and Brazilian practices. I have explored ways to invite and stimulate the participation of members of the Ketu-Nagô in Cuban güemileres. To this end, I have endeavored to make adaptations without distorting or deviating from the Afro-Cuban ritual.

From my observations, Brazilians who belong to Candomblé feel at home dancing to the 12/8 clave pattern, which is identical in Cuba Lucumí and Brazilian Ketu-Nagô music.[23] Brazilian congregants easily fall into step with generic batá rhythms such as *ñongo* or *chachalokafun*. Beyond this common ground, it has always been evident to me that many specific Afro-Brazilian orixá dances conform tightly to the patterns played by atabaque drums in a precise and unique way, just as Afro-Cuban oricha dances adhere directly to distinctive batá rhythms. These divergent Brazilian and Cuban sacred dances are not interchangeable

with their "opposites"; that is, Cuban oricha dances are not easily paired
with atabaque repertoires and Brazilian orixá dances do not sit comfort-
ably with Cuban batá. Nor can the batá and atabaque rhythms and Cuban
and Brazilian dance steps sufficiently be adapted without violating their
identifying character. The dancing, with its formalized steps in both traditions, is so intimately related to the drumming patterns that I believe
it to be impossible to modify either drumming or dancing without seriously distorting the form and content of both of these sacred repertoires.
Nevertheless, Candomblé congregants do dance with the batá without
knowing the specific steps of the Cuban repertoire by attempting to adapt
Brazilian steps.

It is within the chanting that I have been able to find the element that
invites wider congregant participation. In both Brazil and Cuba, the
elemaxó and akpwon respectively often perform arcane and obscure
chants, which can attract great prestige among peers and knowledgeable
congregants. Bringing in songs from Cuba to Ketu-Nagô ceremonies
generates similar curiosity and prestige. When I visited to Brazil in 1985
after fifteen years in the USA, I was surprised to find some Afro-Cuban
chants had already been adapted to Candomblé rhythms. The lyrics of
these chants had been modified to better suit Brazilian Portuguese pronunciations. In some instances, where lyrics were not clear to Brazilian
participants, they insert phrases from related Brazilian chants or even
invent lyrics of their own. At this time (and since), singers and drummers
were always happy to hear me intone Afro-Cuban chants and were eager
to learn them, which I would later hear in modified form as these same
chants were integrated into the repertoire of some cult houses.

Noting the ease with which Lucumí songs were locally adapted, I
decided to reverse the process by modifying Candomblé chants for batá
drumming in order to encourage the participation of congregants. Many
chants in Santería and Candomblé are mutually recognizable; indeed
some related chants have near-identical texts and melodies. For example,
the songs for Echú Eleguá in Cuba and Exú in Brazil (see Figs. 11.5 and
11.6) are very close. As a strategy, I sometimes alternate between the
Cuban and Brazilian versions within this shared repertoire. I have noticed that the chorus strengthens considerably when Candomblé chants
are used with the batá, as knowing the lyrics is core to participation.
Even though the traditional Afro-Brazilian repertoire had already been
infiltrated by Afro-Cuban chants prior to my return from my time in the
USA, the exchange between Cuban and Brazilian chants I am personally
instigating may eventually contribute to a new musical direction in some
houses.

Figure 11.5: Cuban song for Echú Eleguá.

Figure 11.6: Brazilian song for Exú.

Bringing Añá to Brazil

The past decade has opened a new chapter in the history of Añá with the introduction of Cuban-consecrated fundamentos imported into Brazil. To my knowledge, the first batá-Añá in Brazil was brought by a *babalaô* (Ifá divining priest) known as "Beto"; I have been unable to establish when exactly this fundamento arrived.[24] Beto is not a drummer, and at the time we met, he did not have drummers around him capable of performing on his fundamento. I was called in to play in an Oricha Oko ceremony that Beto was leading in his house in Rio de Janeiro in June or July 2008, to which I brought my own fundamento and crew of drummers. To the best of my knowledge his own drums have not been played.

As far as I can ascertain, my fundamento is the second and only other existing batá-Añá in Brazil at the time of writing. My motivation for attaining my own fundamento and bringing it home was never part of a premeditated master plan. I simply wanted to keep on playing batá, and as I saw a growing Lucumí community in Rio, I identified the increasing need for a working fundamento. Since bringing my drums to Rio from Cuba in 1999, I have sworn fifteen Brazilians to Añá and washed the hands of four others.[25] While most are drummers, I initiated several babaláwos, who did the ceremony for religious reasons. In addition to the Brazilians who play batá with me, one Chilean national (sworn to Añá in Havana) and a Cuban babalao, Luis Destrade Despaigne, have both played with me. The latter was sworn by Havana batá drummer and babalao Papo Angarica, who is from one of the most important religious lineages in Havana.[26] I perform regularly in Rio with this crew of drummers at güemileres, consecration rituals, and the presentation of iyawós.[27]

Beyond the two fundamentos owned by Beto and myself, the diffusion of Añá into Brazil continues to be slow and difficult and faces several problems. One of them is the fact that Afro-Cuban religion in Brazil has been introduced from outside and remains largely in the hands of babalaos. Cuban oricha religion is divided along the lines of babalaos and *obás* (also known as *obá oriatés* or *oriatés*), master diviners in a different but related tradition, Santería.[28] Babalaos tend to work with clients privately, rather than with the wider orixá community. There are still very few obás in Brazil with godchildren (devotees initiated personally by them) according to the Cuban Lucumí tradition. It is obás and those initiated by them, rather than babalaos, who are most likely to call drummers for iaô (iyawó) presentations, initiation anniversaries, and other celebrations.

Yet another obstacle to introducing Añá into Brazil is the fact that Candomblé is well established as the primary religion of African descent and it is difficult for Santería to make significant inroads among the faithful. To further complicate matters, batá drumming is difficult for musicians to sufficiently master to conduct a ceremony in its entirety. Most drummers who start their apprenticeship of studying the liturgy do not follow through to the more advanced stages. Additionally, there is a lack of knowledge among congregants about the Cuban oricha dances and chants that the batá accompany. Since most Santería converts in Brazil cross over from Candomblé, the challenges of learning new chants and dance steps is considerable. As I have described above, I have taken the initiative to adapt several chants from Brazilian Candomblé to the rhythms of the batá, which is gradually increasing the participation and hence acceptance of the batá in ceremonies.

Reclaiming and Inventing Tradition

Beyond the introduction of two Cuban fundamentos into Brazil, there is an entirely different development driven by a desire to reclaim Àyàn and climb the musical power hierarchy. This is happening outside of the authoritative exchanges between priests and drummers in two well-established diasporic traditions, Santería and Candomblé. This new movement resides within a much newer (post-1930s) spiritual tradition, Umbanda, which originally developed in Rio and its vicinity and has now spread and established itself throughout Brazil. It is an eclectic tradition that mixes diverse elements from Candomblé de Caboclo (fusing African and indigenous American deities and mistaken by many as being a "Native Brazilian" religious practice), European Kardecism, Christianity, Angola (the Brazilian rough equivalent to Cuban Palo), along with Eastern philosophies such as Ayurvedic medicine and Buddhism. The popular appeal of its internal diversity has contributed to the notion of Umbanda as the truly legitimate, national religion of Brazil—an eclectic religion for an eclectic people—and contributed to its politicization and bureaucratization. By pushing into the public sphere and attracting political and financial support (as Candomblé had done earlier), Umbanda has even been able to establish its own University of Umbanda in São Paulo, which has been recognized by the federal government as an institution of higher education, purportedly supervising the formation of clergy sanctioned by their federation.

In spite of all the attempts to give Umbanda a definitive and uniform structure, its rituals are still only loosely defined in comparison to, say, Candomblé and Santería. Not all houses of Umbanda utilize drumming, and the ones that do appear to be generating rhythms that can be easily identified as grossly simplified versions of Candomblé rhythms. There have been some attempts to standardize these new Umbanda rhythms, but since they are all forged by competing, self-proclaimed authorities within only a loosely unified religion, inventing tradition remains a free-for-all.

I have been approached by several members of the Umbanda community who wish to incorporate elements of Añá (or its Nigerian equivalent Àyàn) into their musical and ritual practices. Those who have approached me do not seem invested in learning the drumming but appear to be more interested in learning about Añá in order to start consecrating drums. Indeed, some have confessed their ambition to consecrate atabaque drums, thus becoming the expert "House of the Drumming Orixá" among the other houses of Brazil.

In the extreme, an Umbanda devotee—who presented himself to me as a master drummer and claims the title mestre—showed me a factory-made, store-purchased set of Cuban batá drums with metal fixings, which he claimed to have consecrated himself, though apparently without information from or involvement in any existing Àyàn or Añá community in Nigeria or Cuba. This individual claims to be the master of a long-lost tradition of Brazilian batá. In the absence of concrete evidence for his claim, he offered me a rather fanciful narrative, explaining that references to the Brazilian batá tradition were lost during a famous destruction of records of Afro-Brazilian data conducted by Ruy Barbosa.[29] Apart from having no handed-down religious accoutrements or community to verify his assertion, this aspiring drummer also lacks musical knowledge and skill. His "Brazilian batá rhythms" present little recognizable musical relationship to the Cuban or African batá/bàtá repertoires, let alone atabaque drumming. Rather, his musical repertoire appears to be either poorly copied or invented.

On Birthing Tradition

On the surface, the liturgical drumming and accompanying rituals and ceremonies as performed by both the Brazilian Ketu-Nagô and Cuban Lucumí traditions appear to have much in common. Shared elements such as formal initiations of drummers, sacred practices around the drums themselves, quite similar structures within festivals, prescribed duties and functions of drummers, plus identical nomenclature for a few rhythms render Ketu-Nagô and Lucumí to be parallel traditions. Yet viewed at a deeper level, the Brazilian and Lucumí drumming traditions constitute two separate and unique systems of liturgical drumming developed along very singular cultural lines of interpretation of musical and religious traditions of African origin.

While I (too) may be seen by some as inventing tradition by bringing Añá and the batá repertoire to Brazil, I proceed from decades of dedication, study, and ritual and musical involvement in Candomblé and Santería. More importantly, I have never acted alone, but rather have instigated Añá's presence in Brazil with the involvement and approval of religious elders in Cuba, as was the case with the successful transfer of the religious and musical tradition into the United States and other areas of Latin America.

A new corpus of chants for the batá and an innovative set of ceremonial practices may be evolving in Brazil as the religious repertoire adapts yet again to a new environment. We may yet see the inclusion of the Lucumí nation as one among the Candomblé nations, which I suspect can only strengthen the presence of batá and Añá in Brazil. Hopefully, the community of Santería priests with enough knowledge to initiate others according to the Cuban tradition will expand Lucumí in Brazil and ensure the future success of the fledgling batá and Añá traditions. As José Roberto Brandão Telles "Ojuani Meyi" (a Brazilian babaláwo and my godson in Añá) likes to say, what we are doing in Brazil with the Lucumí tradition is not for us, but for our grandchildren.

Editor's Notes

1. The author and editor gratefully acknowledge input by the late Michael Marcuzzi on earlier drafts of this chapter.

2. Devotees understand a possessed person to be the orixá, not the individual whose body the spirit has occupied. Although chosen by an embodied orixá, ogãs will not be possessed themselves (as with *omo* Añá in Cuba).

3. In Brazil and Cuba the word *santo* (saint) is used interchangeably with orixá and oricha respectively.

4. Arará is a branch of Afro-Cuban religion that has developed from West African Ewe and Fon practices.

5. See Amira (this volume) for an account of Collazo's importance in the introduction of batá drumming into the USA.

6. Rumba is a secular, percussion-based music and dance form that is unique to Cuba.

7. Pedroso died in 2013.

8. When a new set of batá drums is consecrated, it is said to be "born" from a prior set that is present during the consecration. New sets are named through divination. La Atómica was born in 1945 and refers to the atom bomb in Hiroshima.

9. For English-language texts about Candomblé, see, for example, Wafer (1991); Landes (1994); Johnson (2002); and Capone (2010).

10. For detailed accounts of twentieth-century developments in Candomblé, see Parés (2004); Matory (2005); and Capone (2010). In particular, they discuss the "re-Yorùbárization" or "Nagôization" of Candomblé and the ascendant prestige of Yorùbá roots and contemporary associations.

11. Oxumarê is a rainbow/snake deity and is relatively predominant in Brazil, though is now little known in Nigeria and Cuba, where this deity is known as Òṣùmàrè and Ochumaré respectively. The equivalent of this deity in Cuba is in the Arará tradition and is called Aido-Hwedo. See Capone (2007) and Palmić (2013, 203–5) for an account of Miguel "Willie" Ramos's mission to receive this orisha in Brazil in order to (re)instigate the deity in Santería.

12. *Cabildo de naciónes* were once organized by the Cuban authorities along ethnic lines but over time evolved into localized *casa templos* (house temples). See Brown (2003, 55–67) for a description of how cabildos evolved in Cuba.

13. *Axé* is the transliteration of *àṣẹ* (Yorùbá) and *aché* (Lucumí) appearing in other chapters of this book. A central concept in transatlantic orisha belief systems, àṣẹ/aché/axé refers to a spiritual force and authority that is sought in all rituals and utterances. Àṣẹ/aché/axé can also refer to a consecrated object or packet, sometimes called *fundamento* in Cuba.

14. Cuban drummers also call the medicinal packet placed inside the drum by its Lucumí name, *afouobó*.

15. This practice corresponds with contemporary ritual attire in some cults in Yorùbáland, where a sash is worn by male and female priests to represent a baby sling (*òjá*).

16. This cluster of terms is overdetermined. While scholars agree that *houngan* derives from Fon, in Cuban Iyesá rites the ritual lead singer is called *agan* (see Delgado, this volume), and in Cuban Arará music (of Fon origin) the bell that plays the timeline is called *ogan*. Perhaps closest in spelling and pronunciation to the Nagô term ogã is *ọga*, the Yorùbá word for "boss."

17. These Candomblé terms are likely derived from the Yorùbá religious designations *apá ọtún* and *apá òsì* (right side and left side).

18. The word alabê is likely a transliteration of the Yorùbá word *alágbe* (beggar), which is sometimes used for Yorùbá drummers due to the exchange of praise and money.

19. Different terreiros worship clusters of orixás particular to their religious lineage.

20. See Hagedorn, this volume.

21. See Bascom (1972, 9) and Parés (1997).

22. These terms also correspond to the Cuban batá names recorded by Ortíz (1954, Vol. IV, 210).

23. Referred to as clave in Cuba (along with other timelines), the 12/8 timeline X.X.XX.X.X.X is ubiquitous in West Africa and its diaspora in the Caribbean and Latin America.

24. The Brazilian spelling is *babalaô*.

25. "Swearing" refers to the *juramento* ceremony where drummers become full omo Añá initiates, while the "hand washing" is an entry-level ritual to the cult, allowing drummers to play any *fundamento*.

26. See Quintero, this volume, who describes Angarica's importance in introducing Añá into Venezuela.

27. In the Cuban tradition, new initiates must undergo a ceremony in which they are "presented" to the oricha Añá, but crucially, they are also presented to the wider religious community as fully consecrated priests.

28. While most babaláwos were initiated by obás in an earlier initiation, there is a social division between these two priesthoods. See Brown (2003).

29. Barbosa was a politician and abolitionist who ordered the destruction of slaving records in 1891.

References Cited

Bascom, William. 1972. *Shango in the New World*. Austin: African and Afro-American Research Institute, University of Texas.

Brown, David. 2003. *Santería Enthroned: Art, Ritual, and Innovation in an Afro-Cuban Religion*. Chicago and London: University of Chicago Press.

Capone, Stefania. 2007. "The 'Orisha Religion' between Syncretism and Re-Africanization." In *Cultures of the Lusophone Atlantic*, eds. Nancy Priscilla Naro, Roger Sansi-Roca, and David H. Treece. New York: Palgrave. 219–32.

———. 2010. *Searching for Africa in Brazil: Power and Tradition in Candomblé*. Durham and London: Duke University Press.

Johnson, Paul Christopher. 2002. *Secrets, Gossip, and Gods: The Transformation of Brazilian Candomblé*. New York: Oxford University Press.

Landes, Ruth. 1994 [1947]. *The City of Women*. Albuquerque: University of New Mexico Press.

Matory, J. Lorand. 2005. *Black Atlantic Religion: Tradition, Transnationalism, and Matriarchy in the Afro-Brazilian Candomblé*. Princeton and Oxford: Princeton University Press.

Ortíz, Fernando. 1954. *Los Instrumentos de la Música Afrocubana, vol. IV*. Havana: Editoriales Cárdenas y Cía.

Palmié, Stephan. 2013. *The Cooking of History: How Not to Study Afro-Cuban Religion*. Chicago: University of Chicago Press.

Parés, Luis Nicolau. 1997. *The Phenomenology of Spirit Possession in the Tambor de Mina: An Ethnographic and Audio-Visual Study*. PhD thesis, School of Oriental and African Studies, University of London.

———. 2004. "The 'Nagôization' Process in Bahian Candomblé." In *Yorùbá Diaspora in the Atlantic World*, ed. Tóyìn Fálọlá. Bloomington: Indiana University Press. 185–208.

Wafer, Jim. 1991. *The Taste of Blood: Spirit Possession in Brazilian Candomblé*. Philadelphia: University of Pennsylvania Press.

Glossary of Musical and Religious Terms

· ·

Parallel and Contested Definitions

This glossary does not endeavor to be comprehensive but is designed to assist the reader with religious and musical terminology appearing in the chapters in this volume. As many terms in transatlantic orisha traditions have diverse and often contested meanings, this glossary represents only their most common usage and/or their use by authors in this collection. In the English gloss in column 7, interpretations are brief to assist the reader (with literal translations indicated by "lit:") but do not attempt to reflect the considerable diversity of understanding and discourse attached to each word. Each gloss applies only to the word(s) in white boxes on the same row and only loosely refers to parallels on the same row in shaded boxes. Where there is more than one white box in a row, English spellings of terms are used in the gloss (e.g., *babalórìṣà/ babaloricha/babalorixá*—orisha priest). Only Spanish, Portuguese, and English words in columns 3, 5, and 6 that are used as religious terms by devotees are included in these columns and do not serve as translations. Parallel terms in different languages, dialects, lexicons, and geographical sites are sometimes identical or very close in meaning, and in other instances are only loosely coherent (as used by contributors in the volume) but may be vigorously contested. Hence, this glossary makes no effort to assert authoritative meanings and interpretations or to reflect the political dimension of word spellings and orthography.

Orthography

Yorùbá is a true tone language with three relative tone (pitch) bands represented in writing by acute accent marks over high tones /´/, grave accent marks over low tones / `/, and no diacritical marks over mid tones. Sub-dots indicate the following differences: *e* (roughly as in English "g<u>ay</u>"), *ẹ* (roughly as in English "g<u>e</u>t"), *o* (roughly as in English "g<u>o</u>"), *ọ* (roughly as in British English "g<u>o</u>t"), *s* (roughly as in English "<u>s</u>o"), and *ṣ* (roughly as in English "<u>sh</u>ow"). The letter *n* represents four distinct effects in Yorùbá: 1) When followed by a vowel, it is pronounced like an English [n]. 2) At the end of a word or before a consonant, it nasalizes the preceding vowel (as in French) but is not itself pronounced as a separate sound. Unlike in French, the nasalized vowels otherwise hardly change their pronunciation, though in Standard Yorùbá the sequence *an* becomes almost identical in pronunciation to *ọn*, resulting in near-homophones such as in Àyàn and Àyọ̀n. 3) As a separate word, the single letter *n* represents a "syllabic nasal," forming a syllabic nucleus all by itself. One such example is *ń*, which is a continuous marker: *mò ń lọ* (I am in the act of going). 4) The nasal consonant *n* also sometimes nasalizes a following word-final vowel (as in "Ṣọ̀pọ̀nnọ́"—name of an *òrìṣà*). Written *p* is pronounced as [kp] where [k] and [p] are simultaneously pronounced (as in "Ṣọ̀pọ̀nnọ́"). (There is no English [p] in Yorùbá.) In the consonant *gb*, [g] and [b] are pronounced simultaneously (as in "Elégbá"—name of an *òrìṣà*). Yorùbá also includes English [b] (as in *bàtá*) and English [g] (as in *gúdúgúdú*).

There are three diacritics in Spanish and Lucumí orthography. 1) The acute accent / ´ / denotes stress (amplitude) as in Lucumí (rather than high relative pitch in Yorùbá). 2) The *eñe* /ñ/ is pronounced [ny] (and is frequently used to transliterate nasalized Yorùbá vowels as in Àyàn/Añá). 3) The diaeresis / ¨ / is used to ensure that the *u* in written *gu* is not silent, though both *gu* and *gü* are frequently pronounced [gw] in Lucumí (as in *ague/agwe* and *güemilere*).

There are five diacritics in Portuguese and Nagô. 1) The tilde / ˜ / marks nasal vowels (as in *nação*). 2) The acute accent / ´ / marks stress and open vowels. 3) The circumflex / ^ / on *â, ê,* and *ô* marks stress and close vowels. 4) The cedilla (cedilha) / ¸ / is only used for *ç* and is equivalent to English [s]. 5) The grave accent / ` / marks the contraction of two consecutive vowels such as *a + as = às*.

X in Portuguese and Nagô corresponds with English *sh*.

Placement of Words in the Columns

The words in white boxes are not always in column 1 and are placed vertically in English alphabetical order. In alphabetizing, all diacritics and accents are ignored; thus, for example, *e, ẹ, é, è, ẹ́,* and *ẹ̀* are treated as identical (unlike in Yorùbá alphabetization). When two words with the same meaning have: 1) the same spelling (as in Ifá in Yorùbá and Lucumí); 2) the same spelling with diacritical differences (as in Yorùbá *odù* and Lucumí *odu*); 3) very similar (transliterated) spelling with the same or similar meaning (as in Yorùbá *babalórìṣà* and Lucumí *babalocha*); or 4) are consecutive in alphabetical order (as in Yorùbá *alágbe* and Nagô *alabê*), they are placed in the same row in white boxes. Where capitalized, unitalicized words (proper nouns) and lower case, italicized words (common nouns) have discrete meanings, the capitalized word is placed in the row above (as in Odù/Odú and *odù/odú*). As there are sometimes dialectic and orthographic variations in Yorùbá, Lucumí, and Nagô, the more common orthography (or the one employed in this volume) is placed first and is followed by the alternative after a semicolon (as in Àyàn Àgalú; Àyànàgalú; Àyàngalú). Where the alternative term is a different word, it is place in parentheses and may also present alternative spellings separated by semicolons, for example, *bembé* (*güemilere*; *wemilere*).

Gender and Pluralization

Yorùbá nouns and pronouns are genderless and do not have articles, while Spanish, Portuguese, and occasionally Spanish-Lucumí fusions are gendered by an article (as in La Regla de Ocha) or by the inclusion of an alternative final syllable where the word has masculine and feminine forms (as in *santero/santera*).

Yorùbá nouns do not distinguish singular and plural, whereby *bàtá* may refer to one or more drums. Spanish, Lucumí, Portuguese, and Nagô words are pluralized with *s* or *es*. Lucumí *batá* is one exception, where the word denotes both singular and plural forms.

Repetition and Cross-referencing of Terms

Where Cuban terms mix Lucumí and Spanish words or orthography, the two columns are merged and the word is centered (as in *batalero/a*). Where there is a corresponding term in another language/lexicon, words are placed in a shaded box in the same row in another column (as in *àṣẹ, aché, axé, ashe*). The word in the shaded box can then be cross-referenced at the point it occurs in the alphabetical order of the white boxes, where it may have a slightly or substantially different gloss. Thus *àṣẹ* appears in three different rows in the glossary according to alphabetical order: 1) *àṣẹ, aché, axé,* ashe; 2) *àṣẹ, aché, axé,* ashe; and 3) *àṣẹ, aché, axé,* ashe. Where identical words in different columns have more than one meaning, as well as distinct cultural understandings, they are placed in white boxes in the same row with numbered glosses. For example, *awo* appears in columns 1, 2, and 4 with three glosses in column 7: 1. Esoteric knowledge, secret, mystery (Yorùbá, Lucumí, Nagô). 2. Any *òrìṣà* initiate (Yorùbá). 3. Ifá initiate (Lucumí).

1. Yorùbá	2. Lucumí	3. Spanish	4. Nagô
	Abakuá		
	aberikulá; aberíkula; aberinkulá; aberínkula	*judíos*	
abòrìṣà (ẹlẹsin-àbáláyé)			
àṣẹ	*aché*		*axé*
ìdóṣù	*kariocha*	*asiento*	*adoxu*
oróhùn (ohun àṣẹ)	*afóuobó; afuebo; afowobo; (el aché) (el añá)*	*la carga (el secreto)*	
Ajé	Ayé		Ajé
àjé	*ayé*		*ajé*
Aláàfin			Alafín
alágbe			*alabé*
	aláña (obá Añá)		
alubàtá	*batalero(a)*		*ogã alabé*
Àyàn	Añá		
	akpwon; akpon; akuon (agan)		*elemaxó*
	Arará		Jeje

5. Portuguese	6. English	7. Gloss
		Afro-Cuban brotherhood with loose precedents in eastern Nigeria.
pagão		Unconsecrated *batá* drums.
	traditionalist	One who worships the *òrìṣà*.
	ashe	Spiritual power, sacred power of transformation.
assentamento; assentar o santo		Major orisha initiation in which the head is shaved and painted, and medicine is pressed into the head.
		Consecrated pouch that is ritually sealed inside each *batá* drum (as well as *iyesá* drums).
		Òrìṣà of wealth and money represented by cowrie shells.
		Antisocial female forces, the witches.
		Title for the king of Ọ̀yọ́ (said to be descended from Ṣàngó).
		1. Pejorative nickname for Yorùbá drummers (lit: "beggar"). 2. Transliteration used in *ogã alabê* "sacred drummer" (Nagô).
		Añá ritual specialist; owner of a *fundamento*; sometimes used to mean Añá initiate.
		Bàtá player (lit: "the one who beats *bàtá*").
	Anya	*Oricha* of drumming mostly associated with *batá* drums.
		Ritual singer who leads Santería ceremonies (or Iyesá ceremonies in the case of *agan*).
		Afro-Cuban spiritual tradition loosely derived from Fọ̀n and Ewè peoples in West Africa.

1. Yorùbá	2. Lucumí	3. Spanish	4. Nagô
kúsanrín	aro (osu; osun)	agoya (aro)	
àṣẹ	aché		axé
awo	awo (babalao)		awo
àṣẹ	aché		axé
Àyàn; Àyọ̀n	Añá		
àyán; àyọ́n; àáyán			
Àyàn Àgalú; Àyànàgalú; Àyàngalú	Añá		
Ajé (àjẹ́)	Ayé; ayé		Ajé
babaláwo (awo)	babalao; babaláwo (awo)		babalaô; babalawo
babalórìṣà	babaloricha; babalocha	padrino	babalorixá
Babalúayé; Ọbalúayé (Ṣọ̀pọ̀nnọ́)	Babaluayé; Babalú-Aye		Omolu (Obaluayê)

5. Portuguese	6. English	7. Gloss
		Metal ring that is attached to the outside of each *batá* to represent Ogún. *Aro* is both a Lucumí word, likely transliterated from *aro* (an idiophone comprised of two round metal rings), and a Spanish word for "hoop."
	ashe	Power of authority through utterance, vital power, life force, sacred potential, the power of transformation.
atabaque		Sacred drums of Candomblé traditionally played in sets of three (*rum*, *rumpi*, and *lé*).
		1. Esoteric knowledge, secret, mystery (Yorùbá, Lucumí, Nagô). 2. Any *òrìṣà* initiate (Yorùbá). 3. Ifá initiate (Lucumí).
	ashe	1. Spiritual power. 2. Consecrated object that is buried in the center of the *barracão* (the main structure of the *terreiro*).
	Anya	Yorùbá ancestor and progenitor of drumming; the *òrìṣà* of drumming; the craft lineage of drumming.
		Kind of wood used for *bàtá* drums (usually *Afrormosia laxiflora* or *Pericopsis laxiflora*).
	Anya	Alternative names for Àyàn.
		1. *Oricha* of the witches (transliterated from *àjé*). 2. *Oricha* of wealth or money associated with Ochún (transliterated from Ajé).
		Ifá divining priest.
pai-de-santo		1. Orisha priest (Yorùbá and Lucumí) 2. High priest and head of a *terreiro* (Nagô).
		Orisha of smallpox (or fevers) and healing.

1. Yorùbá	2. Lucumí	3. Spanish	4. Nagô
bàǹtẹ́	banté	bandele	
bàtá	batá		
			batá
alubàtá	batalero(a)		
	bembé (güemilere; wemilere)	tambor (toque de santo)	
bẹ̀ḿbẹ́	bembé		
bílálà		chancleta	
		cabildo	
ibú	ibú	camino	
			Candomblé
oróhùn (ohun àṣẹ)	afóuobó; afuebo; afowobo; (el ache) (el añá)	carga (el secreto)	
ṣáṣá	chachá	culata	
bílálà		chancleta	

5. Portuguese	6. English	7. Gloss
		Decorative apron attached to the *bàtá/batá* which can be made of animal skin, cloth, beads, brass, cowrie shells, and/or other materials.
barracão		Space in Candomblé *terreiros* (ritual houses) where semi-public ceremonies are held.
		Kind of orisha drum originating in Nigeria.
		Name of an *atabaque* rhythm used in Candomblé ceremonies.
		Batá player. (The feminine word *batalera* has come into recent use among female *batá* players.)
festa-de-santo		Drumming celebration for *oricha.*
		1. Kind of drum ensemble associated with Ọ̀ṣun in some areas (Yorùbá) (similar in structure to *iyesá* drums from Matanzas). 2. Kind of Cuban drum differing in structure and repertoire from Yorùbá *bèmbé* drums.
		Rawhide beater used on the *ṣáṣá* in Ọ̀yọ́-style *bàtá* drumming.
terreiro (casa de santo) *(casas de nação roça)*		Mutual aid organizations found throughout Latin America.
caminho	road; avatar	Road or path of the *orixás.*
		Cluster of spiritual systems that developed primarily from African cultural sources.
		Consecrated pouch that is ritually sealed inside each *batá* drum (as well as *iyesá* drums).
		Smaller head of *batá* drums.
		Strip of leather shaped like the sole of a shoe which is sometimes used to beat the *chachá* head of Matanzas *batá* drums.

1. Yorùbá	2. Lucumí	3. Spanish	4. Nagô
Ṣàngó	Changó		Xangô
ṣaworo	chaworó; chaguoró	cascabeles	
ṣèkèrè	chekeré (agué; agwé; agbe) (güiro)		xequeré
kónkóló		clave	
		juramento	
			padê
dinlógún	dinlogún; diloggún	caracoles	dilogun
dùndún			
ẹbọ	ebó; ebbó		ebó
			ebomi
Èṣù	Echú		Exú
èèwọ̀	ewé		quizila
Egbẹ́			
ẹgbẹ́			
Egúngún; Eégún	Egun	los muertos	Egungun; Egun (Baba Egum)
Ẹlẹ́gbára; Ẹlẹ́gbá	Eleguá; Elegbá		
ẹlégùn			
	elekoto		
	akpwon; akpon; akuon (agan)		elemaxó

5. Portuguese	6. English	7. Gloss
	Shango	*Oricha* of thunder and lightning said to be the mytho-logical King of Ọ̀yọ́ (Oyó) in the 14th–15th century. Closely associated with Añá and *batá* drums.
		Metal bells (usually brass) attached around the heads of the *iyá batá*.
	shekere	Gourd idiophone strung with beads and/or shells.
		1. Timeline concept in Cuban music. 2. Idiophone.
confirmação		Confirmation or initiation ceremony undertaken by drummers in Candomblé to become an *ogã alabê* (ritual drummer).
despacho		Ritual dedicated to Exú at the outset of Candomblé ceremonies.
búzios		Contraction of *ẹẹ̀rìndínlógún* (Yorùbá "sixteen"), re-ferring to the sixteen cowrie shells used for divination in most orisha traditions.
	talking drum	Yorùbá variable-pitched pressure drum.
		Sacrificial offering in orisha practice.
		Devotee who has been initiated for more than seven years (probably from Yorùbá *ẹ̀gbón mi* "my senior sibling/kin").
	Eshu	*Oricha* of the crossroads, trickster, and divine messen-ger between heaven and earth.
	taboo	Prohibitions attached to orisha practices.
		Òrìṣà of heavenly accomplices.
		Society, fraternity, or age mates.
		1. The *òrìṣà* of the ancestors (Yorùbá). 2. Ancestral spirits (Lucumí, Nagô).
		Dimension or path of the orisha Eshu.
		Ṣàngó spirit possession medium.
		Fourth, shrine-bound *batá* drum.
		Elite Candomblé musician and priest who is responsi-ble for leading ceremonial drumming and singing.

1. Yorùbá	2. Lucumí	3. Spanish	4. Nagô
ẹlẹ́ṣin-àbáláyé (abọ̀rìṣà)			
ojú òjò	enú	boca	
Èṣù	Echú		Exú
eèwọ̀	ewé		quizila
Èṣù	Echú		Exú
	bembé (güemilere; wemilere)	tambor (toque de santo)	
fújì			
		fundamento	
gúdúgúdú (ọpọ́n)			
	güemilere; wemilere (bembé)	tambor (toque de santo) (fiesta)	
	iban balo; (wemilere; güemilere)	fiesta	
Ìbejì	Ibeyí; Ibedyi	Los Jimaguas	Ibeji; Bêji
ibú	ibú	camino	
idóṣù	kariocha	asiento	adoxu
Iyemọja; Yemọja	Yemayá		Iemanjá
Ifá (Ọ̀rúnmìlà; Ọ̀rùnmlà)	Ifá (Orula; Orunla; Orúnmila)		Ifá

5. Portuguese	6. English	7. Gloss
	traditionalist	One who worships the òrìṣà.
		Larger head of the iyá, itótele and okónkolo (lit: "mouth" from Yorùbá "ẹnu").
	Eshu	Òrìṣà of the oríta (orí mẹ́ta "where three roads meet") and divine messenger between heaven and earth.
	taboo	Prohibitions attached to oricha practices.
	Eshu	Orixá of the crossroads, divine messenger.
festa-de-santo		Candomblé orixá celebration in a terreiro.
		Form of Yorùbá popular music that has evolved from Muslim musical traditions.
fundamento		1. Consecrated batá ensemble (Cuba). 2. Wider reference to consecrated spiritual object (Cuba, Brazil).
		Small Yorùbá kettledrum usually played in the dùndún ensemble and sometimes containing Àyàn.
festa-de-santo		1. Drumming celebration for the oricha. 2. Third and celebratory phase of a tambor.
		Third and celebratory phase of a tambor.
		Orisha of twins.
caminho	dimension; road; avatar	Dimension/road/path of orisha (particular to water orisha).
assentamento; assentar o santo		Major òrìṣà initiation in which the head is shaved and painted, and medicine is pressed into the head. (Ìdóṣù is an elision of dá òṣù which means "create òṣù (a ball of ritual substances").
		Orixá of motherhood associated with the ocean.
		1. Orisha of divination. 2. Sacred literary corpus.

1. Yorùbá	2. Lucumí	3. Spanish	4. Nagô
Ìjèṣà	Iycsá; Yesa		Ijcxá
	iyesá		ijexá
ilé	ilé	cabildo	ilê
ìlù	ilú	tambor	ilú
irúnmọlè			
ìtàn	pataki; patakín		pataki
omele abo	itótele (omelé)	segundo	
iyáàlù	iyá	mayor (caja)	
iyálórìṣà	iyalorichá; iyalocha	madrina (madre de santo)	iyalorixá
iyàwó	iyawó; yawó; yabó		iyawó; iaó
Iyemọja; Yemọja	Yemayá		Iemanjá
Ìjèṣà	Iyesá; Yesa		Ijexá
	iyesá		ijexá
	Arará		Jeje
	aberikulá; aberíkula; aberinkulá; aberínkula	judíos	

5. Portuguese	6. English	7. Gloss
		One of the "nations" in Candomblé said to derive from the Ìjèṣà people in Yorùbáland.
		Drum rhythm.
terreiro (*casa de santo*) (*casas de nação roça*)		1. Ritual house. 2. Community of worshippers.
tambor (*atabaque*)		1. Drum of any kind (Yorùbá). 2. Kind of rhythm (Yorùbá). 3. Ritual drum (Lucumí, Nagô).
		Can be used as a generic term for *òrìṣà* or specifically for the earth spirits (Ògbóni).
		Story, narrative, history.
		Second largest (middle) *batá* drum (transliterated from the Yorùbá *àtèlé/itèlé* "the one that follows").
		1. Generic word for the leading drum in drum ensembles (contraction of *iyá* "mother" *ìlù* "drum") (Yorùbá). 2. Largest and leading drum in the *batá* ensemble (Lucumí).
mãe-de-santo		1. *Òrìṣà* priestess (Yorùbá). 2. *Oricha* priestess and spiritual godmother (Lucumí). 3. High priestess and head of a *terreiro* (Nagô).
		Recent orisha initiate (lit: "bride").
		Orisha of motherhood associated with the Ògún River in Nigeria.
		1. Branch of *oricha* worship most prevalent in Matanzas, said to be derived from the Ìjèṣà people in Yorùbáland.
		Drum rhythm.
		Subgroup (*naçõe*) of Candomblé that has evolved from Yorùbá and Fon peoples in West Africa.
pagão		Unconsecrated or unbaptised *batá* (lit: "Jewish").

1. Yorùbá	2. Lucumí	3. Spanish	4. Nagô
jùjú			
		juramento	
			Kêtu
kónkóló		*clave*	
kúdi (kónkóló)	*okónkolo (omelé)*		
kúsanrín	*aro (osu; osun)*	*agoya; aro*	
		lavada de manos; lavarse las manos; las manos lavados	
			lé
iyálórìṣà	*iyalorichá; iyalocha*	*madrina (madre de santo)*	*iyalorixá*
			Nagô
	obá batá		
Ọbàtálá	Obatalá		Oxalá
òòṣà	*ocha*		
Ọ̀ṣọ́òsì	Ochosi		Oxóssi
Ọ̀ṣun	Ochún		Oxum
Odù	Odu (Olofi; Olofin)		
odù	*odu; odun*		*odù*

5. Portuguese	6. English	7. Gloss
		Kind of Yorùbá popular music which evolved from Christian communities.
confirmação		Añá initiation ceremony (lit: "swearing") undertaken to become *omo* Añá.
		Subgroup (*naçõe*) of Nagô in Candomblé.
		1. Yorùbá timeline (cyclical rhythm). 2. Sometimes used to name drums with rhythmic role, such as the *kúdi*.
		Small accompanying drum in the *bàtá* ensemble that plays a purely rhythmic role.
		Metal ring (or sometimes leather knot) which is attached to the (inside or outside) of the *bàtá* and represents Ògún. It can also be placed inside of the *gúdúgúdú*.
		Entry-level Añá initiation that allows drummers to play the consecrated *batá* (lit: "hand-washing").
		Smallest drum in the *atabaque* ensemble.
mãe-de-santo		1. *Oricha* priestess and spiritual godmother (Lucumí). 2. High priestess and head of a *terreiro* (Nagô).
		1. One of the Candomblé "nations" including the sub-groups Ketu, Efon and Ijexá. 2. Lexicon of Candomblé rituals and songs.
		Caretaker of a *fundamento* (consecrated *batá* set).
		Orisha of creativity (lit: "the king of the white cloth").
		Elision of *oricha*.
		Oricha of hunting.
		Oricha associated with "sweet waters," love, sexuality, fertility, femininity and wealth.
		Female orisha central to the Ifá cult. (An interchangeable term for Olofi in Cuba.)
		256 sets or "signs" of sacred oral texts which are accessed through divination.

1. Yorùbá	2. Lucumí	3. Spanish	4. Nagô
Odùduwà	Odudúwa; Odudúa, Odúwa; Odúa		
ọ̀gá			ogã; ogan
onílù	onilu		ogã alabê
Ògbóni			
Ògún	Ogún		Ogum; Ogún
Ọ̀jẹ̀			Ojé
ojú òjò	enú	boca	
omele akọ (kúdi) (kónkóló)	okónkolo (omelé)		
Olódùmarè; Elédùmarè; Èdùmàrè	Olodumaré (Olófi; Olófin) (Olórun)		
Ọ̀lọ́fin	Olófi; Olófin (Odu)		
olórìṣà; (awo)	oloricha	santero(a)	adoxu (abiã) (iaô)
Ọlọ́run	Olorún		Olorum
ọlọ́sọyìn (oníṣègùn)	osainista (olósain)		
alubàtá	olú batá		
omele; ọmọlé; emele	omelé		
omele abo	itótele (omelé)	segundo	

5. Portuguese	6. English	7. Gloss
		1. Progenitor and *òrìṣà* of the Yorùbá people. 2. *Oricha* (Lucumí).
		1. Ritual post for men in Candomblé. 2. Those who undertake animal sacrifice (from Yorùbá *ògá* "one's superior").
		Sacred drummer.
		Earth cult of jural authority.
		Orisha of iron, hunting and blacksmithing.
		Masquerader lineage associated with Egúngún.
		Larger head of the *ìyáàlù* and *omele abo bàtá* (lit: "face of rain").
		Smallest *bàtá* drum that plays a primarily rhythmic role. The word possibly derives from *kónkóló*, a vocable for a Yorùbá timeline concept similar to *clave*.
		God Almighty (Olófi is used interchangeably by *santeros* in Cuba).
		1. Ọọni (king) of Ilé-Ifè and his royal predecessors including Odùduwà (Yorùbá). 2. Law maker (Yorùbá). 3. Name for Supreme Being used by *santeros* (Lucumí). 4. Interchangeable name for Odu used by *babalaos* (Lucumí).
		Initiate of orisha (lit: "one who owns the *òrìṣà*).
		God Almighty.
		Ọ̀sanyìn devotee specialising in herbs and traditional medicine.
		1. Caretaker of a *fundamento*. 2. Someone who plays a *fundamento*.
		1. Generic term for a supporting drum (Yorùbá). 2. Term often used for the *okónkolo* or less commonly the *itótele* (Lucumí).
		Middle-sized *bàtá* drum (lit: "female accompanying drum").

1. Yorùbá	2. Lucumí	3. Spanish	4. Nagô
omele akọ	okónkolo (omelé)		
omele mẹ́ta			
omìẹ̀rọ̀	omiero		abô
ọmọ Àyàn	omó Añá		ogã alabê
Babalúayé; Ọbalúayé (Ṣọ̀pọ̀nnọ́)	Babaluayé; Babalú-Ayé		Omolu (Obaluayê)
onílù	onilú		ogã alabê
oníṣègùn (ọlọ́sọyìn)	osainista (olósain)		
oògùn	ogún		medicina; brujería
òòṣà	ocha		
	oriaté		
òrìṣà	oricha	santo	orixá
oríkì			
òrìṣà	oricha	santo	orixá
orò	oro; oru		
	oro cantado; oru cantado (oro eyá aranla)		xirê
ìlú ṣíṣẹ̀	oro seco; oru seco (oro igbodú; oru igbodú)		

5. Portuguese	6. English	7. Gloss
		Small accompanying drum in the *bàtá* ensemble comprised of one small drum or two tied together (*omele akọ* and *kúdi*).
		Recent innovation of small accompanying drum in the *bàtá* ensemble comprised of three drums (*omele akọ* or *kúdi*) tied together.
banho de fôlha		Solution made from herbs and other substances for the ritual washing of the initiate and the accoutrements of the orisha.
		1. Àyàn lineage member, devotee and/or drummer (Yorùbá). 2. Añá initiate who has done the *juramento* (Lucumí).
		Orixá of smallpox and healing.
		1. Drummer (Yorùbá). 2. Sacred drummer (Lucumí).
		Specialist in flora and traditional medicine.
		Traditional medicine.
		Elision of *òrìṣà*.
		Dinlogún diviner and ritual specialist who leads *oricha* initiations.
santo	saint	Yorùbá spiritual beings.
		Concise or elaborated attributions or appellations equivalent or alternative to names (often translated as "praise poetry").
santo	saint	Yorùbá spiritual beings.
		1. Ceremony. 2. Sung or drummed recitation.
		Sung liturgy performed during Santería ceremonies (lit: "sung ceremony").
		Instrumental liturgy of *batá* rhythms performed at the beginning of Santería ceremonies (lit: "dry ceremony").

1. Yorùbá	2. Lucumí	3. Spanish	4. Nagô
oróhùn (ohun àṣẹ)	afóuobó; afuebo; afowobo; (el ache) (el añá)	la carga (el secreto)	
Ọ̀rúnmìlà; Ọ̀rùnmilà (Ifá)	Orúnmila; Orula; Orunla; (Ifá)		Ifá
ọlọ́sọyìn (oníṣẹ̀gùn)	osainista (olósain)		
Ọ̀sanyìn	Osáin; Osaín		Ossanha
Ọ̀ṣọ́ọ̀sì	Ochosi		Oxóssi
òṣù	osu; osun		osu; oxu (adoxu)
Ọ̀ṣun	Ochún		Oxum
òsùn	osun; osu; ósun		
Ọbàtálá	Obatalá		Oxalá
Ọ̀ṣọ́ọ̀sì	Ochosi		Oxóssi
Ọ̀ṣun	Ochún		Oxum
Ọ̀ṣùmàrè	Ochumaré		Oxumarê; Oxunmarê
Ọya (Ìyánsàn)	Oyá (Yansa)		Iansã
			padê
babalórìṣà	babaloricha	padrino	babalorixá
	Palo		Angola
ìtàn	patakí; patakín		pataki
	(La) Regla de Ocha (Ocha; Santería; el religión)		
			rum; run

5. Portuguese	6. English	7. Gloss
		Consecrated pouch which is ritually sealed inside various Yorùbá drums.
		Orisha of divination.
		Specialist in herbs and traditional medicine.
		Orisha of flora and traditional medicine.
		Òrìṣà of hunting.
		1. Ball of medicine used in orisha rituals. 2. Sometimes used in place of *aro* (the iron ring on *batá* drums) (Lucumí)
		Riverine, warrior *òrìṣà* associated with motherhood, fertility and wealth. Regarded as queen of the witches in Yorùbáland.
		Staff that protects people from witchcraft.
		Orixá of creativity (lit: "the king of the white cloth").
		Orixá of hunting.
		Riverine *orixá* associated with motherhood, fertility and wealth.
		Orixá associated with the rainbow, popular in Brazil but now marginal in Nigeria and Cuba.
		Mythological wife to Shango who is orisha of the wind, the cemetery and the market place (lit: "mother of nine").
despacho		Ritual dedicated to Exú at the outset of Candomblé ceremonies.
pai-de-santo		1. *Oricha* priest and spiritual godfather (Lucumí). 2. High priest and head of a *terreiro* (Nagô).
		Congolese-derived ritual complex in Cuba.
		Sacred story, narrative.
		Oricha devotion in Cuba.
		Tallest drum in the *atabaque* ensemble.

1. Yorùbá	2. Lucumí	3. Spanish	4. Nagô
	rumba		
			rumpi; runpi
Ṣàngó	Changó		Xangô
	Santería (La Regla de Ocha; Ocha, *le religión*)		
olórìṣà (awo)	*oloricha*	*santero(a)*	*adoxu (abiã) (iaó)*
òrìṣà	*oricha*	*santo*	*orixá*
ṣáṣá	*chachá*	*culata*	
ṣaworo	*chaworó; chaguoró*	*cascabeles*	
omele abo	*itótele (omelé)*	*segundo*	
ṣèkèrè	*chekeré (agué; agwé; agbe) (güiro)*		*xequeré*
		sopera	
Ṣọ̀pọ̀nnọ́ (Babalúayé; Ọbalúayé)	Babalúayé; Babalú-Ayé		Omolu (Obaluayê)
		tambor (tambor de fundamento)	
	bembé (güemilere; wemilere)	*tambor (toque de santo)*	

5. Portuguese	6. English	7. Gloss
		Percussive Afro-Cuban musical tradition with mixed African heritage.
		Middle-sized drum in the *atabaque* ensemble.
	Shango	Mythological king of Ọ̀yọ́ (Oyó) in the 14th-15th century and *òrìṣà* of thunder and lightning. Closely associated with Àyàn and *bàtá* drums.
		Oricha devotion in Cuba.
		Oricha initiate.
santo	saint	Interchangeable word for orisha in Santería and Candomblé.
		Smaller head of the *ìyáàlù* and *omele abo bàtá*, and the upper heads of the *kúdi* and *omele akọ*.
		Brass bells attached to Yorùbá drums, including both heads of the *ìyáàlù* and often *omele abo bàtá* drums.
		Second largest *bàtá* drum.
	shekere	Gourd idiophone strung with cowrie shells and/or beads, also known as Ajé in Ilé Aluṣẹ̀kẹ̀rẹ̀ at present Ọ̀yọ́ town.
		Soup tureen used as a receptacle for the *oricha's* sacred implements.
		Òrìṣà of smallpox and healing.
suspenso		Act by which a male member of a Candomblé community is physically lifted by an *orixá* (possessed devotee) during a ceremony, signalling that the devotee has been chosen to be in this *orixá's* service.
		Set of consecrated *bàtá* drums.
festa-de-santo		Drumming celebration for *oricha*.

1. Yorùbá	2. Lucumí	3. Spanish	4. Nagô
ilé	*ilé*	*cabildo*	*ilê*
	bembé (güemilere; wemilere)	*toque de santo (tambor)*	
		tratado (libreta)	
			Umbanda
Ṣàngó	Changó		Xangô
			xiré
Yemoja; Iyemoja	Yemayá		Iemanjá

5. Portuguese	6. English	7. Gloss
terreiro (*casa de santo*) (*casas de nação roça*)		1. House of worship in Candomblé. 2. Community of worshippers.
festa-de-santo		Drumming celebration for *oricha*.
		Written sources for ritual information in Regla de Ocha (lit: "treatise").
		Brazilian religion that brings together African, Christian, indigenous Indian, Asian and European elements.
	Shango	*Orixá* of thunder and lightning said to be the mytho-logical King of Ọ̀yọ́ (Oyó) in the 14th-15th century.
		Segment of the *festa-de-santo* where devotees dance in the *roda* (circle) for their *orixá*.
		Orisha of motherhood; associated with the Ògún River (in Nigeria) and the ocean (in Cuba).

About the Authors

. . . .

Akínṣọlá A. Akìwọwọ (1922–2014) was Professor Emeritus of sociology and anthropology at Ọbáfẹ́mi Awólọ́wọ̀ University in Ilé-Ifẹ̀, Nigeria, and also taught at universities in Ìbàdàn, Nsukka, Ado Ekiti, Boston, and Los Angeles. His numerous influential articles and lectures include "Àjobí and Àjogbé: Variations on the Theme of Sociation" (1983) and "Indigenization of the Social Sciences and Emancipation of Thought" (1988). As close friend and advisor, he played an important role in the work of Babátúndé Ọlátúnjí, writing the liner notes for several of Ọlátúnjí's ground-breaking albums and co-authoring his autobiography, *The Beat of My Drum* (2005).

K. Noel Amherd is a musician and was initiated as a babaláwo in the town of Ìjẹ̀bu-Rẹ́mọ, Nigeria, and earned his PhD in anthropology at University of Birmingham, UK (2006). His research focuses on orality, textuality, and ritual performance among the traditional babaláwo and òrìṣà devotees in the Ìjẹ̀bu-Rẹ́mọ region of Nigeria. He is currently looking at the overlap of traditional practices of conflict negotiation and restorative justice and the implications upon domestic and international juridical concepts and praxes. Amherd is the author of *Reciting Ifá: Difference, Heterogeneity and Identity* (Africa World Press, 2010).

John Amira, born and raised in New York City, has over fifty years' experience as a ritual drummer of sacred Haitian and Cuban music and has also performed with top Latin artists, including Celia Cruz and Tito Puente. Amira has taught, played, and lectured at universities and institutes including New England Conservatory, Julliard, Yale, New York University, Duke, Middlebury, Brooklyn Academy of Music, and the Museum of Natural History (NYC). With Steven Cornelius, Amira co-authored *The Music of Santería: Traditional Rhythms of the Batá Drums* (White Cliffs Media, 1992).

Kawolèyin Àyángbékún (d. 2007) was a bàtá drummer from Ògbómòsó, Nigeria. While almost all Yorùbá Àyàn drummers are now Muslim, Àyángbékún was a devoted and powerful traditional òrìsà priest of Àyàn, Sàngó, Egbé, and Òsun. In his capacity as a priest of Òsanyìn (the òrìsà of flora), Àyángbékún was an expert in traditional medicine. He was also known for dancing in the full-body ancestral (Egúngún) mask and was a renowned shell (*dínlógún*) diviner who was known for his mastery of traditional Yorùbá orature such as *oríkì* praise poetry and *ìtàn* storytelling and history.

Kevin M. Delgado is an Associate Professor of Music and Coordinator of World Music and Ethnomusicology at San Diego State University. He earned his PhD in ethnomusicology from University of California, Los Angeles (2001), writing about Afro-Cuban Iyesá sacred music and culture within contemporary Cuba. Delgado teaches graduate and undergraduate courses on a wide variety of topics covering the music of the world and the intersection between music, culture, politics, identity, history, and technology. He has published articles in *Black Music Research Journal, Selected Reports in Ethnomusicology,* and *A Contracorriente*, as well as numerous book chapters.

David Font-Navarrete is a musician, artist, initiate of the òrìsà Obàtálá and Añá, and an ethnomusicologist. He earned his PhD in ethnomusicology from York University, Canada (2011), writing about Bugarabu drumming in the Senegambia. As a ritual musician in the Cuban Lucumí tradition, he is a student of Ezequiel Torres, Ángel Bolaños, and other luminaries in Afro-Cuban music. His scholarly publications include articles on Congotronics, the Sublime Frequencies label, and Bass, as well as a book on Lucumí music co-authored with Kenneth Schweitzer (forthcoming, Temple University Press). Font-Navarrete is currently a Lecturing Fellow in the Thompson Writing Program at Duke University.

Katherine Hagedorn (1961–2013) was awarded her PhD in ethnomusicology at Brown University (1995) after joining the faculty of Pomona College in Claremont, California, in 1993, where she became a Professor of Music and Director of the Ethnomusicology Program. Specializing in Afro-Cuban Santería music, Hagedorn won two prestigious teaching awards, the California Professor of the Year (2000) and the Wig Distinguished Professorship Award for excellence in teaching (2002). Also in 2002, the Society for Ethnomusicology (SEM) awarded Hagedorn the Alan Merriam Prize for her monograph *Divine Utterances: The Performance of Afro-Cuban Santería* (Smithsonian Institution Press, 2001).

Debra Klein is a Professor of Anthropology at Gavilan College in California. Since undertaking years of ethnographic research in Nigeria and earning her PhD at UC Santa Cruz (2000), Klein has published in edited volumes on African popular culture and journals including *Research in African Literatures*. She is currently researching Yorùbá popular musical genres of *wéré, fújì*, and "Islamic" for a forthcoming book. Her first monograph, titled *Yorùbá Bàtá Goes Global: Artists, Culture Brokers, and Fans* (University of Chicago Press, 2007), focuses on collaborations between Yorùbá performers and overseas culture brokers and artists.

Fernando "Leo" Leobons began his apprenticeship as a ritual Candomblé drummer as a child in Rio de Janeiro, Brazil. After relocating to the USA in 1970, he studied percussion and ethnomusicology at the University of Maryland and began his studies with Cuban percussionist Julito Collazo in New York. Since returning to Brazil in the mideighties, Leobons has recorded and toured internationally with artists such as Djavan and Ramiro Musotto and led workshops in schools and universities around the world. In 2012 Leobons recorded his solo CD *Bá*, which was nominated for Brazil's prestigious award Premio da Música Brasileira.

Michael Marcuzzi (1966–2012) was a trumpeter, percussionist, composer, and ethnomusicologist cross-appointed as Associate Professor in the Department of Music and Associate Professor in the Faculty of Education, York University, Toronto, where he completed his PhD. His research and creative work straddled North American and Cuban popular music, Afro-Cuban sacred music, classical, and jazz. With credits such as the symphony orchestras in Windsor, Detroit, and Mississauga, Cleo Laine, and the Temptations, Michael formed his own Toronto-based group, Ilede, which performed Cuban bàtá repertoire. Michael published in *Journal of Black Research, Journal of Religion in Africa,* and *Latin American Music Review.*

John Àyánṣoolá Abíọ́dún Ògúnlẹ́yẹ resides in Òdè Rẹ́mọ, Ìjèbu-Rẹ́mọ, Ògún State, Nigeria. Born into the Àyàn lineage of traditional Yorùbá drummers, he has become a leader among the musicians of his town and region, coinciding with his numerous roles within the traditional religious societies such as Agẹmọ, Nàná Bùrùkú, and Ifá. He also works as a babaláwo (divining priest), serving clients who come for initiation, information, and medical treatment. He has traveled internationally and has taught in Brazil and Argentina.

J. D. Y. Peel is Emeritus Professor of Anthropology and Sociology at SOAS, University of London. His main writings on the Yorùbá are *Aladura* (1968), *Ijeshas and Nigerians* (1983), and *Religious Encounter and the Making of the Yoruba* (2000), the last two of these receiving the Herskovits Award for African Studies as well as the Amaury Talbot Prize for African Anthropology. A further (and no doubt his final) book on the Yorùbá, *Christianity, Islam and Orisa-Religion: Comparative Studies of Three Traditions in Interaction and Comparison,* is due to be published by the University of California Press in 2015.

Alberto Quintero is a percussionist from Caracas, Venezuela. He studied classical percussion at the National Conservatory of Music of Mexico, performed with the Caracas-based Orquesta Sinfónica Gran Mariscal de Ayacucho (1977–2004), and began his studies of Afro-Cuban drumming in the 1980s with Orlando Poleo in Venezuela. Apprenticing with several of Cuba's legendary batá masters, Qunitero has been a key figure in the establishment of the Cuban Añá tradition in Venezuela and is now a sought-after and internationally mobile musician and oricha priest, participating in Añá consecrations and ceremonies in Venezuela, Cuba, the United States, Puerto Rico, and beyond.

Kenneth Schweitzer is an ethnomusicologist and percussionist versed in jazz, new music, and Afro-Cuban folkloric styles. Since completing his DMA in percussion (2003) at the University of Maryland, Schweitzer has become an Associate Professor and Chair of Music at Washington College in Chestertown, Maryland, where he teaches courses on Cuban music, Latin American music, jazz history, jazz performance, and music technology. Schweitzer is the author of *The Artistry of Afro-Cuban Batá Drumming Aesthetics: Transmission, Bonding, and Creativity* (University Press of Mississippi, 2013) and a book about Lucumí music co-authored with David Font-Navarrete (forthcoming, Temple University Press).

Amanda Villepastour trained as a composer at University of Western Australia then forged her first career as a keyboardist and songwriter with artists including Boy George, the Gang of Four, and Billy Bragg. Since completing her PhD in ethnomusicology at SOAS, University of London (2006), about sacred drumming in Nigeria and Cuba, she served as a founding curator at the Musical Instrument Museum (MIM) in Phoenix, Arizona. Villepastour is now a lecturer/researcher in the School of Music, Cardiff University, Wales, and is the author of *Ancient Text Messages of the Yorùbá Bàtá Drum* (Ashgate 2010).

Index

Page numbers in *italics* refer to illustrations.

CPSIA information can be obtained at www.ICGtesting.com
Printed in the USA
BVOW02*0349231115

427803BV00003B/9/P